Fodor's 6th Edition

Norway

The Guide for All Budgets, Completely Updated, with Many Maps and Travel Tips

Where to Stay, Eat,
and Explore

On and Off
the Beaten Path

When to Go,
What to Pack

Post-it® Flags,
Web Sites, and More

Excerpted from Fodor's Scandinavia

Fodor's Travel Publications • New York, Toronto, London, Sydney, Auckland
www.fodors.com

Fodor's Norway

EDITORS: Shannon Kelly, John D. Rambow

Editorial Contributors: Satu Hummasti, Sonya Procenko, Helayne Schiff
Editorial Production: Taryn Luciani
Maps: David Lindroth, Inc., Mapping Specialists, Ltd., *cartographers;*
Rebecca Baer and Bob Blake, *map editors*
Design: Fabrizio La Rocca, *creative director;* Guido Caroti, *art director;* Jolie Novak, *senior picture editor;* Melanie Marin, *photo editor*
Cover Design: Pentagram
Production/Manufacturing: Colleen Ziemba
Cover Photo (Kautokeino): Bryan and Cherry Alexander

Copyright

Sixth Edition

ISBN 0–676–90202–2

ISSN 1073–6603

Important Tip

Although all prices, opening times, and other details in this book are based on information supplied to us at press time, changes occur all the time in the travel world, and Fodor's cannot accept responsibility for facts that become outdated or for inadvertent errors or omissions. So **always confirm information when it matters,** especially if you're making a detour to visit a specific place.

Special Sales

Fodor's Travel Publications are available at special discounts for bulk purchases for sales promotions or premiums. Special editions, including personalized covers, excerpts of existing guides, and corporate imprints, can be created in large quantities for special needs. For more information, contact your local bookseller or write to Special Markets, Fodor's Travel Publications, 280 Park Avenue, New York, NY 10017. Inquiries from Canada should be directed to your local Canadian bookseller or sent to Random House of Canada, Ltd., Marketing Department, 2775 Matheson Boulevard East, Mississauga, Ontario L4W 4P7. Inquiries from the United Kingdom should be sent to Fodor's Travel Publications, 20 Vauxhall Bridge Road, London SW1V 2SA, England.

PRINTED IN THE UNITED STATES OF AMERICA

10 9 8 7 6 5 4 3 2 1

CONTENTS

Maps

ON THE ROAD WITH FODOR'S

The more you know before you go, the better your trip will be. Norway's most fascinating small museum or best traditional restaurant could be just around the corner from your hotel, but if you don't know it's there, it might as well be on the other side of the globe. That's where this book comes in. It's a great step toward making sure your next trip lives up to your expectations. As you plan, check out the Web as well. Guidebooks have been helping smart travelers find the special places for years; the Web is one more tool. Whatever reference you consult, be savvy about what you read, and always consider the source. Images and language can be massaged to make places appear better than they are. And one traveler's quaint is another's grimy. Here at Fodor's, and at our on-line arm, Fodors.com, our focus is on providing you with information that's not only useful but accurate and on target. Every day Fodor's editors put enormous effort into getting things right, beginning with the search for the right contributors—people who have objective judgment, broad travel experience, and the writing ability to put their insights into words. They're the kind of people you'd poll for tips yourself if you knew them.

Norwegian-Canadian journalist **Sonya Procenko** covers Norway and the Nordic countries for European and North American publications. In 1998, Sonya returned to her roots by moving back to Norway, where she hikes, climbs, skis, and writes.

Don't Forget to Write

Your experiences—positive and negative—matter to us. If we have missed or misstated something, we want to hear about it. We follow up on all suggestions. Contact the Norway editor at editors@fodors.com or c/o Fodor's, 280 Park Avenue, New York, New York 10017. And have a fabulous trip!

Karen Cure
Editorial Director

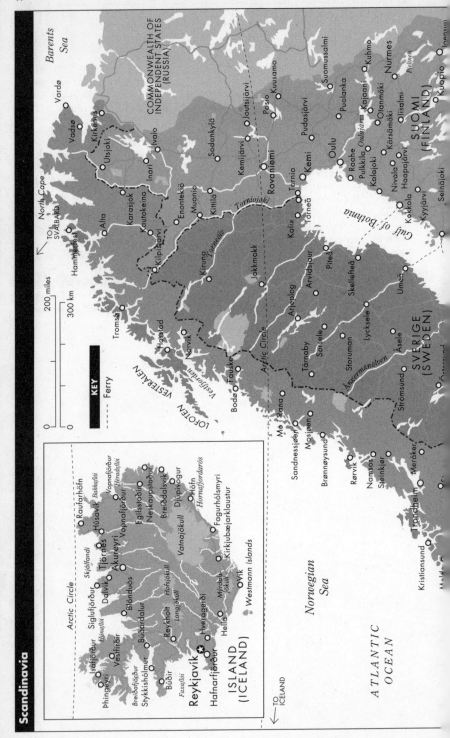

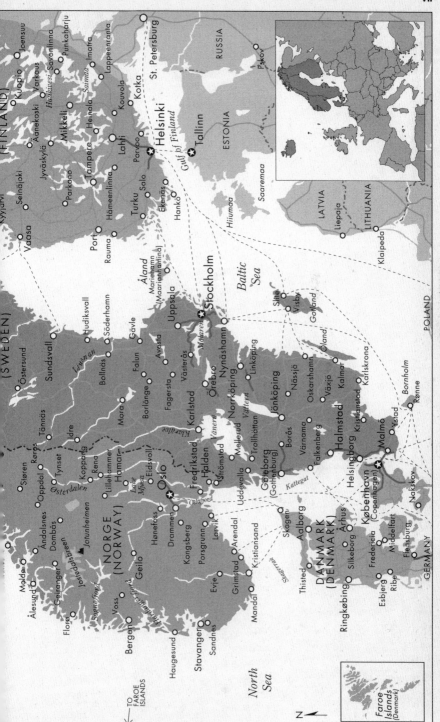

Norway

TO
SVALBARD

North Cape

Vardø

Vadsø

Kirkenes

Hammerfest

Alta

Karasjok

Tromsø

Kautokeino

FINLAND

*ATLANTIC
OCEAN*

*Norwegian
Sea*

Harstad

VESTERÅLEN

Svolvær

Narvik

LOFOTEN

Vestfjorden

Bodø

Fauske

Polarsirkelsenteret

Arctic   Circle

Mo i Rana

Sandnessjøen

Mosjøen

E6

Brønnøysund

SWEDEN

Gulf of Bothnia

Rørvik

Namsos

Steinkjer

Trondheim

Meråker

Støren

Kristiansund

Røros

Molde

70

Oppdal

Ålesund

Åndalsnes

Tynset

Geiranger

Dombås

Nordfjord

Lom

Otta

Koppang

Østerdalen

Florø

Jostedalsbreen

Gudbrandsdalen

Rena

Sognefjorden

Lillehammer

Hamar

Voss

Geilo

Gol

*Lake
Mjøsa*

Baltic Sea

Bergen

Hønefoss

Eidsvoll

Hardangerfjorden

Drammen

⭐ Oslo

Haugesund

Kongsberg

Fredrikstad

Dalen

Larvik

Oslofjord

Halden

Stavanger

Valle

Porsgrunn

Sandnes

Evje

Arendal

Skagerrak

Kattegat

Grimstad

Mandal

Kristiansand

N

0   200 miles

0   300 km

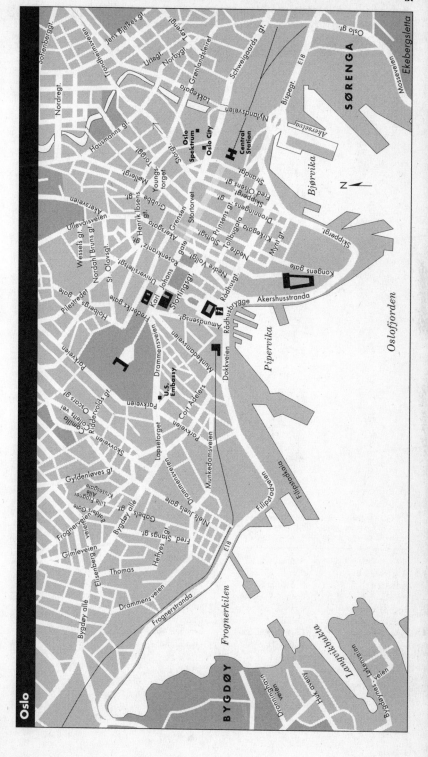

Oslo

IX

World Time Zones

MONDAY
SUNDAY

International Date Line

+12 +13

+11

+12

-9

-10

-11

-10

-11

-10

-7

-8

-6

-5   -4

-3:30

-4

-5

-4

-3

-4

-3

-3

-1

25   0

1 **2** **3** **4** **5** **6** **7** **8** **9** **10** **11** **12** **13** **14** **15** **16** **17** **18** **19** **20** **21** **22** **23** **24** **25**

+11   +12 -   -11   -10   -9   -8   -7   -6   -5   -4   -3   -2

Numbers below vertical bands relate each zone to Greenwich Mean Time (0 hrs.).
Local times frequently differ from these general indications,
as indicated by light-face numbers on map.

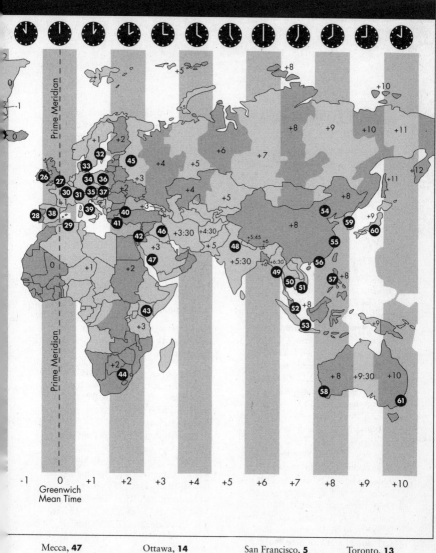

ESSENTIAL INFORMATION

AIR TRAVEL

BOOKING

When you book **look for nonstop flights** and **remember that "direct" flights stop at least once.** Try to avoid connecting flights, which require a change of plane. For more booking tips and to check prices and make on-line flight reservations, log on to www.fodors.com.

CARRIERS

From North America, Scandinavian Airlines (SAS) has daily flights to Oslo (via Copenhagen, Stockholm, Frankfurt, Reykjavik, or London) from Newark, Baltimore, Boston, Chicago, Dallas, Denver, Miami, Montréal, Los Angeles, San Francisco, Seattle, Toronto, Vancouver, and Washington, D.C. Connecting flights depart from more than 45 cities in the U.S. and Canada at least twice a week. From the United Kingdom and Ireland, SAS flies from Heathrow to Oslo, Stavanger, and Bergen, and from Aberdeen and Newcastle to Stavanger. Braathens operates daily flights from London Gatwick and flies six days a week to Oslo, Bergen, Stavanger, and Trondheim. SAS flies to Oslo daily from Sydney and Melbourne via Bangkok and Copenhagen or Stockholm.

Coast Air, an SAS subsidiary, operates scheduled flights on weekdays from Aberdeen to Haugesund and to Bergen. Ryan Air offers twice-daily bargain-price flights from London's Stansted to Oslo's Torp airport, near Sandefjord to the south. British Airways offers five flights a day from Heathrow to Oslo. British Midland Airways flies once a day on the same route. Finnair has service to Oslo.

Within Norway, SAS serves most major cities, including Svalbard. SAS and Braathens are the major domestic airlines, serving cities throughout the country and along the coast as far north as Tromsø and Longyearbyen (on Svalbard). It also has international routes from Oslo to Billund, Denmark; Malmö, Sweden; and Newcastle, England. Widerøe serves smaller airports (with smaller planes), mostly along the coast, and in northern Norway. Coast Air is a commuter airline linking both smaller and larger airports.

Icelandair and American Airlines have direct flights from the U.S. and Canada to Reykjavik or Stockholm, where you can connect with an Oslo-bound flight.

All flights within Norway are no-smoking, as are all airports, except in designated areas.

➤ MAJOR AIRLINES: **American** (☎ 800/433–7300, WEB www.aa.com). **Braathens** (☎ 0191/214–0991 in the U.K.; 81/52–00–00 in Norway). **British Airways** (☎ 0845/773377). **British Midland Airways** (☎ 0870/6070555). **Coast Air** (☎ 01224–725058). **Finnair** (☎ 800/950–5000, WEB www.finnair.com). **Icelandair** (☎ 800/223–5500, WEB www.icelandair.com). **Ryan Air** (☎ 870/1569569). **SAS** (☎ 800/221–2350 in the U.S. and Canada; 0845/607–2772 in the U.K.; 810/03–300 in Norway, WEB www.scandinavian.net). **Widerøe** (☎ 810/01–200).

CHECK-IN & BOARDING

Most carriers require you to check in two hours before your scheduled departure time for domestic flights and 2½ to 3 hours before international flights. Always **ask your carrier about its check-in policy.**

Assuming that not everyone with a ticket will show up, airlines routinely overbook planes. When everyone does, airlines ask for volunteers to give up their seats. In return, these volunteers usually get a certificate for a free flight and are rebooked on the next flight out. If there are not enough volunteers, the airline must choose who will be denied boarding. The first to get bumped are passengers who checked in late and those flying on discounted tickets, so **get to the gate and check in as early as possible,** especially during peak periods.

Always **bring a government-issued photo I.D. to the airport;** even when it's not required, a passport is best.

CUTTING COSTS

A number of special airfares are available within Norway year-round, including air passes, family tickets, weekend excursions, youth (up to the age of 25), student (up to the age of 31), and senior (older than 67) discounts. Youth fares are cheapest when purchased from the automatic ticket machines at the airport on the day of departure.

One or two stopovers can often be purchased more cheaply along with an international ticket. Icelandair, which connects Oslo with North America, gives the option to extend a layover in Reykjavik for up to three days at no extra charge; Icelandair also arranges Fly and Drive specials, which offer discounts on car rental and hotel fees if booking a flight to Oslo.

All Norwegian routes have reduced rates from July through the middle of August, and tickets can be purchased on the spot. Braathens sells a Visit Norway pass, which includes the Scandinavian BonusPass. Widerøe offers a special Summer Pass.

The **SAS Visit Scandinavia/Europe Air Pass** offers up to eight flight coupons for one-way travel within and between Scandinavian cities (and participating European cities such as Frankfurt, Paris, and London). Most one-way tickets for domestic travel within a Scandinavian country cost $65; one-way fares between Scandinavian countries are usually $75, unless you are venturing into the far north, Lapland, Iceland, or Greenland (these flights range from $115 to $225). These passes can only be bought in conjunction with a round-trip ticket between North America and Europe on SAS and must be used

within three months of arrival. SAS also provides family fares.

The cheapest tickets that SAS sells are round-trip, include a Saturday night layover, and must be bought within Scandinavia three weeks ahead of time. Ask about low rates and discounts for hotels and car rental in connection with SAS tickets. Low-price round-trip weekend excursions from one Scandinavian capital to another (minimum three-day stay) can be bought one day in advance from SAS.

It's smart to **call a number of airlines,** and when you are quoted a good price, **book it on the spot**—the same fare may not be available the next day. Always **check different routings** and look into using different airports. Travel agents, especially low-fare specialists (☞ Discounts), are helpful.

Consolidators are another good source. They buy tickets for scheduled international flights at reduced rates from the airlines, then sell them at prices that beat the best fare available directly from the airlines, usually without restrictions. Sometimes you can even get your money back if you need to return the ticket. Carefully read the fine print detailing penalties for changes and cancellations, and **confirm your consolidator reservation with the airline.**

➤ CONSOLIDATORS: **Cheap Tickets** (☎ 800/377–1000). **Discount Airline Ticket Service** (☎ 800/576–1600). **Unitravel** (☎ 800/325–2222). **Up & Away Travel** (☎ 212/889–2345). **World Travel Network** (☎ 800/409–6753).

ENJOYING THE FLIGHT

For more legroom, **request an emergency-aisle seat.** Don't sit in the row in front of the emergency aisle or in front of a bulkhead, where seats may not recline. If you have dietary concerns, **ask for special meals when booking.** These can be vegetarian, low-cholesterol, or kosher, for example. On long flights, try to maintain a normal routine, to help fight jet lag. At night, **get some sleep.** By day, **eat light meals, drink water** (not alcohol), and **move around the cabin** to stretch your legs.

For additional jet-lag tips consult *Fodor's FYI: Travel Fit & Healthy* (available at bookstores everywhere).

FLYING TIMES

A flight from New York to Oslo takes about 11 hours (there are no nonstop flights). A nonstop flight from London to Oslo is about 1¼ hours and about 1½ hours to Stavanger. From Sydney and major cities in New Zealand, the flight to Oslo will be over 20 hours, and will require at least one transfer.

HOW TO COMPLAIN

If your baggage goes astray or your flight goes awry, complain right away. Most carriers require that you **file a claim immediately.**

➤ AIRLINE COMPLAINTS: U.S. Department of Transportation **Aviation Consumer Protection Division** (✉ C-75, Room 4107, Washington, DC 20590, ☎ 202/366–2220, WEB www.dot.gov/airconsumer). **Federal Aviation Administration Consumer Hotline** (☎ 800/322–7873).

AIRPORTS

Gardermoen Airport, about 53 km (33 mi) northeast of Oslo, is the major entry point for most visitors to Norway. Other international airports are in Bergen, Kristiansand, Sandefjord, Stavanger, and Trondheim.

➤ AIRPORT INFORMATION: **Gardermoen Airport** (☎ 47/815–50–250 or 47/64–81–20–00, WEB www.osl.no/english). **Oslo Torp** (✉ Sandefjord, ☎ 33/42–70–00).

BIKE TRAVEL

BIKES IN FLIGHT

Most airlines accommodate bikes as luggage, provided they are dismantled and boxed. Airlines sell bike boxes, which are often free at bike shops, for about $5 (it's at least $100 for bike bags). International travelers can sometimes substitute a bike for a piece of checked luggage at no charge; otherwise, the cost is about $100. Domestic and Canadian airlines charge $25–$50.

BOAT & FERRY TRAVEL

Taking a ferry isn't only fun, it's often necessary in Norway. Many

companies arrange package trips, some offering a rental car and hotel accommodations as part of the deal. The word "ferry" can be deceptive; generally, the ferries are more like small-scale cruise ships, with several dining rooms, sleeping quarters, shopping, pool and sauna, and entertainment.

Ferry crossings often last overnight. The trip between Copenhagen and Oslo, for example, takes approximately 16 hours; most lines leave at about 5 PM and arrive about 9 the next morning. Two ferry lines serve Norway from the United Kingdom. Fjord Line sails from Newcastle to Stavanger, Haugesund, and Bergen. Crossings take about 22 hours.

Smyril Line operates Bergen, Torshavn (Faroe Islands), and Lerwick (Shetland) on Mondays from mid-May to mid-September. DFDS Seaways has a number of crossings, including one from Newcastle to Kristiansand (southern Norway) that continues on to Göteborg (Sweden) and one between Copenhagen and Oslo.

Ferries remain important means of transportation within Norway. Along the west coast, the fjords make car ferries a necessity. More specialized boat service includes hydrofoil-catamaran trips between Stavanger, Haugesund, and Bergen. There are also fjord cruises out of these cities and others in the north.

FARES & SCHEDULES

➤ BOAT & FERRY INFORMATION: **Color Line** (✉ Hjortneskaia, Box 1422 Vika, N–0115 Oslo, ☎ 47/22–94–44–00, FAX 47/22–83–04–30.) **DFDS Seaways** (✉ Travel Centre, 28 Queensway Quay, W2 3RX London, ☎ 020/7616–1400, WEB www.seaeurope.com). **Fjord Line** (✉ Norway House, Royal Quays, near Newcastle NE29 6EG North Shields, ☎ 0191/296–1313, WEB www.fjordline.com). **Smyril Line** (✉ P & O Scottish Ferries, POB 5, Jamieson's Quay, AB9 8DL, Aberdeen, ☎ 0122/457–2615, WEB www.smyril-line.com).

BUS TRAVEL

Bus tours can be effective for smaller regions within Norway, but the train system is excellent and offers much greater coverage in less time. Buses do, however, tend to be a less expensive mode of transport.

Every end station of the railroad is supported by a number of bus routes, some of which are operated by the Norwegian State Railway (NSB), others by local companies. Long-distance buses usually take longer than the railroad, and fares are only slightly lower. Virtually every settlement on the mainland is served by bus, and for anyone with a desire to get off the beaten track, a pay-as-you-go open-ended bus trip is the best way to see Norway.

Most long-distance buses leave from Bussterminalen close to Oslo Central Station. Nor-Way Bussekspress has more than 40 different bus services, covering 10,000 km (6,200 mi) and 500 destinations, and can arrange any journey.

CUTTING COSTS

Eurolines offers 15-, 30-, and 60-day passes for unlimited travel between Stockholm, Copenhagen, and Oslo, and more than 20 destinations throughout Europe.

➤ BUS INFORMATION: **Bussterminalen** (✉ Galleriet Oslo, Schweigaardsgt. 10, ☎ 23/00–24–00 for bus information). **Nor-Way Bussekspress** (✉ Bussterminalen, ☎ 81/44–44–44).

BUSINESS HOURS

BANKS AND OFFICES

Standard bank opening hours are weekdays 8:15–4. On Thursday many banks stay open until 5. Offices are generally open from 9–4.

SHOPS

Most shops are open from 9 or 10 to 5 weekdays, Thursday until 7, Saturday from 9 to 2 or 4, and are closed Sunday. In some areas, especially in larger cities, stores stay open later on weekdays. Large shopping centers, for example, are usually open until 8 weekdays and 6 on Saturday. Supermarkets are open until 8 or 10 weekdays and until 6 on Saturday. In summer, most shops close weekdays at 4 and at 1 on Saturday.

CAMERAS & PHOTOGRAPHY

The *Kodak Guide to Shooting Great Travel Pictures* (available at bookstores everywhere) is loaded with tips.

➤ PHOTO HELP: **Kodak Information Center** (☎ 800/242–2424).

EQUIPMENT PRECAUTIONS

Don't pack film and equipment in checked luggage, where it is much more susceptible to damage. X-ray machines used to view checked luggage are becoming much more powerful and therefore are much more likely to ruin your film. Always **keep film and tape out of the sun.** Carry an extra supply of batteries, and **be prepared to turn on your camera or camcorder** to prove to security personnel that the device is real. Always **ask for hand inspection of film,** which becomes clouded after repeated exposure to airport X-ray machines, and **keep videotapes away from metal detectors.**

CAR RENTAL

Rates in Oslo begin at $70 a day and $284 a week. This does not include tax on car rentals, which is 24%. A service charge is usually added, which ranges from $15–$25.

➤ MAJOR AGENCIES: **Alamo** (☎ 800/ 522–9696; 020/8759–6200 in the U.K.; WEB www.alamo.com). **Avis** (☎ 800/331–1084; 800/879–2847 in Canada; 02/9353–9000 in Australia; 09/525–1982 in New Zealand; 0870/ 606–0100 in the U.K.; WEB www.avis. com). **Budget** (☎ 800/527–0700; 0870/156–5656 in the U.K.; WEB www.budget.com). **Dollar** (☎ 800/ 800–6000; 0124/622–0111 in the U.K., where it's affiliated with Sixt; 02/9223–1444 in Australia; WEB www. dollar.com). **Hertz** (☎ 800/654–3001; 800/263–0600 in Canada; 020/8897– 2072 in the U.K.; 02/9669–2444 in Australia; 09/256–8690 in New Zealand; WEB www.hertz.com). **National Car Rental** (☎ 800/227– 7368; 020/8680–4800 in the U.K.; WEB www.nationalcar.com).

CUTTING COSTS

To get the best deal, **book through a travel agent who will shop around.** Do **look into wholesalers,** companies that do not own fleets but rent in bulk from those that do and often offer better rates than traditional car-rental operations. Payment must be made before you leave home.

➤ WHOLESALERS: **Auto Europe** (☎ 207/842–2000 or 800/223–5555, FAX 207/842–2222, WEB www.autoeurope.com). **DER Travel Services** (✉ 9501 W. Devon Ave., Rosemont, IL 60018, ☎ 800/782–2424, FAX 800/282–7474 for information; 800/860–9944 for brochures, WEB www.dertravel.com). **Kemwel Holiday Autos** (☎ 800/678–0678, FAX 914/825–3160, WEB www.kemwel.com).

INSURANCE

When driving a rented car you are generally responsible for any damage to or loss of the vehicle. Before you rent, see what coverage your personal auto-insurance policy and credit cards provide.

Before you buy collision coverage, check your existing policies—you may already be covered. However, collision policies that car-rental companies sell for European rentals usually do not include stolen-vehicle coverage.

REQUIREMENTS & RESTRICTIONS

Ask about age requirements: the minimum driving age in Norway is 17, but some car-rental companies require that drivers be at least 25. Your own driver's license is acceptable for a limited time; check with the Norwegian Tourist Board before you go. An International Driver's Permit is a good idea; it's available from the American or Canadian Automobile Association, or, in the United Kingdom, from the Automobile Association or Royal Automobile Club.

SURCHARGES

Before you pick up a car in one city and leave it in another, **ask about drop-off charges or one-way service fees,** which can be substantial. Note, too, that some rental agencies charge extra if you return the car before the time specified in your contract. To avoid a hefty refueling fee, **fill the tank just before you turn in the car,** but be aware that gas stations near the rental outlet may overcharge.

CAR TRAVEL

Excellent, well-marked roads make driving a great way to explore Norway, but it can be an expensive choice. Ferry costs can be steep, and reservations are vital. Tolls on some major roads add to the expense, as do the high fees for city parking; tickets for illegal parking are painfully costly.

If you're planning to motor around Norway, call or check the Web site of Vegmeldingsentralen, an information center for the Statens Vegvesen (Public Roads Administration). The center monitors and provides information about roads and road conditions, distances, and ferry timetables. Their phones are open 24 hours a day.

The southern part of Norway is fairly compact—all major cities are about a day's drive from each other. The distances make themselves felt on the way north, where Norway becomes narrower as it inches up to and beyond the Arctic Circle and hooks over Sweden and Finland to touch Russia. It is virtually impossible to visit the entire country from one base.

In a few remote areas, especially in northern Norway, road conditions can be unpredictable, so plan carefully for safety's sake. Should your road trip take you over the mountains in autumn, winter, or spring, make sure that the mountain pass you're heading to is actually open. Some high mountain roads are closed as early as October due to snow, and do not open again until June. When driving in remote areas, especially in winter, let someone know your travel plans, **use a four-wheel-drive vehicle,** and **travel with at least one other car.**

➤ CONTACT: **Vegmeldingsentralen (Road Information Center)** (☎ 175 in Norway; 81/54–89–91 from abroad, WEB www.vegvesen.no).

EMERGENCY SERVICES

Norsk Automobil-Forbund (NAF) offers roadside assistance. They patrol major roads and mountain passes from mid-June to mid-August.

➤ CONTACTS: **Norsk Automobil-Forbund (NAF)** (Norwegian Automobile Association; ✉ Storgt. 2, Box 494 Sentrum, 0155 Oslo, ☎ 22/34–

14–00; 810/00–505 for 24-hour service, WEB www.naf.no).

AUTO CLUBS

➤ IN AUSTRALIA: **Australian Automobile Association** (☎ 02/6247–7311).

➤ IN CANADA: **Canadian Automobile Association** (CAA, ☎ 613/247–0117).

➤ IN NEW ZEALAND: **New Zealand Automobile Association** (☎ 09/377–4660).

➤ IN THE U.K.: **Automobile Association** (AA, ☎ 0990/500–600). **Royal Automobile Club** (RAC, ☎ 0990/722–722 for membership; 0345/121–345 for insurance).

➤ IN THE U.S.: **American Automobile Association** (☎ 800/564–6222).

GASOLINE

Gas stations are plentiful, and *blyfri bensin* (unleaded gasoline) and diesel fuel are sold everywhere from self-service pumps. Those marked *kort* are 24-hour pumps, which take oil-company credit cards or bank cards, either of which is inserted directly into the pump. Gas costs approximately NKr 10 (US$1.13) per liter (that's NKr 38, or US$4.29, per gallon). Don't wait until you're empty before looking for a gas station; hours vary greatly.

INSURANCE

All vehicles registered abroad are required to carry international liability insurance and an international accident report form, which can be obtained from automobile clubs. Collision insurance is recommended.

ROAD CONDITIONS

Four-lane highways are the exception and are found only around major cities. Outside of main routes, roads tend to be narrow and twisting, with only token guardrails, and in summer roads are always crowded. Along the west coast, waits for ferries and passage through tunnels can be significant. Don't expect to cover more than 240 km (150 mi) in a day, especially in fjord country.

Norwegian roads are well marked with directional, distance, and informational signs. Some roads, particularly those over mountains, can close for all or part of the winter. If you drive outside major roads in winter, make sure the car is equipped with studded tires. Roads are not salted but are left with a hard-packed layer of snow on top of the asphalt. If you're renting, choose a small car with front-wheel drive. Also bring an ice scraper, snow brush, small shovel, and heavy clothes for emergencies. Although the weather along the coast is sunny, a few hours inland temperatures may be 15°F (8°F) colder, and snowfall is the rule rather than the exception.

RULES OF THE ROAD

Driving is on the right. Yield to vehicles approaching from the right. Make sure you have an up-to-date map before you venture out, because some highway numbers have changed in the past few years, particularly routes beginning with "E."

The maximum speed limit is 90 kph (55 mph) on major motorways. On other highways, the limit is 80 kph (50 mph). The speed limit in cities and towns is 50 kph (30 mph), and 30 kph (18 mph) in residential areas.

Keep your headlights on at all times; this is required by law. Also by Norwegian law, everyone, including infants, must **wear seat belts.** Children under four years must be in a car seat, and children over four years must ride in the back. All cars must carry red reflecting warning triangles, to be placed a safe distance from a disabled vehicle.

Norway has strict drinking-and-driving laws, and there are routine roadside checks. The legal limit is a blood-alcohol percentage of 0.02%, which effectively means that you should not drink any amount of alcohol before driving. If you are stopped, you may be required to take a breath test. If it is positive, you must submit to a blood test. No exceptions are made for foreigners, who can lose their licenses on the spot. Other penalties include fines and imprisonment. An accident involving a driver with an illegal blood-alcohol level usually voids all insurance agreements, so the driver becomes responsible for his own medical bills and damage to the cars.

Speeding is also punished severely. Most roads are monitored by radar and cameras in gray metal boxes. Signs warning of *Automatisk Trafikkontroll* (Automatic Traffic Monitoring) are posted periodically along many roads.

CHILDREN IN NORWAY

In Norway children are to be seen *and* heard and are genuinely welcome in most public places.

If you are renting a car, don't forget to **arrange for a car seat** when you reserve. For general advice about traveling with young children, consult *Fodor's FYI: Travel with Your Baby* (available in bookstores everywhere).

DISCOUNTS

Children are entitled to discount tickets (often as much as 50% off) on buses, trains, and ferries throughout Norway, as well as reductions on special City Cards. Children under age 12 pay 75% of the adult fare and children under age 2 pay 10% on SAS round-trips. There are no restrictions on the children's fares when booked in economy class. "Family fares," only available in business class, are also worth looking into (☞ Cutting Costs *in* Air Travel).

With the Scanrail Pass (☞ Train Travel)—good for rail journeys throughout Scandinavia—children under age 4 (on lap) travel free; those ages 4–11 pay half-fare and those ages 12–25 can get a Scanrail Youth Pass, providing a 25% discount off the adult fare.

FLYING

If your children are age 2 or older, **ask about children's airfares.** As a general rule, infants under 2 not occupying a seat fly at greatly reduced fares or even for free. When booking, **confirm carry-on allowances** if you're traveling with infants. In general, for babies charged 10% of the adult fare you are allowed one carry-on bag and a collapsible stroller; if the flight is full, the stroller may have to be checked or you may be limited to less.

Experts agree that it's a good idea to use safety seats aloft for children weighing less than 40 pounds. Airlines set their own policies: U.S. carriers usually require that the child be ticketed, even if he or she is young enough to ride free, since the seats must be strapped into regular seats. Do **check your airline's policy about using safety seats during takeoff and landing.** And since safety seats are not allowed everywhere in the plane, get your seat assignments early.

When reserving, **request children's meals or a freestanding bassinet** if you need them. But note that bulkhead seats, where you must sit to use the bassinet, may lack an overhead bin or storage space on the floor. For all airlines servicing Norway, it is necessary to reserve children's and baby meals at least 24 hours in advance; travel of an unaccompanied minor should be confirmed at least three days prior to the flight.

LODGING

Most hotels in Norway allow children under a certain age to stay in their parents' room at no extra charge, but others charge for them as extra adults; be sure to **find out the cutoff age for children's discounts.**

SIGHTS & ATTRACTIONS

Places that are especially appealing to children are indicated by a rubber-duckie icon (☺) in the margin.

CONSUMER PROTECTION

Whenever shopping or buying travel services, **pay with a major credit card,** if possible, so you can cancel payment or get reimbursed if there's a problem. If you're doing business with a particular company for the first time, **contact your local Better Business Bureau and the attorney general's offices** in your state and (for U.S. businesses) the company's home state as well. Have any complaints been filed? Finally, if you're buying a package or tour, always **consider travel insurance** that includes default coverage (☞ Insurance).

➤ BBBs: **Council of Better Business Bureaus** (✉ 4200 Wilson Blvd., Suite 800, Arlington, VA 22203, ☎ 703/276–0100, FAX 703/525–8277, WEB www.bbb.org).

CRUISE TRAVEL

Norway's most renowned boat is *Hurtigruten,* which literally means "Rapid Route." Also known as the Coastal Steamer, the boat departs from Bergen and stops at 36 ports along the coast in six days, ending with Kirkenes, near the Russian border, before turning back. Tickets can be purchased for the entire journey or for individual legs. Tickets are available through Bergen Line travel agents or directly from the companies that run the service: FFR in Hammerfest, OVDS in Narvik, and Hurtigruten Coastal Express Bookings and TFDS in Tromsø.

To learn how to plan, choose, and book a cruise-ship voyage, consult *Fodor's FYI: Plan & Enjoy Your Cruise* (available in bookstores everywhere).

➤ CRUISE LINES: **Bergen Line Travel Agents** (✉ 405 Park Ave., New York, NY 10022, ☎ 212/319–1300). **FFR** (✉ POB 308, 9615 Hammerfest, ☎ 78/40–70–51, WEB www.ffr.no). *Hurtigruten* (✉ Coastal Express, Veiten 2B, 5012, ☎ 55/23–07–90). **Hurtigruten Coastal Express Bookings** (☎ 810/30–000). **OVDS** (✉ POB 43, 8501 8514 Narvik, ☎ 76/96–76–00, WEB www.ovds.no). **TFDS** (✉ 9291 Tromsø, ☎ 77/64–82–00).

CUSTOMS & DUTIES

When shopping, **keep receipts** for all purchases. Upon reentering the country, **be ready to show customs officials what you've bought.** If you feel a duty is incorrect or object to the way your clearance was handled, note the inspector's badge number and ask to see a supervisor. If the problem isn't resolved, write to the appropriate authorities, beginning with the port director at your point of entry.

IN AUSTRALIA

Australian residents who are 18 or older may bring home $A400 worth of souvenirs and gifts (including jewelry), 250 cigarettes or 250 grams of tobacco, and 1,125 ml of alcohol (including wine, beer, and spirits). Residents under 18 may bring back $A200 worth of goods. Prohibited items include meat products. Seeds, plants, and fruits need to be declared upon arrival.

➤ INFORMATION: **Australian Customs Service** (Regional Director, ✉ Box 8, Sydney, NSW 2001, Australia, ☎ 02/9213–2000, FAX 02/9213–4000, WEB www.customs.gov.au).

IN CANADA

Canadian residents who have been out of Canada for at least seven days may bring home C$750 worth of goods duty-free. If you've been away fewer than seven days but more than 48 hours, the duty-free allowance drops to C$200; if your trip lasts 24–48 hours, the allowance is C$50. You may not pool allowances with family members. Goods claimed under the C$750 exemption may follow you by mail; those claimed under the lesser exemptions must accompany you. Alcohol and tobacco products may be included in the seven-day and 48-hour exemptions but not in the 24-hour exemption. If you meet the age requirements of the province or territory through which you reenter Canada, you may bring in, duty-free, 1.14 liters (40 imperial ounces) of wine or liquor *or* 24 12-ounce cans or bottles of beer or ale. If you are 19 or older you may bring in, duty-free, 200 cigarettes and 50 cigars. Check ahead of time with the Canada Customs Revenue Agency or the Department of Agriculture for policies regarding meat products, seeds, plants, and fruits.

You may send an unlimited number of gifts worth up to C$60 each duty-free to Canada. Label the package UNSOLICITED GIFT—VALUE UNDER $60. Alcohol and tobacco are excluded.

➤ INFORMATION: **Canada Customs and Revenue Agency** (✉ 2265 St. Laurent Blvd. S, Ottawa, Ontario K1G 4K3, Canada, ☎ 204/983–3500 or 506/636–5064; 800/461–9999 in Canada, WEB www.ccra-adrc.gc.ca).

IN NEW ZEALAND

Homeward-bound residents 17 or older may bring back $700 worth of souvenirs and gifts. Your duty-free allowance also includes 4.5 liters of wine or beer; one 1,125-ml bottle of spirits; and either 200 cigarettes, 250 grams of tobacco, 50 cigars, or a combination of the three up to 250 grams. Prohibited items include meat products, seeds, plants, and fruits.

➤ INFORMATION: **New Zealand Customs** (Custom House, ✉ 50 Anzac Ave., Box 29, Auckland, New Zealand, ☎ 09/300–5399, FAX 09/ 359–6730, WEB www.customs.govt.nz).

IN NORWAY

Custom regulations have the following duty-free limits: 2 liters of beer, 1 liter of liquor (up to 60% alcohol), 1 liter of wine (up to 22%) or 2 liters of wine or 2 liters of beer if no liquor, 200 cigarettes or 250 grams of tobacco and 200 cigarette papers. You must be over 20 to take in liquor and over 18 years for wine, beer, and tobacco products. You may not bring any vegetables, fruits, dairy products, or other un-cooked foods into Norway. Dried and canned foodstuffs are allowed.

IN THE U.K.

If you are a U.K. resident and your journey was wholly within the European Union (EU), you won't have to pass through customs when you return to the United Kingdom. If you plan to bring back large quantities of alcohol or tobacco, check EU limits beforehand. From countries outside the European Union, including Iceland and Norway, you may bring home, duty-free, 200 cigarettes or 50 cigars; 1 liter of spirits or 2 liters of fortified or sparkling wine or liqueurs; 2 liters of still table wine; 60 ml of perfume; 250 ml of toilet water; plus £145 worth of other goods, including gifts and souvenirs. If returning from outside the EU, pro-hibited items include meat products, seeds, plants, and fruits.

➤ INFORMATION: **HM Customs and Excise** (✉ St. Christopher House, Southwark, London, SE1 OTE, U.K., ☎ 020/7928–3344, WEB www. hmce.gov.uk).

IN THE U.S.

U.S. residents who have been out of the country for at least 48 hours (and who have not used the $400 allowance or any part of it in the past 30 days) may bring home $400 worth of foreign goods duty-free.

U.S. residents age 21 and older may bring back 1 liter of alcohol duty-free. In addition, regardless of your age, you are allowed 200 cigarettes and 100 non-Cuban cigars. Antiques, which the U.S. Customs Service defines as objects more than 100 years old, enter duty-free, as do original works of art done entirely by hand, including paintings, drawings, and sculptures.

You may also mail or ship packages home duty-free: up to $200 worth of goods for personal use, with a limit of one parcel per addressee per day (except alcohol or tobacco products or perfume worth more than $5); label the package PERSONAL USE and attach a list of its contents and their retail value. Do not label the package UNSOLICITED GIFT or your duty-free exemption will drop to $100. Mailed items do not affect your duty-free allowance on your return.

➤ INFORMATION: **U.S. Customs Service** (✉ 1300 Pennsylvania Ave. NW, Room 6.3D, Washington, DC 20229, WEB www.customs.gov; inquiries ☎ 202/354–1000; complaints c/o ✉ 1300 Pennsylvania Ave. NW, Room 5.4D, Washington, DC 20229; registration of equipment c/o Office of Passenger Programs, ☎ 202/ 927–0530).

DINING

Major cities offer a full range of dining choices, from traditional to international restaurants. The restau-rants we list (all of which are indi-cated by a ✗) are the cream of the crop in each price category. Properties indicated by an ✗▥ are lodging establishments whose restaurant warrants a special trip. Price cate-gories are as follows:

CATEGORY	COST*
$$$$	over NKr 250
$$$	NKr 200–NKr 250
$$	NKr 150–NKr 200
$	under NKr 150

*per person for a main course at dinner

Restaurant meals are a big-ticket item in Norway, but there are ways to keep the cost of eating down. Take full advantage of the large, buffet break-fast often included in the cost of a hotel room. At lunch, look for the "menu" that offers a set two- or three-course meal for a set price, or limit yourself to a hearty appetizer. Some restaurants now include a trip to the salad bar in the dinner price. At dinner, pay careful attention to the price of wine and drinks, since the high tax on alcohol raises these costs considerably. For more information on affordable eating, *see* Money Matters.

MEALS & SPECIALTIES

The surrounding oceans and plentiful inland lakes and streams provide Norway with an abundance of fresh fish and seafood: salmon, herring, trout, and seafood delicacies are mainstays, and are prepared in countless ways. Elk, deer, reindeer, and lamb feed in relatively unspoiled areas and have the succulent taste of wild game. Berries and mushrooms are still harvested from the forests; sausage appears in a thousand forms, as do potatoes and other root vegetables such as turnips, radishes, rutabaga, and carrots. Some particular northern tastes can seem unusual, such as the fondness for pickled and fermented fish—to be sampled carefully at first—but are coupled with a universal obsession with sweet pastries, ice cream, and chocolate.

Other novelties for the visitor might be the use of fruit in main dishes and soups, or sour milk on breakfast cereal, or preserved fish paste as a spread for crackers, or the prevalence of tasty, whole-grain crisp breads and hearty rye breads. The *smörgåsbord,* a buffet meal, is less common these days, but is still the traveling diner's best bet for breakfast. A smörgåsbord usually comes with a wide range of cheeses, fresh fish, and vegetables alongside meat and breads and other starches. For more information on Norway's cuisine, *see* Pleasures and Pastimes, *in* chapter 1.

MEALTIMES

Unless otherwise noted, the restaurants listed in this guide are open daily for lunch and dinner.

RESERVATIONS & DRESS

Reservations are always a good idea: we mention them only when they're essential or not accepted. Book as far ahead as you can, and reconfirm as soon as you arrive. We mention dress only when men are required to wear a jacket or a jacket and tie.

WINE, BEER & SPIRITS

Restaurants' markup on alcoholic beverages is often very high in Norway: as much as four times that of a standard retail price.

DISABILITIES & ACCESSIBILITY

Facilities for travelers with disabilities are generally good, and most of the major tourist offices offer special booklets and brochures on travel and accommodations. The Norwegian Association of the Disabled (NHF) gives advice on public and local transportation, sights and museums, hotels, and special interest tours. Notify and make all local and public transportation and hotel reservations in advance to ensure a smooth trip.

➤ LOCAL RESOURCES: **The Norwegian Association of the Disabled** (NHF; ✉ Box 9217 Gronland, N-0134 Oslo, Norway, ☎ 47/22–17–02–55, FAX 47/22–17–61–77, WEB www.nhf.no).

LODGING

Best Western has properties with wheelchair-accessible rooms in Oslo. If wheelchair-accessible rooms on other floors are not available, ground-floor rooms are provided.

➤ WHEELCHAIR-ACCESSIBLE CHAIN: **Best Western** (☎ 800/528–1234).

RESERVATIONS

When discussing accessibility with an operator or reservations agent, **ask hard questions.** Are there any stairs, inside *or* out? Are there grab bars next to the toilet *and* in the shower/tub? How wide is the doorway to the room? To the bathroom? For the most extensive facilities, **opt for newer accommodations.**

SIGHTS & ATTRACTIONS

Although most major attractions in Oslo present no problems, areas in the older sections of city may be challenging for travelers with disabilities.

TRANSPORTATION

With advance notice, most airlines, buses, and trains can arrange assistance for those requiring extra help with boarding. Contact each individual company at least one week in advance, or ideally at the time of booking. Call Oslo Taxi or Taxi 2 for vans and taxis equipped for wheelchairs.

Confirming ahead is especially important when planning travel to less populated regions. The smaller planes and ferries often used in such areas are not all accessible.

➤ RESOURCES: **Oslo Taxi** (☎ 02323). **Taxi 2** (☎ 02202).

➤ COMPLAINTS: **Aviation Consumer Protection Division** (☞ Air Travel) for airline-related problems. **Civil Rights Office** (✉ U.S. Department of Transportation, Departmental Office of Civil Rights, S-30, 400 7th St. SW, Room 10215, Washington, DC 20590, ☎ 202/366–4648, FAX 202/366–9371, WEB www.dot.gov/ost/docr/index.htm) for problems with surface transportation. **Disability Rights Section** (✉ U.S. Department of Justice, Civil Rights Division, Box 66738, Washington, DC 20035-6738, ☎ 202/514–0301 or 800/514–0301; 202/514–0383 TTY; 800/514–0383 TTY, FAX 202/307–1198, WEB www.usdoj.gov/crt/ada/adahom1.htm) for general complaints.

TRAVEL AGENCIES

In the United States, the Americans with Disabilities Act requires that travel firms serve the needs of all travelers. Some agencies specialize in working with people with disabilities.

➤ TRAVELERS WITH MOBILITY PROBLEMS: **Access Adventures** (✉ 206 Chestnut Ridge Rd., Scottsville, NY 14624, ☎ 716/889–9096, dltravel@prodigy.net), run by a former physical-rehabilitation counselor. **CareVacations** (✉ No. 5, 5110–50 Ave., Leduc, Alberta T9E 6V4, Canada, ☎ 780/986–6404 or 877/478–7827, FAX 780/986–8332, WEB www.carevacations.com), for group tours and cruise vacations. **Flying Wheels Travel** (✉ 143 W. Bridge St., Box 382, Owatonna, MN 55060, ☎ 507/451–5005 or 800/535–6790, FAX 507/451–1685, WEB www.flyingwheelstravel.com).

DISCOUNTS & DEALS

Be a smart shopper and **compare all your options** before making decisions. A plane ticket bought with a promotional coupon from travel clubs, coupon books, and direct-mail offers or on the Internet may not be cheaper than the least expensive fare from a discount ticket agency. And always keep in mind that what you get is just as important as what you save.

DISCOUNT RESERVATIONS

To save money, **look into discount reservations services** with toll-free numbers, which use their buying power to get a better price on hotels, airline tickets, even car rentals. When booking a room, always **call the hotel's local toll-free number** (if one is available) rather than the central reservations number—you'll often get a better price. Always ask about special packages or corporate rates.

When shopping for the best deal on hotels and car rentals, **look for guaranteed exchange rates,** which protect you against a falling dollar. With your rate locked in, you won't pay more, even if the price goes up in the local currency.

➤ AIRLINE TICKETS: ☎ **800/247–4537.**

➤ HOTEL ROOMS: **International Marketing & Travel Concepts** (☎ 800/790–4682, WEB www.imtc-travel.com). **Players Express Vacations** (☎ 800/458–6161, WEB www.playersexpress.com). **Steigenberger Reservation Service** (☎ 800/223–5652, WEB www.srs-worldhotels.com). **Travel Interlink** (☎ 800/888–5898, WEB www.travelinterlink.com). **Turbotrip.com** (☎ 800/473–7829, WEB www.turbotrip.com).

PACKAGE DEALS

Don't confuse packages and guided tours. When you buy a package, you travel on your own, just as though you had planned the trip yourself. Fly/drive packages, which combine airfare and car rental, are often a good deal. If you **buy a rail/drive pass,** you may save on train tickets and car rentals. All Eurail- and Europass holders get a discount on Eurostar fares through the Channel

Tunnel. Also check rates for Scanrail Passes (☞ Train Travel).

ELECTRICITY

To use electric-powered equipment purchased in the United States or Canada, **bring a converter and adapter.** The electrical current in Norway is 220 volts, 50 cycles alternating current (AC); wall outlets take Continental-type plugs, with two round prongs.

If your appliances are dual-voltage, you'll need only an adapter. Don't use 110-volt outlets marked FOR SHAVERS ONLY for high-wattage appliances such as blow-dryers. Most laptops operate equally well on 110 and 220 volts and so require only an adapter.

EMBASSIES

➤ AUSTRALIA: (✉ Jerbanetorget 2, Oslo, ☎ 22/47–91–70).

➤ CANADA: (✉ Wergeslandsvn. 7, Oslo, ☎ 22/99–53–00).

➤ NEW ZEALAND: (✉ Billengstad-sletta 19, Oslo, ☎ 66/77–53–30).

➤ UNITED KINGDOM: (✉ Thomas Heftyes gt. 8, Oslo, ☎ 22/13–27–00).

➤ UNITED STATES: (✉ Drammensvn. 18, Oslo, ☎ 22/44–85–50).

EMERGENCIES

Ambulance, fire, and police assistance is available 24 hours.

➤ CONTACTS: **Ambulance** (☎ 113). **Fire** (☎ 110). **Police** (☎ 112).

GAY & LESBIAN TRAVEL

Scandinavian countries were at the forefront of women's rights at the turn of the 20th century, and Scandinavia has also had a liberal attitude toward gays and lesbians. The government of Norway grants to same-sex couples the same or nearly the same rights as those who are married.

➤ GAY- & LESBIAN-FRIENDLY TRAVEL AGENCIES: **Different Roads Travel** (✉ 8383 Wilshire Blvd., Suite 902, Beverly Hills, CA 90211, ☎ 323/651–5557 or 800/429–8747, FAX 323/651–3678, lgernert@tzell.com). **Kennedy Travel** (✉ 314 Jericho Turnpike, Floral Park, NY 11001, ☎ 516/352–4888 or 800/237–7433, FAX 516/354–

8849, WEB www.kennedytravel.com). **Now Voyager** (✉ 4406 18th St., San Francisco, CA 94114, ☎ 415/626–1169 or 800/255–6951, FAX 415/626–8626, WEB www.nowvoyager.com). **Skylink Travel and Tour** (✉ 1006 Mendocino Ave., Santa Rosa, CA 95401, ☎ 707/546–9888 or 800/225–5759, FAX 707/546–9891, WEB www.skylinktravel.com), serving lesbian travelers.

HEALTH

MEDICATIONS

You are permitted to take medicines for your own personal use into the country. To avoid problems with customs, bring a letter from your doctor stating their need. Some medicines bought in Norway are marked with a red triangle, and should not be taken before operating a motorized vehicle.

HOLIDAYS

Major national holidays include: New Year's Eve (Dec. 31); New Year's Day (Jan. 1); Maundy (Holy) Thursday (Mar. 28, 2002; Apr. 17, 2003); Good Friday (Mar. 29, 2002; Apr. 18, 2003), Easter Sunday (Mar. 31, 2002; Apr. 20, 2003); Easter Monday (Apr. 1, 2002; Apr. 21, 2003); May Day (May 1; celebrated as Labor Day); Constitution Day (May 17); Pentecost (May 19, 2002; June 8, 2003); Midsummer Eve and Midsummer Night (June 23 and 24); St. Olav's Day (July 29); Christmas Eve and Christmas Day (Dec. 24 and 25); Boxing Day (Dec. 26).

On major holidays such as Christmas, most shops close or operate on a Sunday schedule. On the eves of such holidays, many shops are also closed all day or are open with reduced hours.

On May Day, the city centers are usually full of people, celebrations and parades. During Midsummer, locals flock to the lakes and countryside to celebrate the beginning of long summer days with bonfires and other festivities.

INSURANCE

The most useful travel-insurance plan is a comprehensive policy that includes coverage for trip cancellation and interruption, default, trip delay, and medical expenses (with a waiver for pre-existing conditions).

Without insurance you will lose all or most of your money if you cancel your trip, regardless of the reason. Default insurance covers you if your tour operator, airline, or cruise line goes out of business. Trip-delay covers expenses that arise because of bad weather or mechanical delays. Study the fine print when comparing policies.

If you're traveling internationally, a key component of travel insurance is coverage for medical bills incurred if you get sick on the road. Such expenses are not generally covered by Medicare or private policies. U.K. residents can buy a travel-insurance policy valid for most vacations taken during the year in which it's purchased (but check pre-existing-condition coverage). British and Australian citizens need extra medical coverage when traveling overseas.

Always **buy travel policies directly from the insurance company**; if you buy them from a cruise line, airline, or tour operator that goes out of business you probably will not be covered for the agency or operator's default, a major risk. Before making any purchase, **review your existing health and homeowner's policies** to find what they cover away from home.

➤ TRAVEL INSURERS: In the U.S.: **Access America** (⊠ 6600 W. Broad St., Richmond, VA 23230, ☎ 800/284–8300, FAX 804/673–1491, WEB www.etravelprotection.com). **Travel Guard International** (⊠ 1145 Clark St., Stevens Point, WI 54481, ☎ 715/345–0505 or 800/826–1300, FAX 800/955–8785, WEB www.travelguard.com).

➤ INSURANCE INFORMATION: In the U.K.: **Association of British Insurers** (⊠ 51–55 Gresham St., London EC2V 7HQ, U.K., ☎ 020/7600–3333, FAX 020/7696–8999, WEB www.abi.org.uk). In Canada: **RBC Travel Insurance** (⊠ 6880 Financial Dr., Mississauga, Ontario L5N 7Y5, Canada, ☎ 905/791–8700; 800/668–4342 in Canada, FAX 905/816–2498, WEB www.royalbank.com). In Aus-

tralia: **Insurance Council of Australia** (⊠ Level 3, 56 Pitt St., Sydney NSW 2000, ☎ 02/9253–5100, FAX 02/9253–5111, WEB www.ica.com.au). In New Zealand: **Insurance Council of New Zealand** (⊠ Level 7, 111–115 Customhouse Quay, Box 474, Wellington, New Zealand, ☎ 04/472–5230, FAX 04/473–3011, WEB www.icnz.org.nz).

LANGUAGE

Despite the fact that Norwegian is in the Germanic family of languages, it is a myth that someone who speaks German can understand it. Fortunately, English is widely spoken. German is the most common third language. English becomes rarer outside major cities, and it's a good idea to **take along a dictionary or phrase book.** Even here, however, anyone under the age of 50 is likely to have studied English in school. Fluent Swedish speakers can generally understand Norwegian.

Norwegian has three additional vowels: æ, ø, and å. Æ is pronounced as a short "a." The ø, sometimes printed as *oe*, is the same as ö in German and Swedish, pronounced very much like a short "u." The å is a contraction of the archaic "aa" and sounds like long "o." These three letters appear at the end of alphabetical listings such as those in the phone book.

There are two officially sanctioned Norwegian languages, Bokmål and Nynorsk. Bokmål is used by 84% of the population and is the main written form of Norwegian and the language of books, as the first half of its name indicates. Nynorsk, which translates as "new Norwegian," is actually a compilation of older dialect forms from rural Norway. Every Norwegian also receives at least seven years of English instruction, starting in the second grade. The Sámi (or Lapps), who inhabit the northernmost parts of Norway, have their own language, which is distantly related to Finnish.

LODGING

The lodgings we list are the cream of the crop in each price category. We always list all the facilities that are available—but we don't specify whether they cost extra. When pricing accommodations, always ask what's included. Price categories are as follows:

CATEGORY	COST*
$$$$	over NKr 1,500
$$$	NKr 1,200–NKr 1,500
$$	NKr 800–NKr 1,200
$	under NKr 800

All prices are for a standard double room, including service and 23% VAT.

In larger cities, lodging ranges from first-class business hotels run by SAS, Sheraton, and Scandic; to good-quality tourist-class hotels, such as RESO, Best Western, and Scandic Budget; to a wide variety of single-entrepreneur hotels. In the countryside, look for independently run inns and motels, called *fjellstuer* or *pensjonat*. Farm holidays have become increasingly available to tourists; there are organizations that can help organize stays in the countryside.

Before you leave home, **ask your travel agent about discounts** (☞ Hotels), including a summer Fjord pass; summer hotel checks for Best Western and Scandic hotels; and enormous year-round rebates at SAS hotels for travelers over 65. All Euro-Class (business class) passengers can get discounts of at least 10% at SAS hotels when they book through SAS.

Two things about hotels in Norway usually surprise North Americans: the relatively limited dimensions of beds and the generous size of breakfasts. Double beds are often about 60 inches wide or slightly less, close in size to the U.S. queen size. King-size beds (72 inches wide) are difficult to find and, if available, require special reservations.

Older hotels may have some rooms described as "double," which in fact have one double bed plus one foldout sofa big enough for two people. This arrangement is occasionally called a combi-room but is being phased out.

Many older hotels, particularly the country inns and independently run smaller hotels in the cities, do not have private bathrooms. Ask ahead if this is important to you.

Breakfasts in Norway resemble what many people would call lunch, usu-ally including breads, cheeses, marmalade, hams, lunch meats, eggs, juice, cereal, milk, and coffee. Generally, the farther north you go, the larger the breakfasts become. Breakfast is usually included in hotel rates.

Make reservations whenever possible. Even countryside inns, which usually have space, are sometimes packed with vacationing Europeans. When making reservations, **ask about high and low seasons.** Some hotels lower prices during what they determine to be "tourist season," whereas others raise them during the same period.

Assume that hotels operate on the **European Plan** (EP, with no meals) unless we specify that they use the **Continental Plan** (CP, with a Continental breakfast), **Modified American Plan** (MAP, with breakfast and dinner), or the **Full American Plan** (FAP, with all meals).

For more information on lodging, *see* Pleasures and Pastimes, *in* chapter 1.

APARTMENT & VILLA RENTALS

If you want a home base that's roomy enough for a family and comes with cooking facilities, **consider a furnished rental.** These can save you money, especially if you're traveling with a group. Home-exchange directories sometimes list rentals as well as exchanges.

➤ INTERNATIONAL AGENTS: **Drawbridge to Europe** (⊠ 98 Granite St., Ashland, OR 97520, ☎ 541/482–7778 or 888/268–1148, ℻ 541/482–7779, WEB www.drawbridgetoeurope.com).

CABINS & CAMPING

Norway has more than 1,000 campsites, all of which are given anywhere from one to five stars based on the standard facilities and activities available. Fees vary but generally each site costs somewhere around NKr 80–160 per day. For camping information and a list of sites, contact local tourist offices. Open fires are illegal in forest or open land between April 15 and September 15.

Many of Norway's campsites also have some cabins available. These are also rated on a five-star system. Most have electricity and heat, but you may have to bring your own bedding. Cost per night is around NKr 250–NKr 750. The DNT hiking organization runs hundreds of the cabins and lodges, especially in the south.

The Norsk Campingkort (Norwegian Camping Card) entitles you to faster check-in service and discounts on cabins and campsites. The cards cost NKr 60 for a year and can be ordered before traveling through the Reiselivsbedriftenes Landsforening (RBL).

➤ CONTACTS: **Den Norske Turistforening (DNT)** (The Norwegian Mountain Touring Association; ✉ Box 7 Sentrum, 0101 Oslo 1, ☎ 22/82–28–22, FAX 22/82–28–23, WEB www.turistforeningen.no). **Reiselivsbedriftenes Landsforening (RBL)** (Norwegian Hospitality Association; ✉ Box 5465, Majorstua, 0305 Oslo, ☎ 23/08–86–20, FAX 23/08–86–21, WEB www.camping.no).

FARM & COTTAGE HOLIDAYS

The old-fashioned farm or countryside holiday, long a staple for Norwegian city dwellers, is becoming increasingly available to tourists. In most cases, you can choose to stay on the farm itself, and even participate in daily activities, or you can opt to rent a private, housekeeping cottage. Seaside fisherman's cabins (or *rorbuer*) are available, particularly in the Lofoten Islands. Contact the local tourist board for details.

HOME EXCHANGES

If you would like to exchange your home for someone else's, **join a home-exchange organization,** which will send you its updated listings of available exchanges for a year and will include your own listing in at least one of them. It's up to you to make specific arrangements.

➤ EXCHANGE CLUBS: **HomeLink International** (✉ Box 47747, Tampa, FL 33647, ☎ 813/975–9825 or 800/638–3841, FAX 813/910–8144, WEB www.homelink.org; $106 per year). **Intervac U.S.** (✉ Box 590504, San Francisco, CA 94159, ☎ 800/756–4663, FAX 415/435–7440, WEB www.intervacus.com; $93 yearly fee includes one catalog and on-line access).

HOSTELS

No matter what your age, you can **save on lodging costs by staying at hostels.** In some 4,500 locations in more than 70 countries around the world, Hostelling International (HI), the umbrella group for a number of national youth-hostel associations, offers single-sex, dorm-style beds and, at many hostels, rooms for couples and family accommodations. Membership in any HI national hostel association, open to travelers of all ages, allows you to stay in HI-affiliated hostels at member rates; one-year membership is about $25 for adults (C$26.75 in Canada, £9.30 in the U.K., $30 in Australia, and $30 in New Zealand); hostels run about $10–$25 per night. If a hostel has nearly filled up, members have priority over others; members are also eligible for discounts around the world, even on rail and bus travel in some countries. The Norwegian branch, Norske Vandrerhjem, maintains a list of Norwegian hostels.

➤ ORGANIZATIONS: **Hostelling International—American Youth Hostels** (✉ 733 15th St. NW, Suite 840, Washington, DC 20005, ☎ 202/783–6161, FAX 202/783–6171, WEB www.hiayh.org). **Hostelling International—Canada** (✉ 400–205 Catherine St., Ottawa, Ontario K2P 1C3, Canada, ☎ 613/237–7884; 800/663–5777 in Canada, FAX 613/237–7868, WEB www.hostellingintl.ca). **Norske Vandrerhjem** (Hostelling International Norway; ✉ Dronningensgt. 26, 0154 Oslo, ☎ 22/13–93–00, FAX 22/13–93–50, WEB www.vandrerhjem.no). **Youth Hostel Association of England and Wales** (✉ Trevelyan House, 8 St. Stephen's Hill, St. Albans, Hertfordshire AL1 2DY, U.K., ☎ 0870/8708808, FAX 01727/844126, WEB www.yha.org.uk). **Youth Hostel Association Australia** (✉ 10 Mallett St., Camperdown, NSW 2050, Australia, ☎ 02/9565–1699, FAX 02/9565–1325, WEB www.yha.com.au). **Youth Hostels Association of New Zealand** (✉ Level 3, 193 Cashel St., Box 436, Christchurch, New Zealand, ☎ 03/379–9970, FAX 03/365–4476, WEB www.yha.org.nz).

HOTELS

All hotels listed have private baths unless otherwise noted.

Inn Checks, prepaid hotel vouchers, offer discounts of up to 50% for accommodations ranging from first-class hotels to country cottages. The vouchers must be purchased from travel agents or from the Scandinavian Tourist Board (☞ Visitor Information) before departure and are sold individually and in packets for as many nights as needed. Winter bargains are often better than those in summer. A *Fjord Pass,* which costs NKr 85, is valid for two adults and any number of children under the age of 15. Valid May through September, the discount card can make it possible to stay at a hotel for NKr 215 per person per day at 225 hotels, guest houses, apartments, and holiday cottages. You can get the Pass from travel agents, tourist information offices, Fjord Pass hotels, some post offices, and railway stations.

ProSkandinavia checks can be used in 400 hotels across Scandinavia for savings up to 50%, for reservations made usually no earlier than 24 hours before arrival, although some hotels allow earlier bookings. One check costs about $35 U.S. Two checks will pay for a double room at a hotel, one check for a room in a cottage. The checks can be bought at many travel agencies in Scandinavia or ordered directly from ProSkandinavia.

➤ CONTACTS: **Best Western Hotels Norway** (☎ 0800/393–130, WEB www.bestwestern.com). **Norway Fjord Pass** (☎ 55/55–76–60, WEB www.fjordpass.com). **ProSkandinavia** (✉ Nedre Slottsgate 13, N-0157 Oslo, ☎ 47/22–42–50–06, FAX 47/22–42–06–57, WEB www.proskandinavia.com). **Scan+ Hotel Pass** (☎ 23/08–02–80, WEB www.norlandia.no). **Scandic Club Card** (☎ 46/85–17–51–700, WEB www.scandic.hotels.com). **Nordic Hotel Pass** (☎ 22/40–13–88, WEB www.choice.no).

➤ TOLL-FREE NUMBERS: **Best Western** (☎ 800/528–1234, WEB www.bestwestern.com). **Choice** (☎ 800/221–2222, WEB www.choicehotels.com). **Comfort** (☎ 800/228–5150, WEB www.comfortinn.com). **Hilton** (☎ 800/445–8667, WEB www.hilton.com). **Holiday Inn** (☎ 800/465–4329, WEB www.basshotels.com). **Quality Inn** (☎ 800/228–5151, WEB www.qualityinn.com). **Radisson** (☎ 800/333–3333, WEB www.radisson.com). **Sheraton** (☎ 800/325–3535, WEB www.starwoodhotels.com).

MAIL AND SHIPPING

Most post offices are open weekdays 8 to 4 or 5, Saturday 9 to 1. In small towns, post offices are often closed on Saturday.

POSTAL RATES

The letter rate for Norway is NKr 5, NKr 6 for the other Nordic countries, NKr 7 for Europe, and NKr 8 for outside Europe for a letter weighing up to 20 grams (¾ ounce).

MONEY MATTERS

Prices throughout this guide are given for adults. Substantially reduced fees are almost always available for children, students, and senior citizens.

Costs are high in Norway. Here are some sample prices: cup of coffee, from NKr 14 in a cafeteria to NKr 25 or more in a restaurant; a 20-pack of cigarettes, NKr 60; a half-liter of beer, NKr 40–50; the smallest hot dog (with bun plus *lompe*—a flat Norwegian potato bread—mustard, ketchup, and fried onions) at a convenience store, NKr 20; cheapest bottle of wine from a government store, NKr 60; the same bottle at a restaurant, NKr 120–200; urban transit fare in Oslo, NKr 20; soft drink, from NKr 20 in a cafeteria to NKr 35 in a better restaurant; sandwich at a cafeteria, NKr 40–50; 1½-km (1-mi) taxi ride, NKr 40–60 depending on time of day.

Be aware that sales taxes can be very high, but foreigners can get some refunds by shopping at tax-free stores (☞ Taxes). City cards can save you transportation and entrance fees in larger cities.

You can **reduce the cost of food by planning.** Breakfast is often included in your hotel bill; if not, you may wish to buy fruit, sweet rolls, and a beverage for a picnic breakfast. Electrical devices for hot coffee or tea should be bought abroad, though, to conform to the local current.

Opt for a restaurant lunch instead of dinner, since the latter tends to be significantly more expensive. Instead of beer or wine, **drink tap water—** liquor can cost four times the price of the same brand in a store—but do specify tap water, as the term "water" can refer to soft drinks and bottled water, which are also expensive. The tip is included in the cost of your meal.

Liquor and strong beer (over 3% alcohol) can be purchased only in state-owned shops, at very high prices, during weekday business hours, usually 9:30 to 6 and in some areas on Saturday until mid-afternoon. (When you visit friends or relatives in Norway, a bottle of liquor or fine wine bought duty-free on the trip over is often much appreciated.) Weaker beers and ciders are usually available in grocery stores.

ATMS

➤ ATM LOCATIONS: **Cirrus** (☎ 800/424–7787).

CREDIT CARDS

Throughout this guide, the following abbreviations are used: **AE,** American Express; **DC,** Diners Club; **MC,** MasterCard; and **V,** Visa.

CURRENCY

Norway is a non-EU country, and has opted to keep its currency while its neighbors convert to the Euro. The Norwegian *krone* (plural: *kroner*) translates as "crown," written officially as NOK. Price tags are seldom marked this way, but instead read "Kr" followed by the amount, such as Kr 10. (In this book, the Norwegian krone is abbreviated NKr.) One krone is divided into 100 *øre,* and coins of 50 øre and 1, 5, 10, and 20 kroner are in circulation. Bills are issued in denominations of 50, 100, 200, 500, and 1,000 kroner. At this writing (winter 2001), the rate of exchange was NKr 9 to the U.S. dollar, NKr 6 to the Canadian dollar, NKr 13 to the pound sterling, NKr 10 to the Irish punt, NKr 5 to the Australian dollar, NKr 4 to the New Zealand dollar, and NKr 1 to the South African rand. Exchange rates fluctuate, so be sure to check them when planning a trip.

No limitations apply to the import and export of currency.

CURRENCY EXCHANGE

For the most favorable rates, **change money through banks.** Although ATM transaction fees may be higher abroad than at home, ATM rates are excellent because they are based on wholesale rates offered only by major banks. You won't do as well at exchange booths in airports or rail and bus stations, in hotels, in restaurants, or in stores. To avoid lines at airport exchange booths, **get a bit of local currency before you leave home.**

➤ EXCHANGE SERVICES: **International Currency Express** (☎ 888/278–6628 for orders, WEB www.foreignmoney.com). **Thomas Cook Currency Services** (☎ 800/287–7362 for telephone orders and retail locations, WEB www.us.thomascook.com).

TRAVELER'S CHECKS

Do you need traveler's checks? It depends on where you're headed. If you're going to rural areas and small towns, go with cash; traveler's checks are best used in cities. Lost or stolen checks can usually be replaced within 24 hours. To ensure a speedy refund, buy your own traveler's checks— don't let someone else pay for them: irregularities such as this can cause delays. The person who bought the checks should make the call to request a refund.

OUTDOORS AND SPORTS

Norway's wilderness and natural beauty, including 18 national parks, affords many special experiences. Whatever your sport or pursuit, the Norwegian Tourist Board advises travelers to use common sense: respect nature, know your physical limitations, take necessary precautions, use proper equipment and dress appropriately, pay attention to local weather forecasts, and take part in group outings if you have little outdoor experience.

Close to 100 recreational and competitive sports are recognized in Norway, each with its own national association. Contact the local tourist office or the Norwegian Tourist Board for more details.

BIKING

Norway has many cycling paths, some of them old roads that are in the mountains and along the western fjords. The Rallarvegen, from Haugastøl in the Hardangervidda National Park to Flåm, is very popular among cyclists. The southern counties of Vestfold and Rogaland have a well-developed network of cycling paths.

Most routes outside large cities are hilly and can be physically demanding. **Wear protective helmets and use lights at night.**

Many counties have produced brochures that have touring suggestions and maps. Syklistenes Landsforening has maps and general information, as well as the latest weather conditions. Several companies, including Lillehammer's Trollcycling, organize cycling tours. Den Norske Turistforening (DNT; ☞ Lodging) provides inexpensive lodging for cyclists planning overnight trips.

If you want to travel with your bike on an NSB long-distance train, you must make a reservation and pay an additional NKr 90. On local or InterCity trains, bikes are transported depending on the amount of space available.

➤ RESOURCES: **Syklistenes Landsforening** (✉ Storgt. 23C, 0028 Oslo, ☎ 22/47–30–30, FAX 22/47–30–31).

➤ CYCLING TOUR COMPANIES: **erik & reidar** (✉ Kirkegt. 34A, 0153 Oslo, ☎ 22/41–23–80, FAX 22/41–23–90). **PedalNor** (✉ Kløvervn. 10, 4326 Sandnes, ☎ 51/66–40–60 or 51/66–48–70). **Trollcycling** (✉ Box 373, 2601 Lillehammer, ☎ 61/28–99–70, FAX 61/26–92–50).

BIRD-WATCHING

Northern Norway has some of northern Europe's largest bird sanctuaries. It teems with fantastic numbers of seabirds, including sea eagles. Another popular spot is the island of Runde, just off Ålesund on the West Coast. A half million birds nest there.

CANOEING AND RAFTING

There are plenty of lakes and streams for canoeing and kayaking in Norway. Popular spots include Aust-Agder, in the Sørlandet; Telemark, and suburban Oslo. Norges Padlerforbund (Norwegian Canoe Association) maintains a list of rental companies and regional canoeing centers.

Rafting excursions are offered throughout Norway. For more information, contact Norwegian Wildlife and Rafting, which operates guided two-day expeditions with accommodation and transport provided. The minimum age limit for white-water rafting is 18 (15 years with parental guidance). Trips are arranged in several places throughout Norway.

➤ RESOURCES: **Norges Padlerforbund** (✉ Service Boks 1, Ullevaal Stadion, 0840 Oslo, ☎ 21/02–98–35, WEB www.padling.no). **Norwegian Wildlife and Rafting** (✉ 2680 Våg, ☎ 61/23–87–27).

DIVING

The Norwegian coast has many diving opportunities. There are many centers with excellent facilities on the west coast, particularly in Møre og Romsdal county, in the west.

There are a few restrictions regarding sites—special permission is required to dive in a harbor, and diving near army installations is restricted. Contact Norges Dykkeforbund or the local tourist office for a list of diving centers and clubs.

➤ RESOURCES: **Norges Dykkeforbund** (✉ Sognsvn. 75L, 0855 Oslo, ☎ 21/02–90–00, WEB www.ndf.no).

FISHING

Norway's fjords, lakes, and rivers make it a fisherman's paradise. Check with fly shops or the local tourist office to see what licenses you may need.

Using live fish as bait is prohibited, and imported tackle must be disinfected before use.

GLACIER WALKING

Glacier walking is an exhilarating way to experience the mountains of Norway. This sport requires the right equipment and training: only try it when accompanied by an experienced local guide. Since glaciers are always moving over new land, the ice and snow may just be a thin covering for a deep crevice. Glacier centers or local tourist offices can recommend guides and tours.

➤ RESOURCES: **Jostedalsbreen Nasjonalparksenter** (✉ Rte. 15 6781 Oppstryn, ☎ 57/87–72–00, ⓦⒺⒷ www.museumsnett.no/jostedalsbreen). **Norsk Bremuseum** (Norwegian Glacier Museum; ✉ Rte. 5, 6848 Fjærland, ☎ 57/69–32–88, ⓦⒺⒷ www.bre.museum.no). **Breheimsenteret** (Jostedalen National Park Visitor's Center ✉ Rte. 604, 6871 Jostedale, ☎ 57/68–32–50).

GOLF

The many golf courses spread out across the country welcome nonmember guests for fees ranging from NKr 150–NKr 350. Local tourist offices and the Norges Golfforbund can provide a list of golf clubs.

➤ RESOURCES: **Norges Golfforbund** (Norwegian Gold Association; ✉ Box 163, Lilleaker, 0216 Oslo, ☎ 22/73–66–20, ⓦⒺⒷ ngf.golf.no).

HANG GLIDING

The mountains and hills of Norway provide excellent take-off spots. However, winds and weather conspire to make conditions unpredictable. For details on local clubs, regulations, and equipment rental, contact Norsk Aeroklubb.

➤ RESOURCES: **Norsk Aeroklubb** (✉ Tollbugt. 3, 0152 Oslo, ☎ 23/10–29–00, ⓦⒺⒷ www.nak.no).

HIKING AND MOUNTAINEERING

Naturally, hiking and mountaineering are popular pastimes in a land of mountain ranges and high plains. Well-known hiking areas include the Jotunheim mountain range; the Rondane and Dovrefjell mountains; the Hardangervidda (Hardanger plateau), the Trollheimen district and Finnmarksvidda. For multiday hikes, you can stay in hostels, camp out in your own tent, or head to one of the DNT's cabins. Throughout the country, DNT also organizes guided hiking tours as well as mountaineering courses in both summer and winter.

➤ RESOURCES: **Den Norske Turistforening** (DNT; The Norwegian Mountain Touring Association; ✉ Box 7 Sentrum, 0101 Oslo 1, ☎ 22/82–28–22, ⒻⒶⓍ 22/82–28–23).

SAILING

Norway's rugged coastline can make for an ideal sailing vacation. Be sure to only sail with up-to-date sea charts, since the water around Norway is filled with skerries and underwater rocks. Contact Norges Seilforbund about facilities around the country.

➤ RESOURCES: **Norges Seilforbund** (Norwegian Sailing Association; ✉ Box Ullevåls Stadion, 0840 Oslo, ☎ 21/02–90–00).

SNOW SPORTS

The Skiforeningen provides national snow-condition reports; tips on trails; and information on courses for cross-country, downhill, Telemark, and snowboarding. If you can't make it to Norway in winter, Stryn Sommerskisenter, in the west, has a summer ski season that runs June–September.

➤ RESOURCES: **Skiforeningen** (✉ Kongevn. 5, 0390 Oslo 3, ☎ 22/92–32–00). **Stryn Sommerskisenter** (✉ 6782 Stryn, ☎ 57/87–40–40).

SPORTS FOR PEOPLE WITH DISABILITIES

Norway encouraged active participation in sports for people with disabilities long before it became popular elsewhere and has many Special Olympics medal winners. Beitostølen Helsesportsenter has sports facilities for people with disabilities as well as training programs for instructors. Sports offered include skiing, hiking, running, and horseback riding. For more information call Norges Funksjonshemmede Idrettsforbund.

➤ RESOURCES: **Beitostølen Helsesportsenter** (✉ 2953 Beitostølen, ☎ 61/34–08–00). **Norges Funksjonshemmede Idrettsforbund** (Norwegian Sports Organization for the Disabled; ✉ 1661 Rolvsøy, ☎ 69/35–49–24, ⓦⒺⒷ www.nfif.no).

SWIMMING

Swimming in the Norwegian outdoors is most enjoyable along the southern coast, where air temperatures can reach 68°F (20°C). In northern Norway, inland temperatures are generally cooler.

PACKING

Bring a folding umbrella and a lightweight raincoat, as it is common for the sky to be clear at 9 AM, rainy at 11 AM, and clear again in time for lunch. **Pack casual clothes,** as Norwegians tend to dress more casually than their Continental brethren. If you have trouble sleeping when it is light or are sensitive to strong sun, **bring an eye mask and dark sunglasses;** the sun rises as early as 4 AM in some areas, and the far-northern latitude causes it to slant at angles unseen elsewhere on the globe. **Bring bug repellent** if you plan to venture away from the cities; large mosquitoes can be a real nuisance on summer evenings.

In your carry-on luggage, **pack an extra pair of eyeglasses or contact lenses and enough of any medication** you take to last the entire trip. You may also ask your doctor to write a spare prescription using the drug's generic name, since brand names may vary from country to country. In luggage to be checked, **never pack prescription drugs or valuables.** To avoid customs delays, carry medications in their original packaging. And don't forget to carry with you the addresses of offices that handle refunds of lost traveler's checks. Check *Fodor's How to Pack* (available in bookstores everywhere) for more tips.

CHECKING LUGGAGE

You are allowed one carry-on bag and one personal article, such as a purse or a laptop computer. Make sure that everything you carry aboard will fit under your seat or in the overhead bin. Get to the gate early, so you can board as soon as possible, before the overhead bins fill up.

If you are flying internationally, note that baggage allowances may be determined not by piece but by weight—generally 88 pounds (40 kilograms) in first class, 66 pounds (30 kilograms) in business class, and 44 pounds (20 kilograms) in economy.

Airline liability for baggage is limited to $1,250 per person on flights within the United States. On international flights it amounts to $9.07 per pound or $20 per kilogram for checked baggage (roughly $640 per 70-pound bag) and $400 per passenger for unchecked baggage. You can buy additional coverage at check-in for about $10 per $1,000 of coverage, but it excludes a rather extensive list of items, shown on your airline ticket.

Before departure, **itemize your bags' contents** and their worth, and label the bags with your name, address, and phone number. (If you use your home address, cover it so potential thieves can't see it readily.) Inside each bag, **pack a copy of your itinerary.** At check-in, **make sure that each bag is correctly tagged** with the destination airport's three-letter code. If your bags arrive damaged or fail to arrive at all, file a written report with the airline before leaving the airport.

PASSPORTS & VISAS

When traveling internationally, **carry your passport** even if you don't need one (it's always the best form of I.D.) and **make two photocopies of the data page** (one for someone at home and another for you, carried separately from your passport). If you lose your passport, promptly call the nearest embassy or consulate and the local police.

ENTERING NORWAY

All U.S. citizens, even infants, need only a valid passport to enter the country for stays of up to three months.

PASSPORT OFFICES

The best time to apply for a passport or to renew is in fall and winter. Before any trip, check your passport's expiration date, and, if necessary, renew it as soon as possible.

➤ AUSTRALIAN CITIZENS: **Australian Passport Office** (☎ 131–232, WEB www.dfat.gov.au/passports).

➤ CANADIAN CITIZENS: **Canadian Passport Office** (☎ 819/994–3500; 800/567–6868 in Canada, WEB www.dfait-maeci.gc.ca/passport).

➤ NEW ZEALAND CITIZENS: **New Zealand Passport Office** (☎ 04/494–0700, WEB www.passports.govt.nz).

➤ U.K. CITIZENS: **London Passport Office** (☎ 0870/521–0410, WEB www.ukpa.gov.uk) for fees and documentation requirements and to request an emergency passport.

➤ U.S. CITIZENS: **National Passport Information Center** (☎ 900/225–5674; calls are 35¢ per minute for automated service, $1.05 per minute for operator service; WEB www.travel.state.gov/npicinfo.html).

SENIOR-CITIZEN TRAVEL

To qualify for age-related discounts, **mention your senior-citizen status up front** when booking hotel reservations (not when checking out) and before you're seated in restaurants (not when paying the bill). When renting a car, ask about promotional car-rental discounts, which can be cheaper than senior-citizen rates.

TRAIN TRAVEL

Seniors over 60 are entitled to discount tickets (often as much as 50% off) on buses, trains, and ferries in Norway, as well as reductions on special City Cards. Eurail offers discounts on Scanrail and Eurail train passes (☞ Train Travel).

➤ EDUCATIONAL PROGRAMS: **Elderhostel** (✉ 11 Ave. de Lafayette, Boston, MA 02111-1746, ☎ 877/426–8056, FAX 877/426–2166, WEB www.elderhostel.org).

STUDENTS IN NORWAY

➤ I.D.s & SERVICES: **Council Travel** (CIEE; ✉ 205 E. 42nd St., 15th floor, New York, NY 10017, ☎ 212/822–2700 or 888/268–6245, FAX 212/822–2699, WEB www.councilexchanges.org) for mail orders only, in the United States. **Travel Cuts** (✉ 187 College St., Toronto, Ontario M5T 1P7, Canada, ☎ 416/979–2406; 800/667–2887 in Canada, FAX 416/979–8167, WEB www.travelcuts.com).

TAXES

VALUE-ADDED TAX

Value-added tax, V.A.T. for short but called *moms* all over Scandinavia, is a hefty 23% on all purchases except books; it is included in the prices of goods. All purchases of consumer goods totaling more than NKr 308 for export by nonresidents are eligible for V.A.T. refunds. Carry your passport when shopping to prove you are a nonresident.

Global Refund is a V.A.T. refund service that makes getting your money back hassle-free. Some 3,000 Norwegian shops subscribe to the service, called "Norway Tax-Free Shopping."

In participating stores, **ask for the Global Refund form** (called a Shopping Cheque). Have it stamped like any customs form by customs officials when you leave the country (be ready to show customs officials what you've bought). Then take the form to one of the more than 700 Global Refund counters—conveniently located at every major airport and border crossing—and 11%–18% of the tax will be refunded on the spot in the form of cash, check, or a refund to your credit-card account (minus a small percentage for processing).

Shops that do not subscribe to this program have slightly more detailed forms, which must be presented to the Norwegian Customs Office along with the goods to obtain a refund by mail. This refund is closer to the actual amount of the tax.

It's essential to have both the forms and the goods available for inspection upon departure. Make sure the appropriate stamps are on the voucher or other forms before leaving the country.

One way to beat high prices is to **take advantage of tax-free shopping.** You can make major purchases free of tax if you have a foreign passport. Ask about tax-free shopping when you make a purchase for $50 (about £32) or more. When your purchases exceed a specified limit (which varies from country to country), you receive a special export receipt. Keep the parcels intact and take them out of the country within 30 days of purchase.

➤ V.A.T. REFUNDS: **Global Refund** (✉ 99 Main St., Suite 307, Nyack, NY 10960, ☎ 800/566–9828, FAX 845/348–1549, WEB www.globalrefund.com). **Global Refund Norge** (☎ 67/15–60–10). **Directorate of Customs and Excise** (✉ POB 8122, 0032 Oslo, ☎ 22/86–03–00, WEB www.toll.no).

TAXIS

Even the smallest villages have some form of taxi service. Towns on the railroad normally have taxi stands just outside the station. All city taxis are connected with a central dispatching office, so there is only one main telephone number, the taxi central. Look in the telephone book under "Taxi" or "Drosje."

Never use an unmarked, or pirate, taxi, since their drivers are unlicensed and in some cases may be dangerous.

TELEPHONES

The telephone system in Norway is modern and efficient; international direct service is available throughout the country. Phone numbers consist of eight digits.

AREA & COUNTRY CODES

The country code for Norway is 47. Numbers in each city start with the same two-digit prefix, such as 22 (Oslo) and 55 (Bergen). You must dial all eight digits whether or not you're in the city. Telephone numbers starting with the prefix 82 cost extra. Toll-free numbers begin with "800" or "810."

In this chapter, phone numbers outside the United States and Canada include country codes; in all other chapters only the area codes are listed.

The country code is 1 for the United States and Canada, 61 for Australia, 64 for New Zealand, and 44 for the United Kingdom.

DIRECTORY AND OPERATOR ASSISTANCE

Dial 180 for information in Norway and other Scandinavian countries; 181 for other international telephone numbers. To place a collect or an operator-assisted call to a number in Norway, dial 115. Dial 117 for collect or operator-assisted calls outside of Norway.

INTERNATIONAL CALLS

AT&T, MCI, and Sprint access codes make calling long distance relatively convenient, but you may find the local access number blocked in many hotel rooms. First ask the hotel operator to connect you. If the hotel operator balks, ask for an international operator, or dial the international operator yourself. One way to improve your odds of getting connected to your long-distance carrier is to travel with more than one company's calling card (a hotel may block Sprint, for example, but not MCI). If all else fails, call from a pay phone.

If you are able to dial directly, dial the international access code, 00, then the country code, and number. All telephone books list country code numbers, including those for the United States and Canada (1), Great Britain (44), and Australia (61). For operator assistance, dial 115. All international operators speak English.

➤ ACCESS CODES: **AT&T Direct** (☎ 800/19011). **MCI WorldPhone** (☎ 800/19912). **Sprint International Access** (☎ 800/19877).

MOBILE PHONES

Scandinavia has been one of the world leaders in mobile phone development; almost 90% of the population owns a mobile phone. Although standard North American cellular phones will not work in Norway, some companies rent cellular phones to tourists. Contact the Norwegian Tourist Office for details.

PHONE CARDS

You can purchase Tellerskritt (phone cards) at Narvesen and Norsk Tipping shops and kiosks. Cards cost NKr 40 to NKr 140 and can be used in the 8,000 green public card telephones. About half of these local phones also take major credit cards.

PUBLIC PHONES

Public telephones are of two types. Push-button phones—which accept NKr 1, 5, and 10 coins (some accept NKr 20 coins)—are easy to use: lift the receiver, listen for the dial tone, insert the coins, dial the number, and wait for a connection. The digital screen at the top of the box indicates the amount of money in your "account." Green public card telephones only accept phone cards or credit cards.

Local calls cost NKr 3 or NKr 5 from a pay phone. If you hear a short tone, it means that your purchased time is almost up.

TIME

Norway is one hour ahead of Greenwich Mean Time (GMT) and six hours ahead of Eastern Standard Time (EST).

TIPPING

Tipping is kept to a minimum in Norway because service charges are added to most bills. It is, however, handy to have a supply of NKr 5 or NKr 10 coins for less formal service. Tip only in local currency.

Room service usually has a service charge included already, so tipping is discretionary. Round up a taxi fare to the next round digit, or tip anywhere from NKr 5 to NKr 10, a little more if the driver has been helpful. All restaurants include a service charge, ranging from 12% to 15%, in the bill. It is customary to add an additional 5% for exceptional service, but it is not obligatory. Maître d's are not tipped, and coat checks have flat rates, usually NKr 10 per person.

TOURS & PACKAGES

Because everything is prearranged on a prepackaged tour or independent vacation, you spend less time planning—and often get it all at a good price. Most tourist information offices have recommended local or regional tours outlined on map and brochures. The Norwegian Tourist Board has lists of tours arranged by region.

BOOKING WITH AN AGENT

Travel agents are excellent resources. But it's a good idea to collect brochures from several agencies as some agents' suggestions may be influenced by relationships with tour and package firms that reward them for volume sales. If you have a special interest, **find an agent with expertise in that area**; the American Society of Travel Agents (ASTA; ☞ Travel Agencies) has a database of specialists worldwide.

Make sure your travel agent knows the accommodations and other services of the place being recommended. Ask about the hotel's location, room size, beds, and whether it has a pool, room service, or programs for chil-

dren, if you care about these. Has your agent been there in person or sent others whom you can contact?

Do some homework on your own, too: local tourism boards can provide information about lesser-known and small-niche operators, some of which may sell only direct.

➤ TOUR-OPERATOR RECOMMENDATIONS: **American Society of Travel Agents** (☞ Travel Agencies). **National Tour Association** (NTA; ✉ 546 E. Main St., Lexington, KY 40508, ☎ 859/226–4444 or 800/682–8886, WEB www.ntaonline.com). **Scantours** (☎ 800/223–7226 or 310/636–4656 in the U.S., WEB www.scantours.com; ✉ 47 Whitcomb St., WC2H 7DH London, ☎ 020/7839–2927). **Scan-Meridian** (✉ 28B Hampstead High St., NW3 1QA London, ☎ 0207/431–5393). **United States Tour Operators Association** (USTOA; ✉ 342 Madison Ave., Suite 1522, New York, NY 10173, ☎ 212/599–6599 or 800/468–7862, FAX 212/599–6744, WEB www.ustoa.com).

BUYER BEWARE

Each year consumers are stranded or lose their money when tour operators—even large ones with excellent reputations—go out of business. So **check out the operator.** Ask several travel agents about its reputation, and try to **book with a company that has a consumer-protection program.** (Look for information in the company's brochure.) In the United States, members of the National Tour Association and the United States Tour Operators Association are required to set aside funds to cover your payments and travel arrangements in the event that the company defaults. It's also a good idea to choose a company that participates in the American Society of Travel Agents' Tour Operator Program (TOP); ASTA will act as mediator in any disputes between you and your tour operator.

Remember that the more your package or tour includes the better you can predict the ultimate cost of your vacation. Make sure you know exactly what is covered, and **beware of hidden costs.** Are taxes, tips, and transfers included? Entertainment and excursions? These can add up.

TRAIN TRAVEL

NSB, the Norwegian State Railway System, has five main lines originating from the Oslo S Station. Its 2,500 mi (4,000 km) of track connect all main cities. Train tickets can be purchased in railway stations or from travel agencies. NSB has its own travel agency in Oslo.

The longest train runs north to Trondheim, then extends onward as far as Fauske and Bodø. The southern line hugs the coast to Stavanger, while the stunning western line crosses Hardangervidda, the scenic plateau that lies between Oslo and Bergen. An eastern line to Stockholm links Norway with Sweden, while another southern line through Göteborg, Sweden, is the main connection with Continental Europe. Narvik, north of Bodø, is the last stop on Sweden's Ofot line, the world's northernmost rail system, which runs from Stockholm via Kiruna. It is possible to take a five-hour bus trip between Bodø and Narvik to connect with the other train.

If you are traveling from south to north in Norway, flying is often a necessity: Stavanger in southern Norway is as close to Rome, Italy, as it is to the northern tip of Norway.

NSB trains are clean, comfortable, and punctual. Most have special compartments for travelers with disabilities and for families with children younger than age two. First- and second-class tickets are available. Both seat and sleeper reservations are required on express and overnight trains. For discounted rates and better availability, reserve at least five days ahead in summer. During major holidays, for Friday and Sunday trains reserve several weeks or a month ahead.

➤ TRAIN INFORMATION: **NSB** (✉ Skolen Tomtekaia 21 0048 Oslo, ☎ 81/50–08–88). **ScanAm World Tours** (✉ N. Main St. 108, Cranberry, NJ 08512, ☎ 800/545–2204). **Victoria Station** (✉ Terminus Pl., London, ☎ 0845/748–4950 in the U.K.).

CUTTING COSTS

A number of special discounted trips are available, including the InterRail Pass, which is available for European residents of all ages, and the Eurail-Pass, sold in the United States only. Norway participates in the following rail programs: EurailPass (and its flexipass variations), ScanRail Pass, Scanrail 'n Drive, InterRail, and Nordturist Card. A Norway Rail Pass is available for three, four, and five days of unlimited rail travel for non-residents within Norway. The ticket is sold in the United States through ScanAm. First-class rail passes are about 30% higher.

Low-season prices are offered October through April. Rail passes do not guarantee that you will get seats on the trains you want to ride, and seat reservations are sometimes required, particularly on express trains. You also need reservations for overnight sleeping accommodations.

Discounted fares also include family, student, senior-citizen (including their not-yet-senior spouses), and off-peak "mini" fares, which must be purchased a day in advance. NSB gives student discounts only to foreigners studying at Norwegian institutions.

Whichever pass you choose, remember that you must **purchase your pass before you leave** for Europe.

Many travelers assume that rail passes guarantee them seats on the trains they wish to ride. Not so. You need to **book seats ahead even if you are using a rail pass**; seat reservations are required on some European trains, particularly high-speed trains, and are a good idea on trains that may be crowded—particularly in summer on popular routes. You will also need a reservation if you purchase sleeping accommodations.

Rail passes may help you save money, but be aware that if you don't plan to cover many miles you may come out ahead by buying individual tickets.

➤ WHERE TO BUY RAIL PASSES: **CIT Tours Corp.** (✉ 342 Madison Ave., Suite 207, New York, NY 10173, ☎ 212/697–2100 or 800/248–8687; 800/248–7245 in western U.S., WEB www.cit-tours.com). **DER Travel**

Services (⊠ Box 1606, Des Plaines, IL 60017, ☎ 800/782–2424, FAX 800/282–7474, WEB www.dertravel.com). **Rail Europe** (⊠ 226–230 Westchester Ave., White Plains, NY 10604, ☎ 800/438–7245, 914/682–5172, or 416/602–4195; ⊠ 2087 Dundas E, Suite 105, Mississauga, Ontario L4X 1M2, ☎ 800/438–7245, 914/682–5172, or 416/602–4195, WEB www.raileurope.com).

FROM BRITAIN

Traveling from Britain to Norway by train is not difficult and takes 20 to 24 hours. The best connection leaves London's Victoria Station, connecting at Dover with a boat to Oostende, Belgium. From Oostende there are overnight connections to Copenhagen, from where there are express and overnight connections on to Oslo. Call Rail Europe for further information.

TRAVEL AGENCIES

A good travel agent puts your needs first. Look for an agency that has been in business at least five years, emphasizes customer service, and has someone on staff who specializes in your destination. In addition, **make sure the agency belongs to a professional trade organization.** The American Society of Travel Agents (ASTA)—the largest and most influential in the field with more than 26,000 members in some 170 countries—maintains and enforces a strict code of ethics and will step in to help mediate any agent-client dispute if necessary. ASTA (whose motto is "Without a travel agent, you're on your own") also maintains a Web site that includes a directory of agents. (If a travel agency is also acting as your tour operator, *see* Buyer Beware *in* Tours & Packages).

➤ LOCAL AGENT REFERRALS: **American Society of Travel Agents** (ASTA; ⊠ 1101 King St., Suite 200, Alexandria, VA 22314, ☎ 800/965–2782 24-hr hot line, FAX 703/739–7642, WEB www.astanet.com). **Association of British Travel Agents** (⊠ 68–71 Newman St., London W1T 3AH, U.K., ☎ 020/7637–2444, FAX 020/7637–0713, WEB www.abtanet.com). **Association of Canadian Travel Agents** (⊠ 130 Albert St., Suite 1705, Ottawa, Ontario K1P 5G4, Canada, ☎ 613/237–3657, FAX 613/237–7052, WEB www.acta.net). **Australian Federation of Travel Agents** (⊠ Level 3, 309 Pitt St., Sydney NSW 2000, Australia, ☎ 02/9264–3299, FAX 02/9264–1085, WEB www.afta.com.au). **Travel Agents' Association of New Zealand** (⊠ Level 5, Paxus House, 79 Boulcott St., Box 1888, Wellington 10033, New Zealand, ☎ 04/499–0104, FAX 04/499–0827, WEB www.taanz.org.nz).

VISITOR INFORMATION

For U.S. Government travel advisories by mail, send a request letter to the U.S. Department of State that includes a self-addressed, stamped, business-size envelope.

➤ TOURIST INFORMATION: **Norwegian Tourist Board** (U.K. ⊠ Charles House, 5 Regent St., London SW1Y 4LR, ☎ 44/207–839–6255, FAX 44/207–839–6014; Norway ⊠ Box 2893, Drammensvn. 40, Solli 0230, Oslo, ☎ 020/7839–6255, FAX 020/7839–6014, WEB www.visitnorway.com). **Scandinavian Tourist Board** (⊠ 655 3rd Ave., New York, NY 10017, ☎ 212/885–9700, FAX 212/855–9710, WEB www.goscandinavia.com). **U.S. Department of State** (⊠ Overseas Citizens Services Office, Room 4811 N.S., 2201 C St. NW, Washington, DC 20520, ☎ 202/647–5225, WEB travel.state.gov/travel/html).

WEB SITES

Do check out the World Wide Web when planning your trip. You'll find everything from weather forecasts to virtual tours of famous cities. Be sure to **visit Fodors.com** (www.fodors.com), a complete travel-planning site. You can research prices and book plane tickets, hotel rooms, rental cars, vacation packages, and more. In addition, you can post your pressing questions in the Travel Talk section. Other planning tools include a currency converter and weather reports, and there are loads of links to travel resources.

➤ RESOURCES: **Norwegian Tourist Board** (WEB www.visitnorway.com). **Oslo Visitors and Convention Bureau** (WEB www.oslopro.no). **Royal Norwegian Embassy in the United States** (WEB www.norway.org).

WHEN TO GO

The tourist season peaks in June, July, and August, when daytime temperatures are often in the 70s (21°C to 26°C) and sometimes rise into the 80s (27°C to 32°C). Detailed temperature charts are below. In general, the weather is not overly warm, and a brisk breeze and brief rainstorms are possible anytime. Nights can be chilly, even in summer.

Visit in summer if you want to experience the delightfully long summer days. Many attractions extend their hours during the summer, and many shut down altogether when summer ends. Fall, spring, and even winter are pleasant, despite the area's reputation for gloom. The days become shorter quickly, but the sun casts a golden light not seen farther south. On dark days, fires and candlelight will warm you indoors.

The Gulf Stream warms the western coast of Norway, making winters there similar to those in London. Even the harbor of Narvik, far to the north in Norway, remains ice-free year round. Away from the protection of the Gulf Stream, however, northern Norway experiences very cold, clear weather that attracts skiers.

CLIMATE

Below are average daily maximum and minimum temperatures for Oslo.

➤ FORECASTS: **Weather Channel Connection** (☎ 900/932–8437), 95¢ per minute from a Touch-Tone phone.

OSLO

Jan.	28F	– 2C	May	61F	16C	Sept.	60F	16C
	19	– 7		43	6		46	8
Feb.	30F	– 1C	June	68F	20C	Oct.	48F	9C
	19	– 7		50	10		38	3
Mar.	39F	4C	July	72F	22C	Nov.	38F	3C
	25	– 4		55	13		31	– 1
Apr.	50F	10C	Aug.	70F	21C	Dec.	32F	0C
	34	1		54	12		25	– 4

1 DESTINATION: NORWAY

Norwegian Landscapes

New and Noteworthy

What's Where

Pleasures and Pastimes

Great Itineraries

Fodor's Choice

NORWEGIAN LANDSCAPES

NORWEGIANS HAVE A STRONG ATTACHMENT to the nature of their homeland. Whether in the verdant dales of the interior, the brooding mountains of the north, or the fjords and archipelagoes of the coast, Norwegians' *hytter* (cabins or cottages) dot even the harshest landscapes.

In almost any kind of weather, blasting or balmy, large numbers of Norwegians are outdoors fishing, biking, skiing, hiking, or playing soccer. Everybody—from cherubic children to hardy, knapsack-toting senior citizens—bundles up for just one more swoosh down the slopes, one more walk through the forest. In a 2001 Norsk Gallup poll, 70% of all Norwegian respondents said that they wanted to spend even more time in nature. Although Norway is a modern, highly industrialized nation, vast areas of the country (up to 95%) remain forested or fallow. When discussing the size of their country, Norwegians like to say that if Oslo remained fixed and the northern part of the country were swung south, it would reach all the way to Rome. Perched at the very top of the globe, this northern land is long and rangy, 2,750 km (1,705 mi) in length, with only 4.5 million people scattered over it—making it the least densely populated land in Europe after Iceland.

Westerly winds carry moisture from the Gulf Stream, leaving the coastal regions with high precipitation, cool summers, and mild winters. The interior and east have a blend of clearer skies, hotter summers, and colder winters.

Norwegians are justifiably proud of their ability to survive the elements. The first people to appear on the land were reindeer hunters and fisherfolk who migrated north, following the path of the retreating ice. By the Bronze Age, settlements began to appear, and, as rock carvings show, the first Norwegians began to ski—purely as a form of locomotion—some 4,000 years ago.

The Viking Age has perhaps left the most indelible mark on the country. The Vikings' travels and conquests took them west to Iceland, England, Ireland (they founded Dublin in the 840s), and North America, and east to Kiev and as far as the Black Sea. Though they were famed as plunderers, their craftsmanship, fearlessness, and ingenuity have always been respected by Norwegians.

Harald I, better known as Harald the Fairhaired, swore he would not cut his hair until he united Norway, and in the 9th century he succeeded in doing both. But a millennium passed between that great era and Norwegian independence. Between the Middle Ages and 1905, Norway remained under the rule of either Denmark or Sweden, even after the constitution was written in 1814.

The 19th century saw the establishment of the Norwegian identity and a blossoming of culture. This Romantic period produced some of the nation's most famous individuals, among them composer Edvard Grieg, dramatist Henrik Ibsen, expressionist painter Edvard Munch, polar explorer Roald Amundsen, and explorer-humanitarian Fridtjof Nansen. Vestiges of nationalist lyricism, including Viking dragonheads and scrollwork, spangle the buildings of the era, all of which symbolize the rebirth of the Viking spirit.

Faithful to their democratic nature, Norwegians held a referendum to choose a king in 1905, when independence from Sweden became reality. Prince Carl of Denmark became King Haakon VII. His baby's name was changed from Alexander to Olav, and he, and later his son, presided over the kingdom for more than 85 years. When King Olav V died in January 1991, the normally reserved Norwegians stood in line for hours to write in the condolence book at the Royal Palace. Rather than simply sign their names, they wrote personal letters of devotion to the man they called the "people's king."

Harald V, Olav's son, is now king, with continuity assured by his own very popular son, Crown Prince Haakon Magnus, who married in August 2001. Norwegians continue to salute the royal family with flag-waving and parades on May 17, Constitution Day, a spirited holiday of independence that transforms Oslo's main boulevard, Karl Johans Gate, into a massive street party.

The 1968 discovery of oil in the North Sea dramatically changed Norway from an outpost for fishing, subsistence farming, and shipping to a highly developed industrial nation. Norway has emerged as a wealthy country, with a per capita income, standard of living, and a life expectancy that are among the world's highest.

Domestically, great emphasis has been placed on social welfare programs. Internationally, Norway is known for the annual awarding of the Nobel Peace Prize and participating in peace talks about the Middle East and other areas.

With one foot in modern, liberal Scandinavia and the other still within a somewhat nationalistic country, Norway, unlike its Nordic siblings, has so far resisted the temptation to join the European Union (EU), keeping a distinct European identity. In a historic national referendum in November 1994, Norwegians rejected EU membership for the second time. However, affluent, oil-rich Norway is aware of its place in a wider Europe and is mirroring and implementing EU requirements and directives.

— Updated by Sonya Procenko

NEW AND NOTEWORTHY

In recent years, Norway's affluence has created a new cosmopolitan attitude that has revitalized its major cities, particularly Oslo. A high standard of living continues to fuel the building of new hotels, restaurants, and shops. Festivals and other cultural events have also expanded, attracting international artists and guests. The boom is thanks in large part to the discovery, between 1995 and 1997, of at least 20 new oil and gas fields in the Norwegian sector of the North Sea. Hotel and restaurant prices remain high, but their owners have become more savvy at catering to travelers through style and enhanced services.

The Cinderella-like courtship and 2001 marriage of single mother (and commoner) Mette-Marit Tjessem Høiby to Norway's

Crown Prince Haakon Magnus captured the hearts and imaginations of many Norwegians. It also sparked a new debate between royalists and republicans over the role of the modern monarchy.

For several years, Norway has been a hip destination for affluent tourists from southern Europe, particularly Spain and Italy, seeking the fresh air and Nordic temperatures and climate. Trendy Norwegians and others have been giving Svalbard, an archipelago in the Arctic, a lot of attention—this exotic area has many opportunities for experiencing the area's austere beauty.

WHAT'S WHERE

Norway, roughly 400,000 square km (155,000 square mi), is about the same size as California. Approximately 30% of this long, narrow country is covered with clear lakes, lush forests, and rugged mountains. Western Norway, bordered by the Norwegian Sea and the Atlantic Ocean, is the fabled land of the fjords—few places on Earth can match its power and splendor. The magnificent Sognefjord, the longest inlet in western Norway, is only one of many fjords found here, including the Hardangerfjord, Geirangerfjord, Lysefjord, and Nordfjord.

Bergen, often hailed as the "Fjord Capital of Norway," is the second-largest city in the country. The cobblestone streets, well-preserved buildings at the Bryggen, and seven mountains that surround the city all add to its storybook charm.

Eastern Norway, bordered by Sweden, and by Finland and Russia to the north, is punctuated by rolling hills, abundant valleys, and fresh lakes—much more subdued than the landscape of the west. Near Gudbrandsdalen (Gudbrands Valley) you'll find Lillehammer. Almost directly south, rising from the shores of the Oslofjord, is the capital of Norway—Oslo. With a population of about a half million, Oslo is a friendly, manageable city.

If you follow the coast south, you'll come to Kristiansand, one of Sørlandet's (the Southland's) leading cities. Sørlandet is known for its long stretches of unspoiled, uncrowded beach. Stavanger, farther west, is one of the most cosmopolitan cities in Scandinavia—its oil and gas industry draws people from around the globe.

Halfway between Oslo and Bergen lies Hardangervidda (Hardanger Plateau), Norway's largest national park. At the foot of the plateau is Geilo, one of the country's most popular ski resorts. Almost directly north is the bustling city of Trondheim.

From here, a thin expanse of land stretches up to the Nordkapp (North Cape). Known as the Land of the Midnight Sun (the display of the northern lights in winter is pretty amazing, too), this region is marked with exquisite landscapes: glaciers, fjords, and rocky coasts. Narvik, a major Arctic port, is the gateway to the Lofoten Islands, where puffins and penguins march about. Even farther north is one of Norway's major universities, Tromsø, the lifeline to settlements and research centers at the North Pole. At the very top of Norway is the county of Finnmark, where many Sami (native Laplanders) live. Access to the area is primarily through Hammerfest, Europe's northernmost city, where the sun is not visible from November 21 to January 21, but is uninterrupted May 17 through July 29.

PLEASURES AND PASTIMES

Beaches

Many Norwegians flock to beaches every summer. Beaches around Mandal in the south and Jaeren's Ogna, Brusand, and Bore, closer to Stavanger, are the country's best, with fine white sand. However, all along the Oslo Fjord are good beaches, too. The western fjords are warmer and calmer than the open beaches of the south—although they have rock, and not sand, beaches—and inland freshwater lakes are chillier still than Gulf Stream–warmed fjords. Topless bathing is common, and there are nude beaches all along the coast.

Dining

The joy of eating is central to Norwegian culture. The Norwegians pride themselves on gracious entertaining and lavish dinner parties using their finest silver and glassware. Dining out in Norway is expensive, so many weekend nights are spent at the houses of friends and family savoring long, candlelit dinners. (The BYOB—Bring Your Own Bottle—policy is common in Norway because alcohol prices are so high.)

However, eating out at restaurants is still popular, especially in Stavanger, on the west coast, and in Oslo. In these large cities, the dining scene is vibrant and thriving. Until the late 1990s, fine Norwegian restaurants were invariably French and based their menus around an entrée of meat. Now, in addition to the traditional Norwegian restaurants that still serve the classic, national dishes, there are many restaurants with such multicultural additions as tapas, Thai curries, and sushi.

Norway's chefs have begun to win cooking awards and become celebrities at home. They're traveling and cooking widely, often inspired by Mediterranean and Asian cuisines as well as from their European neighbors. Fish, from common cod and skate to the noble salmon, naturally still has a prominent place in the Norwegian kitchen. Flavorful Norwegian lamb continues to be popular. Wild game, from birds to moose and reindeer, is often served with sauces made from the wild berries that make up the animals' diet.

Desserts, too, often feature fruit and berries. Norwegian strawberries and raspberries ripen in the long, early summer days and are sweeter and more intense than those grown farther south. Red and black currants are also used. Two berries native to Norway are *tyttebær* (lingonberries), which taste similar to cranberries but are much smaller, and *molter* (cloudberries), which look like orange raspberries but whose taste has been compared to that of a mango or peach. Molter are often served as *moltekrem* (in whipped cream) as a dessert, whereas tyttebær preserves often accompany traditional meat dishes.

For centuries, Norwegians regarded food as fuel, and their dining habits still bear traces of this. *Frokost* (breakfast) is a fairly big meal, usually with a selection of crusty bread, jams, herring, cold meat, and cheese. Norway's famous brown goat cheese or *Geitost* (a sweet, caramel-flavored whey cheese made wholly or in part from goats' milk) and Norvegia (a Norwegian

Gouda-type cheese) are on virtually every table. They are eaten in thin slices, cut with a cheese plane or slicer—a Norwegian invention—on buttered wheat or rye bread.

Lunsj (lunch) is simple and usually consists of *smørbrød* (open-face sandwiches). Most businesses have only a 30-minute lunch break, so unless there's a company cafeteria, people bring their lunch from home.

Middag (dinner), the only hot meal of the day, is early—from 1 to 4 in the country, 3 to 7 in the city—so many cafeterias serving home-style food close by 6 or 7 in the evening. In Oslo it's possible to get dinner as late as midnight at certain dining establishments, especially in summer. Most restaurants in Oslo usually stop serving dinner around 10 PM.

Traditional, home-style Norwegian food is stick-to-the-ribs fare, served in generous portions and blanketed with gravy. One of the most popular meals is *kjøttkaker* (meat cakes), which resemble small Salisbury steaks and are served with boiled potatoes, stewed cabbage, and brown gravy. Almost as popular are *medisterkaker* (mild pork sausage patties), served with brown gravy and caraway-seasoned sauerkraut, and *reinsdyrkaker* (reindeer meatballs), served with cream sauce and lingonberry jam. Other typical meat dishes include *fårikål,* a great-tasting lamb and cabbage stew, and *steik* (roast meat), always served well done. Fish dishes include poached *torsk* (cod) or *laks* (salmon), served with a creamy sauce called Sandefjord butter; *seibiff,* fried pollack and onions; and *fiskegrateng,* something between a fish soufflé and a casserole, usually served with carrot slaw.

Throughout the country, there are also regional specialties such as west coast *smalahove,* sheep's head, and *klippfisk* (also known as bacalao). This dried and salted fish is exported to Portugal, Italy, Spain, South America, and the Caribbean. *Pinnekjøtt,* salted lamb ribs, and *lutefisk* (fish that's been soaked in lye and then simmered) are both popular around Christmas.

Traditional desserts include *karamellpudding* (crème caramel) and *rømmegrøt* (sour-cream porridge served with cinnamon sugar) and a glass of *saft* (raspberry juice). Rømmegrøt—a typical farm dish—

tastes very much like warm cheesecake batter. It's often served with *fenalår* (dried leg of mutton) and *lefsekling,* a thin tortilla-like pancake made with sour cream and potatoes, buttered, and coated with sugar. Christmastime brings with it a delectable array of light, sweet, and buttery pastries. The *bløtkake* (layered cream cake with custard, fruit, and marzipan) is a favorite for Christmas and special occasions but can be purchased in bakeries year-round.

The Norwegians take their *kaffe* (coffee) black and bitter, and they typically drink it several times a day. The tradition of locally brewed *øl* (beer) dates back to the Viking Ages, and most major cities have their signature brew. Wine is imported since Norway is too far north to cultivate wine grapes. A special Norwegian liquor, however, is its *akevitt* or aquavit, which in this rendition is distilled from potatoes and usually flavored with caraway.

CATEGORY	COST*
$$$$	over NKr 250
$$$	NKr 200–NKr 250
$$	NKr 150–NKr 200
$	under NKr 150

*per person for a main course at dinner

Fishing

Fishing has remained a livelihood for many Norwegians and a popular pastime for many others. Whether it's fly-fishing in western rivers or deep-sea fishing off the northern coast, Norway has all kinds of angling possibilities. Some 200 species of saltwater fish either live all year or breed along the coast, particularly cod, pollack, and the smeltlike capelin. In the country's rivers and lakes, salmon, trout, Arctic char, pike, grayling, whitefish, and perch make their home.

Hiking

One of the most common expressions in the Norwegian language is *gå på tur,* or "go for a walk." Naturally, in a mountain and forest-filled country, it's never far to the trails on which many Norwegians spend their weekends hiking and strolling. Much of Norway's 19,000 km (12,000 mi) of marked trails have cabins available for hikers to rest, eat, and even spend the night. Den Norske Turistforening (The Norwegian Mountain Touring Association), a biking group, and affiliated organizations administer cabins and tourist facilities in the central and northern mountainous areas of the country. They also arrange group hikes.

Lodging

Hotel standards in Norway are generally high, and the prices are equally so. Even the simplest youth hostels provide good mattresses with fluffy down comforters and clean showers or baths. Breakfast, usually served buffet style, is almost always included in the room price at hotels, whereas hostels often charge extra for the morning meal. Travelers can reduce accommodation expenses with special summer and weekend specials and discount passes and programs.

Norway has several recommended hotel chains. Radisson SAS, a division of the airline, has the country's best hotels. They're classy and luxurious. Many are above the Arctic Circle and are the only game in town. Throughout Norway, there are numerous individual hotels that stand out, including Dr. Holms Hotel in Geilo; and Fleischer's, a historic wooden hotel in Voss. Rica and Quality hotels, also luxury chains, have expanded extensively in the past few years. Best Western, Golden Tulip Rainbow, Scandic, and Choice Hotels International are moderate-price chains that are found in most major towns.

The Farmer's Association operates simple hotels in most towns and cities. These reasonably priced accommodations usually have "-heimen" as part of the name, such as Bondeheimen in Oslo. The same organization also runs cafeterias serving traditional Norwegian food, usually called Kaffistova. All of these hotels and restaurants are alcohol-free. Rustic cabins and campsites are also available everywhere, as well as some independent hotels.

In the Lofoten and Vesterålen islands, *rorbuer*, fishing cottages that have been converted into lodgings or modern versions of these simple dwellings, are the most popular form of accommodation. These rustic quayside cabins, with minikitchens, bunk beds, living rooms, and showers, are reasonably priced, and staying here can add to your sense of the region.

Norway has more than 100 youth hostels, but in an effort to appeal to vacationers of all ages, the name has been changed to *vandrerhjem* (travelers' home). Norwegian hostels are among the best in the world, squeaky clean and with excellent facilities.

Rooms sleep from two to six, and many have private showers. You don't have to be a member, but members get discounts, so it's worth joining. Membership can be arranged at any vandrerhjem, or you can buy a coupon book good for seven nights, which includes the membership fee. Linens are usually rented per night, so it's a good idea to bring your own—if you haven't, you can buy a *lakenpose* (sheet sleeping bag) at travel-gear at many department stores and at most vandrerhjem.

Norway has more than 500 inspected and classified campsites, many with showers, bathrooms, and hookups for electricity. Most also have cabins or chalets to rent by the night or longer.

CATEGORY	COST*
$$$$	over NKr 1,500
$$$	NKr 1,200–NKr 1,500
$$	NKr 800–NKr 1,200
$	under NKr 800

All prices are for a standard double room, including service and 23% VAT.

Orienteering

One of Norway's most popular mass-participation sports is based on running or hiking over territory with a map and compass to find control points marked on a map. Special cards can be purchased at sports shops to be punched at control points found during a season.

Shopping

Almost no one leaves Norway without buying a hand-knit sweater. Although the prices for these sweaters may seem high here, the quality is outstanding and much more expensive outside the country. While the classic knitting designs, with snowflakes and reindeer, are still best-sellers at *Husfliden* (homecraft) outlets, gift stores tend to sell more contemporary, fashionable designs by Oleana and Dale.

Given the Norwegians' affection for the outdoors, an abundance of high-quality sportsgear and outerwear is available. Good buys include Helly-Hansen rain gear, insulated boots, and the *supertrøye*, a gossamer-thin, insulated undershirt.

Norway's handicrafts include embroidered cloth; handmade pewter and wrought-iron candlesticks; hand-dipped candles; handblown glass; and hand-turned wood bowls, spoons, and platters made of birch roots, decorated with rosemaling (intricate painted or carved floral folk-art designs). Other, more offbeat, items include *ostehøvler* (cheese slicers) and *kransekakeformer,* graduated forms for making almond ring cakes. Silver is a good buy in Norway, especially with the value-added tax refund. Norwegian silver companies produce a wide range of distinctive patterns. Unfortunately, Norwegian rustic antiques may not be exported. However, you can get good replicas of old Norwegian farm furniture.

You're not limited to choosing these typical Norwegian souvenirs either. Norwegian music, traditional to popular, classical to jazz, sung and performed in English and Norwegian, can be a lasting memento. Fiction and nonfiction books by Norwegian authors translated into English sell at bookshops, usually in a "Norway in English" section. Norwegian fashion designers are making a name for themselves on runways from Paris to Milan, and selected shops carry their designs.

Skiing

As the cradle of skiing, Norway has made a major contribution to the world of winter sports. In addition to downhill and cross-country, the 100-year-old Telemark style is also popular across the country. Cross-country skiing is a great way to see Norway's nature; it requires only basic equipment, and rentals are readily available. Most every city has lit trails for evening skiing. Norway's skiing season lasts from November to Easter. But winter's not the only time for skiing in Norway—summer skiing on a glacier can be thrilling.

GREAT ITINERARIES

What sets Norway apart from other European countries is its spectacular natural beauty. What other world capital has subway service to the forest, or lakes and hiking trails within city limits as Oslo does? Although it takes only a few days to explore Oslo and its environs briefly, a full week or more would allow for more leisurely explorations of Norway's stunning countryside, including its fjords, plateaus, mountains, and valleys. We've reviewed accommodations in towns that are preceded by the hotel icon.

If You Have 5 Days

Oslo, Norway's capital, makes a good starting point since most flights to Norway arrive here. Spend your first two days exploring **Oslo.** Take it easy the first day and explore the downtown area—meander on Karl Johans Gate, see Akershus Castle and the Kvadraturen, and walk through Vigelands (Frogner) Park. On day two, head out to Bygdøy and visit the area's museums—the Folkemuseum is a must. On the third day, depart for Bergen by train. This six-hour trip across Norway's interior allows you to see some of the country's spectacular scenery, including **Hardangervidda.** When you get to **Bergen,** check into your hotel and head to Bryggen for dinner. Here along Bergen's wharf are some of the city's oldest and best-preserved buildings. Spend your fourth day exploring Bergen. If you have time, visit Troldhaugen, which was composer Edvard Grieg's house for 22 years; it's a half-day trip from Bergen's center. Spend your last night in Bergen, and on the fifth day, fly back to Oslo.

If You Have 10 Days

Spend your first four days following the tour above. On your fifth day, take the day trip Norway in a Nutshell, which is a bus-train-boat tour that takes you through some of the western fjord country. Spend your fifth night in Bergen, and on your sixth day, fly to **Tromsø,** which is north of the Arctic Circle. Spend the rest of the day touring Tromsø. Overnight here, and on your seventh day, rent a car and head for **Alta.** If you arrive early enough, visit the Alta Museum. Spend the night in Alta, and on the eighth day, continue your voyage, driving farther on to **Hammerfest,** the world's northernmost town. Overnight in Hammerfest, and the next day, take an excursion up the treeless tundra of the **Nordkapp** (North Cape). Return to Hammerfest, and on your last day, fly back to Oslo via Alta.

When to Tour Norway

To experience the endless days of the midnight sun, the best time to visit Norway is mid-May to late July. Hotels, museums, and sights have longer opening hours and the modes of transportation are available and accessible. If you decide to travel in May, try to be in Norway on the 17th, or *Syttende Mai*, Norway's Constitution Day, when flag-waving Norwegians bedecked in national costumes, or *bunader*, fill the streets.

Autumn weather can be quite unpredictable. The days can be cool and crisp, or wet and cold especially on the west coast. However, the Gulf Stream, which flows along the Norwegian coast, keeps the weather surprisingly mild for such a high latitude.

Norway in winter is a wonderland of snow-covered mountains glowing under the northern lights, and few tourists are around to get in your way (although many tourist sights are closed). The days may seem perpetually dark, and November through February can seem especially dreary. If it's skiing you're interested in, plan your trip for March or April, as there's usually still plenty of snow left. Take note that during the week of Easter, many Norwegians head for the mountains, so it's hard to get accommodations, and cities are virtually shut down—even grocery stores close.

FODOR'S CHOICE

Dining
Bagatelle, Oslo. One of the best restaurants in Europe showcases the French-inspired yet Norwegian cuisine of its owner-chef, Eyvind Hellstrøm. *$$$$*

Bølgen & Moi Briskeby, Oslo. Modern and innovative, restaurant duo Toralf Bølgen and Trond Moi keep harvesting culinary successes, from Oslo to Stavanger. At this branch, standouts include the garlic-stuffed leg of lamb—and the chocolate bread is great, too. *$$$–$$$$*

Magma, Oslo. Sumptuous cuisine in sun-kissed surroundings is what this Mediterranean restaurant offers. The menu concentrates on seasonal ingredients and on dishes prepared with the least amount of fuss. *$$$–$$$$*

Oro, Oslo. Chef Terje Ness's Mediterranean-style restaurant is the hottest, hippest thing going in Norway. *$$$–$$$$*

Lodging
Rica Ishavshotel, Tromsø. Docked at the city's harbor, this maritime hotel is shaped like a ship. The rooms feel like spacious cabins. It has Norway's best breakfast buffet, serving almost everything under the Midnight Sun. *$$$–$$$$*

Dr. Holms Hotel, Geilo. Stunning mountain views, timeless luxury, an unforgettable ski bar, a Japanese spa, and superb service all make this Norway's finest resort. *$$–$$$$*

Radisson SAS Plaza Hotel, Oslo. The staff at the Plaza gives every guest the royal treatment. If you stay on an upper floor, you'll have a spectacular view of the capital. *$$–$$$$*

Castles and Churches
Akershus Slott og Festning, Oslo. On the brow of the Oslo fjord, this stone fortress, castle, and royal residence dates back to the 1300s.

Det Kongelige Slottet, Oslo. A neoclassical beauty in vanilla and cream, the Royal Palace can only be visited on special summer tours. Come here early on May 17th and watch the royal family wave to a sea of their subjects.

Stave churches, around Norway. A distinctive symbol of Norway's culture, these medieval churches are always worth a visit. Those in Bergen and Ål and at the Norsk Folkemuseum in Oslo are standouts.

Museums
Munchmuseet, Oslo. Pay homage here to Norway's most famous artist, Edvard Munch, who painted that 20th-century icon, *The Scream*. He bequeathed thousands of his works to Oslo upon his death in 1944.

Norsk Folkemuseum, Bygdøy, Oslo. See Norway in a day at one of Europe's largest open-air museums. An original stave church, sod houses, and other buildings span the country's past.

Norsk Oljemuseum, Stavanger. The Petroleum Museum lays out Norway's rich oil history, showing the impact the product has had on the country's recent history.

Troldhaugen, outside Bergen. Celebrated Norwegian composer Edvard Grieg created and played host to European luminaries here in his home, whose name means Hill of the Trolls. The salon seems frozen in time; you may think for a moment that he's about to walk through the door.

Vikingskiphuset (Viking Ship Museum), Oslo. The Vikings' time has passed, but interest in their world and ways hasn't waned. Three well-preserved Viking ships and relics tell their story in a rounded white-stone building resembling a Viking burial mound.

Special Moments

Basking in the Midnight Sun at the Nordkapp (North Cape)

Dogsledding up the side of a misty glacier on Svalbard

Eating dinner in a Sámi tent, with your reindeer parked outside

Taking in the monumental sculptures in Vigeland Park

2 OSLO

What sets Oslo apart from other European cities is not so much its cultural traditions or its internationally renowned museums as its simply stunning natural beauty. What other world capital has subway service to the forest, or lakes and hiking trails within city limits? But Norwegians will be quick to remind you that Oslo—with thriving theaters, vibrant nightlife, and more—is as cosmopolitan as any world capital. And like other major metropolises, Oslo also has modern architectural monstrosities, traffic problems, and even a bit of urban sprawl.

A S RECENTLY AS 10 YEARS AGO, Oslo had a reputation for being provincial and less sophisticated than its big city peers of Stockholm and Copenhagen. Times have changed. Now a world-class city, Oslo has a cosmopolitan character and prosperity fueled through a strong Norwegian economy. It's one more change for this town of 500,000—a place that has become good at survival and rebirth throughout its nearly 1,000-year history. In 1348, plague wiped out half the city's population, and it has burned down too many times to count. Nearly destroyed entirely by a fire in 1624, it was redesigned and renamed Christiania by Denmark's royal builder, King Christian IV. After that it slowly gained prominence as the largest and most economically significant city in Norway.

During the mid-19th century, Norway and Sweden were both ruled as one kingdom, under Karl Johan. It was then that the grand main street that's his namesake was built, and Karl Johans Gate has been at the center of city life ever since. In 1925, an act of Parliament finally changed the city's name to Oslo, its original Viking name. Today, Oslo is Norway's political, economic, industrial, and cultural capital as well as home to both the Nobel Peace Price and the Norwegian royal family.

Open-minded and outgoing, Oslo has increasingly embraced global and European trends. There are now many more exclusive shops, fancier golf courses, and restaurants with more eclectic menus. This new, hipper Oslo caters to a much broader range of tastes and tempos. For urban souls of all ages, there is an array of cafés, clubs, shops, museums, galleries, entertainment, festivals, and cultural events. For outdoor and sports lovers, there is hiking, sailing, and skiing within the vast expanse of parks, forests, and fjords that make up greater Oslo.

EXPLORING OSLO

Karl Johans Gate, starting at Oslo Sentralstasjon (Oslo Central Station, also called Oslo S Station) and ending at the Royal Palace, forms the backbone of downtown Oslo. Many of Oslo's major museums and historic buildings lie between the parallel streets of Grensen and Rådhusgata. To the southeast of the center of town is Gamlebyen, a historic area with a medieval church and buildings. West of downtown is Frogner and Majorstuen, residential areas known for fine restaurants, shopping, cafés, galleries, and the Vigeland sculpture park. Farther west is the Bygdøy Peninsula, with a castle and five interesting museums that honor different aspects of Norway's taste for exploration. Northwest of town is Holmenkollen, with its stunning bird's-eye view of the city and the surrounding fjords, a world-famous ski jump and museum, and three historic restaurants. On the more multicultural east side, where a diverse immigrant and Norwegian population lives, are the Munch Museum and the Botanisk Hage og Museum (Botanical Gardens and Museum). It's also on the east side that Grünerløkka, a trendy neighborhood of cafés and shops, has sprung up.

Numbers in the text correspond to numbers in the margin and on the Oslo map.

Downtown: The Royal Palace to City Hall

Although the entire city region is huge (454 square km [175 square mi]), downtown Oslo is compact, with shops, museums, historic sights, restaurants, and clubs concentrated in a small, walkable center that's brightly illuminated at night.

12

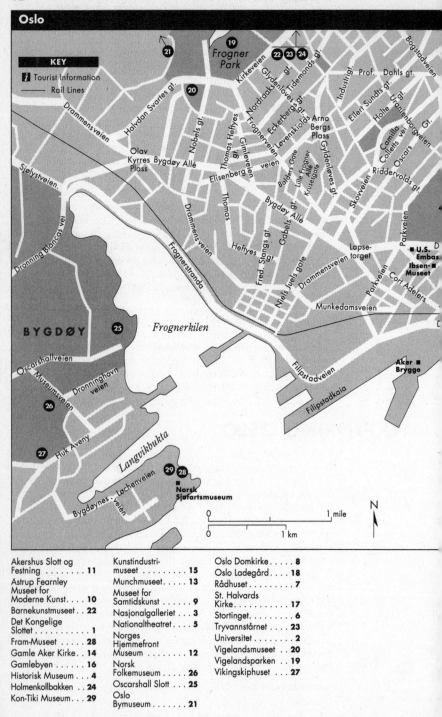

KEY

i Tourist Information
— Rail Lines

Seilduksgt.

Helgesens gt.

Helgesens gt.

Grüners gt.

Sofienberggt.

Waldemar Thranes gt.

Colletts gt.

Akersbakken

Maridalsveien

Akerselva

Møllerveien

Nordregt.

Vår
Frelsers
Gravlund

Parkveien

Ullevålsveien

Pilestredet

Holberg's gate

Frederiksgate

Wessels gt.

Nordahl Bruns gt.

Akersveien

Damstredet

St. Olavsgt.

Trondheimsveien

Botanisk
Hage

Jens Bjelkes gt.

Drammensveien

Universitetsgt.

Henrik Ibsens
Gate

Møllergt.

Torggt.

Hausmanns gt.

Urtegt.

Norbgt.

Tøyengt.

U.S.
Embassy

Munkedamsveien

Karl

Johans

Rosenkrantz Gt.

Akersgata

Grubbe

gt.

Youngs-
torget

Storgt.

Brugt.

Lakkegata

Grønlandsleiret

Stortingsgt.

Gate

Grensen

R. Amundsens gt.

Slottsgt.

Stortorvet

Oslo
Spektrum

Oslo City

Dokkveien

Øvre

Vollgata

Nedre Vollgt.

Prinsens gt.

Basarhallene

Central
(Oslo S)
Station

Schweigaards gt.

Piervika

Akershusstranda

Rådhusgt.

Nedre

Tollbugata

Slottsgt.

Dronningens gt.

Skippergt.

Fred Olsens gt.

Strandgt.

Nylandsveien

Akerselva

Bispegt.

Gamlebyen

St. Halvards Plass

Kirkegata

Revier str.

Mynt gt.

Kongens Gate

Skippergt.

Bjørvika

Bispevika

SØRENGA

Oslo gt.

Oslofjorden

Mosseveien

Ekebergsletta

A Good Walk

Oslo's main promenade, Karl Johans Gate, runs from **Det Kongelige Slottet** ① through town. Before venturing down Karl Johans Gate, walk across the street from the palace to **Ibsen-Museet** to see the playwright Henrik Ibsen's final apartment as well as a museum devoted to his life. Walk down Drammensveien to Munkedamsveien and the **Stenersen-museet,** for its latest temporary exhibition or for permanent works by Edvard Munch and other Norwegian artists. From the gallery, walk back to Karl Johans Gate. Just beyond the castle on your left are three yellow buildings, which were part of the old **Universitet** ②—today they are used only by the law school. Murals painted by Munch decorate the interior walls of these buildings. Around the corner from the university on Universitetsgata is the **Nasjonalgalleriet** ③, which contains hundreds of Norwegian, Scandinavian, and European works. Back-to-back with the National Gallery, across a parking lot, is a big cream-brick art nouveau–style building housing the **Historisk Museum** ④. There's an impressive collection of Viking artifacts on display. Continue along Frederiksgate back to the university and cross Karl Johans Gate to the **Nationaltheatret** ⑤ and Studenterlunden Park. This impressive building is not only the national theater, but a popular meeting place—many buses stop out front, and the T-bane (subway) is right beside it.

Walk past the Lille Grensen shopping area and walk down Karl Johans Gate to see **Stortinget** ⑥, the Norwegian Parliament, on your left. Then go back to Stortingsgata, one of the streets bordering Studenterlunden Park. Head back in the direction of the Nationaltheatret and then turn left on Universitetsgata. Walk toward the water to reach the redbrick **Rådhuset** ⑦, its two block towers a familiar landmark. After visiting Rådhuset, end your tour with an *øl* (mineral water) at one of the many outdoor cafés at Aker Brygge.

TIMING

The walk alone should take no more than two hours. If you happen to be at the Royal Palace midday, you might catch the changing of the guard, which happens every day at 1:30. Note that many museums are closed on Monday.

Sights to See

★ ❶ **Det Kongelige Slottet** (The Royal Palace). At one end of Karl Johans Gate, the vanilla- and cream-color neoclassical palace was completed in 1848. Although generally closed to the public, the palace is sometimes open for special guided tours in summer. An equestrian statue of Karl Johan, King of Sweden and Norway from 1818 to 1844, stands in the square in front of the palace. ⌂ *Drammensvn. 1,* ☎ *22/04–89–52.* ⌸ *NKr 65.* ⊙ *Mid-June–mid-Aug. (guided tours only).*

❹ **Historisk Museum** (Historical Museum). In partnership with the Vikingskiphuset (in Bygdøy), this forms The University Museum of Cultural Heritage, which concentrates on national antiquities as well as ethnographic and numismatic collections. See the intricately carved *stavkirke* (wood church) portals and exhibitions from the Arctic to Asia. You can also gain a deeper understanding of Norway's Viking heritage through artifacts on display here. ⌂ *Frederiksgt. 2,* ☎ *22/85–99–12,* WEB *www.ukm.uio.no.* ⌸ *Free.* ⊙ *Mid-May–mid-Sept., Tues.–Sun. 10–4; mid-Sept.–mid-May, Tues.–Sun. 11–4.*

Ibsen-museet. Famed Norwegian dramatist Henrik Ibsen, known for *A Doll's House* and *Peer Gynt* among many other classic plays, spent his final years here in the apartment on the second floor until his death in 1906. Every morning, Ibsen's wife, Suzannah, would encourage the short literary legend to write before allowing him to head off to the Grand Café for his brandy and foreign newspapers. His study offers some striking glimpses into his psyche. Huge, intense portraits of Ibsen and his archrival, August Strindberg, face each other. On his desk still sits his "devil's orchestra," a playful collection of frog and troll-like figurines that inspired him. Take a guided tour by well-versed and entertaining Ibsen scholars. Afterward, visit the museum's exhibition of Ibsen's drawings and paintings and first magazine writings. ⊠ *Arbiensgt. 1,* ☎ *22/55–20–09,* WEB *www.ibsen.org.* 🖼 *NKr 40.* ☉ *Tues.– Sun., guided tours at noon, 1, and 2.*

❸ **Nasjonalgalleriet.** The National Gallery houses Norway's largest collection of art created before 1945. The deep-red Edvard Munch room holds such major paintings as *The Dance of Life* and several self-portraits. Classic fjord and country landscapes by Hans Gude and Adolph Tidemand—including *Bridal Voyage on the Hardangerfjord*—share space in other galleries with other works by major Norwegian artists. The museum's permanent collection has works by Monet, Renoir, Van Gogh, and Gauguin. ⊠ *Universitetsgt. 13,* ☎ *22/20–04–04,* WEB *www. nasjonalgalleriet.no.* 🖼 *Free.* ☉ *Mon., Wed., Fri. 10–6, Thurs. 10–8, Sat. 10–4, Sun. 11–4.*

❺ **Nationaltheatret** (National Theater). In front of this neoclassical theater, built in 1899, are statues of Norway's great playwrights, Bjørnstjerne Bjørnson, who also composed the national anthem, and Henrik Ibsen, author of *A Doll's House, Hedda Gabler,* and *Peer Gynt.* Most performances are in Norwegian, so you may just want to take a guided tour of the interior, which can be arranged by appointment. ⊠ *Stortingsgt. 15,* ☎ *22/00–17–51.*

★ ❼ **Rådhuset** (City Hall). This redbrick building is best known today for the awarding of the Nobel Peace Prize that takes place here every December. Back in 1915, slums stood on the site, until the mayor had the slums cleared and began plans for the building, which didn't open until 1950. Inside, many museum-quality masterpieces are on its walls. After checking out the Main Hall frescoes, walk upstairs to the Banquet Hall to see the royal portraits. In the East Gallery, Per Krohg's mosaic of a pastoral scene covers all four walls, making you feel like you're part of a painting. On festive occasions, the Central Hall is illuminated from outside by 60 large spotlights that simulate daylight. ⊠ *Rådhuspl.,* ☎ *22/86–16–00.* 🖼 *NKr 30.* ☉ *May–Aug., Mon.–Sat. 9–5, Sun. noon–5; Sept.–Apr., Mon.–Sat. 9–4, Sun. noon–4.*

Stenersen-museet. Named for art collector Rolf E. Stenersen, this city museum often has highly regarded and sometimes provocative temporary exhibitions. Opened in 1994, its permanent collection consists of works from Stenersen's own collection, including art by Edvard Munch, and paintings donated by such artists as Amaldus Neilsen and Ludvig Ravensberg. ⊠ *Munkesdamsvn. 15,* ☎ *23/49–36–00.* 🖼 *NKr 30,* ☉ *Tues., Thurs. 11–7; Wed., Fri., Sat., Sun. 11–5.*

❻ **Stortinget** (The Norwegian Parliament). This classic 1866 building houses the Norwegian Parliament. Take an informative guided tour given daily throughout the summer or on Saturday the rest of the year. In front, the park benches of Eidsvolls Plass are a popular meeting and gathering place. ⊠ *Karl Johans gt. 22,* ☎ *23/31–35–96.* WEB *www. stortinget.no.* 🖼 *Free.* ☉ *Guided tours July 1–Aug. 15, weekdays 10–1; Sept. 15–June 15, Sat. 10–1.*

❷ **Universitetet** (The University). The great hall in the middle building (there are three in all) is decorated with murals by Edvard Munch. Look for *The Sun,* which shows penetrating rays falling over a fjord. This building was the site of the Nobel Peace Prize award ceremony until 1989. ⊠ *Aulaen, Karl Johans gt. 47,* ☎ *22/85–97–11.* 🎫 *Free.* 🕓 *July, weekdays 10–2.*

Kvadraturen and Akershus Castle

The Kvadraturen is the oldest part of Oslo still standing. In 1624, after the town of Oslo burned down for the 14th time, King Christian IV renamed the city Christiania and moved it from the area that is southeast of Oslo S Station, called Gamlebyen, and rebuilt it adjacent to the Akershus fortress. In order to prevent future fires, the king decreed that houses were to be built of stone or brick instead of wood. He also built a stone wall around the newly rebuilt city to protect it from his enemies, the Swedes.

A Good Walk

The Kvadraturen area, which includes Akershus Slott, is bound on the east side of the fortress by Skippergata and on the north side by Karl Johans Gate between Oslo Domkirke and Stortorvet. The boundary follows Øvre Vollgata around to the other side of the fortress. Kvadraturen translates roughly as "square township," which refers to the area's geometrically ordered streets. Be aware that the streets around Skippergata and Myntgata are known as a mini–red-light district and a hangout for drug addicts. Avoid theft by keeping a close eye on your surroundings and by securing purses, wallets, expensive cameras, and other valuables.

Start at Stortorvet, Oslo's main square. To the east of the square is **Oslo Domkirke** ⑧, the city's landmark cathedral. Artists have been contributing to the cathedral's richly decorated interior since the 18th century.

From the cathedral, follow Kirkegata left past Karl Johans Gate to the **Museet for Samtidskunst** ⑨, inside the 1906 Bank of Norway building. Spend time wandering through the museum's halls to admire both its art nouveau architecture and contemporary art. From the museum, take the side street Revierstredet to Dronningensgate, where there's a building that does not seem to fit in with its 17th-century neighbors. Designed and built in the early 1990s, this brick and steel office building houses the **Astrup Fearnley Museet for Moderne Kunst** ⑩. Internationally recognized, the museum's permanent and temporary exhibitions emphasize modern art. Make a right onto Dronningensgate and head up to Rådhusgata. Take a left and walk down the street. Keep an eye out for the 17th-century building at 11 Rådhusgata. It houses the celebrated restaurant Statholdergården. This was the home of the "statholder," the official representative from Copenhagen when Norway was under Danish rule.

Continue on Rådhusgata until you reach the corner of Nedre Slottsgate. The yellow building you see was originally the old city hall (1641), but since the 1800s it has been the Det Gamle Rådhus restaurant. Diagonally across Rådhusgata in two 17th-century buildings are an art gallery and an arty café. The building that houses Kafé Celsius was one of the first buildings erected in Christian IV's town.

Turn left on Akersgata and walk alongside the grassy hill to the entrance of **Akershus Slott og Festning** ⑪, the center of Christian IV's Kvadraturen. It's a worthwhile climb to the hilltop for its incredible Oslo harborfront and fjord views—especially at sunset. The castle became the German headquarters during the occupation of Norway in World War II, and many members of the Resistance were executed on the castle grounds. In a building next to the castle, at the top of the hill, is the **Norges Hjemmefront Museum** ⑫, which tells the gripping story of German occupation and Norwegian resistance.

Walk back to Rådhusgata to see another interesting building, Skogbrand Insurance, at Rådhusgt. 23B. Architects Jan Digerud and Jon Lundberg have won awards for their innovative 1985 vertical addition to this 1917 building. Take a break from history and architecture and head to the **Emanuel Vigelands Museet,** a collection of artistic erotica created by the brother of the celebrated sculptor Gustav Vigeland. To get here, turn right on any of the streets along Rådhusgata back to Karl Johans Gate and take the T-bane (T-bane is short for *tunnelbane,* which is an underground railway, or subway) line 1 from Nationaltheatret station, in the direction of Frognerseteren, and get off at Slemdal, one of Oslo's hillside residential neighborhoods.

TIMING

The walk alone will take at least three hours. Combined with museum visits and breaks, the itinerary could take up more than half a day. Akershus Slott will take at least half an hour. Try to do this tour during daylight hours, catching late-afternoon sun from atop the Akershus grounds. Also note that the T-bane ride to the Emanuel Vigeland Museet in Slemdal takes about 15 minutes and that the museum is open only on Sunday afternoon.

Sights to See

⑪ **Akershus Slott og Festning** (Akershus Castle and Fortress). Dating back to 1299, this stone medieval castle and royal residence developed into a fortress armed with cannons by 1592. After that time, it withstood a number sieges and then fell into decay. It was finally restored in 1899. Summer tours take you through its magnificent halls, the Castle church, the royal mausoleum, reception rooms, and banqueting halls. ⊠ *Akershus Slott, Festningspl.,* ☎ *22/41–25–21.* ⊡ *Grounds and concerts free; castle NKr 20.* ☉ *Grounds daily 6 AM–9 PM; castle May–mid-Sept., Mon.–Sat. 10–4, Sun. 12:30–4; mid-Sept.–Oct., Mon.–Sat. 10–4, Sun. 12:30–4. Guided tours May–Sept., daily at 11, 1, and 3.*

⑩ **Astrup Fearnley Museet for Moderne Kunst** (Astrup Fearnley Museum for Modern Art). This privately funded museum opened in 1993 and earned an international reputation for Norwegian and international art from the post-war period on. In its smaller gallery, "Young British Artist" Damien Hirst's controversial installation *Mother and Child Divided* is on display. Selections from its permanent collection, which include works by post-war Britons as well as such Norwegians as Odd Nerdrum and Olav Christopher Jenssen, are exhibited every summer. There's also a glassed-in sculpture garden with Niki de St. Phalle's sparrow and several other oversize 20th-century figures. ⊠ *Dronningensgt. 4,* ☎ *22/93–60–60,* WEB *www.af-moma.no.* ⊡ *NKr 50, Tuesday free.* ☉ *Tues., Wed., and Fri. noon–4, Thurs. noon–7, weekends noon–5. Guided tours weekends at 1.*

OFF THE BEATEN PATH | **EMANUEL VIGELANDS MUSEET** – Although he never gained the fame of his older brother Gustav, the creator of Vigeland Park, Emanuel is an artist of some notoriety. His alternately saucy, natural, and downright erotic frescoes make even the sexually liberated Norwegians blush. ⊠ *Grimelundsvn. 8,* ☎ *22/14–93–42.* ⊡ *Free.* ☉ *Sun. noon–4.*

⑨ **Museet for Samtidskunst** (The National Museum of Contemporary Art). A stunning granite and marble example of art nouveau architecture, this former 1906 bank building is the largest museum of Norwegian and international visual art from the post-war period. Opened in 1990, its ornate gilded interior contrasts the old with the new in permanent and temporary exhibitions. The permanent collection of 4,300 works spans the genres of graphic art, drawing, photography, sculpture, objects, installations, and video. Take time to ponder the two fascinating permanent installations here: Ilya Kabakov's "The Man Who Never Threw Anything Away" and Per Inge Bjøørlo's "Inner Room V." ⊠ *Bankpl. 4,* ☎ *22/86–22–10,* WEB *www.museumsnett.no/mfs.* 🎫 *Free.* ⊙ *Tues.–Wed. and Fri. 10–5, Thurs. 10–8, Sat. 11–4, Sun. 11–5. Guided tours by appointment only.*

⑫ **Norges Hjemmefront Museum** (Norwegian Resistance Museum). Striped prison uniforms, underground newssheets, and homemade weapons all tell the history of the resistance movement that arose before and during Norway's occupation by Nazi Germany. A gray, winding path leads to two underground stone vaults in which models, pictures, writings, and recordings trace the times between Germany's first attack in 1940 to Norway's eventual liberation on May 8, 1945. Every year, on the anniversaries of these dates, Norwegian resistance veterans gather to commemorate Norway's dark days and honor those who lost their lives. The former ammunitions depot joins the memorial at the exact spot where Norwegian patriots were executed by the Germans. ⊠ *Akershus Slott,* ☎ *23/09–31–38.* 🎫 *NKr 25.* ⊙ *Mid-Apr.–mid-June, Mon.–Sat. 10–4, Sun. 11–4; mid-June–Aug., Mon.–Sat. 10–5, Sun. 11–5; Sept., Mon.–Sat. 10–4, Sun. 11–4; Oct.–mid-Apr., weekdays 10–3, weekends 11–4.*

⑧ **Oslo Domkirke** (Oslo Cathedral). Consecrated in 1697, this dark-brown brick structure has been Oslo's main church ever since. The original pulpit, altarpiece, and organ front with acanthus carvings still stand. Take a look at the endless ceiling murals from 1936 to 1950 and stained-glass windows by Emanuel Vigeland. In the 19th century, the fire department operated a fire lookout point from the bell tower here, which you can visit today. ⊠ *Stortorget 1,* ☎ *23/31–46–00.* 🎫 *Free.* ⊙ *Daily 10–4.*

NEED A   **Pascal Konditori** (⊠ Tollbugt. 11, ☎ 22/42–11–19), a trendy Parisian-
BREAK?   style patisserie inside an old-fashioned Norwegian *konditori* (café), is
              known for its enormous croissants, pastries, and French coffee. It's a
              place to see and be seen.

East, North, and South of Downtown: Munch Museum, Damstredet, and Gamlebyen

The Munch Museum is east of the city center in Tøyen, an area in which Edvard Munch spent many of his years in Oslo. The Tøyen district has a much different feel than Oslo's cushy west side—it's ethnic and more industrial. West of Tøyen, north of the city center near Vär Frelsers Gravlund, is the quiet, old-fashioned district of Damstredet, its streets lined with artisans' shops. If you're an ever curious history buff, you'll probably enjoy the last half of this tour through Gamlebyen. However, if this is your first trip to Oslo and you have a limited amount of time, you may want to end your tour at the Kunstindustrimuseet. Gamlebyen is somewhat off the beaten track, and although the area is interesting, some of the ruins are barely discernible.

A Good Walk

Start by taking any T-bane from the city center (Sentrum) to Tøyen, where **Munchmuseet** ⑬ sits on a hill near the Botanisk Hage, a quiet oasis of plants and flowers. After visiting the museum, head back to town center. Take the T-bane and get off at Stortinget.

Head down Karl Johans Gate and take a left onto Akersgata. Follow it past the offices of *Aftenposten*, Norway's leading daily paper. As you head up the hill, you can see a huge rotund building, Deichmanske Bibliotek, the city's library. When you reach St. Olavs Church, veer gently to the right on Akersveien. You may want to take a detour down Damstredet when you come to it—it's one of the city's oldest streets with well-preserved houses from the 19th century. Afterward, continue back along Akersveien. On your left is Vår Frelsers Gravlund (Our Savior's Graveyard), where you can seek out the gravestones of many famous Norwegians, including Ibsen and Munch. At the graveyard's northeastern corner is **Gamle Aker Kirke** ⑭, the city's only remaining medieval church.

After the church, walk along the north side of the cemetery and then take a left onto Ullevålsveien. Take the road down the hill to the corner of St. Olavs Gate and Akersgata, where **Kunstindustrimuseet** ⑮, one of Europe's oldest museums of decorative arts and design, stands.

If you've got a yen for history and archaeology, visit **Gamlebyen** ⑯, the old town, to the southeast of Oslo S Station. Nearby on Oslo Gate is St. Halvards Plass. During the 13th century, the area was the city's ecclesiastical center. Also here are the still intact foundations of **St. Halvards Kirke** ⑰, which dates from the early 12th century. Some other ruins, including Korskirke and Olavs Kloster, lie in **Minneparken.** Nearby on Bispegata is **Oslo Ladegård** ⑱, a restored Baroque-style mansion that sits on foundations of a 13th-century bishop's palace.

The oldest traces of human habitation in Oslo are the 5,000-year-old carvings on the runic stones near Ekebergsletta Park. They are across the road from the park on Karlsborgveien and are marked by a sign reading FORTIDSMINNE. To reach the park, walk south on Oslo Gate until it becomes Mosseveien. The stones will be on your right. The park is a good spot to rest your feet and end your tour.

TIMING
The Munch Museum will take up most of the morning, especially if you take a guided tour. The second half of the tour, from Gamlebyen to Ekebergsletta, is a perfect way to spend a summer Sunday afternoon. Things are quiet, and locals tend to stroll around this area when the weather is nice.

Sights to See

⑭ **Gamle Aker Kirke** (Old Aker Church). Dating back to 1100, this medieval stone basilica is Oslo's oldest church—it's still in use as a parish church. Inside, the acoustics are outstanding, so inquire about upcoming church concerts. ⊠ *Akersbakken 26,* ☎ *22/69–35–82.* 🎫 *Free.* ⊙ *Mon.– Sat. noon–2, Sun. 9 AM–11 AM.*

⑯ **Gamlebyen** (The Old City). Sometimes referred to as the "Pompeii of Scandinavia," this area contains the last remains of medieval Oslo. Today it's one of the largest homogeneous archaeological sites found in any capital city in Scandinavia. To get here, take *trikk* (as the Norwegians fondly call the streetcars) 18, marked "Ljabru," from Stortorvet to St. Halvards Plass (you can also take trikk 19 from Nationaltheatret). Contact Oslo Byantikvar (☎ 22/20–85–80), the Antiquities Department of Oslo, for information on guided tours of the area. The department and the tourist office have a self-guided tour brochure for the area.

⑮ **Kunstindustrimuseet** (The Museum of Decorative Arts and Design). Rich Baldishol tapestries from 1100, Norwegian dragon-style furniture, and royal Norwegian apparel (including Queen Sonja's wedding gown from 1968) make this a must-see museum. Founded in 1876, it also has exquisite collections of Norwegian 18th-century silver, glass, and faience. A contemporary Scandinavian section follows the history of design and crafts in the region. ⊠ *St. Olavs gt. 1*, ☎ *22/03–65–40*. ▧ *NKr 25. ☉ Tues., Wed., Fri.–Sun. 11–4, Thurs. 11–7.*

Minneparken. Oslo was founded by Harald Hårdråde ("Hard Ruler") in 1048, and the earliest settlements were near what is now Bispegata, a few blocks behind Oslo S Station. Ruins are all that are left of the city's former religious center: the **Korskirke** (Cross Church; ⊠ Egedesgt. 2), a small stone church dating from the end of the 13th century; and **Olavs Kloster** (Olav's Cloister; ⊠ St. Halvards pl. 3), built around 1240 by Dominican monks. ⊠ *Entrance at Oslogt. and Bispegt.*

★ ⓭ **Munchmuseet** (The Munch Museum). Edvard Munch, Norway's most famous artist, bequeathed his enormous collection of works (about 1,800 paintings, 4,500 drawings, and 18,000 graphic works) to the city when he died in 1944. The museum is a monument to his artistic genius, housing the largest collection of his works and changing exhibitions. His most popular painting, *The Scream*, now a 20th-century icon, is not always on exhibition. While most of the Munch legend focuses on the artist as a troubled, angst-ridden man, he moved away from that pessimistic and dark approach to more optimistic themes later in his career. ⊠ *Tøyengt. 53*, ☎ *23/24–14–00*, [WEB] *www.munch.museum.no.* ▧ *NKr 60. ☉ June–mid-Sept., daily 10–6; mid-Sept.–May, Tues.–Wed. and Fri.–Sat. 10–4, Thurs. and Sun. 10–6.*

⓲ **Oslo Ladegård.** The original building, the 13th-century Bispegård (Bishop's Palace), burned down in the famous 1624 fire, but its old vaulted cellar was not destroyed. The present mansion was restored and rebuilt in 1725; it now belongs to the city council and contains scale models of 16th- to 18th-century Oslo. ⊠ *St. Halvards pl., Oslogt. 13*, ☎ *22/19–44–68*. ▧ *NKr 40. ☉ Late May–late Sept., call for hrs; guided tours Sun. at 4.*

⓱ **St. Halvards Kirke** (St. Halvard's Church). This medieval church, named for the patron saint of Oslo, remained the city's cathedral until 1660. ⊠ *Minneparken, entrance at Oslogt. and Bispegt.*

Frogner, Majorstuen, and Holmenkollen

Among the city's most stylish neighborhoods, Frogner and Majorstuen combine old-world Scandinavian elegance with contemporary European chic. Incredibly hip boutiques and galleries coexist with embassies and ambassadors' residences on the streets near and around Bygdøy Allé. Holmenkollen, the hill past Frogner Park, features the famous ski jump and miles of ski trails.

A Good Walk
Catch the No. 12 "Majorstuen" trikk from Nationaltheatret on the Drammensveien side of the Royal Palace grounds. You can also take the No. 15 from Aker Brygge.

Opposite the southwest end of the palace grounds is the triangular U.S. Embassy, designed by Finnish-American architect Eero Saarinen and built in 1959. Look to the right at the corner of Drammensveien and Parkveien for a glimpse of the venerable Nobel Institute. Since 1905 these stately yellow buildings have been the secluded setting where the five-member Nobel Committee decides who will win the Nobel Peace Prize. The library is open to the public.

Stay on the trikk and ride to Frogner Park or walk the seven blocks. To walk, get off at Balders Gate and follow the road to Arno Bergs Plass, with its central fountain. Turn left on Gyldenløves Gate until you reach Kirkeveien. Turn right past the Dutch Embassy, and cross the street at the light. Frogner Park, also called Vigelandsparken, is ahead.

Walk through the front gates of the park and toward the monolith ahead: you are entering **Vigelandsparken** ⑲. This stunning sculpture garden was designed by one of Norway's greatest artists, Gustav Vigeland. Spend a few minutes and walk over to Frogner Stadion (Stadium) and **Skøyte-museet,** which highlights Norway's contribution to the sport of ice skating. Across from the park, you can study the method to Vigeland's madness at **Vigelandsmuseet** ⑳. Cross the street to the **Oslo Bymuse-um** ㉑, a cultural and historical look at the city and its development. After you leave the museum, take a left onto Kirkeveien and continue to the Majorstuen underground station, near the intersection of Bogstad-veien. Here you have two options: you can walk down Bogstadveien, look at the shops, explore the Majorstuen area, and then take the Hol-menkollen line of the T-bane to Frognerseteren; or you can skip the stroll down Bogstadveien and head right up to Holmenkollen. The train ride up the mountain passes some stunning scenery. If you have brought your children, you may want to make a detour at the first T-bane stop, Frøen, and visit the **Barnekunstmuseet** ㉒.

Continue on the T-bane to the end of the line. This is Frognerseteren— a popular destination on winter weekends. The view of the city here is spectacular. The **Tryvannstårnet** ㉓ has an even better panoramic view of Oslo. Downhill is **Holmenkollbakken** ㉔, where Norway's most intrepid skiers prove themselves every March during the Holmenkollen Ski Festival.

TIMING

This is a good tour for Monday, since the museums mentioned are open, unlike most others in Oslo. You will need a whole day for Frogner and Majorstuen since there is some travel time involved. The trikk ride from the city center to Frogner Park is about 15 minutes; the T-bane to Frogn-erseteren is about 20. You're no longer in the compact city center, so distances between sights are greater. The walk from Frognerseteren is about 15 minutes and is indicated with signposts. Try to save Hol-menkollen with its magnificent views for a clear day.

Sights to See

⊙ ㉒ **Barnekunstmuseet** (Children's Art Museum). A brainchild of Rafael Goldin, a Russian immigrant, the museum showcases her collection of children's drawings from more than 150 countries. You can see the world though the eyes of a child in its exhibitions of textiles; drawings; paintings; sculptures; and children's music, dancing, and other activities. ⊠ *Lille Frøens vei 4,* ☎ *22/46–85–73.* ⌘ *NKr 40.* ☉ *Late-June–early Aug., Tues.–Thurs. and Sun. 11–4; mid-Sept.–mid-Dec., late Jan.–late June, Tues.–Thurs. 9:30–2, Sun. 11–4.*

★ ㉔ **Holmenkollbakken** (Holmenkollen Ski Museum and Ski Jump). A distinctive part of the city's skyline, Oslo's ski jump holds a special place in the hearts of Norwegians. A mecca of ski jumping, the 1892 jump was rebuilt for the 1952 Winter Olympics. Still a popular site for international competitions, it attracts a million visitors every year. Take the elevator and walk to the top and imagine what skiers think in the moment before they take off. Back down at the base of the jump, turn right, past the statue of King Olav V on skis, to enter the oldest ski museum in the world. A hands-on exhibition awaits you with the alpine and cross-country skis, poles, and bindings that have been used throughout the ages. See the earliest skis from AD 600, explorer Fridtjof Nansen's wooden skis from his 1888 Greenland crossing, and the autographed specimens used by retired ski champion Bjørn

Daehlie. Then, head to the ski simulator outside for the thrilling sensation of your own ski jump and downhill ski race. ✉ *Kongevn. 5,* ☎ *22/92–32–00,* WEB *www.skiforeningen.no.* ✎ *NKr 60.* ☼ *Jan.–Apr. and Oct.–Dec., daily 10–4; May and Sept., daily 10–5; June–Aug., daily 9–8.*

㉑ **Oslo Bymuseum** (Oslo City Museum). One of the world's largest cities, Oslo has changed and evolved greatly over its thousand years. A two-floor, meandering exhibition covers Oslo's prominence in 1050, the Black Death that came in 1349, the great fire of 1624 and subsequent rebuilding, and the urban development in the 20th century. Among the more interesting relics are the red coats that the first Oslo police, the watchmen, wore in 1700, and the first fire wagon in town, which appeared in 1765. Plan to visit the museum near the beginning of your stay for a more informed understanding of the Norwegian capital. ✉ *Frognervn. 67,* ☎ *23/28–41–70,* WEB *oslobymuseum.no.* ✎ *NKr 30.* ☼ *Tues.–Fri. 10–4, weekends 11–4.*

㉓ **Tryvannstårnet** (Tryvann's Tower). The view from Oslo's TV tower encompasses 36,000 square ft of hills, forests, cities, and several bodies of water. You can see as far as the Swedish border to the east and nearly as far as Moss to the south. ✉ *Voksenkollen,* ☎ *22/14–67–11.* ✎ *NKr 35.* ☼ *May and Sept., daily 10–5; June–Aug., daily 10–6; Oct.–Apr., daily 10–4.*

㉑ **Vigelandsmuseet.** "I am anchored to my work so that I cannot move. If I walk down the street one day a thousand hands from work hold on to me. I am tied to the studio and the road is never long," said Gustav Vigeland in 1912. This museum is the famous Norwegian sculptor's studio and residence. Now, it houses models of almost all his works as well as sculptures, drawings, woodcuts, and the original molds and plans for Vigeland Park. Wander through this intense world of enormous, snowy-white plaster, clustered nudes, and busts of such famous Norwegians as Henrik Ibsen and Edvard Grieg. ✉ *Nobelsgt. 32,* ☎ *22/54–25–30,* WEB *www.vigeland.museum.no.* ✎ *NKr 30.* ☼ *Oct.–Apr., Tues.–Wed. and Fri.–Sun. noon–4, Thurs. noon–7; May–Sept., Tues.–Sat. 10–6, Sun. noon–6.*

★ ⑲ **Vigelandsparken** (Vigeland's Park). Also known as Frogner Park, Vigelandsparken is home to 212 bronze, granite, and wrought-iron sculptures by Gustav Vigeland (1869–1943). Most of the stunning park sculptures are placed on a nearly 1 km (½ mi) long axis and depict the stages of life: birth to death, one generation to the next. See the park's 56-ft-high granite *Monolith Plateau,* a column of 121 upward-striving nude figures surrounded by 36 groups on circular stairs. The most beloved sculpture is a bronze, enraged baby boy stamping his foot and scrunching his face in fury. Known as *Sinnataggen* (The Angry Boy), this famous Oslo image has been filmed, parodied, painted red, and even stolen from the park. It is based on a 1901 sketch Vigeland made of a little boy in London.

Skøytemuseet (The Ice Skating Museum). Tucked away in Frogner Stadium, this is Norway's only museum devoted to ice skates and ice skaters. Gleaming trophies; Olympic medals; and skates, skates, and more skates all serve to celebrate the sport. Photographs of skating legends such as Johan Olav Koss, Hjalmar Andersen, and Oscar Mathisen line the walls. Take a look at ways that skates have evolved, especially the early bone skates from 2,000 BC and the wooden skates that came later. ✉ *Frogner Park, Middelthunsgt. 26,* ☎ *22/43–49–20.* ✎ *NKr 20.* ☼ *Tues. and Thurs. 10–2, Sun. 11–2.*

Bygdøy

Several of Oslo's most well-known historic sights are concentrated on the Bygdøy Peninsula, as are several beaches, jogging paths, and the royal family's summer residence.

A Good Walk

The most pleasant way to get to Bygdøy, from May to September, is to catch a ferry from the Rådhuset. Times vary, so check with NOR-TRA (the Norwegian Tourist Board) for schedules. Another alternative is to take Bus 30, marked "Bygdøy," from Stortingsgata at Nationaltheatret along Drammensveien to Bygdøy Allé, a wide avenue lined with chestnut trees. The bus passes Frogner Church and several embassies on its way to Olav Kyrres Plass, where it turns left, and soon left again, onto the peninsula. The royal family's current summer residence, actually just a big white frame house, is on the right. Get off at the next stop, Norsk Folkemuseum. The pink castle nestled in the trees is **Oscarshall Slott** ㉕, once a royal summer palace.

Next is the **Norsk Folkemuseum** ㉖, which consists of an open-air museum as well as Norwegian folk costumes and art. Around the corner to the right is the **Vikingskiphuset** ㉗, one of Norway's most popular attractions, which houses some of the best-preserved Viking-era remains yet discovered.

Follow signs on the road to the **Fram-Museet** ㉘, a pyramid-shape structure resembling a traditional Viking boathouse. The museum houses the famed *Fram* polar ship as well as artifacts from various expeditions. Beside it, wander through the boat hall and then see marine exhibitions and a movie at the **Norsk Sjøfartsmuseum.** Across the parking lot is the older **Kon-Tiki Museum** ㉙, with Thor Heyerdahl's famous raft, along with the papyrus boat *Ra II.* You can get a ferry back to the City Hall docks from the dock in front of the Fram-Museet. If your children are squirming to break out of the museum circuit, entertain the thought of a trip to Tusenfryd, an amusement park packed with rides.

TIMING

Block out a day for Bygdøy. You could spend at least half a day at the Folkemuseum alone. Note that the museums on Bygdøy tend to be open daily, but close early.

The HMK Sightseeing trip to Tusenfryd is an afternoon trip, so count on spending half a day. It takes between 10 and 20 minutes to reach the park from downtown Oslo by bus. If you decide to go on your own from Oslo S Station, you might want to spend the whole day playing in both parks.

Sights to See

★ ☾ ㉘ **Fram-Museet.** The strongest vessel in the world, the enormous legendary Norwegian polar ship *Fram*, has advanced farther north and south than any other surface vessel. Built in 1892, it made three arctic voyages during expeditions by Fridtjof Nansen (1893–96), Otto Sverdrup (1898–1902) and Roald Amundsen (1910–12). Climb onboard and peer inside the captain's quarters, which has explorers' sealskin jackets and other relics on display. Surrounding the ship are many expedition artifacts. ⊠ *Bygdøynes,* ☎ *22/43–83–70,* WEB *www.fram.museum.no.* ⊠ *NKr 25.* ⊙ *Jan.–Feb. and Nov.–Dec., weekdays 11–2:45, weekends 11–3:45; Mar.–Apr., daily 11–3:45; early–mid-May and Sept., daily 10–4:45; mid-May–mid-June, daily 9–5:45; mid-June–Aug., daily 9–6:45; Oct., daily 10–3:45.*

★ ⓒ ㉙ **Kon-Tiki Museum.** The museum celebrates Norway's most famous 20th-century explorer. Thor Heyerdahl made a voyage in 1947 from Peru to Polynesia on the *Kon-Tiki,* a balsa raft, to lend weight to his theory that the first Polynesians came from the Americas. The *Ra II* sailed from Morocco to the Caribbean in 1970. ⊠ *Bygdøynesvn. 36,* ☎ *22/43–80–50,* ⓦⒺⒷ *www.kon-tiki.no.* 🎟 *NKr 30.* ☉ *Apr.–May and Sept., daily 10:30–5; June–Aug., daily 9:30–5:45; Oct.–Mar., daily 10:30–4.*

★ ⓒ ㉖ **Norsk Folkemuseum** (Norwegian Folk Museum). One of the largest open-air museums in Europe, this is a perfect way to see Norway in a day. From the stoic stave church to farmers' traditional houses made of sod, the old buildings here span Norway's history throughout the ages and regions. Indoors, there's a fascinating display of folk costumes. The displays of richly embroidered, colorful *bunader* (national costumes) from every region includes one set at a Telemark country wedding. The museum also has stunning dragon-style wood carvings from 1550 and some beautiful rosemaling. The traditional costumes of the Sámi (Lapp) people of northern Norway are exhibited around one of their tents. If you're visiting in summer, inquire about "Norwegian Evening," a summer program of folk dancing, guided tours, and food tastings. During Sundays in December, the museum holds Oslo's largest Christmas market. ⊠ *Museumsvn. 10,* ☎ *22/12–37–00,* ⓦⒺⒷ *www.norskfolke.museum.no.* 🎟 *NKr 70.* ☉ *Mid-Sept.–mid-May, weekdays 11–3, weekends 11–4; mid-May–mid-June, daily 10–5; mid-May–mid-Sept., daily 10–6.*

ⓒ **Norsk Sjøfartsmuseum** (Norwegian Maritime Museum). Everything from Norwegian fishing boats, paintings of fishermen braving rough seas, and intricate ship models are all on display here. The Arctic vessel is *Gjøa* docked at the waterfront outside. The breathtaking, panoramic movie *The Ocean: A Way of Life* delves into Norway's unique coastal and maritime past. ⊠ *Bygdøynesvn. 37,* ☎ *22/43–82–40,* ⓦⒺⒷ *www.norsk-sjofartsmuseum.no.* 🎟 *NKr 30.* ☉ *Mid-May–Sept., daily 10–6; Oct.–mid-May, Mon., Wed., Fri.–Sun. 10:30–4, Tues., Thurs. 10:30–6.*

㉕ **Oscarshall Slott.** This small country palace was built (1847–52) in eccentric English Gothic style for King Oscar I. There's a park, pavilion, fountain, and stage on the grounds. The original interior has works by the Norwegian artists Adolph Tidemand and Hans Gude. ⊠ *Oscarshallvn.,* ☎ *22/56–15–39.* 🎟 *NKr 20.* ☉ *Late May–mid-Sept., Tues., Thurs., and Sun. noon–4.*

OFF THE   **TUSENFRYD –** At Norway's foremost amusement park, the thrills are many.
BEATEN PATH   In May 2001, ThunderCoaster, a huge wooden rollercoaster with the
ⓒ   steepest drop in Europe, opened here for the daring. HMK Sightseeing
(☞ Oslo A to Z) provides an afternoon bus excursion from the Norway Information Center. There's also a shuttle bus that departs from Oslo Bussterminalen Galleriet, the city's main train station, which is right by Oslo S Station. ⊠ *Vinterbro,* ☎ *64/97–64–00,* ⓦⒺⒷ *www.tusenfryd.no.* 🎟 *NKr 215.* ☉ *Early June–mid-Aug., daily 10:30–7; May and late Aug., weekends 10:30–7.*

★ ㉗ **Vikingskiphuset** (The Viking Ship Museum). The Viking legacy in all its glory lives on at this classic Oslo museum. Chances are you'll come away fascinated by the three blackened wooden Viking ships *Gokstad, Oseberg,* and *Tune,* which date back to AD 800. Discovered in Viking tombs around the Oslo fjords between 1860 and 1904, the ships have been exhibited since the museum's 1957 opening. In Viking times, it was customary to bury the dead with food, drink, useful and decorative objects, and even their horses and dogs. Many of the well-preserved tapestries, household utensils, dragon-style wood carvings and sledges were found aboard ships. The museum's rounded white walls actually give the feeling of a burial mound. Avoid summertime crowds by visiting at lunchtime. ⊠ *Huk Aveny 35,* ☎ *22/43–83–79,* WEB *www.ukm.no.* ⌷ *NKr 40.* ☉ *May–Aug., daily 9–6; Sept., daily 11–5; Apr. and Oct., daily 11–4; Nov.–Mar., daily 11–3.*

DINING

Cosmopolitan flavors and influences are changing the face of the Oslo restaurant scene and cuisine. Mediterranean and Asian dishes and ingredients have both created a richer menu. Inspired by international experiences and travels, chefs such as Magma's Sonja Lee, are bringing new energy and expertise to their kitchens. Fusion and crossover cooking have come to stay, even in fast-food restaurants. The rise of soup bars, sushi, and sophisticated cafés are all signs of global trends being adopted in the capital.

Take time to taste the exciting variations as well as the traditional dishes coming out of Norway's capital. They're both based on seafood; farm-fresh produce; and game, especially reindeer. Menus change frequently with the seasons.

Most restaurants close through Christmas and the often week-long Easter break. Spend at least one sunny summer afternoon harborside at Aker Brygge eating shrimp and watching the world go by. Floating restaurants serve shrimp in bowls with baguettes and mayonnaise. Or better still, buy steamed shrimp yourself off the nearby docked fishing boats and plan a picnic in the Oslo fjords or Vigeland or another of the city's parks.

Downtown: Royal Palace to the Parliament

$$$–$$$$ ★ ✗ **Oro.** Norwegian celebrity chef Terje Ness opened this Mediterranean restaurant, whose name means "gold" in Spanish, in September 2000. Now the city's hottest restaurant, it requires reservations months ahead. In the restaurant's open kitchen, you can see Ness and his personable staff at work. The dining room's decor is hip and airy. Ness recommends the grilled scallops with eggplant and orange, the turbot with lentils, capers, and truffles, and the Taste of Oro (a 7 or 12 course dinner). For dessert savor the delicious Chocolate Oro, chocolate mousse with passion fruit topped with gold leaf. ⊠ *Tordenskjolds gt. 6,* ☎ *23/01–02–40. AE, DC, MC, V. Reservations essential. Closed Sun. No lunch on weekends.*

$$$–$$$$ ★ ✗ **Theatercafeen.** The window seats at this elegant Norwegian dining institution are *the* place to see and be seen. Open since 1900, the last Viennese-style café in northern Europe reveals its past through the paintings of actors and writers on its walls. Try the reindeer steak in mushroom and cream sauce as well as the chocolate mousse. ⊠ *Hotel Continental, Stortingsgt. 24–26,* ☎ *22/82–40–50. Reservations essential. AE, DC, MC, V.*

$$$ ✗ **Babette's Gjestehus.** Near City Hall, this restaurant's dark-blue walls and lace curtains make it resemble an old-fashioned Norwegian living room. French chef Dominic Choaqa and his staff serve Scandinavian and international dishes with a friendly, welcoming style. Consider the reindeer fillet in port sauce, the lamb with apricots, or the monkfish. ⊠ *Rådhuspassasjen, Roald Amundsensgt. 3,* ☎ *22/41–64–64. AE, DC, MC, V. Closed Sun. No lunch.*

Oslo Dining

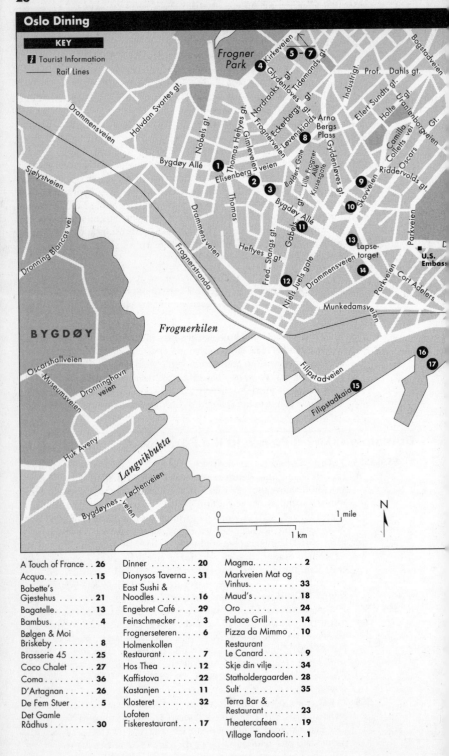

KEY

i Tourist Information
— Rail Lines

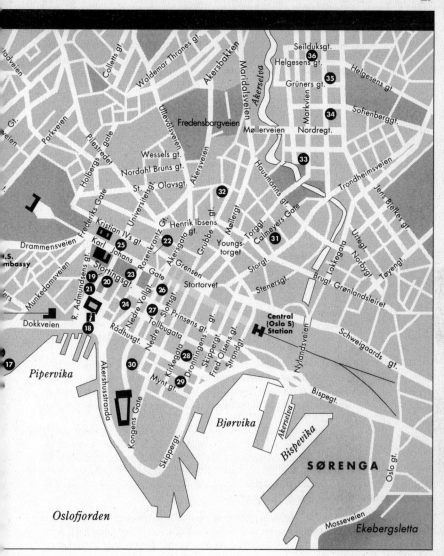

$$$ ✕ **D'Artagnan.** This classic French restaurant carries an intimate feel-
★   ing within its white and sea-blue walls. Owner Freddie Nielsen, one
       of Norway's most celebrated restaurateurs, received both his educa-
       tion and inspiration in France, but do not expect the tiny portions of
       nouvelle cuisine. Try the tartare of king crab with avocado and lime.
       If you're truly famished, embark on the seven-course Grand Menu that
       includes steamed smoked Arctic char. ⊠ *Øvre Slottsgt. 16,* ☎ *22/41–
       50–62. AE, DC, MC, V. Closed Sun. and July. No lunch Jan.–Aug.*

$$$ ✕ **Terra Bar & Restaurant.** Spanish pottery and earth tones hint at the
       Mediterranean-inspired dishes served here. Across the street from the
       Parliament, it attracts its share of politicians. Half the menu is fish—
       you may wish to sample the peppered monkfish or the herbed cod. Terra's
       grilled tenderloin with rioja sauce is also a standout. A special treat is
       the Tired of Everything dessert: homemade vanilla ice cream and cof-
       fee sherbet that's served with hot brandy and espresso syrup. ⊠ *Stort-
       ingt. 2,* ☎ *22/40–55–20. AE, DC, MC, V. No lunch July–mid-Aug.*

$$–$$$ ✕ **A Touch of France.** Downstairs from D'Artagnan, Freddie Nielsen's
        clean, inviting wine bistro is straight out of Paris. The waiters' long,
        white aprons; the art nouveau decor; old French posters; and closely
        packed tables all add to the illusion. The tempting menu includes a steam-
        ing hot bouillabaisse. ⊠ *Øvre Slottsgt. 16,* ☎ *22/42–56–97. AE, DC,
        MC, V.*

$–$$ ✕ **Brasserie 45.** Overlooking the fountain on Karl Johans Gate, this
       candlelit brasserie has a Scandinavian feel to match its cuisine. Fish dishes
       such as grilled salmon and catfish are its signatures. ⊠ *Karl Johans gt.
       45 (upstairs),* ☎ *22/41–34–00. AE, DC, MC, V.*

$–$$ ✕ **Dinner.** The bland name belies the fact that this is one of the best
★   places in Oslo for Chinese food, as well as dishes that combine Nor-
       wegian and Cantonese styles. The four-course Peking duck is a spe-
       ciality. Try the platter of seafood in chili-pepper sauce. ⊠ *Stortingsgt.
       22,* ☎ *23/10–04–66. AE, DC, MC, V. No lunch.*

$ ✕ **Kaffistova.** Norwegian homemade cooking is served cafeteria style
       at this downtown restaurant. Everyday specials in generous portions
       include soup and a selection of entrées, including a vegetarian dish. ⊠
       Rosenkrantz gt. 8, ☎ *22/42–95–30. AE, DC, MC, V.*

Kvadraturen and Aker Brygge

$$$$ **Acqua.** As the name suggests, this popular harborside restaurant and
       bar has a menu swimming in fish and other seafood. Chef Kjell Arne
       Johnsether is well known locally for the time he was chef at the Grand
       Hotel. Consider the seafood platter of lobster, scallops, oysters, and
       mussels or crayfish. Acqua's picture window and blue mosaics rein-
       force the theme. ⊠ *Filipstadkaia 2,* ☎ *22/83–92–99. Reservations es-
       sential May–Sept. AE, DC, MC, V.*

$$$$ ✕ **Statholdergaarden.** Chef Bent Stiansen's Asian-inspired French
       dishes have long been a hit around town. Try his smoked mountain
       trout, monkfish and artichokes, or chicken tarragon. The six-course
       gastronomic menu changes daily, or you can order from the à la carte
       menu. More than 400 years old, the rococo dining room, decorated
       in blue-green and oak, is one of Norway's largest, holding up to 75
       people. ⊠ *Rådhusgt. 11,* ☎ *22/41–88–00. Reservations essential.
       Jacket and tie. AE, DC, MC, V. Closed Sun. and 3 wks in July.*

$$$–$$$$ ✕ **Engebret Café.** This somber, old-fashioned restaurant at Bankplassen
          was a haunt for bohemian literati at the turn of the 20th century. The
          formal, French-tinged Norwegian dinner menu includes traditional sea-
          sonal fare around *Juletide* (Christmastime), including lutefisk and *pin-
          nekjøtt* ("sticks of meat"), which is lamb steamed over branches of birch.
          For a real taste of Norway, try the *smalahove* (a whole sheep's head).

Many Norwegian families consider it a treat to visit the restaurant around Christmas, so book early if that's your plan, too. During the rest of the year, try the reindeer in cream sauce or the poached catfish. ⊠ *Bankpl. 1,* ☎ *22/82–25–25. AE, DC, MC, V.*

$$$–$$$$ ✕ **Lofoten Fiskerestaurant.** Named for the Lofoten Islands off the northwest coast, this Aker Brygge restaurant is considered one of Oslo's best for fish, from salmon to cod to monkfish. Renovated in early 2001, the restaurant has a bright, fresh, minimalistic interior with harbor views and a summertime patio. From January through March, try the cod served with its own liver and roe; April through September, the shellfish; and from October through December, the lutefisk. Call ahead, since sometimes only large groups are served. ⊠ *Stranden 75, Aker Brygge,* ☎ *22/83–08–08. AE, DC, MC, V.*

$$$ ✕ **Det Gamle Rådhus.** In the historic atmosphere of the first city hall, built 1641, this is Oslo's oldest restaurant. Its reputation is based most strongly on its traditional Norwegian fish and game dishes. An absolute must is its specialty, the pre-Christmas lutefisk platter. ⊠ *Nedre Slottsgt. 1,* ☎ *22/42–01–07. AE, DC, MC, V. Closed Sun.*

$–$$ ✕ **East Sushi & Noodles.** The sushi bar trend has hit Norway's capital. This minimalist Japanese-style restaurant is one of a chain. Traditional Nigiri-Sushi and Makimono garner rave reviews from aficionados. Try the Sushi Moriawase, which includes 10 assorted sushi of the day and six maki. Drop by for Sushi Happy Hour between 4 and 7 every evening for three specially priced meals. ⊠ *Bryggetorget 7, Aker Brygge,* ☎ *22/83–63–51. AE, DC, MC, V.*

$–$$ ✕ **Maud's.** The regional Norwegian dishes here are so traditional that they seem exotic to some Norwegian city folk who left the nest long ago. Specialties include medium-rare topside beef and grilled veal steak. ⊠ *Brynjulf Bulls pl. 1,* ☎ *22/83–72–28. AE, DC, MC, V. Closed Sun.*

$ ✕ **Coco Chalet.** Best known for its homemade cakes and pies, the simple Coco Chalet serves affordable Asian-inspired dishes such as baked shrimp. Treat yourself to delicious raspberry cake. ⊠ *Øvre Slottsgt. 8,* ☎ *22/33–32–66. AE, DC, MC, V.*

East of Downtown

$$$ ✕ **Klosteret.** This popular east-side eatery's name means "the cloisters." Its not-very-medieval, informal dining room is in a spacious, candlelit, rounded brick cellar. Saints and other religious figures adorn the walls, and Gregorian chants play in the background. The handwoven menus, bound to look like hymnals, contain a list of appealing meat and fish dishes, plus a daily vegetarian option. Consider the cod with truffles and the heavenly chocolate cake. ⊠ *Fredensborgvn. 13,* ☎ *23/35–49–00. AE, DC, MC, V. Closed Sun. and July.*

$$–$$$ **Coma.** Can you be alive and kicking and eating at a trendy restaurant and still be in a coma? At this strange but very hip place, you can. The offbeat interior uses white, blue, green, and purple ceiling lights, striped walls, and comfy pillows to create a dreamy mood. Tongue-in-cheek signs over the door are there to let you know when you are entering and when you are leaving the coma. From the French inspired menu, try fish dishes such as Completely Nuts and Salmon in a Coma. ⊠ *Helgesensgt. 16,* ☎ *22/35–32–22. AE, DC, MC, V.*

$$–$$$ ✕ **Markveien Mat og Vinhus.** This artsy food and wine house in the heart of the Grünerløkka district serves fresh French-inspired cuisine. The atmosphere is relaxed and the clientele is bohemian. Paintings cover the yellow walls, and the tables are black and somber. Try the fried trout, the reindeer, or the scampi and truffles. ⊠ *Torvbakkgt. 12 (entrance on Markvn. 57),* ☎ *22/37–22–97. AE, DC, MC, V. Closed Sun.*

$$ ✕ **Dionysos Taverna.** Owner Charalambos Eracleous imports fresh fish,
★   wine, and ouzo from Greece to bring to his cobalt blue and whitewashed
restaurant. The *tzatziki* (yogurt and cucumber salad), souvlakia, and
moussaka are authentically prepared, as are the more unusual casseroles,
such as *exohiko* (lamb baked with red wine, tomatoes, and onions).
For a taste of everything, order *mezes*, Greek-style tapas. A bouzouki
trio accompanies your dining experience on Thursday, Friday, and Sat-
urday nights. ⊠ *Calmeyersgt. 11,* ☎ *22/60–78–64. MC, V. No lunch.*

$$ **Sult.** Trendy, Norwegian bohemian informality is the essence of this
small restaurant, whose name means "hunger." Including mostly fish
and seafood dishes done in a contemporary Norwegian style, the ones
worth trying are baked monkfish, catfish, or shark with couscous. Large
picture windows, small square tables, and a simple homemade look
attracts students as well as authors. Next door, the bar/lounge, appropriately named *Tørst* ("thirst"), has it own unique blends of drinks,
including Raspberry Parade, a blend of water, raspberry juice, champagne, and vodka. ⊠ *Thorvald Meyers gt. 26,* ☎ *22/87–04–67. AE,
DC, MC, V.*

$ **Skje din vilje.** Soup bars have been opening up around the capital. This
small and charming example, which has a spoon door handle, has Oslo's
best-tasting soup. Fast and healthy, you can fill up on a big bowl of
hot or cold soup and bread here for less than the cost of a burger and
fries. Try the popular mulligatawny, *borsjtsj clodnik* (borscht), or *ba-
calaosuppe* (soup with dried salt cod). ⊠ *Thorvald Meyers gt. 48,* ☎
22/35–55–68. AE, DC, MC, V.

Frogner and Majorstuen

$$$$ ✕ **Bagatelle.** Chef and owner Eyvind Hellstrøm's has established an
★   international reputation for his modern Norwegian French-inspired
cuisine and superb service, attracting the who's who of Norwegian
society and creating one of Norway's best restaurants. Paintings by
contemporary Norwegian artists accent the understated but elegant
decor. The three-, five-, and seven-course menus change daily. Grilled
cod with truffle sauce and the lobster are both standouts. ⊠ *Bygdøy
Allé 3,* ☎ *22/44–63–97. AE, DC, MC, V. Closed Sun., mid-July–mid-
Aug. No lunch.*

$$$$ ✕ **Restaurant Le Canard.** Behind the Royal Castle, this elegant restaurant is in what looks like a brick manor house. Inside are such antique
furnishings as a stained-glass window by Maria Vigeland, the wife of
Emanuel. Chef Thomas Berg is known for his European dishes, particularly seafood, so try his North Sea turbot with squid lasagna and
artichokes or his grilled scallops. Sample the extensive wine cellar of
30,000 bottles, including rare champagne from 1928. In summer, dine
in special style on Le Canard's stunning garden terrace. ⊠ *Pres. Har-
bitz gt. 4,* ☎ *22/54–34–00. Reservations essential. AE, DC, MC, V.
Closed Sun. No lunch in winter.*

$$$–$$$$ ✕ **Magma.** Vibrant, warm, and intense, the orange- and yellow-
★   splashed interior captures the character of this Mediterranean restau-
rant–bar and its celebrity chef, Sonja Lee. Fresh from successes in
London and Provence, Lee and partner Laurent Surville (also a chef)
opened Magma in April 2000. Since then, it has become one of the
city's hottest restaurants, attracting everyone from businesspeople to
artists. The changing menu is based on seasonal ingredients and fol-
lows the owners' philosophy of rough-hewn simplicity. Consider the
ricotta ravioli and the spit-roasted veal with macaroni gratin. ⊠
Bygdøy Allé 53, ☎ *23/08–58–10. AE, DC, MC, V.*

$$$–$$$$ ✕ **Bølgen & Moi Briskeby.** The restaurateurs Toralf Bølgen and Trond
★   Moi have another winner in this minimalistic restaurant. If you're

tired of eating breakfast in your hotel, you can rise and shine right here. Housed in a redesigned industrial building, the restaurant incorporates the past with an eye-catching, long cement dining table. Well-known Norwegian artists such as photographer Knut Bry showcase their talents throughout the restaurant's bar, brasserie, and formal sections. Try the fresh chocolate bread as well as dishes such as the garlic-stuffed leg of lamb. Most dishes emerge from the wood-burning oven in the corner. ⊠ *Løvenskioldsgt. 26,* ☎ *24/11–53–53. AE, DC, MC, V.*

$$$–$$$$ ✗ **Feinschmecker.** The name is German, but the food is international and Scandinavian. Modern and stylish, the decor's warm earthy tones still make the inside feel homey. Owners Lars Erik Underthun, one of Oslo's foremost chefs, and Bengt Wilson, a leading food stylist, make sure the food looks as good as it tastes. Try the popular steamed fillet of turbot or herb garlic leg of lamb. For dessert, there's raspberries au gratin. ⊠ *Balchensgt. 5,* ☎ *22/44–17–77. Reservations essential. AE, DC, MC, V. Closed Sun. and last 3 wks of July. No lunch.*

$$$ ✗ **Hos Thea.** An intimate yet lively dining experience awaits in this white
★ and blue restaurant, which has fleur de lys accents. From the open kitchen, owner Sergio Barcilon and the other chefs often serve their French and Spanish dishes themselves. The small menu lists four or five choices in each course, but every dish is superbly prepared, from the veal baked in salt to scallops in lemon sauce. Noise and smoke levels can be high late at night. ⊠ *Gabelsgt. 11, entrance on Drammensvn.,* ☎ *22/44–68–74. Reservations essential. AE, DC, MC, V. No lunch.*

$$$ ✗ **Kastanjen.** This rustic Frogner bistro, named after the chestnut trees
★ that line the street, is the kind every neighborhood needs. The food is French and the atmosphere is casual and laid-back. Try the roasted sweetbreads or the fried redfish with glazed artichokes. Be sure to check out the warmly lit downstairs lounge for before- or after-dinner drinks. ⊠ *Bygdøy Allé 18,* ☎ *22/43–44–67. AE, DC, MC, V. Closed Sun. and July.*

$$–$$$ ✗ **Palace Grill.** This tiny, eight-table dining spot near the Royal Palace ranks among the hippest on the Oslo restaurant scene. While you wait for a table, you can sip a beer in the adjoining cowboy rock-and-roll bar. Don't let the "grill" part fool you: it may be relaxed, but it's French-inspired cuisine, not fast food. Consider the breast of duck with orange and fennel or the cod with lentils. The restaurant doesn't take reservations and is usually full, so try to get here before 5 PM for a table. ⊠ *Solligt. 2 (just off Drammensvn.),* ☎ *22/56–14–02. Reservations not accepted. AE, DC, MC, V. Closed Sun. and 1 month in summer.*

$$ **Bambus.** Vietnamese owner Heidi NGuyen and her friendly staff have all lived and cooked throughout Asia, and "Bamboo" reflects this: the menu has delicious and authentic Thai, Japanese, Vietnamese, and Chinese dishes. The Banh Tom Ho Tay (Vietnamese shrimp and sweet-potato pancakes) and Kaeng Phets (Thai duck, shrimp or lamb in coconut milk and vegetables) are both good. The yellow, orange, and pink interior has a bamboo floor and Andy Warhol–type prints of Asian images. ⊠ *Kirkevn. 57,* ☎ *22/85–07–00. AE, DC, MC, V.*

$–$$ **Village Tandoori.** Walking through this restaurant feels like wandering through an Indian or Pakistani village at night 100 years ago. Pakistani owner Mobashar Hussain has collected antique rugs, including vibrant silk ones with embroidery and beadwork. The chicken and lamb curries and tandooris come highly recommended. ⊠ *Bygdøy Allé 65,* ☎ *22/56–10–25. AE, DC, MC, V. No lunch.*

$ **Pizza da Mimmo.** Named for owner Domenico Giardina, aka Mimmo, this is Oslo's best pizzeria. In 1993, Mimmo from Calabria first brought his thin-crusted, authentic Italian pizza recipes to the city. Taste his always popular Pizza Panna and Prosciutto, and Pizza Calabrigella. Earthy colors and hanging rugs help make the restaurant seem cave-like, relaxed, and casual. ⊠ *Behrensgt. 2,* ☎ *22/44–40–20. Reservations essential. AE, DC, MC, V.*

Holmenkollen

$$$$ ✕ **De Fem Stuer.** Near the famous Holmenkollen ski jump, in the his-
★   toric Holmenkollen Park Hotel, this restaurant has first-rate views and
food. Chef Frank Halvorsen's modern Norwegian dishes have strong
classic roots. His fish dishes, particularly those made with salmon, cod,
and wolffish, are his specialty. The three-course "A Taste of Norway"
meal is especially good. ⊠ *Holmenkollen Park Hotel, Kongevn. 26,*
☎ *22/92–27–34. Jacket and tie. AE, DC, MC, V.*

$$$ ✕ **Holmenkollen Restaurant.** An old-fashioned, luxury mountain cabin
café, restaurant, and banquet hall, this Oslo institution dates back to
1892. The spacious café is perfect for afternoon cake and coffee after
walking or skiing. In the more intimate, formal restaurant, dishes
come from the hands of famed chefs Harald Osa and Morten Schak-
enda. The menu focuses on Norwegian fish and game dishes given in-
novative, international twists. Consider their reindeer or their steamed
cod, which comes with a confiture of tomato and pesto. ⊠ *Hol-
menkollvn. 119,* ☎ *22/14–62–26. AE, DC, MC, V.*

$$ ✕ **Frognerseteren.** Just above the Holmenkollen ski jump and therefore full of sweeping views, this is probably Oslo's most famous restau-
rant. Popular with locals and travelers alike, it specializes in fish and
venison. The scrumptious apple cake is legendary and perfect for
dessert or for an afternoon coffee treat. Take the Holmenkollbanen to
the end station and then follow the signs downhill to the restaurant.
⊠ *Holmenkollvn. 200,* ☎ *22/14–05–50. DC, MC, V.*

LODGING

Comfort and convenience at a cost characterize Oslo hotels. Most hotels, from the elegant Radisson SAS classics to the no-frills Rainbows,
are centrally located, just a short walk from Karl Johans Gate. They
are often between the Royal Palace and Oslo S Station, with the newer
ones closer to the station. For a quiet stay, choose a hotel in either Frogner
or Majorstuen, elegant residential neighborhoods just minutes from
downtown.

Special summer and weekend rates may save you money on your hotel
accommodation. Consider cutting costs by buying an Oslo Package combined with an Oslo Card in advance. Inquire at your hotel chains
about their own special discount programs. Through the Rainbow and
Norlandia Hotels, you can purchase their money-saving Scan+ Hotel
Pass. The pass entitles you to receive up to a 50% discount and a fifth
night free at 200 of their hotels in Scandinavia.

Downtown: Royal Palace to the Parliament

$$$–$$$$ ⊞ **Hotel Continental.** An elegant turn-of-the-20th-century facade has
★   put the Continental on Norway's historic-preservation list. Near Na-
tionaltheatret and next door to cafés, clubs, and cinemas, the Conti-
nental's central location makes it ideal for leisure and business travelers.
Theatercafeen is a landmark, and the newest addition, Lipp, a restau-
rant-café-bar-nightclub, is one of Oslo's more hip places. Dagligstuen
(The Sitting Room) is also a popular meeting place for drinks and quiet
conversation. ⊠ *Stortingsgt. 24–26, 0161,* ☎ *22/82–40–00,* FAX *22/42–
96–89. 159 rooms, 23 suites. 3 restaurants, 2 bars. AE, DC, MC, V.*

$$–$$$$ ⊞ **Grand Hotel.** In the center of town on Karl Johans Gate, the
★   Grand has been Oslo's premier hotel since it opened in 1874. The
epitome of elegance, even standard rooms are large, looking more

like guest quarters in an elegant house than hotel rooms. Ibsen used to drink brandy at the Grand Café in the company of journalists. Munch was also a regular guest; you can see him with his contemporaries in Per Krohg's painting on the café's far wall. The Grand has hosted many famous people, including many if not all of the recipients of the Nobel Peace Prize. Many Norwegians book several years in advance for Constitution Day, May 17, in order to have a room overlooking the parades below. ⊠ *Karl Johans gt. 31, 0101,* ☎ *23/21–20–00,* FAX *22/42–12–25,* WEB *www.rica.no. 289 rooms, 51 suites. 3 restaurants, 3 bars, indoor pool, sauna, health club, meeting room. AE, DC, MC, V.*

$$–$$$$ 🏨 **Hotel Bristol.** The Bristol has a dignity and class all its own. Rooms are understated but classy. The lounge and bar were decorated in the 1920s with an intricate Moorish theme and recall Fez much more than Scandinavia. Josephine Baker once performed in the piano bar in the 1920s. Today, the library and bar with their red, burnished leather sofas are among Oslo's places to see and be seen. ⊠ *Kristian IVs gt. 7, 0130,* ☎ *22/82–60–00,* FAX *22/82–60–01,* WEB *www.bristol.no. 252 rooms, 10 suites. 3 restaurants, 3 bars, sauna, health club, nightclub, convention center. AE, DC, MC, V.*

$$–$$$$ 🏨 **Radisson SAS Scandinavia Hotel.** Oslo's established business hotel, built in 1974, has a winning combination of service and Radisson SAS classic style. Simple, elegant rooms come in different styles: art deco, Italian, Asian, Continental, Scandinavian, and—predictably, for a hotel run by an airline—69 high-tech business-class rooms. The Summit 21 Bar has a stunning, panoramic view of Oslo; having a drink there is a special experience. ⊠ *Holbergsgt. 30, 0166,* ☎ *23/29–30–00,* FAX *23/29–30–01,* WEB *www.radissonsas.com. 488 rooms, 3 suites. 2 restaurants, 2 bars, pool, health club, business services. AE, DC, MC, V.*

$$$ 🏨 **Rainbow Hotel Stefan.** This hotel could be a real home away from home. Hot drinks are served for late arrivals, and breakfast tables come with juice boxes and plastic bags for packing a lunch (request this service in advance). The top-floor lounge has magazines in English. The Stefan's kitchen is famous for creating the best buffet lunch in town. ⊠ *Rosenkrantz gt. 1, 0159,* ☎ *23/31–55–00,* FAX *23/31–55–55,* WEB *www.rainbow-hotels.no. 139 rooms. Restaurant, lounge, library, meeting room. AE, DC, MC, V.*

$$–$$$ 🏨 **Rica Victoria.** This modern business hotel occupies one of the city center's taller buildings, giving some top-floor rooms glimpses of Oslo's rooftops. The rooms, built around a center atrium, are elegant and very stylish, furnished with Biedermeier reproductions, brass lamps, and paisley fabrics in bold reds and dark blues. ⊠ *Rosenkrantz gt. 13, 0121,* ☎ *24/14–70–00,* FAX *24/14–70–01,* WEB *www.rica.no. 199 rooms, 5 suites. Restaurant, bar, convention center, meeting rooms. AE, DC, MC, V.*

$$ 🏨 **Best Western Hotell Bondeheimen.** Founded in 1913 for country folk visiting the city, Bondeheimen, which means "farmers' home," still gives discounts to members of Norwegian agricultural associations. In 2000, the rooms were redecorated from a country style to a minimalistic design that uses dark greens and an earthy red. This is a good choice for families, but if you are looking for quiet, ask for a room in back. The country kitchen Kaffistova is in the same building. ⊠ *Rosenkrantz gt. 8 (entrance on Kristian IVs gt.), 0159,* ☎ *23/21–41–00,* FAX *23/21–41–01,* WEB *www.bondeheimen.com. 127 rooms, 5 suites. Cafeteria, shop, meeting rooms. AE, DC, MC, V.*

$$ 🏨 **Norlandia Karl Johan Hotel.** The late-19th-century Karl Johan, once known as the Nobel, is elegant: the wrought-iron railing and stained-glass windows that line the circular staircase bring to mind 19th-cen-

Oslo Lodging

KEY

i Tourist Information

— Rail Lines

Frogner Park

Frognerkilen

BYGDØY

Langvikbukta

N

0   1 mile

0   1 km

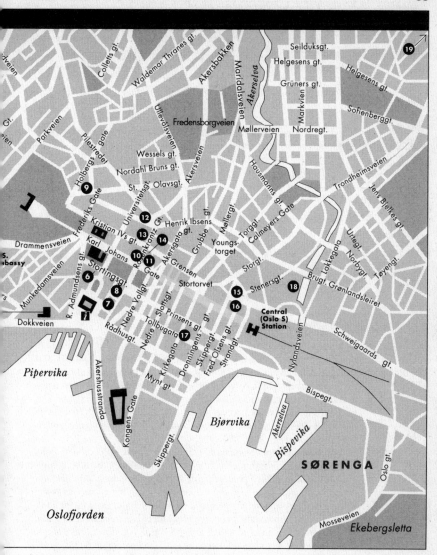

tury Paris. Every room has a different Norwegian antique, but the feel is sophisticated, not rustic. ⊠ *Karl Johans gt. 33, 0162,* ☎ *23/16–17–00,* FAX *22/42–05–19,* WEB *www.norlandia.no. 111 rooms, 1 suite. Restaurant, bar. AE, DC, MC, V.*

$$ ☷ **Rainbow Cecil.** A short walk from Parliament, this modern hotel is
★ a less expensive, centrally located option. Although the rooms are basic, they are perfectly suited to the active, on-the-go traveler. The second floor opens onto a plant-filled atrium, the hotel's "activity center." In the morning it's a breakfast room, but in the afternoon it becomes a lounge, serving coffee, juice, and fresh fruit, with newspapers available in many languages. ⊠ *Stortingsgt. 8, 0130,* ☎ *23/31–48–00,* FAX *23/31–48–50,* WEB *www.rainbow-hotels.no. 112 rooms, 2 suites. Lounge, no-smoking rooms. AE, DC, MC, V.*

East of Downtown

$ ☷ **Haraldsheim.** Named for King Harald, Oslo's hilltop hostel is Europe's largest. Opened in 1954, it has maintained an old-fashioned, typical Scandinavian style. Most of the large rooms have their own toilet and shower, and have four beds. Bring your own sheets or rent them here. A supermarket is close by and local transit is easily accessible. ⊠ *Haraldsheimvn. 4, 0409,* ☎ *22/22–29–65,* FAX *22/22–10–25. 71 rooms, 40 with bath. MC, V.*

Frogner, Majorstuen, and Holmenkollen

$$–$$$$ ☷ **Frogner House.** In the heart of Oslo's West End, this charming, small hotel is popular among business travelers. The five-story redbrick and stone building went up in 1890 as an apartment house and now sits inconspicuously amid rows of other turn-of-the-20th-century town houses. It has a reputation for its quiet rooms, which even have TVs with Internet and e-mail access. ⊠ *Skovvn. 8, 0257,* ☎ *22/56–00–56,* FAX *22/56–05–00,* WEB *www.frogner-house.com. 60 rooms, 8 suites. Meeting room. AE, DC, MC, V.*

$$–$$$$ ☷ **Holmenkollen Park Hotel Rica.** This distinguished, hotel crowns Oslo, to the northwest and above the city center. Dating back to 1894, it commands an unparalleled panorama of the city. The peaceful mountaintop setting is picked up further by the rooms' earth tones and rich wood furniture. Surrounded by open spaces and hills, and next to the Holmenkollen Ski Arena, the property provides the perfect place to cycle, ski, and jog. The hotel is worth a visit even if you don't lodge there, perhaps to dine at its legendary restaurant, De Fem Stuer. ⊠ *Kongevn. 26, 0787,* ☎ *22/92–20–00,* FAX *22/14–61–92,* WEB *www.rica.no. 221 rooms. 2 restaurants, bar, pool, sauna, spa, gym, cross-country skiing, convention center. AE, DC, MC, V.*

$$–$$$ ☷ **Gabelshus.** With only a discreet sign above the door, this ivy-covered brick house in a posh residential area is one of Oslo's most personal hotels. The lounges are filled with antiques, some in the National Romantic style, but the rooms are plain. ⊠ *Gabelsgt. 16, 0272,* ☎ *22/55–22–60,* FAX *23/27–65–60,* WEB *www.gabelshus.no. 43 rooms (plus 48 rooms in Ritz). AE, DC, MC, V.*

$–$$ ☷ **Rainbow Hotel Gyldenløve.** Nestled among the many shops and cafés on Bogstadveien, this hotel is one of the city's most reasonable. Newly renovated rooms are light and airy and have furniture done in a Scandinavian style. It is within walking distance of Vigeland Park, and the trikk stops just outside the door. *Bogstadvn. 20, 0355,* ☎ *22/60–10–90,* FAX *22/60–33–90,* WEB *www.rainbow-hotels.no. 168 rooms. Coffee shop. AE, DC, MC, V.*

Near Oslo Airport and Oslo S Station

$$-$$$$ ⊞ **Clarion Royal Christiania Hotel.** What was once bare-bones hous-
★ ing for 1952 Olympians is now a luxury hotel. Although the original
plain exterior has been retained, inside many rooms were renovated
in 2001 using feng shui principles. The new rooms have white walls
that contrast with the mahogany furniture. ⊠ *Biskop Gunnerus gt. 3,
0106,* ☎ *23/10–80–00,* ℻ *23/10–80–80,* ⓦⒺⒷ *www.royalchristiania.no.
505 rooms, 91 suites. Restaurant, bar, indoor pool, health club, con-
vention center. AE, DC, MC, V.*

$$-$$$$ ⊞ **Radisson SAS Airport Hotel.** Steps away from Oslo Airport, this is
a real beauty of a business hotel. The interiors make use of stone and
metal and have a color scheme that emphasizes burnt-orange and
deep-purple. There are three different room styles: Oriental, Scandinavian, and Maritime. Both the restaurant Toot's International Bar and
Grill and the Lobby Bar are relaxing and inviting. The spacious sports
center is larger than most. There are spinning classes, a trainer on call,
and massage and sauna services. ⊠ *Hotellvegen, Box 163, 2061, Gardermoen,* ☎ *63/93–30–00,* ℻ *63/93–30–30,* ⓦⒺⒷ *www.radissonsas.com.
350 rooms, 88 suites. Restaurant, bar, massage, sauna, health club, business services, meeting room. AE, DC, MC, V.*

$$-$$$$ ⊞ **Radisson SAS Plaza Hotel.** Standing out from other buildings on the
★ city's skyline, Northern Europe's largest hotel is the jewel of the Radis-
son SAS hotel chain. The understated, elegant rooms make use of gilded
fixtures and marble. Many also have spectacular views. The Panorama
Bar on the top floor, the fit-for-a-king breakfast buffets, and luxuriously
grand bathtubs all make a stay in this 37-floor glass extravaganza par-
ticularly memorable. Since it's right next door to Oslo S Station, buses
and other local transit are very convenient. ⊠ *Sonja Henies pl. 3, 0134,*
☎ *22/05–80–00,* ℻ *22/05–80–10,* ⓦⒺⒷ *www.radissonsas.com. 673
rooms, 20 suites. 2 restaurants, bar, indoor pool, health club, conven-
tion center. AE, DC, MC, V.*

$$-$$$ **Rica Oslo Hotel.** Close to Oslo S station, this former office building calls
itself an art hotel. Throughout its lobby and in the rooms, accented in
yellow and redwood, there are paintings by Norwegian artists and many
prints from the National Gallery. Opened in 1998, the Rica attracts
business and leisure travelers due to its location and the convention
center on the premises. ⊠ *Europarådetspl. 1, 0105,* ☎ *23/10–42–00,*
℻ *23/10–42–10,* ⓦⒺⒷ *www.rica.no. 174 room, 2 suites. Restaurant, bar,
sauna, gym, convention center. AE, DC, MC, V.*

$$ **First Hotel Millennium.** This boutique hotel has its own comfortable,
downtown chic. All the simple dark blue, green, and yellow decorated
rooms have bathtubs. Several rooms are geared toward women and
come with a bathrobe, skin products, and women's magazines. The
main-floor lounge has games, a music room, Internet access, and a library. The restaurant–bar, Primo, serves an impressive, international
menu including quail and swordfish. ⊠ *Tollbugt. 25, 0157,* ☎ *21/02–
28–00,* ℻ *21/02–28–30,* ⓦⒺⒷ *www.firsthotels.com. 112 rooms with bath,
10 suites. Restaurant, bar, lounge. AE, DC, MC, V.*

NIGHTLIFE AND THE ARTS

Nightlife

More than ever, the Oslo nightlife scene is vibrant and varied. Cafés,
restaurant bars, and jazz clubs all offer a laid-back, chill atmosphere.
But if you're ready to party, there are many pulsating, live-rock and
dance clubs to choose from. Day or night, people are usually out on
Karl Johans Gate, and many clubs and restaurants in the central area

stay open until the early hours. Drinking out is very expensive, though, starting around NKr 50 for a beer or a mixed drink. Many Norwegians save money by going first to friends' houses before heading out on the town. For special nightlife listings, pick up a copy of the free monthly paper *Natt og Dag*.

Bars and Lounges

Bar Boca (✉ Thorvald Meyers gt. 30, ☎ 22/04–10–80) is a '50s-inspired bar that's intimate. It serves up almost every drink under the sun. The trendiest of the postcollegiate crowd drink the night away at **Beach Club** (✉ Aker Brygge, ☎ 22/83–83–82), a kitschy hamburger joint with tables and booths that wouldn't look out of place in any American diner. If you're more partial to lounging than drinking, try the English pub atmosphere at the **Bristol** (✉ Kristian IVs gt. 7, ☎ 22/82–60–00). **Buddha Bar** (✉ Klingenbergsgt. 40, ☎ 22/82–86–50) may be the hippest bar in town. With its golden Buddha, Chinese lanterns, Asian-inspired cuisine and decor, and inclination for playing world music, it attracts a diverse crowd. With its '70s decor, **Café Con Bar** (✉ Brugt. 11, ☎ 22/05–02–00), is another one of Oslo's trendy crowd pleasers. For a change of pace, get an outdoor table at **Lorry** (✉ Parkvn. 12, ☎ 22/69–69–04), just over from the Royal Palace. Filled with a cast of grizzled old artists, the place advertises 204 brews, but don't be surprised if not all of them are in stock. Serious beer drinkers may find **Oslo Mikrobryggeriet** (✉ Bogstadvn. 6, ☎ 22/56–97–76) worth a stop. Eight different beers are brewed on the premises, including the increasingly popular Oslo Pils. To try out becoming an actual lounge lizard, head to **Tea Lounge** (✉ Thorvald Meyers gt. 33B, ☎ 22/37–07–07), which carries both alcoholic and nonalcoholic tea drinks. The chill-out music, mosaic tile bar, picture window on the world outside, and high-back plush red sofas all add to its cool.

Cafés

In recent years, a cosmopolitan culture has sprung up in the Norwegian capital, bringing with it a desire for cool coffee houses. Now, Oslo's cafés come in as many flavors as the coffee they're serving. **Café Bacchus** (✉ Dronningensgt. 27, ☎ 22/33–34–30), in the old railroad offices by Oslo Domkirke, is tiny but serves a mean brownie. Background music is classical during the day, jazz into the night. **Clodion Art Café** (✉ Bygdøy Allé 63, ☎ 22/44–97–26) has a childlike charm that makes it popular with locals. **Glazed & Amused** (✉ Vestheimgt. 4B, ☎ 22/56–25–18) offers a twist on a normal coffee shop, since you can paint your own ceramic mug here. A cup of coffee to go takes on new meaning. For a slightly bohemian experience, head to **Fru Hagen** (✉ Thorvald Meyers gt. 40, ☎ 22/35–68–71), where the walls are bright and funky and there's a picture-perfect window seat. Hip, little **Java Espresso Bar** (✉ Ullevålsvn. 45B, ☎ 22/59–46–37) has what may be the world's best cup of coffee. **Kaffebrenneriet** (✉ Storgt. 2,) is Oslo's answer to Starbucks, with good coffee and shops throughout town. Norway's indigenous people, the Sámi (also known as Lapp), have their own place, **Sámi GalleriCafé** (✉ Ruseløkkevn. 14, ☎ 22/83–31–95). Sample the Sámi inspired menu (centered around reindeer and wild salmon dishes). There are exhibitions and live indigenous music on Saturday night.

Gay Bars

For information about gay and lesbian activities in Oslo, you can read *Blikk*, the gay newsletter; check out www.gayguideoslo.com; or call **LLH** (Landsforening for Lesbisk of Homofil Frigjøring, ☎ 22/36–19–48), the nationwide gay and lesbian liberation association. The gay nightlife scene has become less active with the closing of popular clubs but several still exist. Now the main bar in town is **London Pub** (✉ C.

J. Hambros pl. 5, ☎ 22/70–87–00), which has **Chairs**, a piano bar on the top floor, and Sunday theme parties. **Potpurriet** (✉ Øvre Vollgt. 13, ☎ 22/41–14–40) organizes well-attended women's dance nights on the last Friday of each month.

Jazz Clubs

Norwegians can't get enough of jazz. Every August, the **Oslo Jazz Festival** (✉ Tollbugt. 28, ☎ 22/42–91–20) brings in major international artists and attracts big crowds. **Blå** (✉ Brennerivn. 9C, ☎ 22/20–91–81), considered the leading club for jazz and related sounds in the Nordic countries, has a popular summer riverside patio. **Herr Nilsen** (✉ C. J. Hambros pl. 5, ☎ 22/33–54–05) features some of Norway's most celebrated jazz artists in a cosmopolitan setting. There's live music three days a week and a jazz café on Saturday afternoon. **Stortorvets Gjæstgiveri** (✉ Grensen 1, ☎ 23/35–63–60) often presents New Orleans–style jazz on Thursday and Saturday nights.

Nightclubs

Most dance clubs open late, so the beat doesn't really start until midnight. Many establishments have a minimum age for entry, which can be as high as 25. There's also usually a cover of around NKr 50. Oslo's beautiful people congregate at the elegant **Barock** (✉ Universitetsgt. 26, ☎ 22/42–44–20). **Bollywood** (✉ Solligt. 2, ☎ 22/55–11–66) has an aggressive red leather and black interior and sometimes shows classic Bombay films. **Cosmopolite** (✉ Møllergt. 26, ☎ 22/20–78–76) has a big dance floor and plays music from all over the world, especially Latin America. **Galleriet** (✉ Kristian IVs gt. 12, ☎ 22/42–29–46), a hot spot in town, has a live jazz club, a disco, and a bar spread over its four art-bedecked floors. **Lipp** (✉ Olav Vs gt. 2, ☎ 22/82–40–60) is an extremely popular restaurant, nightclub, and bar. Most of the big hotels have discos that appeal to the over-30 crowd. **Smuget** (✉ Rosenkrantz gt. 22, ☎ 22/42–52–62) is an institution: live rock and blues every night except Sunday bring crowds who then flock to the in-house discotheque.

Rock Clubs

At Oslo's numerous rock clubs, the cover charges are low, the crowds young and boisterous, and the music loud. **Rockefeller/John Dee** (✉ Torggt. 16, ☎ 22/20–32–32) features alternative acts, including Nick Cave. **Oslo Spektrum** (✉ Sonia Henies pl. 2, ☎ 22/05–29–00) is one of Norway's largest live-music venues. Just behind the Oslo City shopping center, it attracts big names such as Radiohead and Britney Spears. The popular outdoor music festival **Norwegian Wood** (☎ 67/10–34–50, WEB www.norwegianwood.no) is held at the Frognerbadet (Frogner Swimming Pool) in June. Begun in the early '90s, the festival has hosted performers that range from Iggy Pop and Bob Dylan to Norwegian bands just starting out.

The Arts

The monthly tourist information brochure *What's on in Oslo* lists cultural events in Norwegian, as does *Aftenposten,* Oslo's (and Norway's) leading newspaper, in its evening "Oslo Puls" section. The Wednesday edition of *Dagbladet,* Oslo's daily liberal tabloid, also gives an exhaustive preview of the week's events. Tickets to virtually all performances in Norway, from classical or rock concerts to hockey games, can be purchased at any post office.

Film

Filmgoing is a favorite pastime for many Norwegians. Throughout the year, a number of film festivals, including the Oslo Internasjonale

Filmfestival, usually held in November, celebrate the medium. Films are usually subtitled in Norwegian and shown in their original language, though children's films are dubbed. Tickets cost NKr 60 or more and are discounted on some days in summer.

If you like alternative or classic films as well as film festivals, try **Cinemateket** (⊠ Dronningensgt. 16, ☎ 22/47–45–05), the city's only independent cinema. The **IMAX Theatre** (⊠ Aker Brygge, Holmensgt. 1, ☎ 23/11–66–00), is a state-of-the art theater that employs IMAX and IMAX 3-D technology.

Music

The **Oslo Philharmonic Orchestra** is one of Europe's leading ensembles. Its home, **Konserthuset** (⊠ Munkedamsvn. 14, ☎ 23/11–31–11), was built in 1977 in marble, metal, and rosewood. In summer folk dancing is performed here twice a week. **Den Norske Opera** (⊠ Storgt. 23, ☎ 23/31–50–00 for information; 815/44–488 to order tickets) and the ballet perform at Youngstorvet. The breathtaking **Gamle Logen** (⊠ Grev Wedels pl. 2, ☎ 22/33–44–70), Norway's oldest concert hall, often sponsors classical music series, especially piano music.

Theater

Nationaltheatret (⊠ Stortingsgt. 15, ☎ 22/00–14–00) performances are in Norwegian: bring along a copy of the play in translation, and you're all set. The biennial Ibsen festival, which features plays by the great dramatist in both Norwegian and English, takes place in the summer of even-number years. **Det Norske Teatret** (⊠ Kristian IVs gt. 8, ☎ 22/47–38–00) is a showcase for pieces in Nynorsk (a language compiled from rural Norwegian dialects). Guest artists from abroad often perform.

OUTDOOR ACTIVITIES AND SPORTS

Oslo's natural surroundings and climate make it the perfect setting for a wide range of outdoor activities and sports. The Oslo Fjord and its islands, the forested woodlands called the *marka,* a mild year-round temperature, and as many as 18 hours of daylight in the summer all add to its appeal. Just 15 minutes north of the city center by tram is the **Oslomarka,** where locals ski in winter and hike in summer. The area contains 27 small hytter, which are often available free of charge for backpackers on foot or on ski. These can be reserved through the **Den Norske Turistforening** (⊠ Storgt. 3, ☎ 22/82–28–00), which has maps of the marka surrounding Oslo as well as equipment for rent, information, and organized events. The **Villmarkshuset** (⊠ Chr. Krohgs gt. 16, ☎ 22/05–05–22) is an equipment, activities, and excursion center specializing in hiking, climbing, hunting, fishing, cycling, canoeing, books, and maps. There's also an indoor climbing wall, a pistol range, and a diving center and pool. The **Oslo Archipelago** is a favorite destination for sunbathing urbanites, who hop ferries to their favorite isles.

Beaches

Beaches are scattered throughout the archipelago. Sun-loving Scandinavians pack every patch of sand during the long summer days to make up for lack of light in winter. The most popular beach is Paradisbukta at Huk (on the Bygdøy peninsula), which devotes one portion of the beach to nude bathers. To get there, follow signs along Huk Aveny from the Folk- and Viking Ship museums. You can also take Bus 30A, marked "Bygdøy," to its final stop.

Biking

Oslo is a great biking city. One scenic ride starts at Aker Brygge and takes you along the harbor to the Bygdøy peninsula, where you can visit the museums or cut across the fields next to the royal family's summer house.

Glåmdal Cycledepot (✉ Vestbanepl. 2, ☎ 22/83–52–08), just a few doors down from the Norway Information Center, rents bikes and equipment, including helmets. The store also offers five different sightseeing tours and has maps of the area for those braving it on their own. If you feel like roughing the terrain of the Holmenkollen marka, you can rent mountain bikes from **Tomm Murstad** (✉ Tryvannsvn. 2, ☎ 22/13–95–00) in summer. Just take T-bane 1 to Frognerseteren and get off at the Voksenkollen station. **Syklistenes Landsforening** (National Organization of Cyclists; ✉ Stortingsgt. 23C, ☎ 22/41–50–80) sells books and maps for cycling holidays in Norway and abroad and gives friendly, free advice.

Fishing

A national fishing license and a local fee are required to fish in the Oslo Fjord and the surrounding lakes. For information on fishing areas and on where to buy a license, contact **Oslomarkas Fiskeadministrasjon** (✉ Kongevn. 5, ☎ 22/49–07–99). You can also fish throughout the Nordmarka woods area in a canoe rented from **Tomm Murstad** (✉ Tryvannsvn. 2, ☎ 22/13–95–00). Ice fishing is popular in winter, but finding an ice drill could prove difficult—you may want to bring one from home.

Golf

More and more Norwegians are taking up golf. Oslo's international-level golf course, **Oslo Golfklubb** (✉ Bogstad, 0740 Oslo 7, ☎ 22/50–44–02) is private and heavily booked. However, it admits members of other golf clubs (weekdays before 2 PM and weekends after 2 PM) if space is available. Visitors must have a handicap certificate of 24 or lower for men, 32 or lower for women. Fees range from NKr 275 to NKr 325.

Hiking and Running

Head for the woods surrounding Oslo, the marka, for jogging or walking; there's an abundant number of trails here, many of them lit. Frogner Park has many paths, and you can jog or hike along the Aker River, but take extra care late at night or early in the morning. Or you can take the Sognsvann trikk to the end of the line and walk or jog along the Sognsvann stream.

Grete Waitz and Ingrid Kristiansen have put Norway on marathon runners' maps in recent years. Every May, a women's minimarathon is held in Grete Waitz's name; hundreds of women flock to Oslo to enjoy a nice day—and usually night—out. In September, the Oslo Marathon attracts Norwegian and international runners. **Norges Friidretts Forbund** (✉ Sognsvn. 75, 0855 Oslo, ☎ 21/02–99–01) has information about local clubs and competitions.

Health Clubs

If you need a fitness fix, whether aerobics, weight training, spinning, or climbing, try one of the health clubs that use the "klippekort" system. In this method, you pay a charge that entitles you to a certain number of workout sessions, which are marked as "klips" on your card. **Friskis & Svettis** (✉ Munkesdamsvn. 19, ☎ 22/83–94–40) offers free aerobics classes on the green of Frogner Park from mid-May to mid-August. Class types and times vary, so call for the summer schedule. **SATS** (✉ Filipstadbrygge 1, ☎ 22/04–80–80) has some of the better equipped and more attractive clubs around the city and throughout Norway.

Sailing

If sailing floats your boat, then spend a sunny summer afternoon at Oslo's harbor, Aker Brygge, admiring the docked boats. You could also venture out into the fjords yourself on some of the special charter and tour boats that depart there. Sky-high masts and billowing white sails give the **Christian Radich** (☎ 22/47–82–70) a majestic old-world style. This tall ship makes nine different sailing trips, varying from a three-day voyage to an autumn sail across the Atlantic. Although you aren't expected to have prior sailing experience, do expect rough seas, high waves, lots of rain, and being asked to participate in crew-members' tasks.

Skiing

Cross-country, downhill, telemarking, and snowboarding—whatever your snow-sport pleasure, Oslo has miles of easily accessible outdoor areas minutes away from the center of town. Nine alpine ski areas have activities until late at night. More than 2,600 km (1,600 mi) of prepared cross-country ski trails run deep into the forest, of which 90 km (50 mi) are lit up for the special atmosphere of evening tours.

The **Skiforeningen** (✉ Kongevn. 5, 0787 Oslo, ☎ 22/92–32–00) provides national snow-condition reports and can give tips on the multitude of cross-country trails. They also offer cross-country classes for young children (3- to 7-year-olds), downhill for older children (7- to 12-year-olds), and both, as well as instructions on telemark-style racing and snowboarding techniques, for adults.

Among the **floodlit trails in the Oslomarka** are the **Bogstad** (3½ km/2 mi), marked for the disabled and blind; the **Lillomarka** (25 km/15½ mi); and the **Østmarken** (33 km/20½ mi).

Downhill skiing usually lasts from mid-December to March. There are 15 local city slopes as well as organized trips to several outside slopes, including **Norefjell** (☎ 32/15–01–00), 100 km (66 mi) north of the city.

You can rent both downhill and cross-country skis from **Tomm Murstad Skiservice** (✉ Tryvannsvn. 2, ☎ 22/13–95–00) at the Tryvann T-bane station. This is a good starting point for skiing; although there are but few downhill slopes in this area, a plethora of cross-country trails exist for every level of competence.

Swimming

If you don't want to head to the beach, there are several swimming pool facilities within the city. All pools cost NKr 40 but are free with the Oslo Card. **Besserudtjernet** (✉ Holmenkollen) is a small, summer lake at the foot of the Holmenkollen ski jump. The south-facing terraces are ideal for sunbathing. Swimming here is novel due to the fantastic views of Oslo. Lifeguards aren't posted, so swim here at your own risk. **Tøyenbadet** (Tøyen Swimming Pool; ✉ Helgesensgt. 90, ☎ 22/68–24–23) is next to the Munch Museum and Botanical Gardens. The facilities include one indoor and three outdoor swimming pools for all ages, a sauna, a solarium, a water slide, and an exercise area. **Frognerbadet** (Frogner Swimming Pool; ✉ Vigeland Park, ☎ 22/44–

74–29) has four large outdoor swimming pools for all ages and a water slide. The pools are open from mid-May through late August, depending on the weather (weekdays 7 AM–7:30 PM, weekends 10–5:30). Come in June when you can listen to the Norwegian Wood music festival playing close by.

Tennis

There are several tennis clubs throughout the city to consider for a game, set, or match. **Frognerpark** has municipal tennis courts open in the summer. **Holmenkollen Tennisklubb** (⊠ Bjørnvn. 70, ☎ 22/14–67–73) has 11 outdoor courts, a mini-court, and four winter courts inside bubbles that protect them from the elements. **Oslo Tennisklubb** (⊠ Hyllvn. 5, ☎ 22/55–69–81) is the biggest outdoor tennis club in Norway. It has 10 clay courts, two hard courts, and four indoor courts available for winter play. Near Vigelandspark, the easily accessible club has a casual dress code, rents racquets, and charges roughly NKr 150 per hour for court time.

SHOPPING

Oslo is the best place for buying anything Norwegian. Popular Norwegian souvenirs and specialties include knitware, boxes with rosemaling, trolls, wooden spoons, gold and silver jewelry, smoked salmon, and caviar. Some established Norwegian brands include Porsgrund porcelain, Hadeland and Magnor glass, David Andersen jewelry, and Husfliden handicrafts. You may also want to look for popular, classical, or folk music CDs; English translations of Norwegian books; or clothing by a Norwegian designer.

Prices are generally much higher than in other countries. Prices of handmade articles, such as knitwear, are controlled, making comparison shopping useless. Otherwise shops have both sales and specials—look for the words *salg* and *tilbud*. In addition, if you are a resident of a country other than Norway, Sweden, Finland, or Denmark, you can have the Norwegian Value Added Tax (moms) refunded back at the airport when you leave the country. When you are making a purchase, you must clearly state your status in order to have the necessary Global Refund Cheque (export document) filled in by store staff.

Department Stores

GlasMagasinet (⊠ Stortorvet 9, ☎ 22/90–89–00) is an amalgam of shops under one roof rather than a true department store. Traditionally, families visit GlasMagasinet at Christmastime, so the store is usually open on Sundays in December. **Steen & Strøm** (⊠ Kongensgt. 23, ☎ 22/00–40–01), one of Oslo's first department stores, sells the usual: cosmetics, clothing, books, accessories. It also has a well-stocked outdoors floor.

Shopping Centers

Aker Brygge, Norway's first major shopping center, is right on the water across from the Tourist Information Center at Vestbanen. Shops are open until 8 most days, including some on Sunday. **Oslo City** (⊠ Stenersgt. 1, ☎ 22/17–09–92), at the other end of downtown, with access to the street from Oslo S Station, is the largest indoor mall, but the shops are run-of-the-mill, and the restaurants mostly serve fast-food. The elegant **Paleet** (⊠ Karl Johans gt. 39–41, between Universitetsgt. and Rosenkrantz Gt., ☎ 22/41–70–86) opens up into a grand, marbled atrium and has a wide array of shops.

Shopping Neighborhoods

Basarhallene, the arcade behind the cathedral, is worth a browse for glass and crystal and handicrafts made in Norway. From the city center, you can wander up the tree-lined Bygdøy Allé and browse the fashionable **Frogner** area, which is brimming with modern and antique furniture stores, interior design shops, gourmet food shops, art galleries, haute couture, and Oslo's beautiful people. A wide variety of shops fill streets into the downtown area around **Karl Johans Gate,** where many shoppers flock. The concentration of department stores is especially high in this part of town. **Majorstuen** starts at the T-bane station with the same name and proceeds down Bogstadveien to the Royal Palace. As for specialty markets, there's a flower market on Stortorget in front of the Oslo Cathedral and a fruit and vegetable market at Youngstorget. Every Saturday, a flea market is open at Vestkanttorget near Frognerpark. Throughout spring and summer, many local schools also arrange their own fund-raising flea markets.

Specialty Stores

Antiques

Norwegian rustic antiques (those objects considered of high artistic and historic value) cannot be taken out of the country, but just about anything else can with no problem. The Frogner district has many antiques shops, especially on Skovveien and Thomas Heftyes Gate between Bygdøy Allé and Frogner Plass. Deeper in the heart of Majorstuen, Industrigate is famous for its good selection of shops. **Blomqvist Kunsthandel** (⊠ Tordenskolds gt. 5, ☎ 22/70–87–70) has a good selection of small items and paintings, with auctions six times a year. The rare volumes at **Damms Antiqvariat** (⊠ Tollbugt. 25, ☎ 22/41–04–02) will catch the eye of any antiquarian book buff, with volumes in English as well as Norwegian, which could be harder to find back home. **Esaias Solberg** (⊠ Kirkeresten, ☎ 22/86–24–80), behind Oslo Cathedral, has exceptional small antiques. **Kaare Berntsen** (⊠ Universitetsgt. 12, ☎ 22/20–34–29) sells paintings, furniture, and small items, all very exclusive and priced accordingly. **Marsjandisen** (⊠ Paléet, ☎ 22/42–71–68), nestled in the slickest of shopping centers, specializes in Hadeland glass, silver, cups, and mugs. **West Sølv og Mynt** (⊠ Niels Juels gt. 27, ☎ 22/55–75–83) has the largest selection of silver, both old and antique, in town.

Art Galleries

Kunstnernes Hus (The Artists' House; ⊠ Wergelandsvn. 17, ☎ 22/85–34–10, ℻ 22/85–34–11, 🖳 www.kunstnerneshus.no) exhibits contemporary art, hosting an annual art show in the fall.

Books

In Oslo bookshops, you can always find English language books in varying degrees. Some classic Norwegian fiction writers whose works you may want to pick up in translation include Henrik Ibsen and Knut Hamsun as well as the more contemporary authors Jostein Gaarder, Linn Ullmann, and Nikolaj Frobenius. As for Norwegian nonfiction, books by Thor Heyerdahl and Ketil Bjørnstad are worthwhile reads.

ARK Qvist (⊠ Drammensvn. 16, ☎ 22/54–26–00), considered Oslo's "English bookshop," specializes in fiction, crime, and Norwegian–Scandinavian translations. **Avalon** (⊠ Paleet, Karl Johans gt. 39–41, ☎ 22/41–43–36) has Norway's largest selection of science fiction and fantasy (all in English) as well as board, computer, and card games and comics. **Bjørn Ringstrøms Antikvariat** (⊠ Ullevålsvn. 1, ☎ 22/20–78–05), across the street from the Museum of Applied Art, carries a wide selection of used books and records.

Bokkilden Interbok (✉ Akersgt. 34, ☎ 22/41–22–14) stocks an amazing 6,000 maps as well as two walls of travel books. Head to **Nomaden** (✉ Uranienborgvn. 4, ☎ 22/56–25–30) for a wide array of travel-related books and guidebooks as well as photography books and equipment. **Norli** (✉ Universitetsgt. 24, ☎ 22/00–43–00) keeps a substantial number of Scandinavian-language fiction and travel books on hand. **Tanum** (✉ Karl Johans gt. 43, ☎ 22/41–11–00) is very strong in the arts, health and healing, and travel.

Clothing

Norway is famous for its handknit, colorful wool sweaters, and even mass-produced (machine-knit) models are of top quality. The prices are regulated and they are always lower than buying a Norwegian sweater abroad.

Stylish men's, women's, and children's clothing fashions are available at several chains. For designer clothing, Oslo has an increasing number of exclusive boutiques carrying Norwegian and international labels. Take a look at established, international Norwegian design stars such as Paris-based Pia Myrvold.

KNITWEAR

Maurtua Husflid (✉ Fr. Nansens pl. 9, ☎ 22/41–31–64), near City Hall, has a huge selection of sweaters and blanket coats. The designer at **Oleana** (✉ Stortingt., ☎ 22/33–31–63), Solveig Hisdahl, takes traditional women's sweater patterns and updates them in classy, beautiful ways. **Oslo Sweater Shop** (✉ SAS Scandinavia Hotel, Tullinsgt. 5, ☎ 22/11–29–22) is known for having one of the widest selections in the city. **Rein og Rose** (✉ Ruseløkkvn. 3, ☎ 22/83–21–39), in the Vika shopping district, has friendly salespeople and a good selection of knitwear, yarn, and textiles. **William Schmidt** (✉ Karl Johans gt. 41, ☎ 22/42–02–88), founded in 1853, is Oslo's oldest shop. The firm specializes in sweaters and souvenirs.

EMBROIDERY

Husfliden (✉ Møllergt. 4, ☎ 22/42–10–75) sells embroidery kits, including do-it-yourself bunader, the national costumes of Norway.

FASHION AND SPORTSWEAR

H & M (Hennes & Mauritz; ✉ Oslo City and other locations, ☎ 22/17–13–90) carries fresh, up-to-date looks at the most reasonable prices. **Kamikaze** (✉ Hegdehaugsvn. 24, ☎ 22/60–20–25) and the nearby **Kamikaze Donna** (✉ Hegdehaugsvn. 27, ☎ 22/59–38–45) specialize in men's and women's designer fashions, mainly from France and Italy. **Soul** (✉ Vognhallene, Karenlyst Alle 18, ☎ 22/55–00–13) carries Norwegian and international labels from major London, Milan, and Paris fashion houses; shoes and accessories; and home products. **MA** (✉ Hegdehaugsvn. 27, ☎ 22/60–72–90) puts the spotlight on Norwegian designers.

Norwegian sportswear chain stores are easy to spot in the city's malls and on Karl Johans Gate, but also consider checking out some specialty shops. **Skandinavisk Høyfjellutstyr** (✉ Bogstadsvn. 1, ☎ 23/33–43–80) has a great selection of traditional mountain sportswear. **Peak Performance** (✉ Bogstadsvn. 13, ☎ 22/96–00–91) is a top choice for fashionable sportswear.

FUR

Hansson (✉ Kirkevn. 54, ☎ 22/69–64–20), near Majorstuen, has an excellent selection of furs. **Studio H. Olesen** (✉ Karl Johans gt. 31, enter at Rosenkrantz gt., ☎ 22/33–37–50) has the most exclusive designs.

Food

Throughout Oslo, the range of food shops and specialties is tempting. **Åpent Bakeri** (⊠ Inkognito Terrasse 1, ☎ 22/44–94–70) bakes the city's best tasting bread for devoted locals and top restaurants. **Fjelberg Fisk and Vilt** (⊠ Bygdøy Allé 56, ☎ 22/44–60–41) has a reputation for its high-quality fish and seafood, including salmon (smoked, tartar, fresh, and cured), lobster, shrimp, and fish soup. **Hotel Havana** (⊠ Thorvald Meyers gt. 36, ☎ 23/23–03–23) is a hip delicatessen with cheeses, Cuban coffee and cigars, tapas plates, and fresh fish. **Skafferi** (⊠ Elisenbergvn., ☎ 22/44–52–96) is popular with the culinary conscious for many a gourmet delight as well as for their fresh flowers. They are open every day from 10 to 10. **Solbærtorvet** (⊠ Hammerstadsgt. 23, ☎ 22/60–00–63) carries a delectable choice of foods, including cheeses, oils, spices, and fresh produce.

Furniture

There are several established Oslo furniture shops that highlight Scandinavian and international designers. **Expo Nova Møbelgalleri** (⊠ Bygdøy Allé 58B, ☎ 22/44–06–60) is a classic Oslo shop that many designers recommend. **Rom for Idé** (⊠ Jacob Aalls gt. 54, ☎ 22/59–81–17) exhibits international and Norwegian designs by established and up-and-coming names. **Tannum** (⊠ Stortingsgt. 28, ☎ 22/83–42–95) is a perfect starting point for classic and contemporary designs.

Glass, China, Ceramics, and Pewter

Abelson (⊠ Skovvn. 27, ☎ 22/55–55–94), behind the Royal Palace, is crammed with the best modern designs. The shops at **Basarhallene,** behind the cathedral, sell glass and ceramics. **Gastronaut** (⊠ Bygdøy Allé 56, ☎ 22/44–60–90) is an exclusive store selling china, cutlery, linen, glass, spices, and condiments from Spain and Italy.

If there's no time to visit a glass factory outside of town, department stores are the best option: **GlasMagasinet** (⊠ Stortorvet 9, ☎ 22/90–87–00) stocks both European and Norwegian glass designs. **Norway Designs** (⊠ Stortingsgt. 28, ☎ 23/11–45–10) showcases Norwegian and Scandinavian designs in art glass, kitchenware, ceramics, silver, and other household items.

Handicrafts

Basarhallene, the arcade behind the cathedral, is worth a browse for handicrafts made in Norway. **Format Kunsthandverk** (⊠ Vestbanepl. 1, ☎ 22/01–55–70) has a beautiful, colorful array of individual pieces. **Heimen Husflid A/S** (⊠ Rosenkrantz gt. 8, enter at Christian IVs gt., ☎ 22/41–40–50) has small souvenir items and a department for traditional Norwegian costumes. **Husfliden** (⊠ Møllergt. 4, ☎ 22/42–10–75), one of the finest stores for handmade goods in the country, has an even larger selection than that at Husflid. You can find pewter, ceramics, knits, handwoven textiles, furniture, handmade felt boots and slippers, hand-sewn loafers, handmade sweaters, traditional costumes, wrought-iron accessories, Christmas ornaments, and wooden kitchen accessories—all made in Norway.

Jewelry

Gold and precious stones are no bargain, but silver and enamel jewelry, and Viking period productions can be. Some silver pieces are made with Norwegian stones, particularly pink thulite. **David-Andersen** (⊠ Karl Johans gt. 20, ☎ 22/41–69–55) is Norway's best-known goldsmith. He makes stunning silver and gold designs. The **ExpoArte** (⊠ Drammensvn. 40, ☎ 22/55–93–90) gallery specializes in custom pieces and displays the work of avant-garde Scandinavian jewelers. **Heyer-**

dahl (⊠ Roald Amundsensgt. 6, ☎ 22/41–59–18), near City Hall, is a good, dependable jeweler.

Music

More and more Norwegian artists are making names for themselves internationally, often crossing over to singing in English. Some of the bigger Norwegian music names include Sissel and Lene Marlin for pop music, Leif Ove Andsnes for classical music, Silje Nergaard for jazz, and Kari Bremnes for folk singing. Ask informed record store staff to recommend other Norwegian–Scandinavian artists. **Platekompaniet** (⊠ Stortingsgt. 22, ☎ 22/42–77–35) has the most reasonable prices and best overall selection of mainstream music as well as alternative rock, house, and techno. **Benni's** (⊠ Aker Brygge, Stranden 3, ☎ 22/83–70–83) is praised by music-industry types for having Norway's best selection of rap, hard rock, soul, techno, and R & B. They have a lot of new and used vinyl, as well as CDs. **Akers Mic** (⊠ Kongenst. 14, ☎ 23/00–09–28) has two large floors of music for every musical taste, especially pop and rock. Eccentric, eclectic **Los Lobos** (⊠ Thorvald Meyers gt. 30,, ☎ 22/38–24–40) carries rockabilly, surf-guitar, salsa and mambo, and blues music. They also sell vintage clothes: Hawaiian shirts and leather jackets from the '50s.

Perfume

Gimle Parfymeri (⊠ Bygdøy Allé 39, ☎ 22/44–61–42) is a tiny, traditional Oslo perfume institution. Hip perfumery **Gimle Speiz** (⊠ Bygdøy Allé 51B, ☎ 23/27–11–05) carries the latest in fragrances, skin care, jewelry, bags, and accessories from all over.

Watches

For some reason, Swiss watches are much cheaper in Norway than in many other countries. **Urmaker Bjerke** (⊠ Karl Johans gt. 31, ☎ 22/42–20–44; ⊠ Prinsensgt. 21, ☎ 22/42–60–50) has established a reputation for quality and selection. Another good choice is **Thune Gullsmed & Urmaker** (⊠ Rådhuspassasjen, Olav Vs gt. 6, ☎ 22/42–99–66).

OSLO A TO Z

To research prices, get advice from other travelers, and book travel arrangements, visit www.fodors.com.

AIR TRAVEL TO AND FROM OSLO

CARRIERS

SAS Scandinavian Airlines is the main carrier, with both international and domestic flights. The main domestic carriers are Braathens ASA and Widerøe. Other major airlines serving Oslo Airport include British Airways, Air France, Aeroflot, Finnair, and Swissair.

➤ AIRLINES AND CONTACTS: **Aeroflot** (☎ 22/33–38–88). **Air France** (☎ 22/83–56–30). **Braathens** (☎ 815–20–000). **British Airways** (☎ 800–33–142). **Crossair** (☎ 810–00–021). **Finnair** (☎ 810–01–100). **Flyservice a/s** (Air Lithuania, Avianca, China Airlines, TWA) (☎ 22/42–45–60). **LOT Polish Airlines** (☎ 810–00–023). **Sabena** (☎ 810–00–014). **SAS** (☎ 810–03–300). **Swissair** (☎ 810–00–012). **Tap Air Portugal** (☎ 810–00–015). **Widerøe** (☎ 810–01–200).

AIRPORTS AND TRANSFERS

The stunning Oslo Airport is 37 km (23 mi) north of the city. The spacious airport has huge windows that give excellent views of the landscape and Nordic light. State-of-the-art weather systems have decreased the number of delayed flights, but always check ahead with your airline regarding the status of your particular flight.

➤ AIRPORT INFORMATION: **Oslo Airport** (☎ 64/81–20–00; flight information 815–50–250).

Oslo Airport is a 50-minute car ride via the E6 from Oslo's city center. From Oslo S Station, it's a 19-minute ride by Flytoget (express train), with trains scheduled every 10 minutes (4:40 AM–1:16 AM).

Flybussen departs from Oslo Bussterminalen Galleriet every 15 minutes and reaches Oslo Airport approximately 45 minutes later (NKr 90 one-way, NKr 140 round trip; to Oslo weekdays and Sun. 7:30 AM–11:30 PM, Sat. 7:30 AM–11 PM; to Oslo Airport weekdays, 6 AM–9:40 PM, Sat. 6 AM–7:40 PM, Sun. 6 AM–9:50 PM). Another bus departs from the SAS Scandinavia Hotel. At least one of the buses stops at the central train station as well as at Stortinget, Nationalteatret, and near Aker Brygge on the way.

There is a taxi line at the front of the airport. By taxi the trip takes about 50 minutes and is extremely expensive, upward of 600 NKr, so try to catch the Flytoget. All taxi reservations should be made through the Oslo Airport Taxi no later than 20 minutes before pickup time.
➤ TAXIS, SHUTTLES, AND TRAINS: **Flybussen** (☎ 81/50–01–76). **Flytoget** (☎ 815–00–777). **Oslo Airport Taxi** (☎ 23/23–23–23; dial 1 for direct reservation).

BOAT AND FERRY TRAVEL

Several ferry lines connect Oslo with the United Kingdom, Denmark, Sweden, and Germany. Color Line sails to Kiel, Germany, and to Hirtshals, Denmark; DFDS Scandinavian Seaways to Copenhagen via Helsingborg, Sweden; and Stena Line to Frederikshavn, Denmark.

A ferry to the town of Nesodden as well as Hovedøya and other islands in the harbor basin leaves from Vippetangen, behind Akershus Slott (take Bus 29 from Jernbanetorget or walk along the harbor from Aker Brygge). These are great spots for picnics and short hikes. From April through September, ferries run between Rådhusbrygge 3, in front of City Hall, and Bygdøy, the western peninsula, where many of Oslo's major museums are located. There is also ferry service from Aker Brygge to popular summer beach towns along the fjord's coast, including Drøbak.

➤ BOAT AND FERRY INFORMATION: **Bygdøfergene Skibs A/S** (☎ 22/20–07–15). **Color Line** (☎ 810–00–811). **DFDS Scandinavian Seaways** (☎ 66/81–66–00). **Nesodden Bunnefjord Dampskibsselskap** (☎ 22/83–30–70). **Stena Line** (☎ 23/17–91–00).

BUS TRAVEL TO AND FROM OSLO

The main bus station, Oslo Bussterminalen, is across from the Oslo S Station. You can buy local bus tickets at the terminal or on the bus. Tickets for long-distance routes on Nor-Way Bussekspress can be purchased here or at travel agencies. Trafikanten provides transit information.
➤ BUS INFORMATION: **Nor-Way Bussekspress** (✉ Oslo Bussterminalen Galleriet, ☎ 815/44–444, FAX 22/17–59–22). **Oslo Bussterminalen** (☎ 23/00–24–00). **Trafikanten** (☎ 22/17–70–30 or 177, WEB www.trafikanten.no).

BUS TRAVEL WITHIN OSLO

About 50 bus lines, including 16 night buses on weekends, serve the city. Most stop at Jernbanetorget opposite Oslo S Station. Tickets can be purchased from the driver.

CAR RENTAL

➤ MAJOR AGENCIES IN OSLO: **Avis** (☎ 64/81–06–60 at Oslo Airport; 23/23–92–00 downtown). **Hertz** (☎ 64/81–05–50 at Oslo Airport; 22/ 21–00–00 downtown). **Sixt** (✉ Oslo Airport, ☎ 63/94–04–00).

CAR TRAVEL

The E18 connects Oslo with Göteborg, Sweden (by ferry between Sandefjord and Strömstad, Sweden); Copenhagen, Denmark (by ferry between Kristiansand and Hirtshals, Denmark); and Stockholm directly overland. The land route from Oslo to Göteborg is the E6. All streets and roads leading into Oslo have toll booths a certain distance from the city center, forming an "electronic ring." The toll is NKr 12 and was implemented to reduce pollution downtown. If you have the correct amount in change, drive through one of the lanes marked "Mynt." If you don't, or if you need a receipt, use the "Manuell" lane. Car rentals can be made directly at Oslo Airport or downtown.

If you plan to do any amount of driving in Oslo, buy a copy of the *Stor Oslo* map, available at bookstores and gasoline stations. It may be a small city, but one-way streets and few exit ramps on the expressway make it very easy to get lost.

EMERGENCY SERVICES

➤ CONTACTS: **Car Rescue** (☎ 22/23–20–85).

PARKING

Oslo Card holders can park for free in city-run street spots or at reduced rates in lots run by the city (P-lots), but pay careful attention to time limits and be sure to ask at the information office exactly where the card is valid. Parking is very difficult in the city—many spaces have one-hour limits and can cost up to NKr 25 per hour. Instead of individual parking meters in P-lots, a machine dispenses validated parking tickets to display in your car windshield. Travelers with disabilities with valid parking permits from their home country are allowed to park free and with no time limit in specially reserved spaces.

EMBASSIES/CONSULATES

➤ AUSTRALIA: (✉ Jerbanetorget 2, ☎ 22/47–91–70).
➤ CANADA: (✉ Wergelandsvn. 7, ☎ 22/99–53–00).
➤ NEW ZEALAND: (✉ Billengstadsletta 19, ☎ 66/77–53–30).
➤ UNITED KINGDOM: (✉ Thomas Heftyes gt. 8, ☎ 23/13–27–00).
➤ UNITED STATES: (✉ Drammensvn. 18, ☎ 22/44–85–50).

EMERGENCIES

Norway's largest private clinic, Volvat Medisinske Senter, is near the Borgen and Majorstuen T-bane stations, not far from Frogner Park. It is open weekdays 8 AM–10 PM, weekends 10–10. Oslo Akutten is an emergency clinic downtown, near Stortinget. Centrum Legesenter is a small, friendly clinic across from City Hall.

For dental emergencies only, Oslo Kommunale Tannlegevakt at Tøyen Senter is open evenings and weekends. Oslo Private Tannlegevakt, near the American Embassy, is a private dental clinic open seven days a week.

Oslo Kommunale Legevakt, the city's public and thus less expensive, but slower, hospital, is near the Oslo S Station and is open 24 hours. Volvat Medisinske Senter operates an emergency clinic 8 AM–10 PM weekdays, 10–10 weekends. Jernbanetorgets Apotek, across from Oslo S Station, is open 24 hours. Sfinxen Apotek, near Frogner Park, is open weekdays 8:30 AM to 9 PM, Saturday 8:30 AM to 8 PM, and Sunday 5 PM to 8 PM.

➤ DOCTORS AND DENTISTS: **Oslo Akutten** (⊠ Nedre Vollgt. 8, ☎ 22/ 00–81–60). **Oslo Kommunale Tannlegevakt** (⊠ Kolstadgt. 18, ☎ 22/ 67–30–00). **Oslo Private Tannlegevakt** (⊠ Hansteensgt. 3, ☎ 22/44– 46–36). **Volvat Medisinske Senter** (⊠ Borgenvn. 2A, ☎ 22/95–75–00).
➤ EMERGENCY SERVICES: **Ambulance** (☎ 113 or 22/11–70–80). **Fire** (☎ 110 or 22/11–44–55). **Police** (☎ 112 or 22/66–90–50).
➤ HOSPITALS: **Centrum Legesenter** (⊠ Fritjof Nansens pl., ☎ 22/41– 41–20). **Oslo Kommunale Legevakt** (⊠ Storgt. 40, ☎ 22/11–80–80).
➤ LATE-NIGHT PHARMACIES: **Jernbanetorgets Apotek** (⊠ Jernbanetor- get 4B, ☎ 22/41–24–82). **Sfinxen Apotek** (⊠ Bogstadvn. 51, ☎ 22/ 46–34–44).
➤ LOST AND FOUND: **Police** (☎ 22/66–98–65). **NSB (Norwegian State Railway)** (⊠ Oslo S Station; ☎ 23/15–00–00). **Oslo Sporveier (trams, buses, subway)** (☎ 22/08–53–61).

INTERNET SERVICE
➤ CONTACTS: **Akers Mic Netcafé** (⊠ Akersgt. 39, ☎ 22/41–21–90). **Studenten Nett-Café** (⊠ Karl Johans gt. 45, ☎ 22/42–56–80).

LAUNDRY
Self-service laundry facilities are available in several different Oslo neigh- borhoods.
➤ CONTACTS: **A-Vask Selvbetjening** (⊠ Thorvald Meyers gt. 18, ☎ 22/ 37–57–70, ⊙ 10–8). **Majorstua Myntvaskeri** (⊠ Vibesgt. 15, ☎ 22/ 69–43–17, ⊙ weekdays 8–8, weekends 8–5). **Mr. Clean,** (⊠ Parkvn. 6, ☎ 22/60–20–88, ⊙ daily 7 AM–11 PM).

LODGING
The tourist office at Oslo S Station (☞ Visitor Information) can book you in anything from a luxury hotel to a room in a private home for a fee of NKr 20. Usually there are last-minute discount rooms.

If you want to rent an apartment, contact B&B Oslo Apartments. Most of the available apartments are in Bærum, 15 minutes from downtown Oslo. There also also some in Skøyen, a grassy suburban area that's closer to both the airport and city center. All are within a 10-minute walk from public transport.
➤ FEES AND SCHEDULES: **B&B Oslo Apartments** (⊠ Stasjonsvn. 13, Blom- menholm, 1300 Sandvika, ☎ 67/54–06–80, FAX 67/54–09–70, ⊙ week- days 8:30–4).

MONEY MATTERS
CURRENCY EXCHANGE
Foreign currencies can be exchanged at a variety of places throughout the city. At most post offices, hours are limited to weekdays 8–5 and Saturday 9–1. The Tourist Information Center at Vestbanen (☞ Visi- tor Information) also exchanges currency.

At most banks, the hours are weekdays 8:15–3, with many open until 5 on Thursday. The express Flytoget terminal at Oslo S has automatic currency exchange machines available 24 hours. The K Bank Bureau de Change at Oslo S station is open weekdays 7–7, weekends 8–5. At Oslo Airport, there are 16 automatic currency machines as well as a Bureau de Change in the Departure and the Arrival Halls.
➤ CONTACTS: **American Express** (⊠ Fr. Nansens pl. 6, ☎ 22/98–37– 35). **Oslo Central Post Office** (⊠ Dronningensgt. 15, ☎ 22/40–90–50).

SUBWAY TRAVEL
Oslo has seven T-bane (subway) lines, which converge at Stortinget sta- tion. The four eastern lines all stop at Tøyen before branching off, whereas the four western lines run through Majorstuen before emerg-

ing aboveground for the rest of their routes to the northwestern suburbs. Tickets can be purchased at the stations.

➤ CONTACTS: **Trafikantan** (public transportation information; ✉ Jerbanetorget, ☎ 22/17–70–30, ◷ weekdays 7 AM–8 PM, weekends 8–6).

TAXIS

All taxis are connected to a central dispatching office and it can take up to 30 minutes to send one during peak hours. Cabs can be ordered from 20 minutes to 24 hours in advance. (If you leave a cab waiting after you've sent for one, there is an additional fee added to your fare.) Special transport, including vans and cabs equipped for people with disabilities, can be ordered. Taxi stands are located all over town, usually near Narvesen kiosks.

It is possible to hail a cab on the street, but cabs are not allowed to pick up passengers within 100 yards of a stand. It is not unheard of to wait for more than an hour at a taxi stand in the wee hours of the morning, after everyone has left the bars. Never take pirate taxis, only registered company taxis that should have their roof lights on when they're available. Rates start at NKr 18 for hailed or rank cabs and NKr 55 for ordered taxis, depending on the time of day.

➤ TAXI COMPANIES: **Oslo Taxi** (☎ 02323). **Taxi 2** (☎ 02202).

TOURS

Tickets for all tours are available from either tourist office (☞ Visitor Information). Tickets for bus tours can be purchased on the buses. All tours, except the HMK Sightseeing Oslo Highlights tour, operate in summer only. Starting at noon and continuing at 45-minute intervals until 10 PM, the Oslo Train, which looks like a chain of dune buggies, leaves Aker Brygge for a 30-minute ride around the town center. The train runs every day in summer. Contact a tourist center for departure times.

BOAT TOURS

Taking a boat tour in and around the Oslo fjords is a memorable way to tour the capital. The Norway Yacht Charter arranges lunch or evening tours or dinner cruises for 12 to 600 passengers. Taking you back in time, the Viking Cruise, which sets sail on replica Viking ships or sailing yachts, even includes Viking lunches and dinners. The company Marine Service has various boats available for tours. Cruise-Båtene organizes fjord excursions for all occasions on modern luxury or older restored vessels.

➤ CONTACT: **Cruise-Båtene** (✉ H. Heyerdahlsgt. 1, ☎ 22/42–36–98). **Marine Service** (✉ Lindøya, ☎ 22/11–48–15). **Norway Yacht Charter** (✉ Råhusbrygge 3, ☎ 23/35–68–90). **Viking Cruise** (✉ Stranden 89, ☎ 22/83–19–18).

BUS TOURS

HMK Sightseeing offers several bus tours in and around Oslo. Tours leave from the Norway Information Center at Vestbanen; combination boat-bus tours depart from Rådhusbrygge 3, the wharf in front of City Hall. Båtservice Sightseeing has a bus tour, five cruises, and one combination tour.

➤ FEES AND SCHEDULES: **Båtservice Sightseeing** (✉ Rådhusbryggen 3, ☎ 23/35–68–90). **HMK Sightseeing** (✉ Hegdehaugsvn. 4, ☎ 23/15–73–00).

HELICOPTER TOURS

For a bird's-eye view of Oslo, take a helicopter tour through the Pegasus company.

➤ FEES AND SCHEDULES: **Pegasus Helicopter** (✉ Gardermoen Vest, ☎ 64/81–92–00).

PRIVATE GUIDES

A guest agency or the Tourist Information Centre at Vestbanen (☞ Visitors' Information) can provide an authorized city guide. OsloTaxi also gives private car tours.

➤ CONTACTS: **Guideservice** (✉ Akershusstranda 35, ☎ 22/42–70–20). **Oslo Guidebureau** (✉ Øvre Vollgt. 7, ☎ 22/17–56–60). **OsloTaxi** (☎ 02323).

SPECIAL-INTEREST TOURS

For an exhilarating experience, tour the forests surrounding Oslo (the Oslomarka) by dogsled. Both lunch and evening winter tours are available through Norske Sledehundturer. The Tourist Information Center (☞ Visitor Information) can arrange four- to eight-hour motor safaris through the marka, and in the winter Vangen Skistue can arrange an old-fashioned sleigh ride. In summertime, they switch from sleighs to carriages.

➤ FEES AND SCHEDULES: **Norske Sledehundturer** (✉ Einar Kristen Aas, 1514 Moss, ☎ 69/27–56–40, FAX 69/27–37–86). **Vangen Skistue** (✉ Laila and Jon Hamre, Fjell, 1404 Siggerud, ☎ 64/86–54–81).

WALKING TOURS

Organized walking tours are listed in *What's on in Oslo,* available from Tourist Information and at most hotels.

TRAIN TRAVEL

Norway's state railway, NSB (Norges Statsbaner), has two Oslo train stations downtown—Oslo Sentralstasjon (Oslo S), renovated in 2001, and a stop at Nationaltheatret. Long-distance domestic and international trains arrive at and leave from Oslo S Station. Suburban commuter trains use one or the other station. Commuter cars reserved for monthly passholders are marked with a large black "M" on a yellow circle. Trains marked "C," or InterCity, offer such upgraded services as breakfast and "office cars" with phones and power outlets, for an added fee.

➤ TRAIN INFORMATION: **NSB Customer Service** (☎ 81/50–08–88).

TRANSPORTATION AROUND OSLO

The subways and most buses and trikken start running at 5:30 AM, with the last run after midnight. On weekends, there's night service on certain routes. Tickets on all public transportation within Oslo cost NKr 20 with a one-hour free transfer, whereas tickets that cross communal boundaries have different rates. It often pays to buy a pass or multiple-travel card, which includes transfers. A one-day *dags kort* (day card) costs NKr 50 and a seven-day pass costs NKr 150.

A NKr 125 *flexikort,* available at Narvesen and 7-Eleven stores, tourist information offices, T-bane stations, and on some routes, is valid for eight trips by subway, bus, or trikk. The **Oslo Card** offers unlimited travel on all public transport in greater Oslo. A one-day Oslo Card costs NKr 180, a two-day card NKr 290, and a three-day card NKr 390. Children's cards cost NKr 60, NKr 80, and NKr 110 and a family card costs NKr 395. It can be purchased at tourist information offices and hotels. The Oslo Card also includes free admission to museums and sightseeing attractions; a free mini boat cruise; free admission to public swimming pools; discounts on car, ski and skate rentals; and discounts at specified restaurants and theaters.

TRAVEL AGENCIES

The city's travel agencies cater to different markets and different age groups. Ving is a popular overall choice among Norwegians because of the package tours they offer. Bennett BTI Nordic is an international, business travel agency. Kilroy Travels Norway caters to the youth and university market under 33, distributing ISIC cards for students and GO cards for people younger than 25.

➤ LOCAL AGENT REFERRALS: **American Express** (✉ Mariboesgt. 13, ☎ 22/98–37–00). **Bennett BTI Nordic** (✉ Linstowsgt. 6, ☎ 22/59–78–00). **Kilroy Travels Norway** (✉ Universitetssenteret, Blindern, ☎ 02633; ✉ Nedre Slottsgt. 23, ☎ 02633). Scantours UK (☎ 44/207–839–2927, ℻ 44/207–839–5891). **Ving** (✉ Karl Johans gt. 18, ☎ 810–03–810).

VISITOR INFORMATION

➤ IN OSLO: **Oslo Sentralstasjonen (Oslo S Station)** (✉ Jernbanetorget, no phone, ☉ daily 8 AM–11 PM). **Tourist Information Center in Oslo** (✉ Old Vestbanen railway station, Brynjulf Bulls pl. 1, ☎ 23/11–78–80, ℻ 22/83–81–50, ☉ weekdays 9–4).

3 SIDE TRIPS FROM OSLO

If you've got a weakness for the water and things maritime, getting out of Oslo to the windswept fjord beaches might be a good idea. The area northwest of Oslo draws many visitors to its green, hilly countryside. No matter which way you head, you'll find plenty to do.

NORTH OF THE OSLO FJORD

Byrud Gård

This town at the southern end of Lake Mjøsa is home to the **Smaragdgruvene ved Minnesund** (Emerald Mines at Minnesund), the only such mines in Northern Europe. Ask for a special guided tour or go on an exciting treasure hunt: in one section, emerald finders are emerald keepers. Handmade emerald and stone items are available at the gift shop. ⊠ *Rte. 33, off of E6, Byrud Gård,* ☎ *63/96–86–11.* 🔄 *NKr 70.* ☉ *Mid-Apr.–Oct., daily 8–6.*

Gardermoen

The Military Plane Collection, **Forsvarets Flysamling Gardermoen,** at the Sør-Gardermoen Culture and Business Center at Oslo Airport, contains military planes from the early days of flying, rare planes from World War II, and Norwegian air force jets from the Cold War era. By car, take E6 in the direction of Rv 174 to Nannestad. Turn onto Rd. 4 and stay on for approximately 3 km (1½ mi) before turning right and heading toward the airplane collection. ⊠ *Sør-Gardermoen culture and business center, Gardermoen,* ☎ *63/92–86–60.* 🔄 *NKr 50.* ☉ *Tues.–Sun. 11–5.*

Eidsvoll

Norway's Constitution was written and passed at **Eidsvoll,** a manor house about 80 km (50 mi) north of Oslo. May 17, National Day, commemorates that 1814 occasion. Portraits of all the members of the 1814 Norwegian parliament hang here. Trains for Eidsvoll depart from Oslo S Station. ⊠ *Carsten Ankers v.,* ☎ *63/92–22–10,* 🌐 *www.eidsvoll1814.museum.no.* 🔄 *NKr 40.* ☉ *Mid-June–mid-Aug., daily 10–5; mid-May–mid-June and mid-Aug.–mid-Sept., daily 10–3; mid-Sept.–mid-May, weekends 11–2.*

Skibladner, the world's oldest paddle steamer, makes a stop at Eidsvoll, as well as at Hamar, Gjøvik, Lillehammer, and elsewhere. While aboard, dine in the first class lounge on traditional boiled salmon and fresh strawberries. Schedules for the steamer (and for the corresponding train stops) are available at Oslo S Station. ⊠ *Torggt. 1,* ☎ *62/52–70–85.* 🔄 *NKr 150–NKr 300.* ☉ *Sailings late June–mid-Aug., Tues., Thurs., and Sat.*

Årnes

Dating back to 1728, the **Gamle Hvam Museum,** inside a former manor house, looks back at Norwegian country life. In the main building, learn how women lived in 1900 and how farming has changed since 1950. Take a walk outdoors and visit agriculture and handicraft exhibits, rose gardens, and beds of other flowers. To get here, take the train to Årnes. On weekdays you can also take Bus 835. ⊠ *Årnes,* ☎ *63/90–96–09,* 🌐 *www.gamlehvam.museum.no.* 🔄 *NKr 40.* ☉ *Late May–Aug., weekdays 11–4, weekends noon–5; early Sept., Sun. noon–5.*

Bærum

One of Oslo's fashionable suburbs, Bærum is about 20 minutes from the city. The area is mostly residential, but along the banks of the Lomma River is the charming **Bærums Verk.** In the 1960s, the owners of the Bærums Verk iron foundry fixed up their old industrial town and made it into a historical site. Today, the stores, workshops, and exhibitions among the idyllic surroundings attract many visitors to its

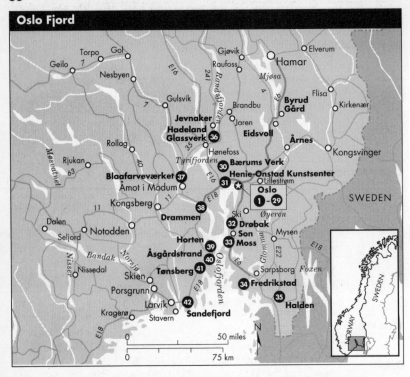

grounds. As you explore the beautifully restored village, notice the cramped wooden cottages lining **Verksgata**, where the workers once lived. Notice that the doors are in the back of the buildings; this was in case a fire from the works spread through the main street. The Museum Bærums Verk has an extensive collection of iron ovens as well as temporary exhibitions. Take Bus 143 or 153 from Grønland or Universitetsplassen. ⊠ *Bærums Verk,* ☎ *67/13–00–18,* WEB *www. baerumsverk.no.* ▣ *Museum NKr 10.* ⊙ *Museum mid-June–mid-Aug., daily noon–4; mid-Aug.–mid-June, weekends noon–4; Verksgata Mon.–Sat. 10–5, Sun. noon–4.*

Dining

$$$ ✕ **Værtshuset Bærums Verk.** Norway's oldest standing restaurant,
★ this spot is a must on any itinerary that includes the neighboring iron works. The inn opened in 1640 and was a frequented stop on the "King's" road from Oslo to Bergen. Restored in 1987, it is now one of the country's finest restaurants specializing in Norwegian cuisine. Low ceilings, pastel-painted wooden floors, shiny pewter tableware, and the tick-tock of a grandfather clock in the dining room all create the impression that you are walking into 19th-century Scandinavia. The fresh mountain trout or fillet of reindeer in cream sauce are particularly popular dishes. ⊠ *Vertshusvn. 10, Bærums Verk,* ☎ *67/80–02–00. AE, DC, MC, V.*

Høvikodden

③① The **Henie-Onstad Kunstsenter** (Henie-Onstad Art Center) is just outside Oslo, about 12 km (7 mi) southwest on E18. It houses Norway's largest collection of international modern art. After the famous skater Sonja Henie married shipping magnate Niels Onstad, they began to put together a fine collection of early 20th-century art, with important works by Munch, Picasso, Bonnard, and Matisse. Henie died in 1969, but she still skates her way through many a late-night movie. The three-time Olympic gold-medal winner was the first to realize the potential of the ice show, and her technical assistant, Frank Zamboni, has been immortalized by the ice-finishing machine he developed just for her, the Zamboni. World-class temporary exhibitions here always prove to be thought-provoking and memorable. Restaurateurs Toralf Bølgen and Trond Moi run the highly regarded restaurant on the premises. Buses 151, 152, and 251 from Oslo S Station stop near the grounds. ✉ *1311 Høvikodden,* ☎ *67/80–48–80,* [WEB] *www.henieonstad.no.* ✇ *NKr 50.* ✆ *Tues.–Thurs. 10–9, Fri.–Mon. 11–6.*

EAST OF THE OSLO FJORD

The eastern side of the Oslo Fjord is summer-vacation country for many Norwegians, who retreat to cabins on the water during July. Many towns along the fjord offer history and culture as well as a place to bathe. Viking ruins and inscriptions, fortified towns, and bohemian 19th-century artists' colonies provide a glimpse into the region's rich past.

Some of the towns mentioned can easily be visited as day trips from Oslo. Roads can be winding, though, so you might want to devote several days to exploring the area. Note that ferries shuttle cars and people back and forth between the archipelago islands and between either side of the fjord, so it is possible to combine this tour with the West of the Oslo Fjord and make a complete circle without backtracking.

Drøbak

㉜ *35 km (21 mi) south of Oslo.*

Mention the summer resort town of Drøbak to many Norwegians, and strangely enough, they'll start talking about Father Christmas. Although there is some question as to where the *Julenisse* (literally, "Christmas elf") came from, Norwegians claim—at least his adopted home—is here in Drøbak.

The inviting **Tregaardens Julehus** (Christmas House) dominates the town's central square. Just around the corner from the post office, this 1876 house was once a mission for seafarers unable to reach Oslo because the fjord was frozen over. Now it sells Christmas wares and gifts such as wooden dolls and mice made of cloth—all handmade by Eva Johansen, the store's creator and owner. ✉ *1440 Drøbak,* ☎ *64/93–41–78.*

NEED A BREAK? Back on the main square, stop in **Det Gamle Bageri Ost & Vinstue** (The Old Bakery Wine and Cheese Room, ☎ 64/93–21–05) for salads, pies, and hearty fare such as salmon in a mouthwatering sweet-mustard sauce. The timber interior is around 250 years old, and the wine list is extensive.

☗ **Jegstad Gård farm,** a traditional Norwegian dairy, has animals to visit and horse carriages to ride. Wander along the nature trail or visit the stable, farm museum, and Viking burial mounds. You can also play ball on the large lawn or walk on stilts. The farm is between Drøbak and Vestby, to the south. ✉ *Rte. E6, Vestby,* ☎ *64/95–00–58,* ✇ *NKr 20.* ✆ *Apr.–Aug., Sun. noon–4; by special arrangement rest of the year.*

Shopping

Take time to stroll the downtown and browse through the charming small shops. **Nautilus** (✉ Niels Carlsens gt. 5, ☎ 64/93–44–55) specializes in blue and maritime-theme gifts. Local artists and craftspeople exhibit and sell their work at such local galleries as **Galleri Havstad** (⊠ Storgt. 15, ☎ 64/93–46–55).

Lodging

$$ ▥ **Reenskaug Hotel.** Old-fashioned, wooden, and white-washed, this 100-year-old hotel is on Drøbak's main road. With its traditional Norwegian country style interior, it is the place to stay. Ask for Room 213. In 1904, Norway's Nobel Prize for Literature winner Knut Hamsun wrote here. ⊠ *Storgt. 32, 1440 Drøbak,* ☎ *64/93–33–60,* ⅂ℵ *64/93– 36–66. 27 rooms. Restaurant, bar, nightclub, meeting room. AE, DC MC, V.*

Son

25 km (15 mi) south of Drøbak.

You can swim, sail, or sun on the banks of Son (pronounced *soon*), just south of Drøbak. An old fishing and boating village, this resort town has traditionally attracted artists and writers. Artists still flock here, as do city folk in summer.

In the summer season, you can count on **Klubben Soon** (☎ 64/95–70– 42) for a good mix of disco, jazz, concerts, and stand-up comedy.

Moss

③③ *10 km (6 mi) south of Son.*

Although the area has been inhabited since Viking times, Moss gained borough status in the 18th century and is one of the area's main commercial and shipping centers.

OFF THE
BEATEN PATH

GALLERI F15 – A 5-km (3-mi) ride outside Moss, on the island of Jeløy, is an art center set in an old farm. Exhibits displayed here range from photography to Scandinavian crafts. ⊠ *Alby Gård,* ☎ *69/27–10–33.* ☉ *June–Aug., Tues.–Sun. 11–7; Sept.–May, Tues.–Sun. 11–5.*

Dining and Lodging

$$$ ✕▥ **Refsnes Gods.** This historic hotel has one of Norway's best
★   kitchens and a fine wine cellar. The French-Norwegian kitchen has a way with seafood, meat, and game dishes. Try the breast of duck and the champagne from 1975. While dining, take a look at one of the four Munch paintings in the dining room, including *Blue Lady.* The main building dates from 1767, when it was a family estate. The Victorian-style, blue-and-beige rooms are airy and pretty. ⊠ *Godset 5, 1502 Moss,* ☎ *69/27–83–00,* ⅂ℵ *69/27–83–01,* Ⅵℰℬ *www.refsnesgods.no. 61 rooms, 4 suites. Restaurant, pool, sauna, gym, beach, boating, meeting room. AE, DC, MC, V.*

Fredrikstad

③④ *34 km (20 mi) south of Moss.*

Norway's oldest fortified city lies peacefully at the mouth of the Glomma, the country's longest river. Its bastions and moat date from the 1600s. After spending time in town browsing the shops and museum, venture outside the city to Hvaler, a popular vacation spot.

Gamlebyen (Old Town) has been preserved and has museums, art galleries, cafés, artisans' workshops, antiques shops, and old bookstores.

The **Fredrikstad Museum** documents the town's history in two separate exhibitions. The first focuses on the town's maritime and shipping heritage and has both period commercial vessels and sailing boats. The second tells the story of the development of the town and city from 1860 to 1960 through pieces of its industrial, commercial, hospital, and day-to-day life. ☎ 69/30–68–75. ☎ NKr 30. ☉ May–Sept., daily noon–5.

In the center of town is **Fredrikstad Domskirke** (Fredrikstad Cathedral). Built in 1860 in a flamboyant neo-Gothic style, it contains interior decorations by leading Norwegian artists of the time. ☎ 69/30–02–80. ☎ Free. ☉ Tues.–Fri. 11–3.

Lodging
$$$–$$$$ 🏨 **Hotel City.** This comfortable, stylish hotel has a central downtown location but is still quiet and peaceful. The restaurant serves international cuisine, particularly Creole, Norwegian, and Italian. ☒ Nygaardsgt. 44–46, 1607 Fredrikstad, ☎ 69/31–77–50, ℻ 69/31–65–83. 110 rooms. Restaurant, sauna, dance club, nightclub, solarium, convention center, meeting rooms. MC, V.

Shopping
Glashytte (☒ Torsnesvn. 1, ☎ 69/32–28–12) is a well-known local glassblowing studio and shop that sells and exhibits in galleries throughout Norway. Before your eyes, watch glassblowers perform their magic, creating shapes from schnapps glasses to vases in primary colors and in the studio's signature style. If you're staying in the area, make a special order and go see your glass object blown. You can pick it up a few days later after it's been cooled slowly in a kiln, which makes it less fragile.

Halden

③⑤ 30 km (18 mi) south of Fredrikstad.

Preserving its past, this idyllic little town has several historical attractions well worth a visit. Since it's close to the Swedish border, it once needed fortifications in order to fend off attacks. Norwegians and Swedes had ongoing border disputes, and the most famous skirmish at Fredriksten fortress resulted in the death of King Karl XII in 1718.

Built in the late 1600s in the shape of a star, the complex of buildings that make up the **Fredriksten Festning** (Fredriksten Fort; ☎ 69/09–09–80) are at the city's highest point. The exhibition in the former prison describes Halden war history from the 17th century to World War II. An old pharmacy in the residence illustrates the history of pharmacology with bird claws used in folk medicine as well as period pots and drawers. At the far end of the inner courtyard, the bakery and brewery could bake enough bread for 5,000 men and brew 3,000 liters of beer. The exhibition Byen brenner, "The Burning City," documents the many fires that attacked Halden's (primarily wood) buildings. Inside the fort itself is **Fredriksten Kro**, a good, old-fashioned pub with outdoor seating. ☎ 69/09–09–80. ☎ NKr 40. ☉ Mid-May–Aug., daily 10–5.

Rød Herregård is one of the finest and best preserved 18th-century manors in Norway. A restored building houses period furniture, artworks, and hunting trophies. The house, open only for tours, has a unique weapons collection. ☒ 1771 Halden, ☎ 69/18–54–11. ☎ NKr 40. ☉ Sun. tours at noon, 1, and 2.

Dining
$–$$ ✕ **Rekekafeen.** Near dockside sheds on a floating pier in the marina, Rekekafeen has a reputation for its fresh fish and seafood. Taste their smoked fish and shrimp. You can also have eel, choosing yours from those swimming in a nearby tank. At a separate fish counter, fish

equipment and bait are sold alongside changing exhibitions of local arts and crafts. Live music is performed on the weekends. ⊠ *Waterfront,* ☎ 69/18–29–06.

East of the Oslo Fjord A to Z

BOAT AND FERRY TRAVEL
A ferry links Drøbak, on the east side of the fjord, with Hurum, on the west side, just north of Horten. Contact Drøbak Turistinformasjon for schedule information.

BUS TRAVEL
Bus 541 from outside Oslo S Station to Drøbak affords great glimpses of the fjord (and its bathers). The trip takes an hour, and buses depart hourly at 10 minutes past the hour during the week, with reduced service on weekends. Bus 100 (E6 Ekspress) departs every three hours during the day, stopping at Svindsen, where you can catch a local bus to Halden. Contact Nor-Way Bussekspress for schedules.

➤ BUS INFORMATION: **Nor-Way Bussekspress** (☎ 815/44–444).

CAR TRAVEL
Follow Route E18 southeast from Oslo to Route E6. Follow signs to Drøbak and Son. Continue through Moss, following signs to Halden, farther south on E6. The route then takes you north to Sarpsborg, where you can turn left to Fredrikstad.

TRAIN TRAVEL
Trains for Halden leave from Oslo S Station and take two hours to make the 136-km (85-mi) trip, with stops in Moss, Fredrikstad, and Sarpsborg.

VISITOR INFORMATION
➤ TOURIST INFORMATION: **Drøbak** (Drøbak Turistinformasjon, ☎ 64/93–50–87). **Fredrikstad** (Fredrikstad Turistkontor, ⊠ Turistsentret vøstre Brohode and ⊠ 1632 Gamle Fredrikstad, ☎ 69/32–03–30 or 69/32–10–60). **Halden** (Halden Turist Kontor, ⊠ Storgt. 6, Box 167, 1751 Halden, ☎ 69/19–09–80). **Moss** (Moss Turistkontor, ⊠ Fleischersgt. 17, 1531 Moss, ☎ 69/25–32–95). **Son** (Son Kystkultursenter, ⊠ 1555 Son, ☎ 64/95–89–20).

WEST OF THE OSLO FJORD

Towns lining the western side of the fjord are more industrial on the whole than their neighbors on the eastern side. Still, the western towns have traditionally been some of Norway's oldest and wealthiest, their fortunes derived from whaling and lumbering. An increasing number of restaurants and museums have made the region more attractive to travelers.

Jevnaker

About 70 km (42 mi) northwest of Oslo. Follow E16 toward Hønefoss, then follow Route 241 to Jevnaker. It's about a 2-hr drive.

A day trip to Jevnaker combines a drive along the Tyrifjord, where you can see some of the best fjord views in eastern Norway, with a visit to Norway's oldest glassworks, in operation since 1762.

36 At **Hadeland Glassverk** you can watch artisans blowing glass, or, if you get there early enough, you can blow your own. Both practical table crystal and one-of-a-kind art glass are produced here, and you can buy first quality pieces as well as seconds at the gift shop. Learn the history of glass at the Glass Museum. For children, there's a Honey House of bees and a Children's House that celebrates Christmas in summer. ⊠ *Rte. 241, Postboks 85,* ☎ *61/31–66–00,* WEB *www.hadeland-glassverk.no.* ✆ *Weekdays 10–5, Sat. 10–4, Sun. 11–5.*

Åmot i Modum

70 km (42 mi) west of Oslo. From Jevnaker, take Route 35 south, along the Tyrifjord. From the E18, take Route 11 west to Hokksund, and Route 35 to Åmot. Then turn onto Route 287 to Sigdal.

The small village of Åmot is famous for its cobalt mines. The blue mineral was used to make dyes for the glass and porcelain industries around the world.

37 The **Blaafarveværket** (Cobalt Works) was founded in 1773 to extract cobalt from the Modum mines. Today the complex is a museum and a national park. A permanent collection displays old cobalt-blue glass and porcelain. For children there's a petting farm, and the restaurant serves Norwegian country fare. Up the hill from the art complex is Haugfossen, the highest waterfall in eastern Norway. Also nearby are Nymoen Nr. 9, a museum of social history, as well as the Th. Kittelsen Museet, which has Norway's largest collection of the haunting, mysterious works of this artist. ⊠ *Rte. 507,* ☎ *32/78–67–00,* WEB *www.blaa.no.* ⌨ *Special exhibitions NKr 50; cobalt works free. Guided tours in English.* ✆ *Mid-May–mid-June, daily 10–5; mid-June–mid-Aug., daily 10–6; mid-Aug.–mid-Sept., Tues.– Sun. 10–5.*

Drammen

38 *40 km (25 mi) from Oslo, 45 km (27 mi) south of Åmot i Modum.*

Drammen, a timber town and port for 500 years, is an industrial city of 55,000 on the Drammen River. Called the River City, it was the former harbor for exported silver from the Kongsberg mines. These days many cars are imported into Norway here. The river divides the city into two: Bragernes (historically more prosperous) and Strømsø. Being a port and having lower costs than places like Oslo, the city has a more diverse population than other Norwegian cities its size. Around the Bragernes Torget (town square) there has been a flowering of shops, cafés, and restaurants. The Gothic Bragernes Church is at the square's head. The city's mountainous hills are ideal spots for fishing, hiking, skiing, and other outdoor activities.

The **Drammen Museum of Art and Cultural History** actually comprises several smaller museums in the city. Marienlyst Manor (1750) has Nøstetangen glass and rustic folk and church art. The Art Department's permanent gallery has many great works of 19th and 20th century Norwegian masters, including Hans Heyerdahl's *The Champagne Girl*. At Spiraltoppen, the Open Air Museum chronicles 300 years of area architecture. ⊠ *Konnerudgt. 7,* ☎ *32/20–09–30.* ⌨ *NKr 30.* ✆ *Tues.–Sat. 11–3, Sun. 11–5.*

Spiralen is the name of the spiraled, more than 1¼-mi-long tunnel cut through Bragernesåsen (Bragernes Hill). **Spiraltoppen,** the area around the tunnel entrance, has a marvelous view of Drammen, the river, and the fjord. Spiraltoppen is also the starting point for many km of downhill and cross-country skiing trails. Several footpaths follow a 2 km (1 mi) nature trail. ⊠ *Spiraltoppen,* ☎ *32/89–69–65.*

Dining and Lodging

$$–$$$ ✕ **Skutebrygga.** Right on the riverbank and just off the square, this popular meeting place has small miniature boats, anchors, and old maps inside, an echo of the real boats outside its windows. Candlelight, an open fireplace, and a summer patio make this a warm, welcoming place. Among the French-inspired, international menu items, seafood dishes such as grilled monkfish in bacon and curry sauce are the most recommended. ✉ *Nedre Strandgt. 2,* ☎ *32/83–33–30. AE, DC, MC, V.*

$–$$ ✕ **Åspavilongen.** This hillside restaurant and bar is known for its panoramic view of the entire valley and fjord. Dating back 100 years, its walls are covered with historic photographs. On the international menu, try the beef steak and onions. ✉ *Bragerenesåsen,* ☎ *32/83–37–47. AE, DC, MC, V. Closed early–mid-Sept. and Nov.–Apr.*

$$ 🏨 **Rica Park.** As with all Rica hotels, the Park is relaxed. The rooms are comfortable, light, and airy. The hotel's dining and entertainment options include a nightclub that attracts an over-30 crowd. Take a walk in the nearby woods, and then have coffee and cake at the Spiraltoppen Café, where great views abound. ✉ *Gamle Kirkepl. 3, 3019,* ☎ *32/26–36–00,* FAX *32/26–37–77,* WEB *www.rica.no. 100 rooms, 6 suites. 2 restaurants, 2 bars, pub, dance club, nightclub. AE, DC, MC, V.*

$–$$ 🏨 **First Hotel Ambassadeur.** One of the better places to stay in Drammen, this hotel is especially popular with business travelers who like its stylish, comfortable guest rooms. The conference center has 30 meeting rooms. It's very close to both the railway station and the bus terminal. ✉ *Strømsø Torg 7, 3044,* ☎ *31/01–21–00,* FAX *31/01–21–11,* WEB *www.first-hotels.no. 230 rooms, 12 suites. Restaurant, 2 bars, sauna, gym, convention center, meeting rooms. AE, DC, MC, V.*

Shopping

The city's main department store, **Steen & Strom Magasinet** (✉ Nedre Storgt. 6, ☎ 32/21–39–90) has 65 shops and restaurants.

About 8 km (5 mi) from Drammen, on route 135 toward Hokksund, is **Buskerud Storsenter** (☎ 32/23–15–45), the region's largest shopping mall, with more than 80 shops and restaurants.

Outdoor Activities and Sports

A few years back, Drammen was voted the Open-Air City of Norway for its outdoor activities, which include fishing, skiing, cycling, boating, and hiking. Four separate cycling trails are outlined on maps available from the Tourist Office. Wherever you are, you are never more than a few minutes from footpaths, nature trails, miles of forest land, lakes or grassy hills, and scenic countryside.

BOATING

MS *Drammen* Charter and Turistbåt (✉ Bragernes Torg 13, ☎ 32/83–50–45) organizes river, fjord tours, fishing trips, and river safaris. A boat with catering and crew is available for hire.

FISHING

The fjord and the river offer great fishing, particularly at Hokksund and Hellefossen. Salmon and trout are most prized; it's not uncommon to catch salmon weighing 22–44 lbs. Forty other fish breeds can also be caught in the river. The fishing season runs from mid-May through September. Contact the **Drammens Sportfiskere** (☎ 32/88–66–73) for information on national and local fishing licenses as well as regulations and events.

HORSE RACING

The **Drammen Racecourse** is one of 10 permanent betting courses in Norway. Tuesday is racing day, beginning at 6 PM with five special Saturday races. The horses can be seen at close range, making the race that much more immediate and exciting. ⊠ *Buskerudvn. 200,* ☎ *32/ 21–87–00.*

Cross-country skiers have 100 km of trails available outside the city, including 42 km of well-maintained tracks that are lit up at night. Downhill skiers can head to Haukåsløypa on the Strømsø side or Aronsløypa on the Bragernes side.

Make a splash poolside at one of Drammen's indoor and outdoor swimming complexes. **Marienlystbadet** (☎ 32/83–34–05, ⊙ late May–mid-Aug.) has an Olympic-size pool, diving pool, and children's pool all heated to nearly 80° F (26°C). The complex also has a water slide, water toys, beach-volleyball courts, a sauna, and places to sunbathe. **Sentralbadet** (☎ 32/83–65–86, ⊙ mid-Aug.–May) has an indoor 25-meter swimming pool and a warm pool that's heated to 93°F (34 °C). There's also a Jacuzzi, water slide, solarium, sauna, Nautilus exercise room, and a lounge.

Nightlife

If you want to have a drink, hear live music, or go dancing, try the hotels or head downtown to one of Drammen's bars, pubs, or clubs. **Rock på Union Scene** (⊠ Gronland 68, ☎ 32/83–77–88) books new bands and concerts every Friday night. **Riggen Pub** (⊠ Amtmann Blomsgt., ☎ 32/83–67–00) has the blues on Friday and Saturday nights. **Pavarotti** (⊠ Nedre Torggt. 9, ☎ 32/83–55–74) is known for its live jazz on Wednesday night and on Saturday starting at 3 PM.

Horten

 35 km (17 mi) south of Drammen.

Off the main route south, the coastal village of Horten has several distinctive museums worth an afternoon's visit. The town was once an important Norwegian Royal Navy station and still retains the officers' candidates school.

The **Marinemuseet** (Royal Norwegian Navy Museum), built in 1853 as a munitions warehouse, displays 16th- and 17th-century Danish and Norwegian relics from the nation's naval history. Outside is the world's first torpedo boat, from 1873, and some one-person submarines. ⊠ *Karl Johans Vern,* ☎ *33/03–33–97.* ▣ *Free.* ⊙ *May–Sept., weekdays noon–4, weekends noon–4; Oct.–Apr., Sun. noon–4.*

The **Norsk Museum for Fotografi: Preus Fotomuseum** (Norwegian Museum for Photography: Preus Photography Museum) houses the fascinating private photographic collection of Leif Preus. First opened in 1994, it was later sold and re-opened in May 2001 on the fourth and fifth floors of the huge naval warehouse. The extensive collection has between 4,500 and 5,000 cameras, including a rare 1840s camera obscura (a kind of projector). All kinds of photographs—documentary, press, portraits, scientific, fine art—are here, including the work of such international photographers as August Sander and Tom Sandberg. The museum has one of the world's largest libraries of photography books. Look for the photographer's studio of a hundred years ago, as well as the tiny camera used for early aerial photographs: it was strapped to a pigeon. ⊠ *Karl Johans Vern,* ☎ *33/ 03–16–30,* WEB *www.foto.museum.no.* ▣ *NKr 35.* ⊙ *Tues.–Sun., daily noon–4.*

The **Horten Bil Museum** traces the car's development from 1900 to 1970 through exhibits of 35 autos and motorcycles. Everything from the earliest cars to modern Porsches are on view. ✉ *Sollistrandvn. 12,* ☎ *33/ 02–08–50.* 🎫 *NKr 35.* ⊙ *Mid-June–mid-Sept., Sun. noon–3.*

Åsgårdstrand

40 *10 km (6 mi) south of Horten.*

Since 1920, the coastal town of Åsgårdstrand has been a popular vacation and bathing spot. A couple decades before that, it was known as an artists' colony for outdoor painting, attracting Edvard Munch, Fritz Thaulow, and others. The local tourist office can arrange guided historic tours of the area given by well-versed guides.

Munchs lille hus (Munch's Little House) was the summer house and studio in which he spent seven summers. Now a museum, it was here that he painted *Girls on the Bridge* and earned a reputation as a ladies' man. ✉ *Munchsgt.,* ☎ *33/08–21–31.* 🎫 *NKr 40.* ⊙ *May and Sept., weekends 11–7; June–Aug., Tues.–Sun. 11–7.*

Lodging

$$ Åsgårdstrand Hotell. Steps away from the harbor, the Åsgårdstrand has large, airy rooms with spectacular ocean views. The waterfront location and a harbor for guests are perfect for those who want to be part of the town's active sailing culture. ✉ *Havnengt. 6, 3167.* ☎ *33/08– 10–40,* FAX *33/08–10–77,* WEB *www.asgardstrand-hotell.no. 70 rooms, 3 suites. Restaurant, bar. AE, DC, MC, V.*

En Route Travel south from Åsgårdstrand toward Tønsberg and you'll pass **Slagen,** the site where the *Oseberg* Viking ship, dating from around 800, was found. (It's now on display at Vikingskiphuset in Oslo.) Look for the mound where it was buried as you pass Slagen's church.

Tønsberg

41 *11 km (6½ mi) south of Åsgårdstrand.*

According to the Sagas, Tønsberg is Norway's oldest non-Sámi settlement, founded in 871. Little remains of Tønsberg's early structures, although the ruins at **Slottsfjellet** (Castle Hill), by the train station, include parts of the city wall, the remains of a church from around 1150, and a 13th-century brick citadel, the **Tønsberghus.** Other medieval remains are below the cathedral and near Storgata 17.

North of the railroad station, the **Vestfold Fylkesmuseum** (Vestfold County Museum) houses a small Viking ship, several whale skeletons, and some inventions. See the whale-factory ships where whales were processed on-board. The open-air museum focuses on farming life. ✉ *Farmannsvn. 30,* ☎ *33/31–24–18.* 🎫 *NKr 30.* ⊙ *Mid-May–mid-Sept., Mon.–Sat. 10–5, Sun. noon–5; mid-Sept.–mid-May, weekdays 10–2.*

The intriguing art in **Haugar Vestfold Kunstmuseum** is mostly done by regional and Norwegian artists. One of Norway's best known artists, Odd Nerdrum, has his own wing in the museum. The dark, rich, evocative character of Nerdrum's paintings (including *The Storyteller*) has been compared to that of Rembrandt's. ✉ *Gråbrødragt. 17,* ☎ *33/30–76–70,* WEB *www.haugar.com.* 🎫 *NKr 40.* ⊙ *Sept.–May, Tues.– Fri. 11–4, weekends noon–5; June–Aug., weekdays 11–5, weekends noon–5.*

Lodging

$$ 🏨 Best Western Grand Hotel. This art deco hotel first opened its doors in 1931. A renovation in 2001 maintained its classic style. The hotel's Grand Restaurant serves a highly regarded international cuisine, including a special seafood platter. The MS *Christina*, a boat owned by the hotel, is available for rent or charter. ⊠ *Øvre Langgt. 5, Tønsberg,* ☎ *33/35–35–00.* 𝔽𝔸𝕏 *33/35–35–01,* 𝕎𝔼𝔹 *www.bestwestern.no. 64 rooms, 3 suites. 2 restaurants, bar, nightclub. AE, DC, MC, V.*

Sandefjord

㊷ *125 km (78 mi) south of Oslo, 25 km (15 mi) south of Tønsberg.*

Back in 1400, Sandefjord was home to Vikings, who had their settlements and grave sites here. A natural harbor, the city was once the whaling capital of the world. Around 1900, it was possibly Norway's wealthiest city. Now that the whales are gone, all that remains of that trade is a monument to it. With many beaches, 116 islands, and an archipelago, Sandefjord earns its nickname of *Badebyen,* or "Bathing City." In summer, boating and tourism thrive. From the Sandefjord Gjestehavn (guest, or public, harbor), take a short walk to the city's restaurants, shopping, and attractions.

Kommandør Christensens Hvalfangstmuseum (Commander Christensen's Whaling Museum) is perhaps best known for the suspended life-size model of a blue whale. The museum traces the development of the industry from small primitive boats to huge floating factories. An especially intriguing display chronicles whaling in the Antarctic. ⊠ *Museumsgt. 39,* ☎ *33/48–46–50.* ⊡ *NKr 25.* ◷ *May–Sept., daily 11–5; Oct.–Apr., daily 11–3.*

Take a break from the beach to see the fascinating **Sandefjords Sjøfartsmuseum** (Sandefjord's Maritime Museum), which chronicles man's life at sea. Discover maritime history at exhibits of the sailing ships of the 19th century as well as more modern vessels. ⊠ *Prinsensgt. 18,* ☎ *33/48–46–50.* ⊡ *NKr 25.* ◷ *Early May–late June and mid-Aug.–late Sept., Sun. 2–4; late June–mid-Aug., daily noon–4.*

Dining and Lodging

$$–$$$ ✕ **Ludls Gourmet Odd Ivar Solvold.** Celebrity chef Odd Ivar Solvold
★ is a former three-time national culinary champion. In a place famous for its seafood, Solvold's grilled crayfish, turbot, catfish, scallops, and mussels all come highly recommended. For dessert, there's a heavenly chocolate truffle cake. ⊠ *Rådhusgt. 7,* ☎ *33/46–27–41. AE, DC, MC, V.*

$$–$$$$ ▥ **Rica Park Hotel.** The old-fashioned decor here is much the same as when it was built in 1958. Ask for one of the 50 redecorated rooms, which are bigger than those in most hotels. A new swimming pool opened in 2001. ⊠ *Strandpromenaden 9, 3200,* ☎ *33/44–74–00,* 𝔽𝔸𝕏 *33/44–75–00,* 𝕎𝔼𝔹 *www.rica.no. 233 rooms, 8 suites. 2 restaurants, bar, indoor pool, health club, nightclub, convention center. AE, DC, MC, V.*

$–$$$ ▥ **Comfort Home Hotel Atlantic.** The Atlantic Home was built in 1914, when Sandefjord was a whaling center. The history of whaling is traced in exhibits in glass cases and in pictures throughout the hotel. There's no restaurant, but the room rate includes *aften,* a supper consisting of bread and cold cuts, and hot soup and light beer. ⊠ *Jernbanealleen 33, 3201,* ☎ *33/42–80–00,* 𝔽𝔸𝕏 *33/42–80–20. 109 rooms. Lobby lounge, sauna, library. AE, DC, MC, V.*

Cafés

Like many other Norwegian cities, Sandefjord has several trendy little spots that serve a great cup of coffee. **Iwonas Kaffebar** (⊠ Kongensgt. 26, ☎ 33/45–86–10) has the city's best coffee, from cappucinos to mochas. The popular café and bar **første etage** (⊠ Torvet 5, ☎ 33/46–27–80) also serves lunch and dinner. If you need to go on-line, head to **cafe 4u.no** (⊠ Storgt. 14, ☎ 33/42–94–98), an Internet café that serves coffees and breakfast, lunch, and dinner. The name's a play on Norway's e-mail country code of "no."

Outdoor Activities and Sports

Sandefjord is probably best known for its beaches and bathing. The tourist office has information on the multitude of sports played by locals, including soccer, handball, badminton, and tennis.

BIKING

Rent a bike at **Sykkelutleie,** (⊠ Hotel Kong Carl, Torggt. 9, ☎ 33/46–31–17) and buy "Sandefjords Reiselivsforening," a good bike map for the area.

SWIMMING/DIVING

Sandefjord has a beautiful, 146 km (90 mi) coastline brimming with wonderful beaches, especially those at the following islands and locations:

Vesterøya: Asnes, Sjøbakken, Langeby, Grubesand, Vøra og Fruvika. **Østerøya:** Flautangen, Skjellvika, Truber, and Yxnøy. **Along Highway 303 toward Larvik:** Granholmen. **Along Highway 303 toward Tønsberg:** Solløkka.

Neptun Dykkersenter (⊠ Bjerggt. 7, Sandefjord, ☎ 33/46–14–90) is a diving center that teaches classes and sells and rents diving and water sports equipment.

West of the Oslo Fjord A to Z

To research prices, get advice from other travelers, and book travel arrangements, visit www.fodors.com.

BOAT AND FERRY TRAVEL

The most luxurious and scenic way to see the region is by boat: there are guest marinas at just about every port.

BUS TRAVEL

Because train service to towns south of Drammen is infrequent, bus travel is the best alternative to cars. Check with Nor-Way Bussekspress for schedules.

➤ Bus Information: **Nor-Way Bussekspress** (☎ 815–44–444).

CAR TRAVEL

Route E18 south from Oslo follows the coast to this region's towns.

TRAIN TRAVEL

Take a suburban train from Nationaltheatret or trains from Oslo S Station to reach Horten, Tønsberg, and Sandefjord.

VISITOR INFORMATION

➤ Tourist Information: **Blaafarveværket** (☎ 32/78–49–00). **Drammen** (Drammen Kommunale Turistinformasjonskontor, ⊠ Bragernes Torg 6, 3008 Drammen, ☎ 32/80–62–10). **Hadeland** (☎ 61/31–66–00). **Horten and Åsgårdstrand** (Horten Turist Kontor, ⊠ Tollbugt. 1A, 3187 Horten, ☎ 33/03–17–08). **Sandefjord** (Sandefjord Reiselivsforening, ⊠ Torvet, 3201 Sandefjord, ☎ 33/46–05–90). **Tønsberg** (Tønsberg og Omland Reiselivslag, ⊠ Nedre Langgt. 36B, 3110 Tønsberg, ☎ 33/31–02–20).

4 TELEMARK AND THE SETESDAL VALLEY

The interior region of southern Norway, Telemark, and the Setesdal Valley, lies in the shadow of the famed beaches and fjords of the coast, but certainly doesn't lack majestic scenery—forested hills meet deeply etched valleys, and lakes stretch across the serene countryside.

A LAND OF WIDE-OPEN VISTAS and deep forests, Telemark is the interior region of southern Norway. It lies in the shadow of the famed beaches and fjords of the coast but doesn't lack majestic scenery. The region is veined with swift-flowing streams and scattered with peaceful lakes—a natural setting so powerful and silent that a few generations ago, trolls were the only reasonable explanation for what lurked in, or for that matter plodded through, the shadows.

Telemark was the birthplace of skiing as well as the birthplace of many Norwegian-American ancestors: the poor farmers of the region were among the first to emigrate to the United States in the 19th century.

Numbers in the margin correspond to points of interest on the Telemark and Sørlandet map.

Kongsberg

❶ *84 km (52 mi) southwest of Oslo.*

Kongsberg, with 23,000 people today, was Norway's silver town for more than 300 years. In 1623, two children discovered a large ox butting the cliff with his horns, revealing a silver vein in the hillside. News of the silver find reached King Christian IV in Copenhagen. He saw the town's natural potential and sent experts to investigate. A year later, the king came and founded the mining town of "Konningsberg." Norway's first industrial town was prominent until the mine closed in 1805.

Kongsberg Kirke (Kongsberg Church), finished in 1761, was built during the heyday of the silver mines. Along one wall is an impressive gilded Baroque altar, organ, and pulpit. The famous large glass chandeliers were made at Nøstetangen glassworks (☎ 32/73–19–02).

The Arts
In the last week of July jazz fans descend on Kongsberg for its annual **jazz festival** (☎ 32/73–31–66, WEB www.kongsberg-jazzfestival.no).

Dining and Lodging
$$ ✕ **Gamle Kongsberg Kro.** This café, next to the waterfall at Nybrofossen, has a reputation for traditional, hearty Norwegian dishes at reasonable prices. Try the broiled salmon with horseradish sauce or pepper steak. ⊠ *Thornesvn. 4,* ☎ *32/73–16–33,* FAX *32/73–26–03. DC, MC, V.*

$$–$$$ 🏨 **Quality Grand Hotel.** A statue of Kongsberg's favorite son, Olympic ski jumper Birger Ruud, stands in the park in front of this modern, centrally located hotel. The rooms are in a minimalistic style of white walls contrasting with dark furniture. ⊠ *Kristian Augusts gt. 2, 3600,* ☎ *32/77–28–00,* FAX *32/73–41–29,* WEB *www.quality-grand.no. 99 rooms, 2 suites. Restaurant, 2 bars, indoor pool, nightclub, meeting room. AE, DC, MC, V.*

Skien

❷ *88 km (55 mi) south of Kongsberg on Routes 32 and 36.*

Best known as the birthplace of playwright Henrik Ibsen, Skien, with a population of 50,000, is the capital of the Telemark region. Ibsen's home town celebrates its favorite son every summer with the **Ibsen-Kul-tur-festival** (☎ 35/90–55–20), which includes concerts as well as drama.

The Telemark Museum, **Brekkeparken,** a manor house from 1780, has a collection of Ibsen memorabilia that includes his study and bedroom and the "blue salon" from his Oslo flat (other interiors are at Ibsen-museet in Oslo). The Telemark collection of folk art dates back to the

Telemark and Sørlandet

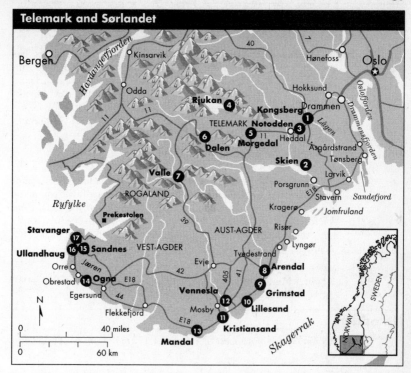

18th and 19th centuries. Brekkeparken is Northern Europe's largest tulip park. The exhibit "From Runes to E-mail" chronicles human communication from the past millennium. ⊠ *Øvregt. 41,* ☎ *35/52–35–94.* 🖃 *NKr 40.* ⊘ *Garden mid-May–Aug., daily 10–6; museum mid-May–Aug., daily 10–6.*

Now the Henrik Ibsen Museum, **Venstøp** looks just as it did when the Ibsen family lived here from 1835 to 1843. The dark attic was the inspiration for *The Wild Duck.* This house, part of Skien's County Museum, is 5 km (3 mi) northwest of the city. ☎ *35/52–35–94.* 🖃 *NKr 40.* ⊘ *Mid-May–Aug., daily 10–6; Sept., Sun. 10–6.*

OFF THE
BEATEN PATH

Bø SOMMARLAND – Norway's largest water park has wave pools, slides, and Las Bøgas, a *tivoli* (amusement park). Always a sure-fire hit with families, it has more than 100 activities each year on the land and in the water here, including live concerts. The park is 50 km (30 mi) from Skien and 25 km (15 mi) from Notodden. ⊠ *3800 Bø,* ☎ *35/95–16–99,* 🕸 *www.sommarland.no.* 🖃 *NKr 195.*

En Route Running 105 km (65 mi) from Skien to Dalen with a detour to Notodden, **Telemarkskanalen** (Telemark Canal; ☎ 35/90–00–30, 🕸 www.telemarkskanalen.com) was carved into the mountains more than 100 years ago. It took 500 men five years to blast through the mountains to create 28 locks. The canal became "the fast route" between east and west Norway and upper and lower Telemark. Telemarkskanalen still has its original stone walls, locks, and closing mechanism.

Dining and Lodging

$$ ✕ **Boden Spiseri.** Boden has earned a well-deserved reputation for its excellent Continental kitchen. One of the recommended dishes on the

French-inspired Norwegian menu is the fillet of reindeer. For dessert, savor the strawberry ice cream or the passionfruit cake. ✉ *Landbrygga 5,* ☏ *35/52–61–70. AE, DC, MC, V. No lunch.*

$$ ☒ **Rainbow Høyers Hotell.** Centrally located, this venerable hotel has style and sophistication. The exterior of cornices and pedimented windows is reflected in the Høyers's lobby, which is an incongruous mixture of old and new. The large rooms are modern and bright, thanks to big windows. ✉ *Kongensgt. 6, 3700,* ☏ *35/90–58–00,* ℻ *35/90–58–05,* ⓦ *www.rainbow-hotel.no. 69 rooms, 1 suite. Restaurant, bar, meeting room. AE, DC, MC, V.*

Outdoor Activities and Sports

BIKING

"The Coastal Route" goes along the Telemark coastline and is part of the North Sea Cycle Route, which goes through six other countries. There's also a 115 km (71 mi) route along the Telemark Canal from Ulefoss to Dalen. **Telemark Reiser** (✉ Skien, ☏ 35/90–00–30) has special cycling maps, and ready-made cycle package trips that include accommodation and transport.

GOLF

About 7 km (4½ mi) north of Skien is **Jønnevald** (☏ 35/59–07–03), an 18-hole championship golf course.

Notodden

❸ *68 km (42 mi) northwest of Skien and 35 km (21 mi) west of Kongsberg.*

Notodden today is not much more than a small industrial town. It's believed that the area must have been a prosperous one in the Middle Ages, though, because of the size of the town's stavkirke—85 ft high and 65 ft long. Notodden is also known for its **summer blues festival** (ⓦ www.bluesfest.no), which lasts four days in August and brings in Norwegian and American acts such as the Robert Cray Band.

Heddal Stave Church is Norway's largest still in use. Dating back to the 12th century, the church is resplendent with rosemaling from the 17th century, a bishop's chair, and incense vessels from medieval times. There is stylized animal ornamentation, along with grotesque human heads on the portals. ☏ *35/02–08–40.* ☒ *NKr 30.* ⊙ *Mid-May–mid-June and mid-Aug.–mid-Sept., Mon.–Sat. 10–5, Sun. 1–5; mid-June–mid-Aug., Mon.–Sat. 9–7, Sun. 1–7.*

Rjukan

❹ *96 km (59 mi) northwest of Notodden.*

The town of Rjukan may not ring a bell, but mention "heavy water," and anyone who lived through World War II or saw the film *The Heroes of Telemark* with Kirk Douglas knows about the sabotage of the heavy water factory there, which thwarted German efforts to develop an atomic bomb. Rjukan's history actually began in the decade between 1907 and 1916, when the population grew from a few hundred to 10,000 because of a different kind of water, hydroelectric power.

Heavy water (used in nuclear reactors) was produced as a by-product in the manufacture of fertilizer at Vemork, 6 km (4 mi) west of Rjukan along Route 37, where a museum, **Industriarbeidermuseet Vemork** (The Norwegian Industrial Workers Museum) has been built. Vemork was the world's largest power station in 1911. In the machine hall, you can see a demonstration of a mini power plant. Exhibitions document both the development of hydroelectric power and the World War II events. ☎ *35/09–51–53.* ✆ *NKr 55.* ☉ *May–mid-Aug., daily 10–6; mid-Aug.–Sept., weekdays 10–4, weekends 11–6; Oct. and Mar.–Apr., Sat. 11–4.*

Rjukan is the site of northern Europe's first cable car, **Krossobanen** (Krosso Cable Car), built in 1928 by Hydro (the hydroelectric company) as a gift to the Rjukan population so they could escape the shadowed valley and see Hardanger Mountain Plateau and Mount Gausta. ☎ *35/09–00–27.* ✆ *NKr 35.* ☉ *Times vary; call Rjukan tourist information for details.*

Lodging

$$$ ⊞ **Gaustablikk Høyfjellshotell.** At the foot of Mount Gausta, the highest mountain in southern Norway, this wooden ski cabin welcomes guests to a popular ski resort. There are nine downhill slopes and 80 km (50 mi) of cross-country trails. In summer these marked trails are ideal for walks and hikes. ⊠ *3660,* ☎ *35/09–14–22,* FAX *35/09–19–75,* WEB *www.gaustablikk.no. 98 rooms, 6 suites. Restaurant, bar, indoor pool, sauna, gym. AE, DC, MC, V.*

$–$$ ⊞ **Park Hotell.** This small tourist hotel in the center of town has a traditional family atmosphere. Rooms are decorated in light colors. The restaurant, curiously named Ammonia, recalls the World War II sinking of a Norwegian ship of the same name. On the typically Norwegian menu, try the pepper steak. ⊠ *Sam Eydes gt. 67, 3660,* ☎ *35/ 08–21–88,* FAX *35/08–21–89. 39 rooms. Restaurant, bar, pub, nightclub. AE, DC, MC, V.*

Outdoor Activities and Sports

CYCLING

Rjukan's local tourist office rents bikes weekdays 9–7 and weekends 10–6.

FISHING

Telemark has more than 1,000 good fishing lakes. Contact the tourist office to find out about maps, licenses, and guides.

HORSEBACK RIDING

Take the reins of an Icelandic horse on a riding trip organized by **Kalhovd Turisthytte** (⊠ Atrå, ☎ 35/09–05–10) on Hardangervidda. Contact the tourist office for more information.

MOUNTAINEERING

Whether you're an experienced mountain climber or a beginner, **Telemark Opplevelser** (☎ 99/51–31–40) can show you the ropes. They teach all levels of climbing courses and organize wilderness climbing and camping trips.

Morgedal

❺ *77 km (46 mi) southwest of Rjukan via Åmot.*

In the heart of Telemark is Morgedal, the birthplace of modern skiing, thanks to a persistent Sondre Norheim, who in the 19th century perfected his skis and bindings and practiced jumping from his roof. His innovations included bindings that close behind the heel and skis that narrow in the middle to facilitate turning. In 1868, after revamping his skis and bindings, he took off for a 185-km (115-mi) trek to Oslo just to prove it could be done. A hundred years ago, skiers used one long pole, held diagonally, much like high-wire artists. Eventually the use of two short poles became widespread, although purists still feel that the one-pole version is the "authentic" way to ski.

☾ The **Norsk Skieventyr** (The Norwegian Skiing Adventure Center) in Morgedal guides you through the 4,000-year history of the winter sport with life-size exhibits of typical ski cottages and authentic skis and costumes. Displays include the inside of Norway's original and last ski-wax factory, where specialists melted a variety of secret ingredients, including cheese, to make uphill and downhill slides smoother. Visit Norheim's cottage, Øvrebø, above the edge of the forest, where the Olympic flame was actually lit. Several action-packed 3-D skiing films can be seen here. ⊠ *On Rte. 11 between Brunkeberg and Høydalsmo,* ☎ *35/05–42–50.* ⌨ *NKr 50.* ⊙ *Late May–mid-June, daily 11–4; mid-June–mid-Aug., daily 9–7; mid-Aug.–late Aug., daily 11–4.*

Dalen

❻ *60 km (37 mi) southwest of Morgedal.*

The area around Dalen is the place to hike, bike, and be outdoors. From Skien you can take boat tours on the Telemark waterways, a combination of canals and natural lakes between Skien and either Dalen or Notodden.

The trip to Dalen takes you through Ulefoss, where you can leave the boat and visit the neoclassical **Ulefoss Manor** (⊠ Hovedgård, ☎ 35/94–56–10), which dates from 1807. It's open weekdays June through September from 2 PM to 4 PM and Sunday from noon to 3.

The historic **Dalen Hotel** is worth a peek, whether or not you stay there. A number of royal families have been guests, and locals are said to think ghosts haunt its creaky wooden walls. *For trips to Dalen, contact the Telemarkreiser tourist organization,* ☎ *35/90–00–20,* 🌐 *www.telemarkreiser.no.*

Dining and Lodging

$$$ ✕▥ **Dalen Hotel.** At one end of the Telemark Canal, this opulent, Victorian "Swiss-style" hotel has retained its classic original style. Look for the dragonhead carvings and stained-glass windows on the balcony that overlooks the stunning entrance hall. When the weather's fine, you can take a rowboat out for a quiet float or play croquet in the garden. ⊠ *3880,* ☎ *35/07–70–00,* 🄵🄰🄷 *35/07–70–11,* 🌐 *www.dalenhotel.no. 38 rooms. Breakfast room, lobby lounge, meeting room. AE, V. Closed Christmas–Easter.*

Valle

❼ *56 km (35 mi) southeast of Dalen. The Setesdal road, Route 39, follows the Otra River downstream and then runs alongside the Byglandsfjord.*

Near Valle sits **Sylvartun,** a clump of grass-roof cottages that house a local silversmith's workshop, a jewelry shop, and an art gallery. It's also a cultural center that hosts concerts and displays local crafts, including many Hardanger fiddles. Every summer during the "Setesdal Evenings," professional musicians and folk dancers perform during a traditional Norwegian dinner. ⊠ *Rte. 19, Nomeland (near Valle),* ☎ *37/93–63–06.* ⊙ *Silversmith's shop: May–Oct., Mon.–Sat. 10–6, Sun. 11–6. Call for hrs and program schedules.*

OFF THE BEATEN PATH   **SETESDAL MINERAL PARK –** About 97 km (57 mi) south of Valle, just south of Evje, in Hornnes, is an interesting park where rock formations from Norway and elsewhere are displayed inside a dim mountain. ⊠ *Rte. 39, 4737 Evje,* ☎ *37/93–13–10.* ⌨ *NKr 60.* ⊙ *Late June–late Aug., daily 10–6.*

Telemark and the Setesdal Valley A to Z

To research prices, get advice from other travelers, and book travel arrangements, visit www.fodors.com.

BUS TRAVEL

The many bus lines that serve the region are coordinated through Nor-Way Bussekspress in Oslo. Buses in the region rarely run more than twice a day, so get a comprehensive schedule from the tourist office or Nor-Way Bussekspress in Oslo.

➤ BUS INFORMATION: **Nor-Way Bussekspress** (⊠ Oslo Bussterminalen Galleriet, ☎ 815/44–444, FAX 22/17–59–22).

CAR TRAVEL

On Route E18 from Oslo, the drive southwest to Kongsberg takes a little more than an hour. If you arrive by way of the Kristiansand ferry, the drive up Route 37 to Evje takes about an hour as well.

Roads in the southern part of the interior region are open and flat, but others are still curvy and mountainous. Route 11 passes through Heddal and Morgedal, and connects with 37, which goes north to Rjukan and south toward Dalen. Route 11 also connects with 37, the main Setesdal road, which goes through Valle and Evje all the way to Kristiansand.

TRAIN TRAVEL

The train from Oslo S Station to Kongsberg takes 1 hour and 25 minutes; bus connections to Telemark are available. The only train service in the southern part of the region is the Oslo–Stavanger line (via Kristiansand).

VISITOR INFORMATION

➤ TOURIST INFORMATION: **Kongsberg** (⊠ Storgt. 35, ☎ 32/73–50–00). **Notodden** (⊠ Teatergt. 3, ☎ 35/01–50–00). **Rjukan** (⊠ Torget 2, ☎ 35/09–12–90). **Setesdal** (4735 Evje, ☎ 37/93–14–00). **Skien** (⊠ Reiselivets Hus, N. Hjellegt. 18, ☎ 35/90–55–20). **Telemarkreiser** (Telemark Canal tourist organization; ⊠ Nedre Hjellegt. 18, 3702 Skien, ☎ 35/90–00–20, FAX 35/90–00–21, WEB www.telemarkreiser.no).

5 SØRLANDET TO STAVANGER: THE NORTH SEA ROAD

In summer, Oslo's residents migrate to the southern coast to soak up some sunshine. Southern Norway is an outdoor paradise, with a mild summer climate and terrain varying from coastal flatland to inland mountains and forests.

ANY SPLENDID POINTS mark the route of the North Sea Road. Beginning in the relaxed resort town of Kristiansand, the road winds west along the major section of Norway's southern coast, Sørlandet. Wide, sun-kissed, inviting beaches have their blue waters warmed by the Gulf Stream. Sandy terrain turns to coastal flatlands, inland mountain peaks and green forests ideal for cycling, hiking, and mountaineering. Freshwater lakes and rivers, and this section of the ocean, are some of the best places to go salmon fishing—they're also superb for canoeing, kayaking, and rafting. The conditions make the land perfect for such wildlife as beavers, deer, foxes, and many birds.

When the North Sea Road reaches its final destination, it's in a landscape of fjords, islands, mountains, and valleys. It's here where the other major city, Stavanger, lies. Norway's oil capital is cosmopolitan yet small-town charming, with some of the country's best restaurants, hotels, museums, nightlife, and festivals.

Numbers in the margin correspond to points of interest on the Telemark and Sørlandet map in chapter 4.

Arendal

8 *260 km (418 mi) south of Oslo.*

In Arendal's Tyholmen, the old town, there are many painted houses bearing window boxes filled with pink and red flowers. Such dwellings are a common sight in this area. A popular speedboat race attracts international competitors to Arendal each summer.

A rather unusual gallery space, the restored **Bomuldsfabriken** (Cotton Factory) operated from 1898 to 1960 producing jeans, shirts, and cotton flannel clothing. Today, it's home to changing art exhibitions and a permanent collection of 35 works by some of Norway's foremost painters. ⊠ *Oddenvn. 5,* ☎ *37/02–65–19,* WEB *www.bomuldsfabriken.com.* ☉ *Tues.–Sun. noon–4.*

Originally established in 1832, the **Aust-Agder Museet** displays fascinating coastal artifacts and relics, from toys to farm tools. Find out about the 1767 slave ship the *Fredensborg*, and learn more about the region's folk art and geology. ⊠ *Langsægård, Arendal,* ☎ *37/07–35–00.* ☉ *Late June–late Aug., weekdays 10–5, Sat. 9–1, Sun. noon–5; early Aug.–early June, weekdays 9–3, Sat. 9–1, Sun. noon–5.*

OFF THE BEATEN PATH **MERDØGAARD MUSEUM –** On the island of Merdøy, a 30-minute boat ride from Arendal's Langbrygga (long wharf), is an early 18th-century sea captain's home, from 1736, now a museum. After visiting, enjoy a swim on the beach or walk around the island. ⊠ *Merdøy,* ☎ *37/07–35–00.* ☐ *NKr 20.* ☉ *Late June–mid-Aug., daily noon–5.*

Lodging

$$–$$$ 🏨 **Clarion Tyholmen Hotel.** This maritime hotel has the sea at close quarters and a magnificent view of the fjord. The modern decor makes use of much blue and wooden furniture. The hotel's outdoor restaurant, Bryggekanten, serves fish and steak dishes. It's a popular summer spot. ⊠ *Teaterpl. 2, Tyholmen 4801,* ☎ *37/02–68–00,* FAX *37/02–68–01. 60 rooms. 2 restaurants, bar, sauna. AE, DC, MC, V.*

Grimstad

❾ *15 km (9 mi) south of Arendal.*

Grimstad's glory was in the days of sailing ships—about the same time the 15-year-old Henrik Ibsen worked as an apprentice at the local apothecary shop from 1844 to 1850.

Grimstad Apotek is now a part of **Ibsenhuset - Grimstad Bymuseum** (the Ibsen House) and has been preserved with its 1837 interior intact. Ibsen wrote his first play, *Catlina,* here. Every summer Grimstad holds an Ibsen festival celebrating the world famous playwright. The museum also has a maritime department and section honoring Terje Vigen, a folk hero who was the subject of a poem by Ibsen. He is credited with a life-saving ride to Denmark that brought back food for the starving Norwegians. ⊠ *Henrik Ibsens gt. 14, 4890,* ☎ *37/04–04–90.* 🎫 *NKr 25.* ☉ *Mid-May–mid-Aug., Mon.–Sat. 11–5, Sun. 1–5, mid-Aug.–mid-May weekdays 9–2.*

Lillesand

❿ *20 km (12 mi) south of Grimstad.*

An idyllic summer vacation town, Lillesand has one of Norway's best guest (public) harbors, which is usually bustling. The town has many of the region's typical white wooden houses.

In an 1827 Empire-style building, the **Lillesand By og Sjøfartsmuseum** (Lillesand City and Maritime Museum) reconstructs maritime-related work places. You can see how sail makers did their craft and also see the city's first fire pump. ⊠ *Carl Knudsen gården,* ☎ *37/27–04–30.* 🎫 *NKr 15.* ☉ *Mid-June–Aug., weekdays 11–3, Sat. 11–2.*

Dating back to AD 1,000, the 33 ft-long stone **Høvåg Kirke** was lengthened and restored in 1768 and 1828. It wasn't completely finished until 1966. ☎ *37/27–43–31.* ☉ *May–Sept., daily 9–4.*

Lodging

$$–$$$ 🏨 **Lillesand Hotel Norge.** Right on the harbor, this old Norwegian hotel definitely offers rooms with views. The sea-inspired decor in the rooms and public areas is classic yet modern. The restaurant is well regarded by locals as well as visitors. ⊠ *Strandgt. 3, 4790,* ☎ *37/27–01–44,* 🆗 *37/27–30–70,* 🌐 *www.hotelnorge.no. 25 rooms. Restaurant, bar. AE, DC, MC, V.*

Outdoor Activities and Sports

DIVING

ProDykk Norway (⊠ Skottevig, ☎ 37/27–31–10) dive center rents and sells diving equipment, arranges tours, and teaches courses.

Kristiansand

⓫ *55 km (34 mi) south of Grimstad on E18.*

Nicknamed *Sommerbyen* ("the Summer City"), Norway's fifth largest city has 73,000 inhabitants. Kristiansand has good national and international travel connections. Norwegians come here for its sun-soaked beaches and its beautiful harbor. It has also become known internationally for the **Quart Festival** (☎ 38/07–02–88, 🌐 www.quartfestival.com), which brings in cool bands from all quarters every July.

According to legend, in 1641 King Christian IV marked the four corners of Kristiansand with his walking stick, and within that framework the grid of wide streets was laid down. The center of town, called the

Kvadrat, still retains the grid, even after numerous fires. In the north-east corner is **Posebyen,** one of northern Europe's largest collections of low, connected wooden house settlements. Kristiansand's **Fiske-torvet** (fish market) is near the south corner of the town's grid, right on the sea. **Christiansholm Festning** (◷ mid-May–Aug., daily 9–9) is a fortress on a promontory opposite Festningsgata. Completed in 1672, the circular building with 15-ft-thick walls has played more a decorative role than a defensive one; it was used once, in 1807, to defend the city against British invasion. Now it contains art exhibits.

The Gothic Revival **Kristiansand Domkirke** (Kristiansand Cathedral) from 1885 is the third-largest church in Norway. It often hosts summer concerts in addition to the weeklong International Church Music Festival (☎ 38/12–09–40) in mid-May. Organ, chamber, and gospel music are on the bill. ✉ *Kirkegt., 4610,* ☎ *38/02–11–88,* WEB *www.kirkefestspill.no.* ◻ *Free.* ◷ *June–Aug., daily 9–2.*

A wealthy merchant-shipowner built **Gimle Gård** (Gimle Manor) around 1800 in the Empire style. It displays furnishings from that period, including paintings, silver, and hand-blocked wallpaper. To get there from the city center, head north across the Otra River on Bus 22 or drive to Route E18 and cross the bridge over the Otra to Parkveien. Turn left onto Ryttergangen and drive to Gimleveien; take a right. ✉ *Gimlevn. 23, 4630,* ☎ *38/09–02–28,* WEB *www.museumsnett.no/gimlegaard.* ◻ *NKr 45.* ◷ *Mid-June–mid-Aug., weekdays noon–4, Sun. noon–6; May–mid-June and mid-Aug.–early Jan., Sun. noon–5.*

The **Agder naturmuseum og botaniske hage.** (Agder Nature Museum and Botanical Gardens) takes on Sørlandet's natural history from the Ice Age to the present, examining the coast and moving on to the high mountains. There's a rainbow of minerals on display, as well as a rose garden with varieties from 1850. There's even the country's largest collection of cacti. ✉ *Gimlevn. 23, 4630,* ☎ *38/09–23–88,* WEB *www. museumsnett.no/naturmuseum.* ◻ *NKr 45.* ◷ *Mid-June–mid-Aug., Tues.–Fri. 10–6; Sat.–Mon. noon–6; mid-Aug.–mid-June, Tues.–Fri. 10–3, Sun. noon–5.*

The striking runestone in the cemetery of **Oddernes Kirke** (Oddernes Church) tells that Øyvind, godson of Saint Olav, built this church in 1040 on property he inherited from his father. One of the oldest churches in Norway, it is dedicated to Saint Olav. ✉ *Oddernesvn., 6430,* ☎ *38/09–01–87.* ◻ *Free.* ◷ *May–Aug., Sun.–Fri. 9–2.*

At the **Kristiansand Kanonmuseum** (Cannon Museum) you can see the cannon that the occupying Germans rigged up during World War II. With calibers of 15 inches, the cannon was said to be capable of shooting a projectile halfway to Denmark. In the bunkers, related military materials are on display. ✉ *Møvik,* ☎ *38/08–50–90.* ◻ *NKr 50.* ◷ *May–early June and early Sept., Thurs.–Sun. 11–6; early June–early Sept., Mon.–Sun. 11–6; Oct.–Apr., Sun. noon–5.*

☝ **Vest-Agder Fylkesmuseum** (County Museum), the region's largest cultural museum, has more than 40 old buildings on display. The structures, transported from other locations in the area, include two *tun*—farm buildings traditionally set in clusters around a common area, which suited the extended families. If you have children with you, check out the old-fashioned toys, which can still be played with. The museum is 4 km (2½ mi) east of Kristiansand on Route E18. ✉ *Kongs-gård,* ☎ *38/09–02–28,* WEB *www.museumsnett.no/vafymuseum.* ◻ *NKr 30.* ◷ *Mid-June–mid-Aug., Mon.–Sat. 10–6, Sun. noon–6; mid-Aug.–mid-June, Sun. noon–5.*

A favorite with hikers and strolling nannies, **Ravnedalen** (Raven Valley) is a lush park that's filled with flowers in springtime. Wear comfortable shoes to hike the narrow, winding paths up the hills and climb the 200 steps up to a 304-ft lookout. ✉ *Northwest of Kristiansand.*

One of Norway's most popular attractions, **Kristiansand Dyreparken** is actually five separate parks, including a water park (bring bathing suits and towels); a forested park; an entertainment park; a theme park; and a zoo, which contains an enclosure for Scandinavian animals such as wolves and elk, and a large breeding ground for Bactrian camels. The theme park, **Kardemomme By** (Cardamom Town), is named for a book by Norwegian illustrator and writer Thorbjørn Egner. A new attraction, My Africa, allows you to move along a bridge observing native savanna animals such as giraffe and zebras. The park is 11 km (6 mi) east of town. *Kristiansand Dyreparken, Kardemomme By,* ☎ *38/04–97–25,* WEB *www.dyreparken.no.* ✉ *NKr 200 includes admission to all parks and rides.* ⊙ *Mid-May–Sept., weekdays 10–7; Sept.–mid-May, daily 10–3:30.*

Dining and Lodging

$$$ ✕ **Luihn.** This fine restaurant in the center of the city makes an elegant, intimate setting for a quiet dinner. The five special fish dishes, such as catfish with pesto and pasta stand out; the wine selection is impressive. ✉ *Rådhusgt. 15,* ☎ *38/10–66–50. AE, DC, MC, V.*

$$–$$$ ✕ **Sjøhuset Restaurant.** Considered one of the city's best restaurants, Sjøhuset was built in 1892 as a salt warehouse. Now the white-trimmed red building has developed a well-earned reputation for seafood, its specialty. Take a seat on the sunny patio and dine on fresh lobster. ✉ *Østre Strandgt. 12A,* ☎ *38/02–62–60. AE, DC, MC, V.*

$–$$ ✕ **India Tandoori Restaurant.** Near Slotts Kvartalet, you can sample traditional Indian fare in a rich red interior. Vegetarians have their own menu. Try the Mixed Tandoori or Tandoori Sangam, both combinations of several popular dishes that are cooked in the emblematic oven of the same name. ✉ *Tordenskjolds gt. 12,* ☎ *38/02–52–20. AE, DC, MC, V.*

$$–$$$ 🏨 **Rica Dyreparken Hotel.** Built like Noah's Ark, this 2001 hotel was designed to delight children of all ages. Inspired by the park, many of the rooms go a little wild, with tiger-stripe chairs and paw prints on walls. Children have their own playroom and cinema on board the ark. ✉ *Dyreparken, Kristiansand 4609.* ☎ *38/14–64–00,* FAX *38/14–64–01,* WEB *www.rica.no. 160 rooms. Restaurant, bar, children's programs.*

$$ 🏨 **Clarion Ernst Park Hotel.** Convenience is the main reason to stay at this rather traditional city hotel. Centrally located, the hotel is close to the city beach and shopping street Markens. You can stay connected on-line at the Internet café, an uncommon sight in Norway. A small tourist office makes it easy to inquire about local attractions and buy tickets to Dyreparken. ✉ *Rådhusgt. 2, 4601,* ☎ *38/12–86–03,* FAX *38/02–03–07,* WEB *www.ernst.no. 112 rooms, 4 suites. Restaurant, 2 bars, nightclub, meeting rooms. AE, DC, MC, V.*

$ 🏨 **Quality Hotel Kristiansand.** Nicknamed "the children's hotel," this chain hotel is perfect for young families on the go. Inside, there's a huge children's playroom, activity leaders, childcare, and a children's buffet. Even more toys are outdoors. Rooms are comfortable, with cheerful pastel walls and wood furniture. ✉ *Sørlandsparken, 4696,* ☎ *38/17–77–77,* FAX *38/17–77–80,* WEB *www.quality-kristiansand.no. 210 rooms. Restaurant, indoor pool, baby-sitting, children's programs, nursery, playground. AE, DC, MC, V.*

Nightlife and the Arts

Markens gate, the city's main street, is the place for clubbing, pubbing, and live music. **Kick Café** (✉ Dronningensgt. 8, ☎ 38/02–62–44) has become a hip spot for warm summer evenings. **Dr. Fjeld** (✉ Rådhusgt. 2, ☎ 38/12–86–03) at Clarion Ernst Park Hotel has become a popular place to dance the night away. Party types head to **Lobbybaren** (✉ Vestre Strandgt. 7, ☎ 38/11–21–00) at Radisson SAS Caledonien Hotel. Every summer **Agder Teater** (✉ Kongensgt. 2A, ☎ 38/02–43–00) moves its performances outdoors to Fjøreheia near Grimstad. **Musikkens Hus** (✉ Kongensgt. 54, ☎ 38/14–87–30) schedules musical concerts throughout the year. The **Kristiansand Symfoniorkester** (Kristiansand Symphony Orchestra; ✉ Kongensgt. 6, ☎ 38/02–24–40) performs year-round.

Outdoor Activities and Sports

Troll Mountain (✉ Setesdal Rafting og Aktivitetssenter, Rte. 9, Evje, ☎ 37/93–11–77), about one hour's drive from Kristiansand, organizes many activities. Be it mountain climbing, sailing, biking, rafting, paintball, or even beaver or deer safaris, this is the place for outdoorsy types.

BIKING

Kristiansand has 70 km (42 mi) of bike trails around the city. The tourist office can recommend routes and rentals. **Kristiansand Sykkelsenter** (Grim Torv, ☎ 38/02–68–35) rents a range of bicycles and off-road vehicles.

CLIMBING

Whether you're an experienced pro or just a gung-ho beginner, you can rent climbing equipment or learn more about the sport from **Klatrehuset på Samsen** (✉ Vestervn. 2, ☎ 38/07–54-17).

FISHING

Just north of Kristiansand there's excellent trout, perch, and eel fishing at Lillesand's **Vestre Grimevann** lake. You can get a permit at any sports store or at the tourist office.

GOLF

Enjoy Kristiansand's sunny weather and a round of golf at **Kristiansand Golfklubb** (☎ 38/14–85–60), which has a 9-hole course, equipment rentals, instruction, and a café. On rainy days, there's always **Kristiansand Sørlandsparken** (✉ Barstølv 28B, ☎ 38/09–80–08), which has a modern simulator, courses, driving range, and billiards.

HIKING

In addition to the gardens and steep hills of Ravnedalen, the **Baneheia Skog** (Baneheia Forest) is full of evergreens, small lakes, and paths that are ideal for a lazy walk or a challenging run. It's just a 15-minute walk north from the city center.

RIDING

If you're at home in the saddle, then head to **Islandshestsenteret** (The Icelandic Horse Center; ✉ Søgne, ☎ 38/1116–98–82). Specializing in the Icelandic horse breed, this center offers courses, various trips, and camping for children and adults.

WATER SPORTS

Kuholmen Marina (✉ Roligheden Camping, ☎ 38/09–67–22) rents boats, water skis, and water scooters. **Dykkeren** (✉ Dvergsnestangen, ☎ 38/05–86–20) has everything related to diving, including organized trips and classes as well as equipment.

Combining history with sailing, the magnificent square-rigger **Sørlandet** (✉ Gravene 2, Kristiansand, ☎ 38/02–98–90), built in 1927, takes passengers for two weeks, usually stopping for several days in a northern European port. The price is about NKr 7,000.

Shopping

Kristiansand has a broad range of shops next to Dyreparken. **Sørlands Senteret** (☎ 38/04–91–00) is one of the region's larger shopping centers, with 96 stores, a pharmacy, and a post office. **Kvadraturen** (☎ 38/02–44–11) has 300 stores and eating spots.

Vennesla

⑫   *15 km (9 mi) north of Kristiansand. Follow Route 39 from Kristiansand to Mosby, veer right onto 405, and continue to Grovane.*

Untouched forests and excellent salmon fishing in the Otra river have made Vennesla a popular outdoor destination.

Setesdalsbanen (Setesdal Railway), a 7-km-long (4½ mi) stretch of narrow-gauge track, has a steam locomotive from 1896 and carriages from the early 1900s that are available for round-trip rides. The railway remained in normal use until 1962. An exhibition back at Grovane station explains the history of the locomotive. ⊠ *Vennesla Stasjon*, ☎ *38/15–64–82*, WEB *www.setesdalsbanen.no.* ⊡ *NKr 70.* ☼ *Mid-June–early Sept., Sun. 11:30 and 2; Mar.–June, Tues.–Fri. 6, Sun. 11:30 and 2.*

Mandal

⑬   *42 km (28 mi) southwest from Kristiansand and 82 km (51 mi) from Evje.*

Mandal is Norway's southernmost town, famous for its historic core of well-preserved wooden houses and its beautiful long beach, Sjøsanden.

Mandal Kirke, built in 1821, is Norway's largest Empire-style wooden church. ☎ *38/26–35–77.* ☼ *Tues.–Thurs. 11–2.*

Lindesnes Fyr, Norway's first lighthouse, was lit in the Lindesnes municipality in February 1656, at the southernmost point in Norway. It was closed the same year by the Danish king after complaints of fire and didn't re-open until 69 years later. Many different lighting methods have been used since, including coal in the early 1800s. An exhibition in the museum traces the changing methods. ⊠ *Mandal*, ☎ *38/26–19–02.* ☼ *Open during daylight hrs.*

Ogna

⑭   *93 km (57 mi) from Flekkefjord on Route 42.*

Ogna has a stretch of sandy beach that inspired many Norwegian artists, among them Kitty Kielland (1843–1914), who was best known for her impressionist landscape paintings.

The complex making up **Hå Gamle Prestegaard** (Old Parsonage) was built in 1637 to face the ocean. It now houses a gallery of changing art and cultural exhibitions that are often worth visiting. ⊠ *Ogna*, ☎ *51/43–39–44.* ⊡ *NKr 20.* ☼ *May–mid-Sept., weekdays 11–6, Sat. noon–5, Sun. noon–7; mid-Sept.–Apr., Sat. noon–5, Sun. noon–6.*

Many ancient monuments are still around, notably the **Hå gravesite** below the Hå parsonage near the Obrestad lighthouse. The roughly 60 mounds, including two shaped like stars and one shaped like a boat, date from around AD 500. To get here take coastal Route 44.

Outdoor Activities and Sports

FISHING

Three of the 10 best fishing rivers in Norway, the Ognaelva, Håelva, and Figgjo, are in Jæren, just south of Stavanger. Fishing licenses, sold in grocery stores and gas stations, are required at all of them.

Sandnes

🚩 *25 km (16 mi) south of Stavanger, 52 km (32 mi) north of Orre.*

For good reason, this city of 53,000 is called Bicycle Town. Local company Øglend DBS, founded in 1898, has manufactured nearly two million bicycles here. Sandnes has 200 free city bicycles, miles of bicycle paths, a bicycle museum, the Bicycle Blues Festival, a bicycle library, and an active racing club. Besides bicycles, brickworks, pottery, and textiles have been the traditional industries. Eleven factory outlets and art galleries sell historical and modern Sandnes crafts and products at reduced prices.

Even oatmeal gets its own museum in Norway. **Krossens Havremølle Museum** (Krossen's Oatmeal Museum) shows the significance oats have played in the region and the country. National, industrial, and cultural artifacts are on display, as is an authentic model of a mill showing how oats are processed. ⊠ *Storgt. 26,* ☎ *51/67–06–96,* WEB *www.havre.museum.no.* ☉ *Mid-June–mid-Aug., daily noon–5; mid-Aug.–mid-June, Sun. noon–3.* ☒ *NKr 30.*

Dining and Lodging

$ ✕🏨 **Hotel GamlaVærket Gjæstgiveri og Tracteringsted.** A former brick and pottery works, this intimate hotel has a warm, old-fashioned charm. Simple white-wall rooms have slanted ceilings and dark wood furniture. The well-regarded restaurant has a menu that ranges from sandwiches to seven-course meals. ⊠ *St. Olavs gt. 38, 4306,* ☎ *51/68–51–70,* FAX *51/68–51–71,* WEB *www.gamlavaerket.no. 14 rooms. Restaurant. AE, DC, MC, V.*

Outdoor Activities and Sports

BICYCLING

Can you actually visit Norway's bicycle town and not spin a few wheels yourself? If the cycling mood strikes, borrow one of the 200 that are available for free downtown. You can rent one at **Spinn Sykkelshop** (☎ 51/68–62–65) or **Naboen** (☎ 51/57–07–10). Ask at the tourist office for the bicycle maps it has of the area. **Scan One Tours** (☎ 51/89–39–00) organizes and sells packaged bicycle trips.

WATER SPORTS

Scandinavia's largest indoor swimming facility, **Havanna Badeland** holds a total of 264,000 gallons (1 million liters) of water. A 300-ft water slide, playhouse, reading corner, whirlpool baths, saunas, and a Turkish bath all entertain children and adults. The Havanna Lekeland next door has a ball pool, play equipment, climbing labyrinths, and five slides. ⊠ *Hanavn. 17, Sandnes,* ☎ *51/62–92–00 water park; 51/68–48–98 playland,* WEB *www.havanna.no.* ☒ *NKr 110 for playland and water park.* ☉ *Daily 10–8.*

OUTLET STORES

Sandnes has a tempting selection of factory outlets offering as much as 70% off regular priced goods. Several times a year, the local tourist board organizes free bus trips there. The region's most visited factory outlet, **Byrkjedalstunet** (⊠ Rte. 45, Dirdal, ☎ 51/61–29–00), has a candle-maker, children's activities, and a mountain farm as well as stores selling handicrafts and souvenirs. For fine quality porcelain, go to **Figgjo** (☎ 51/68–35–70), in the nearby town of the same name. It's the largest supplier to professional kitchens in Norway. **Skjæveland** (⊠ Ålgård, ☎ 51/61–24–19) carries high-quality knit sweaters and jackets for men and women.

Ullandhaug

16 *15 km (9 mi) west of Sandnes.*

Although reconstructed, this Jernaldergarden Iron Age farm complex from the Migration Period (AD 350–550) feels like the real thing. The reconstructed historical buildings have been positioned on original foundations. Relics such as a Bronze Age gravestone have been discovered here. Research is still underway. Taste some mead, the Vikings' favorite drink, or have breakfast or lunch on wooden benches before fireplaces. ⊠ *Ullandhaugvn. 3, Ullandhaug,* ☎ *51/84–60–00.* ▣ *NKr 30.* ⊙ *Mid-June–mid-Aug., daily 11–4; May–mid-Oct., Sun. noon–6; mid-Aug.–mid-June, by appointment.*

The site where Norway was founded has been memorialized by the **Sverd i fjell** (Three Swords Monument). The three huge bronze swords were unveiled by King Olav in 1983 and done by artist Fritz Røed. The memorial is dedicated to King Harald Hårfagre (Harald the Fairhaired), who through an 872 battle at Hafrsfjord managed to unite Norway into one kingdom. The Viking swords' sheaths were modeled on others found throughout the country; the crowns atop the swords represent the different Norwegian districts that took part in the battle. ⊠ *1½ km (1 mi) east on Grannesveien Ullandhaug to the Hafrsfjord.*

OFF THE BEATEN PATH
> **UTSTEIN KLOSTER** – Originally the palace of Norway's first king, Harald Hårfagre, and later the residence of King Magnus VI, Utstein was used as a monastery from 1265 until 1537, when it reverted to the royal family. Buses depart for Utstein weekdays from Stavanger at 12:15, returning from the monastery at 4:05. It's about a half-hour drive from Stavanger. Travel north on coastal highway 1, through the world's second-longest undersea car tunnel. There's a toll of NKr 75 for the tunnel passage.

Stavanger

17 *3 km (2 mi) north of Ullandhaug, 256 km (123 mi) from Kristiansand, 4½ hrs from Bergen by car and ferry, 8–9 hrs from Oslo.*

Stavanger has always prospered from the riches of the sea. During the 19th century, huge harvests of brisling and herring established it as the sardine capital of the world. A resident is still called a Siddis, from S (tavanger) plus *iddis,* which means "sardine label." The city's symbol, fittingly enough, is the key of a sardine can.

During the past three decades, a different product from the sea has been Stavanger's lifeblood—oil. Since its discovery in the late 1960s, North Sea oil hasn't just transformed the economy. Stavanger has emerged as cosmopolitan and vibrant, more bustling than other cities with a population of only 110,000. Norway's most international city, it has attracted residents from more than 90 different nations. Roam its cobblestone streets or wander the harborfront and you're likely to see many cozy cafés and fine restaurants as well as lively clubs and pubs. For many visitors, Stavanger is a place to be entertained.

The charm of the city's past is on view in **Old Stavanger,** Northern Europe's largest and best preserved wooden house settlement. The 150 houses here were built in the late 1700s and early 1800s. Wind down the narrow, cobblestone streets past small, white houses and craft shops with many-paned windows and terra-cotta roof tiles.

Construction on Stavanger's cathedral began in 1125. Legend has it that Bishop Reinald of Winchester constructed the **Stavanger Domkirke**

(Stavanger Cathedral) to marry the king to his third wife after accepting his divorce from Queen Malmfrid. Originally the church was built in an Anglo-Norman style, probably with the aid of English craftsmen. Patron saint St. Svithun's arm is believed to be among the original relics. Largely destroyed by fire in 1272, the church was rebuilt to include a Gothic chancel. The result: its once elegant lines are now festooned with macabre death symbols and airborne putti. Of all of Norway's churches from the Middle Ages, the cathedral is the only one that has generally retained its original style and been continually in use. Next to the cathedral is **Kongsgård,** formerly a residence of bishops and kings but now a school and not open to visitors. ⊠ *Near Torget,* ☏ *Free.* ☉ *Mid-May–mid-Sept., Mon.–Tues. 11–6, Wed.–Sat. 10–6, Sun. 11–6; mid-Sept.–mid-May, Wed.–Sat. 10–3.*

☾ Designed to help children learn about the prehistoric past, the **Arkeologisk Museum** (Museum of Archaeology) has changing exhibitions, instructive models, open archives, and movies designed to make learning history fun. Children can research their ancestors in computer games, treasure hunts, and other activities. In summer, children can look through stones in search of fossils and other signs of life. There's also old-fashioned games and toys, which have become popular attractions. ⊠ *Peder Klowsgt. 30A,* ☏ *51/84–60–00.* ⊡ *NKr 20.* ☉ *June–Aug., Tues.–Sun. 11–5; Sept.–May, Tues. 11–8, Wed.–Sat. 11–3, Sun. 11–4.*

Stavanger Museum is made up of four other local museums: Stavanger Sjøfartsmuseum, Norsk Hermetikkmuseum, Ledaal, and Breidablikk.

A collection of preserved birds and animals from around the world is permanently on display at the **Stavanger Museum.** Re-enactments of church life, school, and artisans at work trace the city's growth from its 12th-century start to the oil city it is today. ⊠ *Muségt. 16,* ☏ *51/84–27–00,* WEB *www.stavanger.museum.no.* ⊡ *NKr 40.* ☉ *Mid-June–mid–Aug., daily 11–4; early–mid-June and mid-Aug.–late Aug., Mon.–Thurs. 11–3, Sun. 11–4; Sept.–May, Sun. 11–4 or by appointment.*

Breidablikk manor house has a perfectly preserved interior and exterior and feels as if the owner has only momentarily slipped away. An outstanding example of what the Norwegians call "Swiss-style" architecture, this house was built by the Norwegian merchant and ship owner Lars Berentsen, from 1881 to 1882. In spite of its foreign label, the house is uniquely Norwegian, inspired by National Romanticism. ⊠ *Eiganesvn. 40A,* ☏ *51/84–27–00,* WEB *www.stavanger.museum.no.* ⊡ *NKr 40.* ☉ *Mid-June–mid-Aug., daily 11–4; mid-Aug.–mid-June, Sun. 11–4 or by appointment.*

Ledaal, the royal family's Stavanger residence, is a mansion museum and is used for receptions by the Stavanger Council. From 1799 to 1803, it was built for shipping magnate Gabriel Schanche Kielland. A prime example of neoclassical style in western Norway, its interior furnishings are done in rococo, Empire, and Biedermeier styles. The second-floor library is dedicated to famed writer Alexander Kielland, a social critic and satirist. ⊠ *Eiganesvn. 45,* ☏ *51/84–27–00,* WEB *www.stavanger. museum.no.* ⊡ *NKr 40.* ☉ *Mid-June–mid-Aug., daily 11–4; mid-Aug.–mid-June, Sun. 11–4 or by appointment.*

The fascinating **Norsk Hermetikkmuseum** (Norwegian Canning Museum) is within an authentic, former canning factory. From the 1890s to the 1960s, canning fish products like brisling, fish balls, and sardines was Stavanger's main industry. On special activity days, the public can try their hands at parts of the production process, sometimes tasting newly smoked brisling. On the first Sunday of every month and Tuesdays and Thursdays in summer, the ovens used for smoking fish are stoked up once again. ⊠ *Øvre Strandgt. 88A,* ☎ *51/84–27–00,* 𝖶𝖤𝖡 *www.stavanger.museum.no.* 🖾 *NKr 40.* ☉ *Mid-June–mid-Aug., daily 11–4; early June and late Aug., Mon.–Thurs. 11–3, Sun. 11–4; Sept.–May, Sun. 11–4 or by appointment.*

Along Strandkaien, warehouses face the wharf; the shops, offices, and apartments face the street on the other side. Housed in the only two shipping merchants' houses that remain completely intact is the **Sjøfartsmuseet** (The Stavanger Maritime Museum). Dating back to 1770–1840, the restored buildings trace the past 200 years of trade, sea-traffic, and shipbuilding. Visit a turn-of-the-20th-century general store, an early 1900s merchant's apartment, and a sail maker's loft. A reconstruction of a shipowner's office as a well as a memorial are also here, as are two ships: *Anna af Sand* (1848) and *Wyvern* (1896). ⊠ *Nedre Strandgt. 17–19,* ☎ *51/84–27–00,* 𝖶𝖤𝖡 *www.stavanger.museum.no.* 🖾 *NKr 40.* ☉ *Mid-June–mid-Aug., daily 11–4; early June–mid-June and mid–late Aug., Mon.–Thurs. 11–3, Sun. 11–4; Sept.–May, Sun. 11–4 or by appointment.*

★ Resembling a shiny offshore oil platform, the dynamic **Norsk Oljemuseum** (Norwegian Petroleum Museum) is an absolute must-see. In 1969, oil was discovered off the coast of Norway. This 1999 museum explains how oil forms, how it's found and produced, its many uses, and its impact on Norway. Interactive multimedia exhibits accompany original artifacts, models, and films. A reconstructed offshore platform includes oil workers' living quarters—as well as the sound of drilling and the smell of oil. The highly recommended museum café, by restaurateurs Bølgen & Moi, serves dinners as well as lighter fare. ⊠ *Kjeringholmen, Stavanger Havn,* ☎ *51/93–93–00,* 𝖶𝖤𝖡 *www.norskolje.museum.no.* 🖾 *NKr 75.* ☉ *Sept.–May, Mon.–Sat. 10–4, Sun. 10–6; June–Aug., daily 10–7.*

If you have a Norwegian branch on your family tree, trace your roots at **Det Norske Utvandresenteret,** in a harborside wharf house from the early 1700s. The Norwegian Emigration Center has passenger lists, parish registers, census records, and a comprehensive collection of books on Norway's rural past. Bring along any information you have, especially the dates and places from which your ancestors left Norway. Every year, the center organizes the annual Norwegian Emigration Festival, with exhibitions, concerts, and excursions to historical sites. ⊠ *Strandkaien 31,* ☎ *51/53–88–60,* 𝖥𝖠𝖷 *51/53–88–63,* 𝖶𝖤𝖡 *www.emigrationcenter.com.* 🖾 *NKr 35.* ☉ *Mon. and Wed.–Fri. 9–3, Tues. 9–7.*

Rogaland Kunstmuseum (Rogaland Museum of Fine Arts) has the country's largest collection of works by Lars Hertervig (1830–1902), the greatest Romantic painter of Norwegian landscapes. With Norwegian paintings, drawings, and sculptures, the museum's permanent collection covers the early 19th century to the present. The Halvdan Haftsten Collection has paintings and drawings done between the two world wars. There's also a collection of works by Kitty Kielland. The museum is near Mosvannet (Mos Lake), which is just off highway E18 at the northern end of downtown. ⊠ *Tjensvoll 6, Mosvannsparken,* ☎ *51/53–05–20.* 🖾 *NKr 50.* ☉ *Tues.–Sun. 11–4.*

As Stavanger began to become an important town in the Middle Ages, "watchmen" were hired to look out for fires, crime, and anything else out of the ordinary. The **Vektermuseet i Valbergtårnet** (The Watchman's Museum in the Valberg Tower) examines the role the watchmen played in keeping the town safe. The Valbergtårnet was built in 1850–53 to give a panoramic view of the town below. With so many wooden houses, an early warning was essential. The view remains as incredible as ever. ⊠ *Valbergtårnet,* ☎ *51/89–55–01,* 𝖶𝖤𝖡 *www.stavanger.kommune.no/solverg.* 🖾 *NKr 10.* ☉ *Mon.–Wed. and Fri. 10–4, Thurs. 10–6, Sat. 10–2.*

Opened at the end of 2001, the **Norsk Barnemuseum** (Norwegian Children's Museum) has Norway's largest collection of children's toys. Storytelling, dramatic performances, and other activities focus on the country's culture and history. ⊠ *Sølvberget (Stavanger Culture Center),* ☎ *51/91–23–90,* WEB *www.norskbarne.museum.no.* ☐ *NKr 65.* ☉ *Wed–Fri. 1–7, Sat. noon–5, Sun. 1–5.*

Take a scented stroll in Stavanger's wild rose garden. At the **Botanisk Hage** (Botanical Gardens), you can find many leaved and flowered earthly delights. Some 2,000 herbs and perennials are here. ⊠ *Rektor Natvig Pedersensv. 40,* ☎ *51/50–78–61.* ☐ *Free.* ☉ *Apr.–Sept., weekdays 7 AM–8 PM, weekends 10–8; Oct.–Mar., weekdays 7–5, weekends 10–5.*

More than 35 historical military and civilian planes make up the collection at the **Flyhistorisk Museum Sola** (History of Flying Museum, Sola municipality), which emphasizes the history from World War II on. Besides checking out changing exhibitions, you can sit in a passenger seat of 1950s Metropolitan and see the changing designs that the Norwegian Air Force's jet fighters have gone through. ⊠ *Sjøflyhaven, Stavanger Lufthavn,* ☎ *51/65–56–57.* ☐ *NKr 40.* ☉ *Late June–mid-Aug., daily noon–4; May–late June and late Aug.–Nov., Sun. noon–4.*

☾ **Kongeparken** amusement park has go-carts, radio cars, bumper boats, Norway's longest bobsled run, and its largest merry-go-round. In the Chocolate Factory, children can make their own real Freia-brand milk chocolate. ⊠ *4330 Ålgård,* ☎ *51/61–71–11,* WEB *www.kongeparken.no.* ☐ *NKr 125; free for children shorter than 35 inches.* ☉ *May–Sept., daily 10–6.*

OFF THE BEATEN PATH

PREIKESTOLEN – The Pulpit Rock, a huge cube with a vertical drop of 2,000 ft, is not a good destination if you suffer from vertigo. It has a heart-stopping view. The clifflike rock sits on the banks of the finger-shape Lysefjord. You can join a tour to get to the region's best-known attraction, or you can do it on your own from early June to early September by taking the bus costing NKr 45 one-way from the town of Tau to the Pulpit Rock. The buses are paired with morning ferry departures from Stavanger at 8:20 and 9:15. Then you can either hike the two-hour walk on a marked trail or ride horseback. (The ferry and bus take a total of about 40 minutes from Stavanger.)

LYSEFJORDSENTERET – Lysefjord Center has a shape that mimics the mountains. The multimedia simulation, *Saga of the Fjord*, shows how a trickling brook created this sliver of a fjord. You'll also learn about the geology and culture of Lysefjord. A ferry to the bottom of Pulpit Rock drops off passengers midway (for more information, call **Rogaland Trafikk** (☎ 51/86–87–00) or **Clipper Fjord Sightseeing** (☎ 51/89–52–70). The center is free but the multimedia simulation costs NKr 20. ⊠ *Oanes, Forsand,* ☎ *51/70–31–23.* ☉ *May–Aug., weekdays noon–6, Sat. noon–7, Sun. noon–8.*

Dining

Stavanger has established a reputation for culinary excellence. In fact, the city has the distinction of having the most bars and restaurants per capita in Norway. Many restaurant menus burst with sumptuous international dishes. Throughout the year, the Culinary Institute of Norway, Gladmat festival, Garlic Week, Stavanger Wine Festival, Chili Festival, and Creole Week all call the city home.

$$$–$$$$ ✕ **Cartellet Restaurant.** The elegant dining room reflects the timelessness of this classic restaurant that goes back to 1890. The gold-accented

decor makes use of stone walls, dark wood interior and leather furniture, and richly colored paintings. Based on fresh, seasonal ingredients from Norway's fjords and mountains, the highly regarded menu changes every day. ✉ *Øvre Holmegt. 8,* ☎ *51/89–60–22. Reservations essential. AE, DC, MC, V.*

$$–$$$$ ✕ **Straen Fiskerestaurant.** Right on the quay, this esteemed fish restaurant is "world famous throughout Norway." An old-fashioned grandmother's decor of memorabilia and white-clothed tables make it feel like home. If you're traveling in groups, reserve the bookshelf-lined library dining room. Try the famous fish soup of salmon and cream of shellfish, grilled monkfish, or lutefisk. The three-course meal of the day is always the best value. The aquavit bar carries more than 30 different kinds. ✉ *Nedre Strandgt. 15,* ☎ *51/84–37–00. AE, DC, MC, V.*

$$$ ✕ **Craigs Kjøkken & Bar.** Oklahoman Craig Whitson's café–restaurant is a great place for wining as well as dining. Stylish glass cabinets house the collection of more than 600 bottles of wine, which focus on Italy, and the Rhone and Alsace regions of France. This is one of the city's best places to dine, and the food here is seasonal, experimental, and eclectic, its influences ranging from Mediterranean to Asian. Try the popular spring lamb burger, or the juicy, huge Babe burger. The café hosts popular annual events such as the chili and wine festivals. Whitson's offbeat sense of humor comes through in the "12 disciples" that sit against one wall—12 smoked, salted, and dried pigs' heads. ✉ *Breitorget,* ☎ *51/93–95–90. AE, DC, MC, V.*

$$–$$$ ✕ **Gaffel & Karaffel.** Framed shiny forks playfully line the red walls of this hip restaurant, whose name means "fork and carafe." Called a tapas restaurant, its international menu boasts delights such as cheese-filled salmon rolls, beefsteak sukiyaki, and herb-marinated catfish. ✉ *Øvre Holmegt. 20,* ☎ *51/86–41–58. AE, DC, MC, V.*

$$–$$$ ✕ **Harry Pepper.** Norway's first Tex-Mex restaurant is still considered one of the country's best. Earthtones, cacti, and tacky souvenirs combine to make the joint light-hearted and playful. Try the sizzling fajitas or the lime grilled fish kebab served with triple pesto. Have a tequila shot or two at its lively bar. ✉ *Øvre Holmegt. 15,* ☎ *51/89–39–93. AE, DC, V.*

$$–$$$ ✕ **Saken er Biff.** A Norwegian country-style steakhouse, this restaurant has a whole lot more than beef on its menu. Be daring and try venison, reindeer, or moose prepared rare, medium, or well-done. ✉ *Skagenkaien 28,* ☎ *51/89–60–80. AE, DC, MC, V.*

$$–$$$ ✕ **Sjøhuset Skagen.** A sort of museum, this 18th-century former boathouse is filled with wooden beams, ship models, lobster traps, and other sea relics. The Norwegian and international menu has such dishes as chicken confit or the Hunter's Dream, grilled medallions of reindeer, potatoes, and vegetables, which comes highly recommended. ✉ *Skagenkaien 16,* ☎ *51/89–51–80. AE, DC, MC, V.*

$$–$$$ ✕ **Timbuktu Bar and Restaurant.** Timbuktu is closer than you might think. But it's not the African city or a far-off, vague state of mind. Instead, it's one of Stavanger's trendier places to eat. Within its airy interior of blonde wood and yellow and black, enthusiastic chefs serve Asian-inspired cuisine with African ingredients such as tuna fish from Madagascar. Known for its NKr 350 three-course dinners and its sushi, the restaurant often has celebrity chefs visiting and hosts special events such as salsa parties and nights of Spanish tapas. ✉ *Nedre Strandgt. 15,* ☎ *51/84–37–40. AE, DC, MC, V.*

$$–$$$ ✕ **Vertshuset Mat & Vin.** Traditional Norwegian dishes served in a decor to match is the signature style here. Amid wood walls, white lace curtains and traditional paintings, you can enjoy popular dishes such as monkfish with saffron and *komler* (dumplings) with salted meats. ✉ *Skagen 10,* ☎ *51/89–51–12. AE, DC, MC, V.*

$–$$$ ✕ **N. B. Sørensen's Dampskibsexpedition.** Norwegian emigrants waited
★   here before boarding steamships crossing the Atlantic to North Amer-
ica 150 years ago. Restored in 1990, the historic wharfhouse is now
a popular waterfront restaurant and bar. Emigrants' tickets, weathered
wood, nautical ropes, old maps, photographs, and gaslights may make
you feel that you're at sea as well. The Norwegian and international
menu has popular dishes such as barbecued spareribs. Upstairs, the din-
ing room has an understated elegance. It is there where the highly rec-
ommended grilled entrecôte with garlic is served. ⊠ *Skagen 26,* ☎ *51/
84–38–20. AE, DC, MC, V.*

Lodging

$$–$$$ 🏨 **Radisson SAS Atlantic Hotel Stavanger.** In the heart of downtown,
the Atlantic overlooks Breiavatnet pond. All rooms are elegantly dec-
orated in understated yellow, beiges, and reds as well as plush furni-
ture. Special rooms have been designed for disabled guests. The King
Oscar lobby bar, Alexander Pub, and Café Ajax have become popu-
lar meeting places. ⊠ *Olav Vs gt. 3, 4001 Stavanger,* ☎ *51/52–75–
20,* FAX *51/53–48–69,* WEB *www.radisson.com. 350 rooms, 5 suites.
Restaurant, bar, café, lounge, pub, sauna, dance club, nightclub, meet-
ing rooms. AE, DC, MC, V.*

$$–$$$ **Rica Park Hotel.** Understandably popular among business travelers, this
hotel has been designed for people who need space and facilities to work.
Several rooms are equipped with a computer and a fax machine. One
room is wheelchair accessible. Stylish and comfortable, the decor is a
conservative blend of understated colors and patterns, dark wood fur-
niture, and sea-theme paintings. ⊠ *Kannikgt. 7, 4000 Stavanger.* ☎
51/50–05–00, FAX *51/50–04–00,* WEB *www.rica.no. 59 rooms. Restau-
rant, bar, saunas, meeting rooms. AE, DC, MC, V.*

$$–$$$ 🏨 **Skagen Brygge Hotell.** A symbol of Stavanger, this classic hotel's
white wooden wharfhouses are common subjects for city postcards and
photographs. Not only does it have a reputation for superb service,
but this hotel has a real seaside soul. The blue-accented, wood-beamed
rooms tend to have somewhat irregular shapes. Request a room fac-
ing the harbor and watch the world dock outside your window. Have
a coffee anytime on the fourth floor's relaxing Kaffekroken lounge. On
weekends Hovemesteren Bar heats up, becoming a popular nightspot.
Skagen Brygge's has a convenient arrangement with 14 restaurants in
the area—the hotel makes the reservations and the tab ends up on your
hotel bill. ⊠ *Skagenkaien 30, Postboks 793, 4004,* ☎ *51/85–00–00,*
FAX *51/85–00–01,* WEB *www.skagenbryggehotell.no. 110 rooms, 2 suites.
Restaurant, bar, sauna, Turkish baths, health club, solarium, conven-
tion center. AE, DC, MC, V.*

$$–$$$ 🏨 **Victoria Hotel.** Stavanger's oldest hotel was built at the turn of the
20th century and still retains a clubby, Victorian style, with elegant carved
furniture, floral patterns, and a gold-accented decor. Ask for a room
overlooking the harbor. Museums, Gamle Stavanger, and shopping are
all within short walking distances. ⊠ *Skansegt. 1, Postboks 279, 4001
Stavanger,* ☎ *51/86–70–00,* FAX *51/86–70–10,* WEB *www.victoria-hotel.no.
107 rooms, 3 suites. Restaurant, bar, breakfast room, meeting rooms.
AE, DC, MC, V.*

$$ 🏨 **Clarion Hotel Stavanger.** This downtown business hotel has an up-
to-the-minute design. Famed local artist Kjell Pahr Iversen's vibrant
paintings grace the hotel's walls. Within the light, simple interior there
are the clean lines of Phillipe Starck lamps and Erik Jørgensen chairs.
The rooms are also bright and simply furnished. ⊠ *Ny Olavskleiv 8,
4008, Stavanger,* ☎ *51/91–00–00,* FAX *51/91–00–10,* WEB *www.clhs.no.
251 rooms, 22 suites. Restaurant, café, bar, meeting rooms. AE, DC,
MC, V.*

Festivals

Stavanger has earned the title *festivalbyen,* or "festival city" for its year-round celebrations. More than 20 official festivals are held throughout the year—comedy, garlic, chili, food, chamber music, jazz, literature, beach volleyball, wine, belly dancing, vintage boats, emigrants, immigrants. There are probably just as many unofficial events, since locals love any reason to have a party. Contact Destination Stavanger (☎ 51/85–92–00, WEB www.visitstavanger.com) for a listing.

Nightlife and the Arts

CAFÉS

Stavanger has its share of cozy and hip locations to have a drink, read the papers, listen to live music, or just hang out. News junkies head to Norway's first news café, **Newsman** (⊠ Skagen 14, ☎ 51/84–38–80), for CNN on the TV and for the Norwegian and foreign periodicals. **Café Sting** (⊠ Valberget 3, ☎ 51/89–38–78), a combination restaurant, nightclub, art gallery, and performance venue, is an institution. **Amys Coffeebar** (⊠ Salvåergt. 7, ☎ 51/86–07–65) is a sweet little spot for an afternoon coffee or takeaway lunch. At **Café Italia** (⊠ Skagen 8, ☎ 51/85–92–90), there's a one-stop Italian coffee bar, a restaurant, and even a boutique selling Italy's top fashion names. **Stavanger Sportscafé** (⊠ Skagenkaien 14A, ☎ 51/89–17–41) is a big hit with sports fans.

CLUBS AND PUBS

Stavanger clubs and pubs can show you a very, very good time year-round. Walk along **Skagenkaien** and **Strandkaien** streets for a choice of pubs and nightclubs. In the summertime, harborside places with patios don't usually close until dawn—around 3 AM in the summer. Sun-kissed **Hansen Hjørnet** (⊠ Skagenkaien 18, ☎ 51/89–52–80, ☉ mid-May–mid-Sept.) is a bar and restaurant that always attracts a crowd. Dance the night away to pulsating sounds at **Taket Nattklubb** (⊠ Nedre Strandgt. 15, ☎ 51/84–37–20), popular among those in their 30s and under. **Checkpoint Charlie Hard Rock Café** (⊠ Lars Hertevigs gt. 5, ☎ 51/53–22–45) is a local version of the famous chain. With its open fireplace and stone walls, **Nåloyet** (⊠ Nedre Strandgt. 13, ☎ 51/84–37–60) is Stavanger's answer to the London pub. Step into the stylish wine cellar **Flaskehalsen** (⊠ Øvre Holmegt. 20, ☎ 51/86–41–58) if you're seeking some quiet romantic moments.

THE ARTS

Stavanger Konserthus (⊠ Concert Hall, Bjergsted, ☎ 51/53–70–00) features local artists and hosts free summertime concerts in the foyer. **Stavanger Symphony Orchestra** (☎ 51/50–88–30) gives performances throughout the year. **Stavangeren Kultur & Revyscene** (⊠ Vaisenhusgt. 37, ☎ 51/84–38–50) is a popular meeting place and venue for cultural activities and events. In the heart of the city, **Sølvberget** (Stavanger Culture House; ⊠ Sølvberggt. 2, ☎ 51/50–71–70) has exhibitions, cultural events, a library, Internet access, and movie theaters.

Built on an island in the archipelago in the Middle Ages and once a palace as well as a monastery, **Utstein Kloster** (⊠ Mosterøy, ☎ 51/72–01–00, WEB www.herlige-stavanger.no) puts its superior acoustics to use during the classical and jazz concerts performed there from June to August. **Rogaland Theatre** (☎ 51/91–90–90) performs plays throughout the region. **Rogaland Kunstsenter** (Rogaland Art Center; ⊠ Nytorget, ☎ 51/59–97–60) has a respected gallery and art shop. Every May, Norwegian and international jazz artists play at the acclaimed **MaiJazz** (☎ 51/84–66–67) festival. If chamber music's more your style, plan to attend the **International Chamber Music Festival** (⊠ ☎ 51/84–66–70), held every August. For literary types, there's **Chapter 01** (☎ 51/50–

72–57), the "International Festival of Literature and Freedom of Expression."

Outdoor Activities and Sports

CYCLING

See Stavanger and the surrounding countryside on bicycle. The tourist map has several maps with route suggestions and information about places to visit. Bikes are available for rent at **Sykkelhuset** (⊠ Løkkevn. 33, ☎ 51/53–99–10).

FISHING

Angling for saltwater fish doesn't require a license or a fee of any kind. The local tourist office can help you get the proper permits required for other types of fishing.

North of Stavanger is the longest salmon river in western Norway, the Suldalslågen, made popular 100 years ago by a Scottish aristocrat who built a fishing lodge there. **Lindum** (⊠ Lakseslottet Lindum, 4240 Suldalsosen, ☎ 52/79–91–61) still has cabins and camping facilities, as well as a dining room. The main salmon season is July through September. Wear diving gear and you can go on a **Salmon Safari** (⊠ Mo Laksegard, ☎ 52/79–76–90), floating in the river 2 km (1 mi) to study wild salmon in their natural environment.

On the island of Kvitsøy, in the archipelago just west of Stavanger, you can rent an apartment, complete with fish-smoking and -freezing facilities, and arrange to use a small sail- or motorboat. Contact **Kvitsøy Kurs & Konferanse** (⊠ Box 35, 4090 Kvitsøy, ☎ 51/73–51–88).

GOLF

Golf enthusiasts can work on their game at several local golf courses. The **Stavanger Golf Klubb** (⊠ Longebakken 45, Hafrsfjord, ☎ 51/55–50–06) has a lush park and forest near its 18-hole, international-championship course.

The **Sola Golf Klubb** (⊠ Åsenveien, Sola, ☎ 51/70–91–70) also sets its 18-hole course amid a forest. If you'd like to golf next to the sea, head to **Sandnes og Sola Golfklubb** (⊠ Solastranden Golfbane, ☎ 51/69–88–83) 20 km (12 mi) from Stavanger.

HIKING

Specialized books and maps are available through Stavanger Turistforening (⊠ Postboks 239, 4001 Stavanger, ☎ 51/84–02–00). They can help you plan a hike through the area, particularly in the rolling Setesdalsheiene and the thousands of islands and skerries of the Ryfylke Archipelago. The tourist board oversees 33 cabins for members (you can join on the spot) for overnighting along the way.

HORSEBACK RIDING

Fossanmoen (☎ 51/70–37–61) organizes riding camps and trips on Iceland ponies that go through scenic surroundings. They last anywhere from an hour to all day.

ICE SKATING

Stavanger Ishall (⊠ Siddishallen, ☎ 51/53–74–50) has ice skating mid-September–mid-April. From November through March, you can skate outdoors at **Kunstisbanen** (⊠ Åsen, Sørmarka, ☎ 51/58–06–44).

SKIING

Skiing in the Sirdal area, 2½ hours from Stavanger, is possible from January to April. Special ski buses leave Stavanger on the weekends at 8:30 AM during the season. Especially recommended is **Sinnes** (☎ 38/37–12–65) for its non–hair-raising cross-country terrain. Downhill skiing is available at **Alsheia** on the same bus route. Other places to ski include **Gullingen skisenter, Suldal** (☎ 52/79–99–01), **Stavtjørn alpinsenter** (☎ 51/45–17–17), and **Svandalen skisenter, Sauda** (☎ 52/78–56–56). Contact **SOT Bustrafikk** (✉ Treskevn. 5, Hafrsfjord, Stavanger, ☎ 51/59–90–66) for transportation information.

Diving is excellent all along the coast—although Norwegian law requires all foreigners to dive with a Norwegian as a way of ensuring that wrecks are left undisturbed. If you just want to take a swim, plan a trip to **local beaches** such as Møllebukta and Madia, which are both deep inside the Hafrsfjord. **Solastranden** has 2⅓ km (1½ mi) of sandy beach ideal for windsurfing and beach volleyball. Other prime beach spots are Vaulen badeplass, Godalen badeplass Viste Stranden, and Sande Stranden.

The local swimming pool is **Stavanger Svømmehall** (☎ 51/50–74–51). **Gamlingen Friluftsbad** (✉ Tjodolfsgt. 53, ☎ 51/52–74–79) is an outdoor heated swimming pool that's open year-round.

Shopping

Stavanger Storsenter Steen & Strøm (✉ Domkirkepl. 2) is centrally located but doesn't have the best selection. **Kvadrat Kjøpesenter** (✉ Lura, between Stavanger and Sandnes, ☎ 51/96–00–00) is the area's best shopping center, with 155 shops, restaurants, a pharmacy, post office, a state wine store, and a tourist information office. In an early 17th century wharfhouse, **Straen Handel** (✉ Strandkaien 31, ☎ 51/52–52–02) has an impressive collection of knitted items, rosemaling, Norwegian dolls, trolls, books, and postcards. Bookworms might find literary treasures in the aptly titled **Odd Book Shop** (✉ Kirkegt. 30, ☎ 51/89–47–66). Reindeer hides and sheepskin and other souvenirs are sold at **Olaf Pettersen & Co.** (✉ Kirkegt. 31, ☎ 51/89–48–04). If jewelry's your passion, head to the city's best shop: **Sølvsmeden på Sølvberget** (✉ Sølvberggt. 5, ☎ 51/89–42–24).

Sørlandet to Stavanger A to Z

To research prices, get advice from other travelers, and book travel arrangements, visit www.fodors.com.

AIR TRAVEL
Kristiansand is served by Braathens, with nonstop flights from Oslo, Bergen, and Stavanger, and SAS, with nonstop flights from Copenhagen. MUK Air serves Aalborg, Denmark; Agder Fly serves Göteborg, Sweden, and Billund, Denmark. Tickets on the last two can be booked through Braathens or SAS.

Braathens flies to Stavanger from Oslo, Kristiansand, Bergen, Trondheim, and Newcastle. SAS has nonstop flights to Stavanger from Bergen, Oslo, Copenhagen, Aberdeen, Göteborg, London, and Newcastle. Widerøe flyveselskap specializes in domestic flights within Norway.
➤ AIRLINES AND CONTACTS: **Braathens** (☎ 81/52–00–00). **SAS** (☎ 81/00–33–00). **Widerøe** (☎ 81/00–12–00).

AIRPORTS
Kristiansand's Kjevik Airport is about 16 km (10 mi) outside town. The airport bus departs from the Braathens office approximately one hour before every departure and proceeds to Kjevik, stopping at downtown hotels along the way. A similar bus makes the return trip from the airport.

In Stavanger, Sola Airport is 17 km (11 mi) from downtown. The Fly-bussen (airport bus) leaves the airport every 20 minutes. It stops at hotels and outside the railroad station in Stavanger. It then heads back to the airport.

➤ AIRPORT INFORMATION: **Stavanger Airport Bus** (☎ 91/63–51–65).

BOAT AND FERRY TRAVEL

Color Line has four ships weekly on the Stavanger–Newcastle route. High-speed boats to Bergen are operated by Flaggruten. Fjord Line offers car ferries that go from Stavanger to Newcastle, England, and from Egersund to Hanstholm, in Northern Denmark. Another line connects Larvik to Frederikshavn, on Denmark's west coast. For information about this crossing, contact DSB in Denmark; or Color Line or DFDS Scandinavian Seaways in Norway.

➤ BOAT AND FERRY INFORMATION: **Color Line A/S** (✉ Nygt. 13, 4006 Stavanger, ☎ 810–00–811, WEB www.colorline.no). **DSB** (☎ 33/14–17–01 or 42/52–92–22 in Denmark, WEB www.dsb.dk). **DFDS Scandinavian Seaways** (☎ 22/41–90–90, WEB www.seaeurope.com). **Fjord Line** (☎ 81/53–35–00, WEB www.fjordline.com). **Flaggruten** (☎ 51/86–87–80).

BUS TRAVEL

Aust-Agder Trafikkselskap, based in Arendal, has one departure daily in each direction for the 5½- to six-hour journey between Oslo and Kristiansand. Sørlandsruta, based in Mandal, has two departures in each direction for the 4½-hour trip from Kristiansand bus terminal to Stavanger.

For information about both local and regional buses in Stavanger, call the number below; the bus terminal is outside the train station. Bus information for Kristiansand is listed below also.

Bus connections in Sørlandet are infrequent; the tourist office can provide a comprehensive schedule. HAGA Reiser operates buses between Stavanger and Hamburg.

➤ BUS INFORMATION: **Aust-Agder Trafikkselskap** (☎ 37/02–65–00). **HAGA Reiser** (☎ 51/67–65–00 or 38/12–33–12). **Kristiansand Bus Information** (✉ Strandgt. 33, ☎ 38/00–28–00). **Sørlandsruta** (☎ 38/03–83–00). **Ruteservice Stavanger, Norway Busekspress** (☎ 51/53–96–00).

CAR TRAVEL

From Oslo, it is 320 km (199 mi) to Kristiansand and 452 km (281 mi) to Stavanger. Route E18 parallels the coastline but stays slightly inland on the eastern side of the country and farther inland in the western part. Although seldom wider than two lanes, it is easy driving because it is so flat.

Sørlandet is also flat, so it's easy driving throughout. The area around the Kulturhus in the Stavanger city center is closed to car traffic, and one-way traffic is the norm in the rest of the downtown area.

CAR RENTALS

➤ MAJOR AGENCIES: **Avis Bilutleie** (☎ Stavanger 51/93–93–60; Kristiansand 38/07–00–90). **Budget** (☎ Stavanger 51/52–21–33; Kristiansand 38/06–37–97). **Hertz Bilutleie** (☎ Stavanger 51/52–00–00; Kristiansand 38/02–22–88).

EMERGENCIES

For emergency medical care in Kristiansand, go to Kristiansand Legevekt, open daily 4 PM–8 AM. For an emergency in Stavanger, you can call Rogaland Sentralsykehusgo or go to Forus Akutten medical center, open 8–8 weekdays.

In Kristiansand, Elefantapoteket (Elefant Pharmacy) is open weekdays 8:30–8, Saturday 8:30–6, Sunday 3–6. In Stavanger, Løveapoteket is open daily 9 AM–11 PM all year except only until 8 PM on Christmas, New Year's, and Easter.

➤ CONTACTS: **Ambulance** (☎ 113). **Egil Undem, Stavanger dentist** (✉ Kannikbakken 6, ☎ 51/52–84–52). **Elefantapoteket** (Elefant Pharmacy; ✉ Gyldenløvesgt. 13, 4611, Kristiansand, ☎ 38/12–58–80). **Emergency Doctor, Stavanger** (☎ 51/51–02–02). **Fire** (☎ 110). **Forus Akutten medical center, Stavanger** (☎ 51/70–94–94). **Kristiansand Legevakt** (✉ Egsvn. 102, ☎ 38/07–69–00). **Løveapoteket** (Løve Pharmacy; ✉ Olav Vs gt. 11, 4005, Stavanger, ☎ 51/52–06–07). **Police** (☎ 112). **Rogaland Sentralsykehus** (☎ 51/51–80–00).

TAXIS

All Kristiansand and Stavanger taxis are connected with a central dispatching office. Journeys within Stavanger are charged by the taxi meter, elsewhere strictly by distance.

➤ TAXI INFORMATION: **Norgestaxi Stavanger** (☎ 08000).**Taxi Sør** (Kristiansand ☎ 38/02–80–00). **Stavanger Taxisentral** (☎ 51/90–90–90).

TOURS

Tours of Kristiansand are only in summer. The City Train is a 15-minute tour of the center part of town. The MS *Maarten* offers two-hour tours of the eastern archipelago and a three-hour tour of the western archipelago daily at 10 AM, early June–August 8.

In Stavanger, a two-hour bus tour leaves from the marina at Vågen daily at 1 between June and August. Rødne Clipper Fjord Sightseeing offers three different tours. FjordTours operates sightseeing and charter tours by boat.

➤ FEES AND SCHEDULES: **City Train** (✉ Nedre Torv,, ☎ 38/03–05–24). **FjordTours** (☎ 51/53–73–40). **MS *Maarten*** (✉ Pier 6 by Fiskebrygga, ☎ 38/12–13–14)). **Rødne Clipper Fjord Sightseeing** (✉ Skagenkaien 18, 4006, ☎ 51/89–52–70).

TRAIN TRAVEL

The Sørlandsbanen leaves Oslo S Station four times daily for the five-hour journey to Kristiansand and five times daily for the 8½- to nine-hour journey to Stavanger. Two more trains travel the 3½-hour Kristiansand–Stavanger route. Kristiansand's train station is at Vestre Strandgata. For information on trains from Stavanger, call Stavanger Jernbanestasjon.

➤ TRAIN INFORMATION: **Kristiansand Train Station** (☎ 38/07–75–32). **NSB** (Norwegian State Railways; ☎ 815–00–888). **Stavanger Jernbanestasjon** (Stavanger Train Station; ☎ 51/56–96–10).

VISITOR INFORMATION

➤ TOURIST INFORMATION: **Arendal** (SørlandsInfo, ✉ Arendal Næringsråd, Friholmsgt. 1, 4800, ☎ 37/00–55–44). **Destinajon Sørlandet: Kristiansand** (✉ Vestre Torv, Vestre Strandgt. 32, Box 592, 4665, ☎ 38/12–13–14). **Destinasjon Sørlandet: Lillesand** (✉ Rådhuset, 4790, ☎ 37/26–15–00). **Destinasjon Sørlandet: Vennesla** (✉ Vennesla stasjon, 4700, ☎ 38/15–55–08). **Destinasjon Stavanger** (✉ Rosenkildetorget, ☎ 51/85–92-00). **Hå Tourist Information** (✉ Hå Folkebiblioteket, ☎ 51/43–40–11). **Mandal** (Mandal og Lindesnes Turistkontor, ✉ Bryggegt., 4500, ☎ 38/27–83–00). **Sandnes Tourist Board** (✉ Våsgt. 22, ☎ 51–97–55–55).

6 BERGEN

Bergen is the gateway to Norway's fjord country, and though it's Norway's second largest city, it's managed to maintain an intimate, small-town feeling.

Many fall in love at first sight with Bergen, Norway's second largest city. Seven rounded, lush mountains, pastel-color wooden houses, historic Bryggen, winding cobblestone streets, and Hanseatic relics all make it a place of enchantment. It has earned many titles, including *Trebyen* ("Tree City"; it has many wooden houses), *Regnbyen* ("Rainy City," due to its 200 days of rain a year), and *Fjordbyen* (it's a gateway to the many fjords nearby). Surrounded by forested mountains and fjords, it's only natural that most Bergensers feel at home either on the mountains (skiing, hiking, walking, or at their cabins) or at sea (fishing and boating). As for the rainy weather, most locals learn the necessity of rain jackets and umbrellas early. In 2001, Bergen even became the site of the invention and construction of the world's first umbrella vending machine.

Town residents take legendary pride in their city and its luminaries. The composer Edvard Grieg, the violinist Ole Bull, and Ludvig Holberg, Scandinavia's answer to Molière, all made great contributions to the culture of their city and to Norway itself. Today, that legacy lives on in nationally acclaimed theater, music, film, dance, and art. The singer Sissel Kyrkjebø, pianist Leif Ove Andsnes, choreographer Jo Strømgren, author Gunnar Staalesen, and other artists all call Bergen home. Every year, a whole host of lively arts festivals take center stage and attract national and international artists.

This international harbor city has played a vital role in the Norwegian economy as well, since it has long been a center of fishing and shipping and, more recently, oil. In fact, Bergen was founded in 1070 by Olav Kyrre as a commercial center. During the 14th century, Hanseatic merchants from northern Germany settled in Bergen and made it one of their four major overseas trading centers. The surviving Hanseatic, wooden buildings on Bryggen (the quay) are topped with triangular cookie-cutter roofs and painted in red, blue, yellow, and green. A monument in themselves (they are on the UNESCO World Heritage List), the buildings tempt travelers and locals to the shops, restaurants, and museums that are now housed inside. In the evenings, when the Bryggen is illuminated, these modest buildings, together with the stocky Rosenkrantz Tower, the Fløyen, and the yachts lining the pier, are reflected in the water— and provide one of the loveliest cityscapes in northern Europe.

EXPLORING BERGEN

The heart of Bergen is at Torgalmenningen, the city's central square that runs from Ole Bulls Plass to Fisketorget, which sits on the harbor and faces *Bryggen* (the quay). From here, the rest of Bergen spreads up the sides of the seven mountains that surround it, with some sights concentrated near the university or a small lake called Lille Lungegårdsvann. Fløyen, the mountain to the east of the harbor, is the most accessible for day-trippers. Before you begin your walking tour, you can take the funicular up to the top of it for a particularly fabulous overview of the city.

Numbers in the text correspond to numbers in the margin and on the Bergen map.

Historic Bergen: Bryggen to Fløyen

A Good Walk

Start your tour in the center of town at Torget, also called **Fisketorget** ① or the Fish Market, where fishermen and farmers deal their goods. Next, walk over to **Bryggen** ②, the wharf on the northeast side of Bergen's harbor. The gabled wood warehouses lining the docks mark the site of the city's original settlement. Take time to walk the narrow passageways between buildings; shops and galleries are hidden among the wooden facades. Follow the pier to the **Hanseatisk Museum** ③ at Finnegårdsgaten and have a look inside. Afterward, continue your walk down the wharf, past the historic buildings to the end of the Holmen promontory and to **Bergenhus Festning** ④ (Bergenhus Fort), which dates from the 13th century; the nearby Rosenkrantztårnet is a 16th-century tower residence. After you've spent some time out here, retrace your steps back to the Radisson SAS Royal Hotel. Beside the hotel is **Bryggens Museum** ⑤, which houses some magnificent archaeological finds. Just behind the museum is the 12th-century church called **Mariakirken** ⑥. Around the back of the church up the small hill is Øvregaten, a street that's the back boundary of Bryggen. Walk down Øvregaten four blocks to **Fløibanen** ⑦, the funicular that runs up and down Fløyen, one of the city's most popular hiking mountains. Don't miss a trip to the top, whether you hike or take the funicular—the view is like no other. When you've returned, walk south on Øvregaten to the **Domkirke** ⑧ (Bergen Cathedral). It's on your left, at the intersection with Kong Oscars Gate. Finally, head back to Torgalmenningen in the center of town for a late afternoon snack at one of the square's cafés.

TIMING

This tour will take a good portion of a day. Be sure to get to the Fisketorget early in the morning, as many days it may close as early as 1 or 2. Also, try to plan your trip up Fløyen for a sunny day. It may be difficult, as Bergen is renowned for rain, but you may want to wait a day or two to see if the skies clear up.

Sights to See

OFF THE BEATEN PATH

AKVARIET (Bergen Aquarium) – This is one of the largest collections of North Sea fish and invertebrates in Europe. The aquarium has 70 tanks and three outdoor pools of seals, carp, and penguins. On a realistic nesting cliff, adorable penguins rest, waddle by, and stare back curiously at onlookers. Watch Lina, the first harbor seal born in captivity in Norway, or her companions as they zoom by like swimming torpedoes. Inside, there are schools of brilliant Amazon rainforest fish as well as common eels, which tend to wrap around each other. *The Aquarium: Bergen and the Local Coastline* is a 360° video directed by one of Norway's most beloved animators, Ivo Caprino. The aquarium is on Nordnes Peninsula, a 15-minute walk from the fish market, or take Bus 11 or the ferry from the Fish Market. ✉ *Nordnesbakken 4,* ☎ *55/55–71–71,* WEB *www. akvariet.com.* 🎫 *NKr 80.* ⊙ *May–Sept., daily 9–8; Oct.–Apr., daily 10– 6. Feeding times: 11, 3, and 6 May–Sept.; noon and 3 Oct.–Apr.*

❹ **Bergenhus Festning** (Bergenhus Fortress). The buildings here date from the mid-13th century. **Håkonshallen,** a royal ceremonial hall erected during the reign of Håkon Håkonsson between 1247 and 1261, was badly damaged by the explosion of a German ammunition ship in 1944 but was restored by 1961. Erected in the 1560s by the governor of Bergen Castle (Bergenhus), Erik Rosenkrantz, **Rosenkrantztårnet** (Rosenkrantz Tower), served as a combined residence and fortified tower. ✉ *Bergenhus,* ☎ *55/31–60–67,* WEB *www.hd.uib.no/haakon.htm.* 🎫 *NKr 20.* ⊙ *Mid-May–mid-Aug., daily 10–4; Sept.–mid-May, Fri.–Wed. noon–3, Thurs. 3–6. Guided tours every hr. Closed during Bergen International Music Festival.*

❷ **Bryggen** (The Wharf). A trip to Bergen is incomplete without a trip to Bryggen. This row of mostly reconstructed 14th-century wooden build-

Bergen

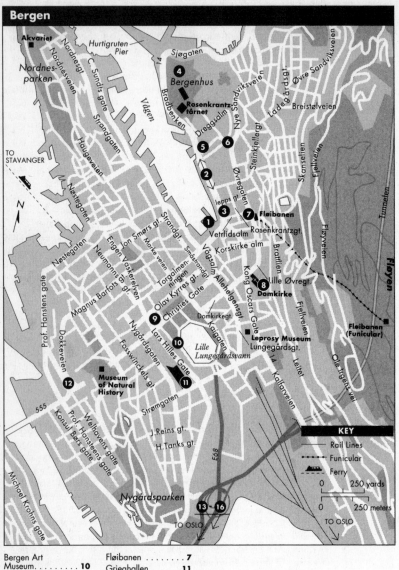

Akvariet

Nordnes-
parken

Hurtigruten
Pier

Sjøgaten

Bergenhus

Rosenkrantz
tårnet

TO
STAVANGER

Fløibanen

Vetrlidsalm

Korskirke alm

Lille Øvregt.

Domkirke

Museum
of Natural
History

Leprosy Museum
Lungegårdsgt.

Bergen Art
Museum

Lille
Lungegårdsvann

Fløibanen
(Funicular)

Fløyen

Nygårdsparken

TO OSLO

TO OSLO

KEY

— Rail Lines

···· Funicular

🚢 Ferry

0   250 yards

0   250 meters

ings that face the harbor make this one of the most charming walkways in Europe, especially on a sunny day. The originals were built by Hansa merchants, while the oldest reconstruction dates from 1702. Several fires, the latest in 1955, destroyed the original structures.

⑤ Bryggens Museum. This museum has an amazing array of archaeological finds from the Middle Ages. An exhibit on Bergen circa 1300 shows the town at its zenith of importance and has reconstructed living quarters as well as artifacts such as old tools and shoes. Back then, Bergen was the largest town in Norway, a cosmopolitan trading center and the national capital. ⊠ *Dreggsalmenning 3, 5000,* ☎ *55/58–80–10,* WEB *www.uib.no/bmu.* ⊠ *NKr 30.* ☉ *May–Aug., daily 10–5; Sept.–Apr., weekdays 11–3, Sat. noon–3, Sun. noon–4.*

⑧ Domkirke (The Bergen Cathedral). The Cathedral's long turbulent history has shaped the eclectic architecture of the current structure. The Gothic-style choir and the lower towers are oldest, dating from the 13th century. Note the bullet holes in the tower wall. From June to August, a Sunday service is held in English at 9:30 AM, an organ recital is held Thursday at noon, and music played on Sunday evening at 7:30. ⊠ *Kong Oscars gt. and Domkirkegt.,* ☎ *55/31–23–09.* ☉ *Late May–Aug., Mon.–Sat. 11–5, Sun. 10–1; Sept.–late May, Tues.–Fri. 11–2, Sat. 11–3, Sun. 10–1.*

① Fisketorget (Fish Market). Turn-of-the-20th-century photographs of this pungent square show fishermen in Wellington boots and mackintoshes and women in long aprons. Now, the fishmongers wear bright-orange rubber overalls as they look over the catches of the day. In summer, they cater to tourists, who are mostly looking for shrimp, salmon, and monkfish. The rest of the year, more Bergensers come, and the selection is greater. There's also fruit, vegetables, flowers, handicrafts, and souvenirs at this lively market: even the world's first umbrella vending machine. Have a lunch of smoked shrimp or salmon on a baguette with mayonnaise and cucumber. ☉ *Summer Mon.–Wed. and Fri. 7–4, Thurs. 7–7, Sat. 7–3. Off season the market opens later.*

⑦ Fløibanen (Fløyen Funicular). A magnificent view of Bergen and its suburbs can be taken in from the top of **Fløyen,** the most popular of the city's seven mountains. The eight-minute ride on the funicular (a cable car) takes you to the top at 1,050 ft above the sea. A car departs every half hour. Take a break at the restaurant and café (open daily in summer and weekends the rest of the year), the gift shop, or the children's playground. Summer concerts play every evening from June 17 to August 19. Stroll down the mountain walking path back downtown or explore the mountains that lead to Ulriken, the highest mountain surrounding Bergen. *Vetrlidsallmenning 21,* ☎ *55/33–68–00,* WEB *www.floibanen.no.* ⊠ *NKr 50.* ☉ *May–Aug. weekdays 7:30 AM–midnight, Sat. 8 AM–midnight, Sun. 9 AM–midnight. Sept.–Apr. weekdays 7:30 AM–11 PM, Sat. 8 AM–11 PM, Sun. 9 AM–11 PM.*

③ Hanseatisk Museum. One of the best-preserved buildings in Bergen, the Hanseatic Museum was the 16th-century office and home of an affluent German merchant. The apprentices lived upstairs, in boxed-in beds with windows cut into the wall. Although claustrophobic, the snug rooms retained body heat, practical in these unheated buildings. ⊠ *Bryggen,* ☎ *55/31–41–89,* WEB *www.hanseatisk.museum.no.* ⊠ *NKr 40; off-season NKr 25.* ☉ *June–Aug., daily 9–5; Sept.–May, daily 11–2.*

⑥ Mariakirken (St. Mary's Church). Considered one of the most outstanding Romanesque churches in Norway, this is the oldest building in Bergen that's still in use. It began as a church in the 12th century but gained a Gothic choir, richly decorated portals, and a splendid Baroque pulpit, much of it added by the Hanseatic merchants 1408–1766. See the gilded triptych at the High Altar that dates from the late Middle Ages. Organ recitals are held Tuesday, Thursday, and Sunday mid-June through late August and during the International Festival in late May. ⊠ *Dreggen,* ☎ *55/31–59–60.* ☜ *NKr 10 in summer.* ☉ *Mid-May–mid-Sept., weekdays 11–4; mid-Sept.–mid-May, Tues.–Fri. noon–1:30.*

Rasmus Meyers Allé and Grieghallen

A Good Walk

From Torgalmenningen, walk to Nordahl Bruns Gate and turn left for the **Vestlandske Kunstindustrimuseum** ⑨, the West Norway Museum of Decorative Art. After viewing some of the museum's elaborately crafted works, exit the museum and head for Christies Gate. Follow it along the park and turn left on Rasmus Meyers Allé, which runs along the small lake, Lille Lungegårdsvann, to reach the **Bergen Art Museum,** which encompasses side-by-side the **Bergen Billedgalleri,** the **Stenersen Collection,** and the **Rasmus Meyer Collection** ⑩. Near these galleries, right on Lars Hilles Gate, is **Grieghallen** ⑪, Bergen's famous music hall.

At the back of the hall, on Nygårdsgaten, walk up Herman Foss gate to Muséplass to the **Bergen Museum** ⑫. Heading back into the center of the city, walk down Nygårdsgaten to Strømgaten to Kong Oscars gate to the **Leprosy Museum.**

TIMING

All of the museums on this tour are quite small and very near to each other, so you probably won't need more than half a day to complete this tour.

Sights to See

⑩ **Bergen Billedgalleri.** Part of the Bergen Art Museum (which also includes the Rasmus Meyers and the Stenersen collections), the City Art Collection stresses contemporary art. Standouts include Bjørn Carlsen's "Mother, I don't want to die in Disneyland" mixed-media piece, Tom Sandberg photography, and poetry and installations by Yoko Ono. *Bergen Art Museum, Rasmus Meyers allé 3 and 7, Lars Hilles gt. 10,* ☎ *55/56–80–00,* WEB *www.bergenartmuseum.no.* ☜ *NKr 50.* ☉ *Mid-May–mid-Sept., daily 11–5; mid-Sept.–mid-May, Tues.–Sun. 11–5.*

⑫ **Bergen Museum.** Part of the University of Bergen, this museum has two collections. The **Cultural History Collections** emphasize archaeological artifacts and furniture and folk art from western Norway. There's also an exhibit on the Viking way of life. The **Natural History Collections** is perfect for lovers of the outdoors, since it includes botanical gardens. ⊠ *Haakon Sheteligs pl. 10 and Musépl. 3,* ☎ *55/58–31–40 or 55/58–29–20,* WEB *www.bm.uib.no.* ☜ *NKr 30.* ☉ *Mid-May–Aug., Tues.–Sat. 10–3, Sun. 11–4; Sept.–mid-May, Tues.–Sat. 11–2, Sun. 11–3.*

OFF THE
BEATEN PATH

GAMLE BERGEN MUSEUM – (Old Bergen Museum) This family-friendly open-air museum transports you to 18th- and 19th-century Bergen. Streets and narrow alleys of 40 period wooden houses show the town life of 200–300 years ago. A baker, dentist, photographer, jeweler, shopkeeper, and sailor are all represented. Local artists hold exhibitions here. The grounds and park are open free of charge year-round. ⊠ *Elseros, Sandviken,* ☎ *55/39–43–04.* ☜ *NKr 25; NKr 50 with guided tour.* ☉ *Late May–early Sept., guided tours every hour 10–5.*

⑪ **Grieghallen.** Home of the Bergen Philharmonic Orchestra and stage for the annual International Festival, this music hall is a conspicuous slab of glass and concrete. The acoustics are marvelous. Built in 1978, the hall was named for the city's famous son, composer Edvard Grieg (1843–1907). From September to May, every Thursday and some Fridays and Saturdays at 7:30 PM, the orchestra gives concerts. Throughout the year, the hall is a popular venue for cultural events. ⊠ *Lars Hills gt. 3A,* ☎ *55/21–61–50.*

Leprosy Museum. St. George's Hospital houses the Bergen Collection of the History of Medicine, which includes this museum. Although the current buildings date from the start of the 1700s, St. George's was a hospital for lepers as long ago as the Middle Ages. This unusual museum profiles Norway's contribution to leprosy research. Many Norwegian doctors have been recognized for their efforts against leprosy, particularly Armauer Hansen, for which the modern term ("Hansen's disease") is named. ⊠ *St. George's Hospital, Kong Oscars gt. 59,* WEB *www.lepra.uib.no.* ⊠ *NKr 30.* ☉ *Late May–Aug., daily 11–3.*

OFF THE
BEATEN PATH **NORWEGIAN MUSEUM OF FISHERIES –** The sea and its resources, territorial waters, management and research, boats and equipment, whaling and sealing, and fish farming are all covered in the exhibits here. There are also substantial book, video, and photographic collections. ⊠ *Bontelabo 2,* ☎ *NKr 20.* ☉ *June–Aug., weekdays 10–6, weekends noon–4; Sept.–May, weekdays 10–4, weekends noon–4.*

⑩ **Rasmus Meyer Collection.** When the businessman Rasmus Meyer (1858–1916) was assembling his superb collection of works by what would become world-famous artists, most of them were unknowns. On display are the best Edvard Munch paintings outside Oslo, as well as major works by J. C. Dahl, Adolph Tidemand, Hans Gude, Harriet Backer, and Per Krogh. Also head to the Blumenthal to see interiors from fine 18th-century houses and some incredible frescoes. ⊠ *Bergen Art Museum, Rasmus Meyers allé 3 and 7, Lars Hilles gt. 10,* ☎ *55/56–80–00,* WEB *www.bergenartmuseum.no.* ⊠ *NKr 50.* ☉ *Mid-May–mid-Sept., 11–5; mid-Sept.–mid-May, Tues.–Sun. 11–5.*

⑩ **Stenersen Collection.** This is an extremely impressive collection of modern art for a town the size of Bergen. Modern artists represented include Max Ernst, Paul Klee, Vassily Kandinsky, Pablo Picasso, and Joan Miró, as well as Edvard Munch. There's also a large focus here on Norwegian art since the mid-18th century. ⊠ *Bergen Art Museum, Rasmus Meyers allé 3 and 7, Lars Hilles gt. 10,* ☎ *55/56–80–00,* WEB *www.bergenartmuseum.no.* ⊠ *NKr 50.* ☉ *Mid-May–mid-Sept., daily 11–5; mid-Sept.–mid-May, Tues.–Sun. 11–5.*

⑨ **Vestlandske Kunstindustrimuseum** (West Norway Museum of Decorative Art). This eclectic collection contains many exquisite art and design pieces. Its permanent "People and Possessions" spans 500 years and has everything from Bergen silverware to Ole Bull's violin, which was made in 1562 by the Italian master Saló. Bull's violin has a head of an angel on it carved by none other than by Benvenuto Cellini. A fine collection of chairs traces the history of their design. "The Art of China," the other permanent exhibition, presents one of Europe's largest collections of Buddhist marble sculptures alongside porcelain, jade, bronzes, textiles, and paintings. The silk robes embroidered with dragons and other ceremonial dress are stunning. Changing exhibitions focus on paintings, artifacts, and design. ⊠ *Permanenten, Nordahl Bruns gt. 9,* ☎ *55/32–51–08,* WEB *www.vk.museum.no.* ⊠ *NKr 30.* ☉ *Mid-May–mid-Sept., Tues.–Sun. 11–4; mid-Sept.–mid-May, Tues.–Sun. noon–4.*

Troldhaugen, Fantoft, Lysøen and Ulriken

A Good Drive

Once you've gotten your fill of Bergen's city life, you can head out to the countryside to tour some of the area's interesting, and lesser known, low-key attractions. Follow Route 1 (Nesttun/Voss) out of town about 5 km (3 mi) to **Troldhaugen** ⑬, the villa where Edvard Grieg spent 22 years of his life. After you've spent some time wandering the grounds, head for **Lysøen** ⑭, the Victorian dream castle of Norwegian violinist Ole Bull. Getting here is a 30-minute trek by car and ferry, but it's well worth the effort. From Troldhaugen, get back on Route 1 or Route 586 to Fana, over Fanafjell to Sørestraumen. Follow signs to Buena Kai. From here, take the ferry over to Lysøen. After visiting Lysøen, on your way back to Bergen, you can see the **Fantoft Stavkirke** ⑮, which was badly damaged in a fire in 1992 but has been completely rebuilt. Lastly, end your day with a hike up **Ulriken Mountain** ⑯, the tallest of Bergen's seven mountains. If you're too worn out from your day of sightseeing, but still want take in the view from the top, you can always take the Ulriken cable car.

About 12 km (7 mi) from Bergen city center, following Route 553 to the airport, is Siljustøl, the home of late composer Harald Sæverud.

TIMING

Driving and visiting time (or bus time) will consume at least a day or several depending on your pace and interest. Visiting these sights is a pleasant way to explore Bergen's environs with some direction.

Sights to See

★ ⑮ **Fantoft Stavkirke** (Fantoft Stave Church). During the Middle Ages, when European cathedrals were built in stone, Norway used wood to create unique stave churches. These Norwegian wooden cultural symbols stand out for their dragon heads, carved doorways, and walls of "staves" or vertical planks. Though as many as 750 stave churches may have once existed, only some 30 remain standing. The original stave church here, built in Fortun in Sogn in 1150 and moved to Fantoft in 1883, burned down in 1992. Since then, the church has been reconstructed to its original condition. From *sentral bystasjonen* (the main bus station next to the railway station), take any bus leaving from Platform 19, 20, or 21. ✉ *Paradis,* ☎ *55/28–07–10.* 🎫 *NKr 30.* ☉ *Mid-May–mid-Sept., daily 10:30–2 and 2:30–6.*

⑭ **Lysøen.** The beautiful villa of Norwegian violin virtuoso Ole Bull (1810–1880) is on Lysøen, which means the "island of light." Bull, not as well known as some of Norway's other cultural luminaries, was a musician and patron of great vision. In 1850, after failing to establish a "New Norwegian Theater" in America, he founded the National Theater in Norway. He then chose the young, unknown playwright Henrik Ibsen to write full time for the theater and later encouraged and promoted another neophyte—15-year-old Edvard Grieg.

Built in 1873, this villa, with an onion dome, gingerbread gables, curved staircase, and cutwork trim just about everywhere, has to be seen to be believed. Once you're here, you can stroll along the 13 km (8 mi) of pathways Bull created, picnic or swim in secluded spots, and even rent a rowboat. Throughout the summer (the only season that Ole Bull lived here), concerts are performed in the villa.

To get here by bus (Monday–Saturday), take the "Lysefjordruta" bus from Platform 19 or 20 at the main bus station to Buena Kai then the *Ole Bull* ferry across the fjord to the island. By car, it's a 25 km (15 mi) trip from Bergen to the ferry. Take road E39 south out of the city.

Fork right onto Route 553, signposted FANA, then continue straight over Fana Mountain to Sørestraumen and follow signs to Buena Kai from there. ☎ 56/30–90–77. ⌨ NKr 25. ⊙ Mid-May–late Aug., Mon.–Sat. noon–4, Sun. 11–5; Sept., Sun. noon–4.

OFF THE BEATEN PATH **SILJUSTØL.** Norway's most important composer of the last century, Harald Sæverud (1897–1992), called this unusual house home. He built it in 1939 of wood and stone and followed old Norwegian construction methods. Every Sunday in July concerts are held here at 2 PM (admission NKr 200). By bus, take Bus 30 from the Bergen bus station, Platform 20. By car, drive 12 km (7 mi) from Bergen center to Route 553 heading toward the airport. ⌂ Rådal, ☎ 55/92–29–92, WEB www.bergen.by.com/museum/siljustol. ⌨ NKr 50. ⊙ Mid-June–early Aug., Wed.–Fri. and Sun. 11–4; early Aug.–early Nov., Sun. noon–4.

⑬ Troldhaugen (Trolls' Hill). Built in 1885, this was the home of Norway's most famous composer, Edvard Grieg (1843–1907). In the little garden hut by the shore of Lake Nordås, he composed many of his best known works. In 1867, he married his cousin Nina, a Danish soprano. They lived in the white clapboard house with green gingerbread trim for 22 years beginning in about 1885. A salon and gathering place for many Scandinavian artists then, it now houses mementos—a piano, paintings, prints—of the composer's life. Its 1907 interior shows it the way that Grieg knew it. At Troldsalen, a concert hall seating 200, chamber music is performed. Summer concerts are held on Wednesday and weekends. They're daily during the Bergen International Festival. To get here, catch a bus from Platform 19, 20, or 21 at the bus station, and get off at Hopsbroen, turn right, walk 200 yards, turn left on Troldhaugsveien, and follow the signs for roughly 2 km (1 mi). ⌂ Troldhaugv. 65, ☎ 55/92–29–92, WEB www.troldhaugen.com. ⌨ NKr 50. ⊙ May–Sept., daily 9–6; Oct.–Nov. and Apr., weekdays 10–2, weekends noon–4; mid-Jan.–Mar., weekdays 10–2.

⑯ Ulriken Mountain. There's a great view of the city, fjords, islands, and coast from the top of the highest of the seven Bergen mountains. The famous Ulriken cable car, running every seven minutes, transports you here. Bring a lunch and hike on well-marked trails in unspoiled mountain wilderness. Or take a break at Ulriken Restaurant and Bar. To get here from downtown, take the Bergen in a Nutshell sightseeing bus along the harbor and Bryggen, through the town center, up to Mount Ulriken's cable car. The same bus returns you to town afterward. ⌂ Ulriken 1, 5009 Bergen, ☎ 55/20–20–20. ⌨ Round-trip cost (including shuttle bus and cable car) is NKr 120. ⊙ 9 AM–10 PM May–Sept., Oct.–Apr. 10–5.

DINING

"Bergen is the city with the ocean and sea completely in its stomach," someone once said. Bergensers love their seafood dishes: *Fiskepudding* (fish pudding), *fiskekaker* (fish cakes), *fiskeboller* (fish balls), and *Bergensk fiskesuppe* (Bergen fish soup)—delicious renditions of such classic recipes show up on local menus with great regularity.

Any Bergen dining experience should start at *Fisketorget*, the fish market. Rain or shine, fresh catches of the day go on sale here in shiny, stainless-steel stalls. The fishmongers dole out shrimp, salmon, monkfish, and friendly advice. Usually, they have steamed *rekker* (shrimp), or smoked *laks* (salmon), served on a baguette with mayonnaise and cucumber—a perfect quick lunch. As for desserts, *skillingsbolle*, a big cinnamon roll that often has a custard center, is popular. *Lefse* is a round flat cake from oatmeal or barley that has a sugar or cream filling. As

Bergen Dining

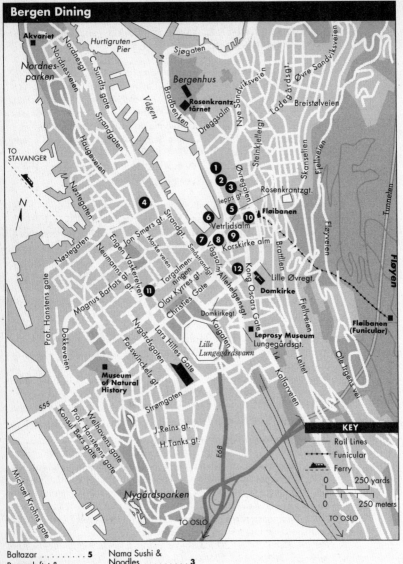

in other major Norwegian cities, Bergen's local chefs have introduced the town to international cuisine through crossover dishes. The popularity of Tex-Mex, tapas, Mediterranean dishes, sushi, and cafés are all signs of a changing Bergen restaurant scene.

$$$$ ✕ **Lucullus.** Although the decor seems a bit out of kilter—modern art matched with lace doilies and boardroom chairs—the French food in this restaurant is always good. The four-course meal offered here is a good splurge. ⊠ *Hotel Neptun, Walckendorfsgt. 8,* ☎ *55/30–68–00. Jacket and tie. DC, MC, V. Closed Sun. No lunch.*

$$$–$$$$ ✕ **Fiskekrogen.** Right at the fish market, the Fishhook is a quintessential fish restaurant. The market's last original fish tank from 1888 holds the fresh lobster, codfish, and crab on offer here. The blue-and-white country decor and open kitchen make the place feel rustic, as does the stuffed brown bear that still growls. Although Fiskekrogen also serves game, stick to seafood dishes such as the grilled monkfish in a goat cheese sauce or the mixture of catfish, salmon, shellfish, and mussels with vegetables. ⊠ *Zachariasbryggen,* ☎ *55/55–96–55. Reservations required. AE, DC, MC, V.*

$$$–$$$$ ✕ **Kafé Kristall.** This small, intimate restaurant is one of the most
★ fashionable in town. The chef here combines his own eclectic contemporary style with traditional Norwegian ingredients. Try the chili grilled angler with tomato or the fish soup with grilled scampi. ⊠ *Kong Oscars gt. 16,* ☎ *55/32–10–84. AE, DC, MC, V. Closed Sun. No lunch.*

$$–$$$$ ✕ **Bryggeloftet & Stuene.** Dining here on lutefisk at autumn and Christmastime is a time-honored tradition for many Bergensers. Also try the pinnkjøtt (lumpfish) or the reindeer fillets. Since it serves *husmannskost,* traditional everyday dishes, the heavy wooden decor, fireplace, and circa 1900 oil paintings are quite fitting. ⊠ *Bryggen 11,* ☎ *55/31–06–30. AE, DC, MC, V.*

$$–$$$$ ✕ **Smauet Mat & Vinhus.** Inside a cozy blue cottage is one of Bergen's least expensive fine restaurants. Chef Per Trygve Bolstad has a reputation for being innovative with Mediterranean and Norwegian cuisine. Try the ostrich or one of the seafood dishes. ⊠ *Vaskerelvssmauet 13,* ☎ *55/21–07–00. Reservations essential. AE, DC, MC, V.*

$$$ ✕ **Baltazar.** In the cellar of a historic meat market, Kjøttbasaren, this candlelit restaurant with exposed brick walls is warm and romantic. Underneath the floor there's the keel of a wooden ship from 1300 that was discovered during the restoration of the building. The international menu emphasizes Norwegian ingredients. Try the fried ocean catfish on a bed of spinach greens. The restaurant's chef, Knut Tau Hatlestad, is also behind several of the city's other successful restaurants, including von Lippe and Pasta Basta. ⊠ *Vetrlidsalmenning 2,* ☎ *55/55–22–00. Reservations essential. AE, DC, MC, V.*

$$$ ✕ **Finnegaardstuene.** This classic Norwegian restaurant near Bryggen
★ has four snug rooms. Some of the timber interior dates from the 18th century. The seven-course menu emphasizes seafood, although the venison and reindeer are excellent. Traditional Norwegian desserts such as cloudberries and cream are irresistible. ⊠ *Rosenkrantzgt. 6,* ☎ *55/ 55–03–00. AE, DC, MC, V. Closed Sun.*

$$$ ✕ **To Kokker.** Ranked among Bergen's best restaurants by many, To
★ Kokker is on Bryggen wharf. The quaint 300-year-old building has crooked floors and slanted moldings. The seafood and game are excellent—especially the lobster and crayfish. ⊠ *Enhjørningsgården,* ☎ *55/32–28–16. Reservations essential. AE, DC, MC, V. Closed Sun. No lunch.*

$$$ ✕▣ **von der Lippe.** Elegant and regal, this restaurant is in the catacombs of Kjøttbasaren, a restored meat market. Chef Knut Tau Hatlestad keeps the mainly poultry and seafood dishes simple. The lob-

ster and the scallops both stand out. If you're traveling in a group, reserve one of the two private rooms, which are like wine cellars. ⊠ *Vetrlidsalmenningen 2,* ☎ *55/55–22–22. Jacket and tie. Reservations essential. AE, DC, MC, V.*

$–$$$ ✕ **SkiBet.** One of Norway's best bets for Tex-Mex, SkiBet is shaped like a sailboat. Since it overlooks the harbor, ask for a window table and take in the special view day or night. Consider the fajitas, made from beef, chicken, jumbo prawns, or lamb, or the Beef El Paso, in Mexican pepper sauce. ⊠ *Zachariasbryggen,* ☎ *55/55–96–55. AE, DC, MC, V.*

$$ ✕ **Nama Sushi & Noodles.** The city's best sushi bar ("nama" means "fresh and raw" in Japanese) has garnered good reviews for its minimalistic, aquatic decor and half-sushi, half-noodles menu. Their fish comes fresh daily from the market nearby. There are daily "Happy Hour" sushi specials here. The sashimi *moriawase* (assortment), the breast of duck, and the banana mousse dessert all come highly recommended. The café/bar is perfect for an afternoon coffee break. ⊠ *Lodin Leppes gt. 2,* ☎ *55/32–20–10. AE, DC, MC, V.*

$–$$ ✕ **Pasta Basta.** Renovated to bring to mind a Mediterranean vineyard, this small, fresh-faced restaurant serves the city's finest Italian food at reasonable prices. The Penne con Pollo (grilled breast of chicken with penne served with lime and cilantro sauce and sautéed peppers) is popular. ⊠ *Zachariasbryggen,* ☎ *55/55–22–22. AE, DC, MC, V.*

$ ✕ **Escalón.** Near the Fløibanen, this tiny tapas restaurant bar is a trendy place to meet friends for a bite or a drink. Taste the Gambas al Ajillo (scampi in wine and garlic) or the Albódigas en salsa de tomate (meatballs in tomato sauce). ⊠ *Vetrlidsalmenningen 21,* ☎ *55/32–90–99. AE, DC, MC, V.*

LODGING

From the elegance of the Radisson SAS Hotels to the no-frills Crowded House, Bergen has a good selection of accommodation options for every traveler's budget and style. Most of the hotels are within walking distance of the city's shopping, restaurants, entertainment, and other attractions. In recent years, the Tourist Office has offered the Bergen Package, which includes lodging in one of many of the city's hotels, breakfast, and the Bergen Card starting at NKr 410 per person per double room per day. It's available weekends throughout the year, daily May 21–August 31, and during the Easter and Christmas holidays. In summer, June 18 through August, most Bergen hotels offer a special last-minute rate for booking 48 hours before arrival. During the off season, September to May, many have special weekend rates.

$$–$$$$ ⊞ **Radisson SAS Hotel Norge.** Since it's a real class act and has superb service, this luxury hotel attracts a who's who of guests, from prime ministers to musicians. The architecture is standard modern, with large salmon-colored, dark-wood rooms that blend contemporary Scandinavian comfort with traditional warmth. The second-floor American Bar is a popular meeting place for a drink. Every morning, the hotel's fresh smörgåsbord breakfast is the perfect way to start your day. Ask for a room facing Lille Lungegårdsvann for a scenic view. Those facing Ole Bull Square can be noisy at night. ⊠ *Ole Bulls pl. 4, 5012,* ☎ *55/57–30–00,* ℻ *55/57–30–01,* 🕸 *www.radissonsas.com. 347 rooms, 12 suites. 2 restaurants, 2 bars, indoor pool, health club, nightclub, meeting room. AE, DC, MC, V.*

$$–$$$$ ⊞ **Radisson SAS Royal Hotel.** Opened in 1982 behind Bryggen, this hotel was built where old warehouses used to be. Ravaged by nine fires since 1170, the warehouses were repeatedly rebuilt in the same style,

Bergen Lodging

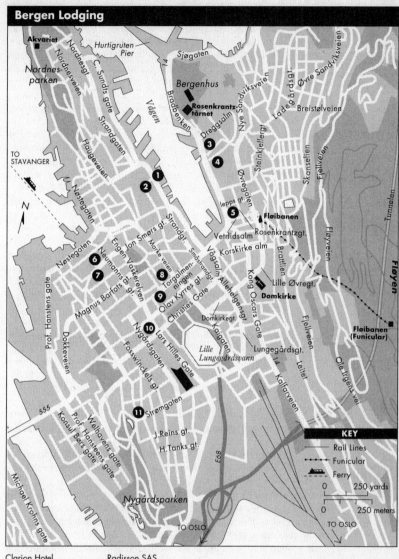

Akvariet

Hurtigruten Pier

Nordnes-parken

Sjøgaten

Bergenhus

Rosenkrantz-tärnet

TO STAVANGER

Dreggsalm

Nordnesveien

C. Sunds gate

Strandgaten

Haugeveien

Nøstegaten

Vågen

Bradbenken

Øvregaten

Nye Sandviksveien

Lade gårds gt.

Øvre Sandviksveien

Breistølveien

Steinkjellergt.

Skanselien

Fjellveien

Tunnelen

lepps gt.

Vetrlidsalm

Rosenkrantzgt.

Korskirke alm

Fløibanen

Fløyen

Fløyenveien

Fløibanen (Funicular)

Nøstegaten

Neumanns gt.

Engen Vaskerelven

Jon Smørs gt.

Strandgt.

Marke veien

Småstrandgt.

Torgalmenningen

Vågsalm. Allehelgensgt.

Bratflien

Lille Øvregt.

Domkirke

Prof. Hansten gate

Dokkeveien

Magnus Barfots gt.

Olav Kyrres gt.

Christies Gate

Domkirkegt.

Kong Oscars Gate

Fjellveien

Leitet

Ole Irgens vei.

Nygårdsgaten

Lars Hilles Gate

Fosswinckels gt.

Kaigaten

Lille Lungegårdsvann

Lungegårdsgt.

Kalfarveien

555

Welhavens gate

Prof. Hansteens gate

Konsul Børs gate

Strømgaten

J. Reins gt.

H. Tanks gt.

F68

Michael Krohns gate

Nygårdsparken

TO OSLO

TO OSLO

KEY

— Rail Lines

•••• Funicular

⛴ Ferry

0 ——— 250 yards

0 ——— 250 meters

Clarion Hotel
Admiral **1**

Crowded House **7**

First Hotel Marin **5**

Hotel
Hordaheimen **2**

Hotel Park
Pension **11**

Radisson SAS
Hotel Norge **9**

Radisson SAS
Royal Hotel **4**

Rainbow Hotel
Bristol **8**

Rica Travel
Hotel **10**

Scandic Hotel
Bergen City **6**

Tulip Inn
Rainbow Hotel
Bryggen Orion **3**

which has been carried over into Radisson's facade. The small but comfortable rooms have light gold walls and many wood accents. Under a glass ceiling, the Café Royal Restaurant serves a wide range of Scandinavian and international dishes as well as light snacks. The Madam Felle pub and bar on the waterfront is known for its live jazz and blues, as well as its wide range of whiskeys. ⊠ *Bryggen, 5003,* ☎ *55/54–30–00,* FAX *55/32–48–08,* WEB *www.radissonsas.com. 273 rooms, 10 suites. 3 restaurants, bar, pub, indoor pool, sauna, health club, dance club, nightclub, convention center. AE, DC, MC, V.*

$$–$$$ ✕ **First Hotel Marin.** This harborside business hotel is near Bryggen. Every room has a bathtub and is decorated in yellows and blues, with oak furniture and wooden floors. The penthouse suites have magnificent views of Bergen. Buses, ferries, and trains are all within walking distance. ⊠ *Rosenkrantzgt. 8, 5003,* ☎ *53/05–15–00,* FAX *53/05–15–01,* WEB *www.firsthotels.com. 122 rooms, 28 suites. 2 restaurants, café, sauna, Turkish bath, gym. AE, DC, MC, V.*

$$–$$$ ✕ **Hotel Hordaheimen.** Dating back to 1913, one of the city's oldest and most distinctive hotels is on a quiet, central street. The lobby has a memorable collection of painted Norwegian furniture by Lars Kinsarvik (1846–1928). The hotel's café–restaurant, Hordastova, is well known for its home-cooked fare, especially klippfisk, fried mackerel, and smoked cod. Rooms are very small but ideal for active travelers intending only to sleep at the hotel. ⊠ *C. Sundtsgt. 18, 5004,* ☎ *55/33–50–00,* FAX *55/23–49-50. 64 rooms. Restaurant. AE, DC, MC, V.*

$$–$$$ ✕ **Rainbow Hotel Bristol.** The Bristol is minutes away from many popular attractions. Built in the 1930s, the rooms are small but comfortable. Several are designed to be wheelchair-accessible and allergen-free. ⊠ *Torgalmenningen, 5014,* ☎ *55/23–23–44,* FAX *55/23–23–19,* WEB *www.rainbow-hotels.no. 128 rooms, 1 suite. Restaurant, bar. AE, DC, MC, V.*

$$–$$$ ⊠ **Rica Travel Hotel.** Popular with business travelers, this hotel is steps away from Torgalmenningen. The rooms are stylish and the location is ideal, but facilities are few. A public swimming pool and a popular local fitness center are nearby. ⊠ *Christiesgt. 5–7, 5808,* ☎ *55/31–54–00,* FAX *55/31–32–50,* WEB *www.rica.no. 144 rooms. Restaurant, bar, meeting rooms, parking (fee). AE, DC, MC, V.*

$$–$$$ ✕ **Scandic Hotel Bergen City.** This business hotel runs Bergen Congress Center, the city's largest convention center, and has warm, stylish, comfortable rooms. Take a seat in a wicker chair in the spacious lobby bar to meet people or relax. Located beside Bergen Kino, it's a short walk to Den Nationale Scene theater, Grieghallen, and restaurants. ⊠ *Håkonsgt. 2, 5015,* ☎ *55/30–90–90,* FAX *55/23–49–20,* WEB *www. scandic-hotels.com. 171 rooms, 4 suites. Restaurant, bar, convention center. AE, DC, MC, V.*

$–$$$ ⌘ **Tulip Inn Rainbow Hotel Bryggen Orion.** Facing the harbor in the center of town, the Orion is within walking distance of many of Bergen's most famous sights, including Bryggen and Rosenkrantztårnet. Now part of the Rainbow Hotel chain, the rooms in this budget hotel are small but comfortable. ⊠ *Bradbenken 3, 5003,* ☎ *55/30–87–00,* FAX *55/32–94–14,* WEB *www.rainbow-hotels.no. 229 rooms. Restaurant, bar, nightclub. AE, DC, MC, V.*

$–$$ ⌘ **Hotel Park Pension.** Near the university, this small family-run hotel is in a well-kept Victorian building dating back to the 1890s. Both the public rooms and the guest rooms are furnished with antiques. It's a short distance to Grieghallen, downtown, and the bus and railway stations. ⊠ *Harald Hårfagres gt. 35, 5007,* ☎ *55/54–44–00,* FAX *55/54–44-44. 21 rooms. Breakfast room. AE, DC, MC, V.*

$ ⌘ **Crowded House.** Named after an Australian band of the '80s, this no-frills travel lodge is perfect for students and budget travelers. Newly renovated, it's a short walk from shopping, restaurants, entertainment, and local attractions as well as train, bus, and ferry connections. Most of the spartan rooms have good beds, telephones, and wash basins. Showers and toilets are in the corridor. ⊠ *Håkonsgt. 27, 5015,* ☎ *55/23–13–10,* FAX *55/23–13–30,* WEB *www.crowded-house.com. 34 rooms without bath. Café. AE, DC, MC, V.*

NIGHTLIFE AND THE ARTS

Nightlife

Bars and Clubs

Most nightlife centers are downtown and in the harbor area. **Banco Rotto** (⊠ Vågsalmenning 16, ☎ 55/55–49–60) has pulsating music, much of it live, that attracts those in their 20s and 30s. **Dickens** (⊠ Kong Olavs pl. 4, ☎ 55/36–31–30), across from the Hotel Norge, is a relaxed place good for an afternoon or evening drink. **Engelen Discoteque** (the Angel; ⊠ Radisson SAS Royal Hotel, Bryggen, ☎ 55/54–30–00) attracts a mixed weekend crowd when it blasts hip-hop, funk, and rock. Several Irish style pubs, including **Finnegans** (⊠ Ole Bulls pl. 9, ☎ 55/55–31–31), attract native English speakers, both locals and visitors. The **Hotel Norge** (⊠ Ole Bulls pl. 4, ☎ 55/57–30–00) piano bar and disco are low-key, with an older crowd. The three-story **Rick's Café & Salonger** (⊠ Veiten 3, ☎ 55/55–31–31) has a disco, an Irish pub, and Bergen's longest bar; the decor is straight out of *Casablanca*. **Wesselstuen** (⊠ Ole Bulls pl. 6, ☎ 55/55–49–49) is a cozy gathering place for local students and academics. **Zachariasbryggen** is a restaurant and entertainment complex right on the water.

Bergen has an active gay community. Call or check the Web site of **Landsforeningen for Lesbisk og Homofil Frigjøring** (⊠ Nygårdsgt. 2A, ☎ 55/32–13–16, WEB home.powertech.no/llhbg), the National Association for Lesbian and Gay Liberation, Wednesday 7–9 to ask about events in the city. In the same building as the Landsforeningen, there's the popular gay hangout **Kafé Fincken** (⊠ Nygårdsgt. 2A, ☎ 55/32–13–16), which is open daily until 1 AM.

Cafés

Café Opera (⊠ 24 Engen, ☎ 55/23–03–15) is a classic, both sumptuous and stylish. It's often crowded on Friday and Saturday nights. Next to the **Mr. Bean Bar & Coffee Shop**, there's **Dr. Livingstone's Traveller's Café**, (⊠ Kong Oscars gt. 12, ☎ 55/56–03–12), a special bar and café whose walls are covered with photographs, maps, and memorabilia from world travels. If you're traveling by train, stop for a coffee at **Kaffehuset Friele** (⊠ Railway Station). **Kafe Klippers** (⊠ Georgernes Verft 12, ☎ 55/31–00–60), Bergen's largest outdoor café, has a spectacular view of the water at sunset. **På Folkemunne** (⊠ Ole Bulls pl. 9–11, ☎ 55/30–71–37) is a trendy, candelit café with clever quotes on its walls. Lunch and dinner are served. As the name implies, **Say Cheese** (⊠ Finnegården 2A, ☎ 55/56–30–90) is a cute wine and cheese bar. **Vågen Fetevare** (⊠ Kong Oscars gt. 10, ☎ 55/31–65–13) is a homey and bohemian coffeehouse. Books are sold and readings are held here.

Live Music

Bergensers love jazz. The **Bergen Jazz Forum** (⊠ Georgernes Verft 3, 5011 Bergen, ☎ 55/32–09–76) is *the* place to find it, both in winter and summer, when there are nightly jazz concerts. The international **Nattjazz** festival is held here in late May to early June. For live pop and rock, see local listings for concerts at **Den Stundesløse** (⊠ Ole Bulls pl. 9–11, ☎ 55/30–71–36), **Det Akademiske Kvarter** (⊠ Olav Kyrres gt. 49–53, ☎ 55/30–28–00), and **Maxime** (✉ Ole Bulls pl. 9–11, ☎ 55/30–71–35), and **Det Akademiske Kvarter** (✉ Olav Kyrresgt. 49–53, ☎ 55/30–28–00).

The Arts

Bergen is known for its **Festspillene** (International Music Festival), held each year during the last week of May and the beginning of June. It features famous names in classical music, jazz, ballet, the arts, and theater. Tickets are available from the Festival Office at **Grieghallen** (✉ Lars Hilles gt. 3, 5015, ☎ 55/21–61–50).

Folk Music

Twice a week in summer the **Bergen Folklore Dance Group** performs a one-hour program of traditional dances and music from rural Norway at the Bryggens Museum. Tickets are sold at the tourist office and at the door. ✉ *Bryggen*, ☎ *55/31–95–50.* 🎫 *NKr 95.*

The extensive **Fana Folklore** program is an evening of traditional wedding food, dances, and folk music, plus a concert—at the 800-year-old Fana Church. The event has been going on for more than 40 years. ✉ *A/S Kunst (Art Association), Torgalmenning 9, Fana,* ☎ *55/91–52–40.* 🎫 *NKr 230 (includes dinner and return bus transportation).* ☉ *June–Aug., Mon.–Tues. and Thurs.–Fri. at 7* PM. *Catch the bus from the center of Bergen and return by 10:30* PM.

Film

If you're in the mood for a movie, all foreign films are shown in their original language, with subtitles in Norwegian. **Bergen Kino** (✉ Konsertpaleet, Neumannsgt. 3, ☎ 55/56–90–50) is a complex of several different theaters. The **Forum** (✉ Danmarkspl.) is the big, old cinema in town.

Classical Music

Recitals are held at **Troldhaugen** (☎ 55/92–29–92, WEB www. troldhaugen.com), home of composer Edvard Grieg, all summer. Tickets are sold at the tourist office or at the door. Performances are given late June–August, Wednesday and Sunday at 7:30, Saturday at 2; and September–November, Sunday at 2.

Bergen International Chamber Music Festival (✉ ☎ 55/99–07–55) is played every August at Fløien Restaurant atop Fløyen. The **Bergen Filharmonsike Orkester** (Bergen Philharmonic Orchestra; ✉ Grieghallen, Lars Hilles gt. 3, 5015, ☎ 55/21–61–50) plays from September to May.

Revues and Cabarets

There are a number of locations that perform revues and cabaret shows, including **Logen** (✉ Ole Bulls pl., ☎ 55/23–20–15) and **Ole Bull Teater** (✉ Ole Bulls pl. 9–11, ☎ 55/30–71–35). **Radisson SAS Hotel Norge,** (✉ Ole Bulls pl. 4, ☎ 55/57–30–00) stages performances in July and August.

Theater

Although theater is generally performed in Norwegian, check listings for occasional English performances. The **Den Nationale Scene** (✉ Engen, ☎ 55/54–97–10) has performances on three stages. It's closed in July and most of August. **Bergen International Theater (BIT)** (✉ Nøstegt. 54, ☎ 55/23–22–35) has Norwegian and international theatrical and modern dance performances. **Nye Carte Blanche** (✉ Danseteatret, Sigurdsgt. 6, ☎ 55/30–86–80) stages ballet and modern dance performances.

OUTDOOR ACTIVITIES AND SPORTS

Fishing

The **Bergen Angling Association** (✉ Fosswinckelsgt. 37, ☎ 55/32–11–64) has information and fishing permits. Among the many charters in the area, the **Rjfylke Fjord Tour** (☎ 911/59–048 or 946/09–548) offers two-hour journeys from Bergen twice daily along the coast. Anglers can catch coal fish, cod, mackerel, and haddock.

Golf

North of Bergen at Fløksand, in a scenic setting, **Meland Golf Club** (✉ Frekhaug, ☎ 56/17–46–00) has an 18-hole championship course with high-quality golf clubs and carts for rent.

Hiking

Mountainous and forest-filled Bergen and the surrounding region make it ideal for long walks and hikes in fresh, mountain air and lush, green surroundings. Take the funicular up **Fløyen,** and minutes later you'll be in the midst of a forest. For a simple map of the mountain, ask at the tourist office for the cartoon "Gledeskartet" map, which outlines 1½- to 5-km (1- to 3-mi) hikes. **Ulriken Mountain** is popular with walkers. Maps of the many walking tours around Bergen are available from bookstores and from **Bergens Turlag** (✉ Tverrgt. 2–4, 5017 Bergen, ☎ 55/32–22–30) a touring club that arranges hikes and maintains cabins for hikers.

Racket Sports

Take your favorite racket and head to a couple of sports facilities outside downtown Bergen. **Racquet Center** (✉ Fjellsdalen 9, ☎ 55/12–32–30) has tennis, badminton, squash, soccer, and handball. The well-equipped **Paradis Sports Senter** (☎ 55/91–26–00) has five indoor tennis courts, four squash courts, and badminton courts. There's also spinning, aerobics, and sunbeds.

Swimming

These days, the most exciting place to swim in Bergen is the new **Vannkanten** (☎ 55/50–77–77) a water complex of several pools, cosmic bowling, a coffee bar, and restaurants. **Sentralbadet** (✉ Teatergt.), is the city's main swimming pool, in the center of town. **Nordnes sjøbad** (✉ near the Akvariet/Bergen Aquarium) is a popular recreational facility that has an outdoor, heated swimming pool.

Yachting

The 100-year-old Hardanger yacht *Mathilde* (✉ Stiftinga Hardangerjakt, 5600 Kaldestad, ☎ 56/55–22–77), with the world's largest authentic yacht rigging, does both one- and several-day trips, as well as coastal safaris.

SHOPPING

Shopping Centers

Bergen's shopping centers Galleriet, Kløverhuset, and Bergen Storsenter are open weekdays 9–8 and Saturday 9–6. The pedestrian shopping streets Gamle Strandgaten, Torgallmenningen, Hollendergaten, and Marken are all worth browsing. **Sundt City** (✉ Torgalmenningen 14,

☎ 55/31–80–20) is the closest thing Norway has to a traditional department store, with everything from fashion to interior furnishings. However, you can get better value for your kroner if you shop around for souvenirs and sweaters. **Kløverhuset** (✉ Strandkaien 10, ☎ 55/31–37–90), between Strandgaten and the fish market, has 40 shops under one roof, including outlets for the ever-so-popular Dale knitwear, souvenirs, leathers, and fur. **Galleriet,** on Torgalmenningen, is the best of the downtown shopping malls. Here you will find **Glasmagasinet** and more exclusive small shops along with all the chains, including **H & M (Hennes & Mauritz)** and **Lindex. Bergen Storsenter,** by the bus terminal, is a fairly new shopping center that's conveniently located for last-minute items.

Specialty Stores

Antiques
There are many antiques shops on **Øvregaten,** especially around Fløibanen. **Cecilie Antikk** (✉ Kong Oscars gt. 32, ☎ 55/96–17–53) deals primarily in antique Norwegian glass, ceramics, and old and rare books.

Books
Melvær (✉ Galleriet and other locations downtown, ☎ 55/96–28–10), has a wide selection of maps, postcards, books about Norway, dictionaries, travel guides, novels, children's books, and books in English.

Clothing
Viking Design (✉ Strandkaien 2A, ☎ 55/31–05–20) carries lots of sweaters, including many by Oleana.

Glass, Ceramics, Pewter
Viking Design (✉ Strandkaien 2A, ☎ 55/31–05–20) specializes in pewter. Some pieces can be picked up quite reasonably. **Tilbords, Bergens Glasmagasin** (✉ Olav Kyrres gt. 9, ☎ 55/31–69–67) claims to have the town's largest selection of glass and china, both Scandinavian and European designs. **Hjertholm** (✉ Olav Kyrres gt. 7, ☎ 55/31–70–27) is the ideal shop for gifts; most everything is of Scandinavian design. Available are pottery and glassware of the highest quality—much of it from local artisans.

Handicrafts
Husfliden (✉ Vågsalmenning 3, ☎ 55/31–78–70) caters to all your handicrafts needs, including a department for Norwegian national costumes. This is one of the best places to pick up handmade Norwegian goods, especially handwoven textiles and hand-carved wood items. **Berle Bryggen** (✉ Bryggen 5, ☎ 55/10–95–00) has the complete Dale of Norway collection in stock and other traditional knitwear and souvenir items—don't miss the troll cave. **Amerie** (✉ Finnegårdsgt. 6, ☎ 55/31–18–20) has traditional and modern handicrafts and designs in knitwear, jewelry, souvenirs, leather goods, china, and crystal.

Fishing Supplies
Campelen (✉ Strandkaien 2A and 18, ☎ 55/32–34–72 or 55/23–07–30) has fishing equipment for sports and working anglers. Its staff also arranges fishing trips that leave from Bergen harbor.

Food
Kjøttbasaren (✉ Vetrlidsalmenning 2, ☎ 55/55–22–23) is in a restored 1877 meat market. The "Meat Bazaar" is known as Bergen's temple of food for its array of everything from venison to sweets. Famous all over Norway, **Søstrene Hagelin** (✉ Olav Kyrres gt. 33, ☎ 55/32–69–49) sells traditional fish balls, fish pudding, and other seafood products made from its secret recipes.

Interior Design

Norwegian designers recommend the **Black & White Studio** (⊠ Kong Oscard gt. 4, ☎ 55/90–35–40) for Scandinavian furniture and lamps.

Jewelry

Theodor Olsens (⊠ Ole Bulls pl. 7, ☎ 55/55–14–80) stocks silver jewelry of distinctive Norwegian and Scandinavian design. **Juhls' Silver Gallery** (⊠ Bryggen, ☎ 55/32–47–40), has its own exclusive jewelry called "Tundra," which is inspired by the nature of the Norwegian north.

Toys

Take a stroll through **Troll** (⊠ Audhild Viken, Bryggen, ☎ 55/21–51–00) for adorable, mean-looking trolls of all shapes and sizes. The same complex that holds Troll also has an all-year **Julehuset** (⊠ Audhild Viken, Bryggen, ☎ 55/31–14–32) or Christmas House, full of cheery Norwegian Christmas "Nisser" (elves).

BERGEN A TO Z

To research prices, get advice from other travelers, and book travel arrangements, visit www.fodors.com.

AIR TRAVEL TO AND FROM BERGEN
CARRIERS

SAS, Braathens, and Widerøe Airlines are the main domestic carriers.
➤ AIRLINES AND CONTACTS: **Braathens** (☎ 815/20–000). **SAS** (☎ 810/03–300). **Widerøe** (☎ 810/01–200).

AIRPORTS AND TRANSFERS

Flesland Airport is 20 km (12 mi) south of Bergen. Braathens, SAS, and Widerøe's have the most frequent flights here.
➤ AIRPORT INFORMATION: **Braathens** (☎ 55/99–82–50). **SAS** (☎ 55/11–43–00). **Widerøe** (☎ 810/01–200).

AIRPORT TRANSFERS

Flesland is a 30-minute bus ride from the center of Bergen at off-peak hours. The Flybussen (Airport Bus) departs three times per hour (less frequently on weekends) from the SAS Royal Hotel, the Braathens office at the Hotel Norge, and from the bus station. Tickets cost NKr 45.

Driving from Flesland to Bergen is simple, and the road is well marked. Bergen has an electronic toll ring surrounding it, so any vehicle entering the city weekdays between 6 AM and 10 PM has to pay NKr 5. There is no toll in the other direction.

A taxi stand is outside the Arrivals exit. The trip into the city costs about NKr 250.
➤ TAXIS AND SHUTTLES: **Bergen Taxi** (☎ 07000 or 55/99–70–60).

BOAT AND FERRY TRAVEL

Boats have always been Bergen's lifeline to the world.

Fjord Line serves North Norway, Stavanger and Haugesund, and Hardangerfjord and Sunnhordland. There's also service to Sognefjord, Nordfjord, and Sunnfjord.

The Smyril Line has a ferry that departs once a week in summer to the Shetland Islands, the Faroe Islands, and Iceland. Smyril also has service between Bergen and Scotland.

Hurtigruten (the Coastal Steamer) departs daily from Frielenes Quay, Dock H, for the 11-day round-trip to Kirkenes in the far north.

Fjord and express boats depart from Strandkai Terminalen. International ferries depart from Skoltegrunnskaien.

➤ BOAT AND FERRY INFORMATION: **Fjord Line,** (☎ 81/53–35–00, WEB www.fjordline.com). *Hurtigruten* (✉ Coastal Express, Veiten 2B, 5012, ☎ 55/23–07–90). **Smyril Line** (☎ 55/32–09–70, WEB www. smyril-line.com). **Strandkai Terminalen** (☎ 55/23–87–80).

BUS TRAVEL TO AND FROM BERGEN

The summer-only bus from Oslo to Bergen, Geiteryggekspressen (literally, "Goat-Back Express," referring to the tunnel through Geiteryggen Mountain, which looks like a goat's back, between Hol and Aurland) leaves the Nor-Way bus terminal at 8 AM and arrives in Bergen 12½ hours later. Buses also connect Bergen with Trondheim and Ålesund. Western Norway is served by several bus companies, which use the station at Strømgaten 8.

➤ BUS INFORMATION: **Central Bus Station** (Strøgt. 8, ☎ 177). **Geiteryggekspressen** (✉ Oslo Bussterminalen Galleriet, ☎ 815/44–444).

BUS TRAVEL WITHIN BERGEN

Tourist tickets for 48 hours of unlimited travel within the town boundaries cost NKr 90, payable on the yellow city buses. All buses serving the Bergen region depart from the central bus station at Strømgaten 8.

➤ BUS INFORMATION: **Central Bus Station** (✉ Strømgt. 8, ☎ 177).

CAR TRAVEL

Bergen is 478 km (290 mi) from Oslo. Route 7 is good almost as far as Eidfjord at the eastern edge of the Hardangerfjord, but then it deteriorates considerably. The ferry along the way, crossing the Hardanger Fjord from Brimnes to Bruravik, runs continually 5 AM to midnight and takes 10 minutes. At Granvin, 12 km (7 mi) farther north, Route 7 joins Route E68, which is an alternative route from Oslo, crossing the Sognefjorden from Refsnes to Gudvangen. From Granvin to Bergen, Route E68 hugs the fjord part of the way, making for spectacular scenery.

Driving from Stavanger to Bergen involves two to four ferries and a long journey packed with stunning scenery. The Stavanger tourist information office can help plan the trip and reserve ferry space.

Downtown Bergen is enclosed by an inner ring road. The area within is divided into three zones, which are separated by ONE WAY and DO NOT ENTER signs. To get from one zone to another, return to the ring road and drive to an entry point into the desired zone. It's best to leave your car at a parking garage (the Birkebeiner Senter is on Rosenkrantz Gate, and there's a parking lot near the train station) and walk. You pay a NKr 5 toll every time you drive into the city—but driving out is free.

➤ CAR EMERGENCIES: **Vehicle Breakdown Service** (✉ Inndalsvn. 22, ☎ 55/59–40–70) operates 24 hours a day.

➤ CAR RENTAL AGENCIES: **Avis** (✉ Lars Hilles gt. 20B, ☎ 55/55–39–55). **Budget** (✉ Lodin Lepps gt. 1, ☎ 55/90–26–15). **Hertz** (✉ Nygårdsgt. 91, ☎ 55/96–40–70).

EMERGENCIES

The dental emergency center at Vestre Strømkai 19 is open weekdays 4–9 and weekends 3–9. An emergency room at the outpatient center at the same location is open 24 hours. Apoteket Nordstjernen, by the bus station, is open Monday–Saturday from 8:00 AM to midnight, Sunday from 9:30 AM.

➤ DOCTORS AND DENTISTS: **Emergency Dental Care** (✉ Vestre Strømkai 19, ☎ 55/32–11–20).

➤ HOSPITALS: **Emergency Room** (⊠ Vestre Strømkai 19, ☏ 55/32–11–20).

➤ LATE-NIGHT PHARMACIES: **Apoteket Nordstjernen** (⊠ Central Bus Station, Strømgt. 8, ☏ 55/21–83–84).

INTERNET SERVICE

➤ CONTACTS: **Allezzo, Galleriet** (⊠ Torgallm., ☏ 55/31–11–60). **Cyberhouse** (⊠ Vetrlidsallm. 13, ☏ 55/36–66–16, WEB cafe.cyberhouse.no). **Netropolis** (⊠ Teatergt. 20, ☏ 55/55–85–44).

LAUNDRY

➤ CONTACTS: **Jarlens Vaskoteque** (⊠ Lille Øvregt. 17, ☏ 55/32–55–04).

MONEY MATTERS

Most Bergen banks in downtown are open Monday–Wednesday and Friday 8:15–3:30, Thursday 8:15–6. Some are open on Saturday 10–1. From mid-May–September, most close a half hour earlier. The 24-hour **Bergen Card,** which costs NKr 150 (NKr 230 for 48 hours), gives free admission to most museums and attractions, and rebates of 25% to 50% off sightseeing, rental cars, transportation to and from Bergen, and free parking (limited to marked areas). It's available at the tourist office and in most hotels. The **Bergen Package** cuts your lodging costs by including a special deal on hotel rates, a full breakfast, and the Bergen Card. It costs from NKr 465 (NKr 585 in summer) per person in double room and you may choose from 24 hotels in all categories. Children under the age of 16 sleeping in extra beds in their parents' room, pay only NKr 50 per night.

CURRENCY EXCHANGE

The post office exchanges money and is open weekdays 8–6 and Saturday 9–3. The Tourist Information Office in Bergen exchanges money outside banking hours.

➤ CONTACTS: **Post Office** (☏ 55/54–15–00).

TAXIS

Taxi stands are in strategic locations downtown. All taxis are connected to the Bergen Taxi central dispatching office and can be booked in advance.

➤ TAXI COMPANIES: **Bergen Taxi Dispatching Office** (☏ 07000 or 55/99–70–60 for reservations).

TOURS

Bergen is the guided-tour capital of Norway because it is the starting point for most fjord tours. Tickets for all tours are available from the tourist office.

Check with the tourist office (☞ Visitor Information) for additional recommendations. The ambitious all-day "Norway-in-a-Nutshell" bus-train-boat tour (you can book through the tourist office) goes through Voss, Flåm, Myrdal, and Gudvangen—truly a breathtaking trip—and is the best way to see a lot in a short amount of time.

BOAT TOURS

Traveling by boat is an advantage because the contrasts between the fjords and mountains are greatest at water level. The boats are comfortable and stable (the water is practically still), so seasickness is rare. Stops are frequent, and all sights are explained. Fjord Sightseeing offers a four-hour local fjord tour. Fylkesbaatane (County Boats) i Sogn og Fjordane has several combination tours. Tickets are sold at the tourist office (☞ Vistor Information) and at the quay.

Norway's largest and oldest tall sailing ship, *Statsraad Lehmkuhl,* is
the pride of Bergen. Sailing cruises, short skerry cruises, and charters
are available. The *TMS Weller* (☎ 55/19–13–03 or 905/32–367), can
be booked for charter and fishing tours.

➤ FEES AND SCHEDULES: **Fjord Sightseeing** (☎ 55/25–90–00). **Fylkesbaatane i Sogn og Fjordane** (☎ 815/00–888). **Statsraad Lehmkuhl** (✉
Bradbenken, ☎ 55/30–17–00). *TMS Weller* (☎ 55/19–13–03 or 905/
32–367).

BUS AND WALKING TOURS

Bergen Guided Tours offers three city tours that leave from the Tourist
Office, including one to Edvard Grieg's home and the Fantoft Stave
Church. Bergen Guide Service has 100 authorized Bergen guides who
give two different city walking tours: "The Unknown Bergen" and
"Bergen Past and Present."

Bergens-Expressen, a "train on tires," leaves from Torgalmenningen
for a one-hour ride around the center of town, summer only.

➤ FEES AND SCHEDULES: **Bergens-Expressen** (☎ 55/53–11–50). **Bergen
Guide Service** (☎ 55/32–77–00). **Bergen Guided Tours** (☎ 55/55–
44–00).

TRAIN TRAVEL

The Bergensbanen has five departures daily, plus an additional one on
Sunday, in both directions on the Oslo–Bergen route; it's widely ac-
knowledged as one of the most beautiful train rides in the world.
Trains leave from Oslo S Station for the 7½- to 8½-hour journey. For
information about trains out of Bergen, call the number below.

➤ TRAIN INFORMATION: **Bergen Train Information** (☎ 55/96–69–00 or
815–00–888).

TRANSPORTATION AROUND BERGEN

The best way to see the small center of Bergen is on foot. Most sights
are within walking distance of the marketplace.

VISITOR INFORMATION

Bergen's Tourist Information Office is in the Fresco Hall in Vågsall-
menning Square opposite the fish market. The opening hours are June–
August, daily 8:30 AM–10 PM; May and September, daily 9–8; and October–May, Monday–Saturday 9–4. The office's staff sells the Bergen
Card, Bergen Package, brochures and maps, arranges accommodations
and sightseeing, and exchanges currency.

For more information on fjord travel, go to the Galleriet shopping mall
and check out Fjord Norway's information center there.

➤ TOURIST INFORMATION: **Fjord Norge–Fjord Norway** (✉ Galleriet, ☎
55/55–07–30). **Tourist Information in Bergen** (Vågsallmenningen 1,
☎ 55/32–14–80).

7 CENTRAL NORWAY: THE HALLINGDAL VALLEY TO HARDANGERFJORD

In summer, the rugged peaks and flat plateaus of central Norway provide a spectacular backdrop for hikers and bikers: crystal clear streams ramble down mountainsides, flocks of sheep graze in the pastures, and snowcapped summits glisten in the distance. Come winter this area—especially Geilo, Gol, and Hemsedal—teems with skiers, both cross-country and downhill.

T HE STUNNING MOUNTAIN COUNTRY between Hallingdal Valley and Hardangerfjord is a feast for the eyes—here there are Europe's tallest peaks, the largest national park, and the highest plateau. No wonder it has become a popular destination for Norwegian outdoor lovers. Take the much-heralded, spectacular Oslo-Bergen train ride and gaze at the amazing views passing you by. Along the way, there are many places to cross-country or downhill ski, cycle, or hike in the mountains. Fish, canoe, and raft in the shimmering lakes and rivers. Ride Fjord horses over the Hardangervidda plateau. Walk back in time through medieval stave churches or relics-filled folk museums. Experience country living and local hospitality at friendly mountain farms, or bask in the charm of a resort town like Geilo.

Numbers in the margin correspond to points of interest on the Central and Interior Norway map.

Hallingdal Valley

Route 7 from Drammen winds through the historic Hallingdal Valley, which is lined with small farming communities and ski resorts. Hallingdal is known for its many well-preserved wooden log buildings.

Outdoor Activities and Sports

BIKING

The **Eventyrvegen** (Adventure Road) is a group of bicycle routes that go through the forest and country. They follow the Hallingdal and Hemsil rivers and go near the idyllic Krøderen Lake. Along the way, you'll see wild, majestic mountains and lush, green valleys. Eventyrvegen's Route 52, for example, goes from Gol to Hemsedal following the Hemsil River, which is known for its fishing. You can buy the Adventure Road cycling map at tourist offices or bookshops. One-way bike rentals (to be dropped off in another town along the route) can be made at **Fjell og Fjord Ferie A/S** (⊠ Sentrumsvegen 93, Gol, ☎ 32/07–61–35). When looking for a place to stay, look for SYKLIST VELKOMMEN-signs. This means that the lodgings are "bicycle friendly," welcoming cyclists with bike repair kits, safe parking, and laundry facilities.

En Route   Between Hallingdal and Valdres lies **Vassfaret,** a forested, 30 km (18 mi) mountain valley of large lakes, rivers and streams, steep rocky areas, mountain farms, and abandoned settlements. Many brown bear and elk make their homes here. After the Black Death swept through in medieval times, the valley remained uninhabited until the 1740s. It was then that land was cleared and permanent settlements established, which lasted until 1921. In the 1980s, Vassfaret was declared a preserved nature area.

At the **Vassfaret Bjørnepark,** the brown bear is king. Actually, five brown bears (Rugg, Berte, Birgjit, Frigg, and Frøya) and two bear cubs call their 10-acre enclosure at the Vassfaret Bear Park home. Moose roam freely in the park's surroundings, and there's also a separate enclosure with a male, female, and calf. The children's zoo has a rabbit, hen, goat, and other farm animals. Sit in a Sámi tent or go on a picnic—the picnic area provides grills and sells meat. Throughout the summer, the park organizes special events such as tours and horseback riding. ⊠ *3539, Flå,* ☎ *32/05–35–10,* WEB *www.vassfaret-bjornepark.no.* ☒ *NKr 90.* ☉ *Early May–mid-June and mid-Aug.–mid-Sept., weekends 11–6; mid-June–mid-Aug., daily 11–6.*

Nesbyen

❶ *120 km (74½ mi) northwest of Oslo, 92 km (57 mi) from Drammen.*

This small town in the heart of Hallingdal valley has some memorable attractions. The **E.K.T. Langedrag Villmarkspark/Fjellgård og Leirskole** (Langedrag Wild Life Park and Mountain Farm) has a park and farm with more than 250 animals of 25 species. The park has great mountain and lake views. Visit the farm and milk one of the 40 goats. Wander through the wildlife park, where wolves, lynxes, boar, elk, deer, and wild reindeer are kept. There are also the ponylike Fjord horses here, which are available for rides, riding lessons, and carriage rides. The park and farm has year-round fishing and theme activities. ⊠ *Tunhovd Nesbyen,* ☎ *32/74–25–50,* WEB *www.numedal.net/langedrag.* ☉ *Daily 10–6.* ☑ *NKr 100.*

A visit to the **Hallingdal Folkemuseum** can help you understand what the area was like a century ago. Twenty-five period sod houses display an extensive collection of regional clothes, weapons, and art. In summer, handicrafts are demonstrated every Wednesday. An emigrant center shows changing exhibitions and has a genealogical archive for those with Norwegian roots. ⊠ *Møllevn. 18, Nesbyen,* ☎ *32/07–14–85,* WEB *www.museumsnett.no/hallingdal.* ☉ *Early June–mid-June and mid-Aug.–late Aug., daily 11–3; mid-June–mid-Aug., daily 10–5; Sept.–May, Sat. 11–3.* ☑ *NKr 50.*

Gol

❷ *About 21 km (13 mi) northwest of Nesbyen.*

This small town is popular with campers in summer and skiers in winter who throng the mountains to the north and east of Gol during ski season. The original 12th-century **Gol stavkyrkje** (Gol Stave Church) still stands today, but it's in Oslo's Norsk Folkemuseum. In Gol, though, a replica church was built. An exhibition highlights the principles of stave church architecture. The Nørront religious museum is nearby. ⊠ *Storeøyni,* ☎ *32/07–54–11.* ☑ *NKr 60.* ☉ *Late May–late June and mid-Aug.–mid-Sept., daily 9–4; late June–mid-Aug., daily 9–4.*

Historic Norwegian farmhouses from 1600 to 1800 inhabit the grounds of **Gol bygdemuseum - Skaga.** Folk dancing and folk music programs and handicraft demonstrations can be arranged through the local tourist office. ☎ *32/02–97–00.* ☑ *NKr 20.* ☉ *July–mid-Aug., Wed.–Sun. noon–5.*

While you're in Gol, check out the beautiful handmade crystal glass designs sold at **Halling Glass** (⊠ *Sentrumsvn. 18, Gol,* ☎ *32/07–53–11*).

OFF THE
BEATEN PATH

HUSO FJELLGÅRD is a popular *støl,* or mountain summer farm. You can visit farm animals, venture into the valley on horseback or its rivers via canoe, and also go on fishing trips. See the house from the time of the Vikings, a dozen log houses, and several exhibits and presentations on the area's culture and business life. ⊠ *Take Rte. 52 north from Gol to Robru, then take Øvrevegen to Huso,* ☎ *32/07–54–11,* WEB *www.pers.no.* ☑ *NKr 60.* ☉ *Late June–early Aug., daily 11–6; early Aug.–Sept., weekends 11–6.*

Hemsedal

❸ *35 km (21½ mi) from Gol.*

Spring, summer, winter, or fall, the valley of **Hemsedal,** and its surrounding area, is always a special destination for those who love the outdoors. Striking mountains and lakes, fjords and glaciers, cascad-

Central and Interior Norway

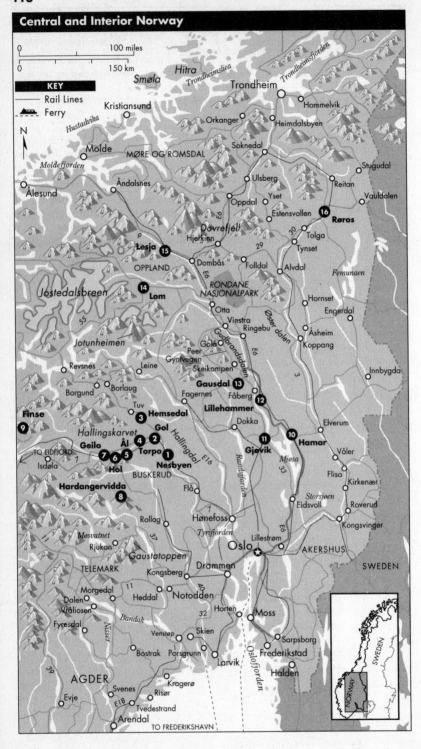

KEY
— Rail Lines
🚗 Ferry

N

100 miles
150 km

Hitra
Smøla
Trondheimsleia
Trondheimsfjorden
Trondheim
Hommelvik
Kristiansund
Orkanger
Heimdalsbyen
Hustadvika
Soknedal
Molde
MØRE OG ROMSDAL
Moldefjorden
Stugudal
Ulsberg
Åndalsnes
Reitan
Vauldalen
Ålesund
Oppdal
Yset
Estensvollen
Røros **16**
Dovrefjell
Hjerkinn
Tolga
Lesja **15**
Dombås
Tynset
OPPLAND
Folldal
Alvdal
Jostedalsbreen
Lom **14**
RONDANE
NASJONALPARK
Femunaen
Otta
Hornset
Engerdal
Vinstra
Ringebu
Åsheim
Jotunheimen
Gola
Koppang
Revsnes
Leine
Peer
Gyntvegen
Skeikampen
Gausdal **13**
Fagernes
Fåberg
Borgund
Borlaug
Tuv
Lillehammer **12**
Finse
Hemsedal **3**
Gol
Dokka
Elverum
9
Hallingskarvet
Ål **4** **2** Torpo **1**
Geilo **7** **6** **5**
Nesbyen
Gjøvik **11** **10** Hamar
TO EIDFJORD
Hol
BUSKERUD
Dokka
Våler
Isdøla
Hardangervidda **8**
Flå
Flisa
Kirkenær
Rollag
Hønefoss
Eidsvoll
Roverud
Møsvatnet
Tyrifjorden
Storsjøen
Kongsvinger
Rjukan
Gaustatoppen
Lillestrøm
AKERSHUS
Oslo
TELEMARK
Kongsberg
Drammen
SWEDEN
Morgedal
Heddal
Notodden
Horten
Moss
Dalen
Wråliosen
Fyresdal
Bandak
Venstøp
Skien
Sarpsborg
Frederikstad
Nisser
Bøstrak
Porsgrunn
Larvik
Halden
AGDER
Kragerø
Evje
Svenes
Risør
Oslofjorden
Tvedestrand
Arendal
TO FREDERIKSHAVN

SWEDEN
NORWAY

ing waterfalls, clear streams—they're all here. In fact, here in Hemsedal, Norwegian World Cup skiers often practice in the top local ski center.

Outdoor Activities and Sports

FISHING

The fishing season runs June–mid-September, in Hemsedal's 18 mountain lakes and four rivers. Inquire at the tourist office about licenses and equipment rental.

HORSEBACK RIDING

Elvestad Fjellridning (☎ 97/63–99–70) offers half-day riding trips in the forest and mountains for experienced to beginner riders. From late June through August, rides start at 9:30, last 3 to 3½ hours, and cost NKr 320.

KAYAKING AND CANOEING

Norske Opplevelser (☎ 32/06–00–03) organizes mountain river kayaking and canoeing trips for half-days at NKr 450 and whole days at NKr 600.

MOUNTAIN CLIMBING

Norske Opplevelser (✉ 3560 Hemsedal, ☎ 32/06–00–03) has introductory courses and guides to mountain climbing. It costs NKr 600 for a whole-day course.

PARAGLIDING

Oslo Paragliding Klubb (☎ 22/10–90–50) has its main base in Hemsedal. Paragliding in tandem with an experienced instructor costs NKr 800.

SKIING

Hemsedal Skisenter (☎ 32/05–53–00) has 34 km (21 mi) of alpine slopes, 175 km (108 mi) of cross-country trails, and 17 ski lifts. The **Vinterlandkortet ski pass** is accepted at all 71 ski slopes in Geilo, Hemsedal, Gol, Nesbyen, and Ål, and is available at ski centers and tourist offices.

Torpo

❹ *52 km (32 mi) from Hemsedal.*

Driving from Gol to Geilo, you'll pass through the tiny town of Torpo, known for its church. **Torpo stave church** is the only church in Hallingdal left preserved from the 1100s. Rich medieval paintings show scenes from the life of Saint Margaret. ☎ *32/08–31–37.* ✉ *NKr 30.* ☉ *June–Aug., daily 8:30–6.*

Ål

❺ *30 km (18 mi) east of Geilo.*

On the road to Geilo, you'll pass through another small town, Ål, best known for the **Ål Stavkyrkjemuseum** (Ål Stave Church Museum). Richly decorated, the museum highlights and explains stave church history and architecture. See the museum's copy of the famous west portal, which no longer exists. ✉ *Prestegardslåven,* ☎ *32/08–10–11.* ☉ *Year-round by appointment.*

Hol

❻ *25 km (15 mi) east of Geilo.*

Hol is best-known in the valley for its *Holsdagen* (☎ 32/09–59–00) festival, held annually on the first Saturday in July or August. Back in 1957, the festival began as a way of keeping local traditions and customs alive. During the festival, a traditional wedding ceremony is performed in the 11th century Hol Gamle Kyrkje. Then the bridal pair rides in a lively procession to Hol Bygdemuseum, where folk music, dance, performances, and traditional Hallingdal dishes await them.

At the **Hol bygdemuseum,** you can see reconstructed buildings from the 1700s. In its 17 sod houses, which include a tenant farmer's house, a barn, stables, and a smithy, costumed museum staff reenact early Norwegian farm life. Rosemaling, Norwegian folk art from the late 1700s, and local costumes from the region are all on view. ⊠ *Hagafoss, Hol,* ☎ *32/08–81–40.* ☉ *Late June–mid-Aug., Tues.–Sun. 11–5.*

Geilo

❼ *35 km (21 mi) west of Torpo; 251 km (155½ mi) from Oslo; 256 km (159 mi) from Bergen.*

Situated halfway between Bergen and Oslo, Geilo is Norway's most popular winter resort and its third biggest tourist draw. More than a million visitors a year head to its alpine slopes and cross-country trails; many people ski directly from their hotels and cabins. Now also a popular summer destination, Geilo is a great place to experience the outdoors. Plan ahead if you want to visit at Easter, since Norwegians flock here then for a final ski weekend.

In the center of Geilo, the 17th-century farm of **Geilojordet** is a part of Hol bygdemuseum. The cattle house, storage house, farmer's living quarters, and other buildings were brought here from the surrounding area and then restored. Special cultural activities and events such as rosemaling, wood carving, and folk music performances are held here. A café serves coffee, waffles, *rømmebrød* (sour-cream cookies), *lefse* (flat cakes filled with sugar or cream), and other traditional local sweets. ⊠ *Geilo center.* ☉ *July, daily 11–5.*

Dining and Lodging

This resort town features an impressive selection of accommodations: major hotels, mountain lodges, traditional cabins, apartments, and camping sites. During high season, they book up early, so contact **Geilo Booking** (☎ 32/09–59–40, WEB www.geilo.no) for advice on choosing lodgings.

$$–$$$ ✕ **Halling-stuene.** Considered one of the region's best chefs, Frode Aga has a high profile in Norwegian culinary circles. The restaurant's simple and elegant interior is in keeping with the Norwegian, international-inspired cuisine. Taste the reindeer fillet with fresh vegetables and mushrooms or the "bacalao tomat," which is dried salt cod with tomato, onion, and paprika. ⊠ *Geilovn. 56,* ☎ *32/09–12–50. AE, DC, MC, V. Closed May.*

$–$$ ✕ **Ro Kro.** Whether you're a rosy-cheeked skier or just passing through, ★ Ro Kro is a worthwhile part of the local experience. The cafeteria-style restaurant serves Norwegian meals and European dishes. The decor uses wood from wall to wall. Near Geilo railway station, it's a convenient place for a quick coffee or meal. ⊠ *Ro Hotell,* ☎ *32/09–08–99. AE, DC, MC, V.*

$$–$$$$ ✕▥ **Dr. Holms Hotel.** "People find pleasure in a beautiful building and ★ a congenial hotel stay," Dr. Ingebrikt Christian Holm once said. Grand pleasure, indeed, can be found at his timeless hotel. Resembling a luxury mountain cabin, this resort hotel has soul and sophistication. Back in 1909, the Norwegian doctor, who specialized in respiratory illnesses, opened it as a sanitorium for asthma sufferers. Soon the hotel earned a reputation for excellence in service and style for its elegantly decorated rooms and its Galleriet restaurant, which serves Continental-Norwegian dishes. Have drinks by the fire in the classy Ski bar, one of Norway's five most popular après-ski bars. Panoramic mountain views surround you amid old wooden skis and sporting relics. Reflect or read in the peaceful library amid its 2,000 volumes. The pub Recepten ("Prescription") has a lively, laid-back atmosphere that includes stand-up comedy, live bands, and special theme nights. Be pampered in the popular Japanese-style Shiseido spa, Dr. Holms Spa Klinikk. Make reservations early and inquire about such events as wine tastings. ⊠ *Timrehaugvn., 23580,* ☎ *32/09–57–00,* ℻ *32/09–16–20,* WEB *www.drholms.com. 127 rooms. Restaurant, 3 bars, lounge, pub, 2 indoor pools, spa, gym, library, meeting rooms. AE, DC, MC, V.*

$$–$$$ ⊞ **Bardøla Høyfjellshotel.** This classic mountain hotel provides thorough personal service. One kilometer (½ mile) from the center of Geilo in peaceful surroundings, the 19th-century wooden buildings are a short distance away from alpine and cross-country ski areas. Sofia's Café and Bar and the Barock Dance Bar have become popular night spots. ⊠ *3580,* ☎ *32/09–41–00,* ℻ *32/09–41–01,* WEB *www.bardoela.no. 104 rooms, 42 suites. Bar, café, lounge, 2 pools, tennis courts, dance club, solarium. AE, DC, MC, V.*

Outdoor Activities and Sports

The informative **Geilo Aktiv** (☎ 32/09–59–30, tourist center) has details and suggestions on local outdoor activities and sports.

BIKING

Ask for bike maps at Geilo Tourist information. Besides Rallarvegen, the Adventure Road, and Numedalsruta, there's excellent cycling in the countryside around Geilo on "summer" roads up into the mountains. **Bike rentals** are available through Geilo Aktiv and **Intersport Geilo** (☎ 32/09–09–70). They cost NKr 100–NKr 200 per day.

FISHING

Geilo's 90 mountain lakes and river stretches are open to the public from June to September. Inquire about the Walks and Recreation Maps for Geilo and Hallingskarvet at the tourist office. All fishers over 16 need a **fishing license.** They are valid for one year and cost NKr 45 at any post office or tourist office. **Fishing permits,** needed for fishing in certain areas, are available at local shops and the tourist office for NKr 40 per day. **Fishing tackle and boat rentals** can be made through **Geilo Camping** (☎ 32/09–07–33) for NKr 120 a day, while rowboats cost NKr 90 for three hours.

HORSEBACK RIDING

Various Geilo businesses offer horseback riding for beginners as well as experienced riders by the hour or day. There are also weekly tours available. **Eivindsplass Fjellgard** (☎ 32/09–48–45, ⊙ July). **Geilo Hestesenter** (☎ 32/09–01–81, ⊙ June–Oct.). **Hakkesetstølen** (☎ 32/09–09–20, ⊙ mid-June–late Sept.). **Hallingskarvet Høyfjellshotell** (☎ 32/08–85–25, ⊙ June–Aug.). **Prestholtseter** (☎ 92/03–75–14, ⊙ July–Aug.). **Ustaoset Hesteridning** (☎ 94/49–39–59, ⊙ July–mid-Aug.).

HIKES AND WALKS

Den Norske Turistforening (DNT) (The Norwegian Mountain Touring Association), has marked trails across the Hardangervidda plain and in the countryside around Hallingskarvet. Inquire at the tourist office about DNT routes and the use of their cabins.

RAFTING AND CANOEING

Dagali Rafting (☎ 32/09–38–20) has an array of organized river rafting trips in the Sjoa and Dagali areas. Prices range from a weekday rate of NKr 250–650 to weekends NKr 300–700. Canoes and rowboat rentals can be made through Geilo Camping, Geilo Aktiv, **Fagerli Leirskole** (☎ 32/09–47–25), and **Hakkesetstølen** (☎ 32/09–09–20).

SKIING

Geilo has 33 pistes and 18 lifts on both sides of the valley. Your down-hill ski pass applies to all the lifts. A free shuttle service goes between each ski center. For cross-country skiers, there are 220 km of groomed and marked cross-country trails that take you through woodland, to Hardangervidda's hills and moors, or around Hallingskarvet, 6,342 ft (1,933 m) above sea level. Geilo has also brought forth a strange new sport to try: rubber rafts outfitted with wooden rudders are sent down snowy slopes for a bracing swoosh. Contact Geilo Aktiv for details.

Geilo Skiheiser (☎ 32/09–59–20) has 24 km of alpine slopes, 130 km of cross-country trails, 18 lifts, and also a ski-board tunnel. Among the area's other four ski centers, **Vestlia** (☎ 32/09–55–10), west of the Ustedalsfjord, is a good choice for families; **Halstensgård** (☎ 32/09–10–20) and **Slaatta** (☎ 32/09–02–02) have a range of alpine and cross-country trails; and **Havsdalsenteret** (☎ 32/09–17–77) attracts a young crowd to its long alpine slopes.

Ski passes give access to all lifts in all five centers (a day pass costs NKr 220 and a week pass NKr 900). The **Vinterlandkortet ski pass** is ac-cepted at all 71 ski slopes in Geilo, Hemsedal, Uvdal, and Ål and is available at ski centers and tourism offices.

Hardangervidda

❽ *90 km (56 mi) from Geilo to Eidfjord following Route 7, the main road that crosses Hardangervidda.*

Norwegians take great pride in their largest national park, which is also Europe's largest mountain plateau—10,000 square km (3,861 square mi). Hardangervidda is home to the largest wild reindeer herds in Eu-rope and the southernmost outpost of the Arctic fox, snowy owl, and other arctic animals and plants. A plateau with a thousand lakes, it has gentle rolling hills and wide stretches of level ground. In the west, the mountains become more dramatic, the plant life richer, the climate wetter, and temperatures more moderate. In the east, the small amount of snow means that it's an almost barren, windswept moorland.

Some 250 Stone Age sites have been found in Hardangervidda. The earliest date from 6,300 BC, which proves that man reached the plateau at the same time as the reindeer. When touring the plateau, either on horseback or on foot, you can find a trail for any level of ability. Den Norske Turistforening (DNT; The Norwegian Mountain Touring As-sociation) has built cabins along the trails. They also organize special tours and activities. All plant and animal life is protected by law. Re-spect the area to make sure it remains a thing of beauty.

At the foot of Vøringfossen waterfall and Måbødalen valley, the **Hardangervidda Natursenter Eidfjord** (Hardangervidda Nature Cen-ter at Eidfjord) focuses on the area's geology, biology, and archaeol-ogy. Over half a billion years ago, Norway was actually south of the equator. Twenty-five million years ago, glaciers began their descent over Norway. An interactive program explains how glaciers form, grow, and recede over time. ✉ Øvre Eidfjord, ☎ 53/66–59–00, WEB *www. hardangervidda.org.* 🎫 *NKr 70.* ☼ *June–Aug., daily, 9–8; Sept.–Oct. and Apr.–May, daily 10–6; Nov.–Mar. by arrangement.*

About an hour's drive north of Geilo is Hardangervidda's highest peak, **Hardangerjøkulen** (Hardanger Glacier), at 6,200 ft. Near Hardan-gerjøkulen you can take a guided hike to the archaeological digs of 8,000-year-old Stone Age settlements. Contact the Geilo Tourist Office (☎ 32/09–59–00).

Finse

❾ Norway's highest railway station on the Bergen line, Finse is a place of pilgrimage for those seeking adventures in the outdoors. Long cross-country ski trips, telemarking, ski sailing, glacier walking, dogsledding, hiking, and cycling are common pastimes. On the last Saturday in April, the traditional end to the ski season, Norwegian skiers gather here for the Skarverennet race. One of the most frigid places in southern Norway, snow can be found on the ground in August. It was here that the polar explorers Fridtjof Nansen and Robert Scott tested their equipment.

The **Rallarmuseet Finse** (Rallar Museum Finse) recalls the legendary turn-of-the-20th-century construction of the Bergen Railway. One exhibition shows how the railway's high mountain section was built, 1871–1909. Another exhibition, *Kampen mot snøen,* or "The Fight Against the Snow," chronicles nature's opposing winter forces. ⊠ *Østre lokomotivstall, Finse stasjon,* ☎ *56/52–69–66,* ⅦⅠⅦ *www.rallarmuseet.no.* ⊡ *NKr 30.* ☉ *Early July–Sept., daily 10–10; early Feb.–early June, weekdays 9–3.*

Outdoor Activities and Sports

BIKING

The most popular bike trek in Norway is the 80-km (50-mi) **Rallarvegen,** which follows the Bergen Railway, westbound over the Hardangervidda, from Haugastøl to Flåm. Carved by hand, the route was originally a construction and transportation track during the building of the Bergen Railway. (*Rallar* was the Norwegian word for the railway workmen). In 1974, the bikeway was established and today attracts 20,000 cyclists every year. Experience southern Norway's highest mountains starting at 3,280 ft above sea level and dropping to 16 ft. Rent a bicycle at Finse and return it at Flåm. Take the bicycle train from Oslo. **Bike rental** is available through Haugastøl Tourist Center (☎ 32/08–75–64) or at the Finse 1222 hotel.

Lodging

$$ ▥ **Finse 1222.** Welcoming guests as soon as they step off the station platform, this *villmarkshotell* (wilderness hotel) is suitably rustic, with signs and other touches that recall the nearby railway. The rooms are cozy and bring to mind a country inn. Countless organized summer and winter outdoor activities, tours, courses, and ski and bike rentals are available. Spend some time at the wellness center. Make your reservations early, especially for weekends. ⊠ *Next to the train station, 3590 Finse,* ☎ *56/52–71–00,* ℻ *56/52–67–17,* ⅦⅠⅦ *www.finse1222.no. 44 rooms. Restaurant, bar, pub, sauna, Turkish bath, dance club. AE, DC, MC, V.*

Central Norway A to Z

To research prices, get advice from other travelers, and book travel arrangements, visit www.fodors.com.

BY TRAIN

This region is served by the Oslo–Bergen line of the NSB. Between late June and mid-September, a special bicycle train runs between Oslo and Voss, departing Oslo at 6:31 AM, arriving at Haugastøl at 11:52 AM, and Voss at 1:06 PM. It departs Voss at 5:20 PM, Myrdal at 6:40 PM, Finse at 7:22 PM, Haugastøl at 7:50 PM, and finally arrives at 12:27 AM in Oslo. Price per bicycle with valid ticket is NKr 90. For a trip between Geilo and Myrdal, the cost is NKr 50.

➤ CONTACTS: **NSB (Norwegian State Railway)** (☎ 81/50–08–88).

BY BUS

Nor-Way Bussekspress operates several different routes between Oslo and Bergen.

➤ CONTACTS: **Nor-Way Bussekspress** (☎ 81/54–44–44).

BY CAR

Follow Route 7 between Oslo–Hønefoss and Bergen.

TOUR OPERATORS

Several companies organize special activities and tours.

➤ CONTACTS: **Fjellferie** (✉ Rotneim, Gol, ☎ 32/07–60–33). **Geilo Aktiv** (☎ 32/09–59–30). **Norske Opplevelser** (☎ 32/06–00–03).

VISITOR INFORMATION

The main tourist offices of the region are in Ål, Geilo, Hemsedal, Gol, and Hallingdal (Nesbyen).

➤ TOURIST INFORMATION: **Ål** (☎ 32/08–10–60). **Geilo** (☎ 32/09–59–00). **Gol** (☎ 32/02–97–00). **Hallingdal (Nesbyen)** (☎ 32/07–01–70). **Hemsedal** (☎ 32/05–50–30).

8   INTERIOR NORWAY: LILLEHAMMER TO RØROS

Colorful farmhouses dot Norway's interior countryside, where rivers run wild through rolling valleys and mountains reach up to the sky. See medieval stave churches, preserved mining towns, open-air museums, and the world's oldest paddleboat in this land with a rich heritage. Lillehammer hosted the 1994 Winter Olympics.

THE LAND TURNS TO ROLLING HILLS and green forests northward in Norway's inner midsection. The main town of Lillehammer draws thousands of skiers from around the world to its slopes and trails. As you travel north, you'll enter Gubrandsdalen (*dal* means valley), one of the longest and most beautiful valleys in the country. Gudbrandsdalen extends from Lake Mjøsa, north of Oslo, diagonally across the country to Åndalsnes. At the base of the lake is Eidsvoll, where Norway's constitution was signed on May 17, 1814.

Venture still farther north to reach the copper-mining town of Røros, which is listed on UNESCO's World Heritage list. This bucolic little town seems to have stood still for the past 100 years. This triangle between Oppland and Hedmark counties, heading south to Lillehammer, is called Troll Park.

Numbers in the margin correspond to points of interest on the Central and Interior Norway map in chapter 7.

Hamar

⑩ *134 km (83 mi) from Oslo, 66 km (41 mi) from Eidsvoll.*

During the Middle Ages, Hamar was the seat of a bishopric. Four Romanesque arches, which are part of the cathedral wall, remain the symbol of the city today. Ruins of the town's 13th-century monastery now form the backbone of a glassed-in exhibition of regional artifacts that include some from the Iron Age.

☾ Also on the grounds of the **Hedmarksmuseet and Domkirkeodden** (Hedemark Museum and Cathedral Point) sit 50 or so idyllic grass-roof houses from the region. The organic garden has 375 different types of herbs. ⊠ *Hamar,* ☎ *62/54–27–00,* WEB *www.hedmarksmuseet.museum.no.* ▱ *NKr 60.* ☾ *Late-May–mid-June and mid-Aug.–Sept., daily 10–4; mid-June–mid-Aug., daily 10–6.*

Hamar got a new lease on life in 1994 when the **Hamar Olympiahall** played host to the speed- and figure-skating events of the Lillehammer Winter Olympics. The multipurpose stadium is now used for exhibitions, conferences, fairs, concerts, and sports events. Shaped like an upside-down Viking ship, Olympiahall was voted most magnificent structure of the previous century by the national Norwegian newspaper *Dagbladet.* Contact Hamar Olympiahall (⊠ Hamar, ☎ 62/55–01–00, WEB www.noa.no) for details on tours and sports facilities.

☾ One of Europe's first railway museums, the **Jernbanemuseet** documents how Norway's railways developed. Exhibits with train memorabilia are inside, while various locomotives and carriages are on narrow-gauge tracks outside and in sheds. Tertittoget, the last steam locomotive built by Norway's state railway, gives rides from mid-May to mid-August. ⊠ *Strandvn. 132,* ☎ *62/51–31–60,* WEB *www.jernbaneverket.no.* ▱ *NKr 30.* ☾ *late May–June and Aug.–early Sept. daily 10–4; July, daily 10–6.*

The world's oldest paddle steamer still in operation, DS *Skibladner,* also called the "White Swan of the Mjøsa," was first launched in 1856. She departs daily from Hamar, connecting the towns along the lake. The steamer creeps up to Lillehammer three days a week. The other days it stops at Eidsvoll. The "Gentlemen's Saloon" and "Ladies Saloon" have been restored. A traditional dinner, consisting of poached salmon and potatoes, with strawberries and cream for dessert, is available for an extra fee. ⊠ *Torggt. 1, Hamar,* ☎ *62/52–70–85,* WEB *www.skibladner.no.* ☾ *Mid-May–mid-Sept.*

Gjøvik

⑪ *45 km (27 mi) from Hamar.*

The *Skibladner* stops several times a week at this quiet, hillside town, which claims to be home to the world's largest underground auditorium. If you're able to make a stop here, check out the **Gjøvik Olympiske Fjellhall** (Olympic Mountain Hall), buried 400 ft below the mountain in the middle of town. ✉ *Town Center,* ☎ *61/13–82–00.* 🎫 *NKr 20.*

OFF THE
BEATEN PATH

GILE GÅRD – Farmhouses dot the rolling green countryside along this side of the Mjøsa. Some of them serve as lodgings, and others are just picturesque stops along the way. The Gile family has owned the Gile Farm since the 18th century, although the land has been used as farmland for some 5,000 years. In addition to seasonal activities, you can eat in the traditional restaurant. ✉ *Off Rte. 33, Lena,* ☎ *61/16–03–73.* ☉ *Mid-May–mid-Sept. Call for more information.*

Lillehammer

⑫ *40 km (25 mi) from Gjøvik, 60 km (37 mi) from Hamar, 180 km (111 mi) from Oslo, 450 km (280 mi) from Bergen.*

Many Norwegians have great affection for Lillehammer, the winter-sports center that was used for the 1994 Winter Olympics. In preparation for the games, the small town built a ski-jumping arena, an ice-hockey hall, a cross-country skiing stadium, and a bobsled and luge track. These days, "Winter City" is known for the skiing mountains of Nordseter and Sjusjøen as well as its many old wooden buildings.

Kulturhuset Banken, a magnificent, century-old bank building, is the main locale for cultural events. It's decorated with both contemporary and turn-of-the-20th-century art. Don't miss the murals on the ceiling of the ceremonial hall. ✉ *Kirkegt. 41,* ☎ *61/26–68–10.* ☉ *Tours for groups by appointment only.*

The **Olympiaparken** (Lillehammer Olympic Park) includes the Lysgårdsbakkene Ski Jump Arena,where the Winter Olympics' opening and closing ceremonies were held. From the tower you can see the entire town. Also in the park are **Håkons Hall,** used for ice hockey; the **Birkebeineren Stadion** (ski stadium), which holds cross-country and biathlon events, and a bobsled and luge track. ✉ *Elvegt. 19,* ☎ *61/25–11–40,* 🌐 *www.olympiaparken.no.* 🎫 *Arena NKr 15; admission fee charged at individual facilities during athletic events.*

The **Norges Olympiske Museum** displays the history of the games from their start in ancient Greece in 776 BC to their current international incarnation. Multimedia presentations and artifacts accompany Norwegian sporting history's Gallery of Honor. The architects of Maihaugen's "We Won the Land" have also created the exhibits here. ✉ *Håkons Hall, Olympic Park.* ☎ *61/25–21–00.* 🎫 *NKr 50 or NKr 100 with joint Mailhaugen.* ☉ *June–Sept., daily 10–6; Oct.–May, Tues.–Sun. 11–4.*

The winter-sports facilities provide amusement year-round in Lillehammer. You can try the **Downhill and Bobsled simulator** between Håkons Hall and Kristins Hall in the Olympic Park. It's a five-minute ride that replicates the sensations of being on a bobsled. 🎫 *NKr 25.* ☉ *Jan.–late June and late Aug., daily 11–4; late June–mid-Aug., daily 10–7.*

If you're older than age 12, you can try the **Bobsled on Wheels**—it's the real thing with wheels instead of blades—at the Lillehammer Bobsled and Luge Stadion. Speeds of 100 km (60 mi) per hour are reached, so you'll get a distinct impression of what the sport is all about. ☎ 94/ 37–43–19. 🎫 *Wheeled bobsled NKr 125.* 🕙 *Late May–early June and mid-Aug.–mid-Sept., daily noon–5; June–mid-Aug., daily 11–7.*

A highlight of Lillehammer's ski year is the **Birkebeineren cross-coun- try ski race,** which commemorates the trek of two warriors whose legs were wrapped in birchbark (hence *birkebeiner*—birch legs), which was customary for people who couldn't afford wool or leather leggings.

★ 🕙 Lillehammer claims fame as a cultural center as well. Sigrid Undset, who won the Nobel Prize in literature in 1928, lived in the town for 30 years. It's also the site of **Maihaugen,** Norway's oldest open-air mu- seum, founded in 1887. The massive collection was begun by Anders Sandvik, an itinerant dentist who accepted folksy odds and ends—and eventually entire buildings—from the people of Gudbransdalen in ex- change for repairing their teeth. Eventually Sandvik turned the collection over to the city of Lillehammer, which provided land for the museum.

Maihaugen's permanent indoors exhibit, **"We Won the Land,"** is an inventive meander through Norway's history. It begins in 10,000 BC when life was somewhere inside a mere drop of melting ice. After walk- ing past life-size, blue-hue dolls representing periods from the Black Death and 400 years of Danish rule, you will arrive in the 20th cen- tury to unsettling visions of the postwar West. ✉ *Maihaugvn. 1,* ☎ *61/28–89–00.* 🎫 *NKr 70, or NKr 100 joint with the Norges Olymp- iske Museum.* 🕙 *June–Aug., daily 9–6; May and Sept., daily 10–5; Oct.– Apr., Tues.–Sun. 11–4. Admission includes guided tour.*

One of the most important art collections in Norway is housed at the **Lillehammer Kunstmuseum** (Lillehammer Museum of Art). In addition to significant pieces by masters from Edvard Munch to Odd Nerdrum, the gallery also has one of the largest collections of works from the National Romantic period. ✉ *Stortorgt. 2,* ☎ *61/26–94–44,* 🌐 *www.lillehammerartmuseum.com.* 🎫 *NKr 30.* 🕙 *May–Sept., daily 10– 5; Sept.–May, Tues.–Sun. 11–4.*

OFF THE BEATEN PATH 🕙

HUNDERFOSSEN PARK – The world's biggest troll sits atop a cave in this amusement park. The glittering gold Eventyrslottet, or fairytale castle, is a must-see. There's a petting zoo for small children; plenty of rides; plus an energy center, with Epcotlike exhibits about oil and gas; and a five- screen theater. The park is 13 km (8 mi) north of Lillehammer. ✉ *Fåberg,* ☎ *61/27–72–22,* 🌐 *www.hunderfossen.no.* 🎫 *NKr 160.* 🕙 *Early June–mid-Aug., daily 10–8.*

Dining and Lodging

$–$$$ ✕ **Blåmann Restaurant & Bar.** Named after a Norwegian folktale about a buck called "Blueman," this popular city restaurant has a com- pletely blue interior spread over two spacious floors. Try the Mexican tacos or a reindeer or ostrich steak. ✉ *Lilletorvet 1,* ☎ *61/26–22–03. Reservations essential. AE, DC, MC, V.*

$ ✕ **Vertshuset Solveig.** This informal restaurant is down one of the quain- test streets and in one of the oldest buildings in Lillehammer. The rus- tic wood interior has homey touches like hanging brass pots. The traditional Norwegian fare, which varies depending on the season, is reasonably priced. ✉ *Storgt. 68B,* ☎ *61/26–27–87. AE, DC, MC, V.*

$$$ 🏨 **Comfort Home Hotel Hammer.** This hotel is named after the origi- nal Hammer farm, which first opened its doors to guests in 1665. The rooms are decorated in shades of green with oak furniture, both mod- ern and rustic. Waffles, coffee, light beer, and an evening meal are in- cluded in the price. ✉ *Storgt. 108, 2600,* ☎ *61/26–35–00,* 📠 *61/26–*

37–30. 67 rooms with bath. Lobby lounge, sauna, meeting room. AE, DC, MC, V.

$$–$$$ ⊞ **First Hotel Breiseth.** Within walking distance of the Olympic Park and close to the railroad station and bus stations, this classic hotel attracts many different types of travelers. Rooms are modern and stylish, and there's even a special wing for allergy sufferers. The intimate restaurant Thorvald's Bar & Spiseri has a good reputation for its food and service. ⊠ *Jernbanegt. 1–5,* ☎ *61/24–77–77,* 🖷 *61/26–95–05. 89 rooms. Bar, brasserie, sauna. AE, DC, MC, V.*

$$–$$$ ✕⊞ **Rica Victoria Hotel.** This classic, centrally located hotel has small, relaxing rooms, some of which look out on the main street and the outdoor café it owns, Terassen. **Victoria Stuene,** the hotel's restaurant, is quite good. ⊠ *Storgt. 84B, 2600,* ☎ *61/25–00–49,* 🖷 *61/25–24–74. 121 rooms. 2 restaurants, lobby lounge, outdoor café, pub, nightclub, meeting room. AE, DC, MC, V.*

$$ ⊞ **Mølla Hotell.** In this converted mill, the intimate reception area on the ground floor gives the feeling of a private home. The yellow-walled rooms, which once held grain, are cozy and hold antiques like rocking chairs. At the sky bar, Toppen Bar, you get a panoramic view of the Olympic ski jumping hill and Lake Mjøsa. The Egon Restaurant is a beautiful outdoor retreat in the former 130-year-old grinding mill along Mesna river. ⊠ *Elvegt. 12,* ☎ *61/26–92–94,* 🖷 *61/26–92–95,* 🌐 *www.molla.ol.no. 58 rooms with bath. Restaurant, bar, sauna, gym. AE, DC, MC, V.*

$$ ⊞ **Radisson SAS Lillehammer Hotel.** This classic hotel is between Mailhaugen and the Olympic Park. Rooms are modern and comfortable. There's an 8-acre private park on the premises.⊠ *Turisthotelvn. 6, 2609 Lillehammer,* ☎ *61/28–60–00,* 🖷 *61/25–73–33,* 🌐 *www.lillehammerhotel.no. 250 rooms. Restaurant, 3 bars, pool, sauna, gym, library, solarium, children's programs, meeting rooms. AE, DC, MC, V.*

$–$$ ⊞ **Gjestehuset Ersgaard.** Dating from the 1500s and originally called Eiriksgård (Eirik's Farm), this white manor house has all modern facilities but retains its homeyness. Since it's very close to Olympic Park, there are fantastic views of the city. ⊠ *Olympic Park, Nordsetervn. 201,* ☎ *61/25–06–84,* 🖷 *61/25–31–09,* 🌐 *www.ersgaard.no. 30 rooms, 21 with bath. AE, DC, MC, V.*

$ ⊞ **Birkebeineren Hotel, Motell & Apartments.** Ski trails and hiking terrain are steps away from this hotel's doors. You can choose from new, modern, and well-equipped apartments, hotel rooms, or basic rooms. ⊠ *Olympiaparken,* ☎ *61/26–47–00,* 🖷 *61/26–47–50,* 🌐 *www.birkebeineren.no. 52 hotel rooms, 35 motel rooms, 40 apartments. Dining room, sauna. AE, DC, MC, V.*

Outdoor Activities and Sports

FISHING

Within Troll Park, the **Gudbrandsdalåen** is touted as one of the best-stocked rivers in the country, and the size of Mjøsa trout (locals claim 25 pounds) is legendary. For seasons, permits (you'll need a national and a local license), and tips, contact local tourist boards.

HIKING

Hiking through the mountains is a tried-and-true pastime here. The Nordseter and Sjusjøen tourist centers are both good starting points. From **Nordseter Aktivitets-og Skisenter** (⊠ Lillehammer, ☎ 61/26–40–37), you can hike to Mount Neverfjell, at 1,089 m (3,573 ft). There you can see the Jotunheimen and Rondane mountain ranges. The center rents out mountain bikes for NKr 135 a day and canoes and boats for NKr 120 a day. Mount Lunkefjell (1,012 m) is a popular hikers destination from **Sjusjøen Sport & Aktiviteter** (⊠ Sjøen, ☎ 62/36–30–04). Regular bicycles and mountain bikes can be rented for NKr 45–

150 a day. The center also organizes walks, bicycle and fishing trips, and canoeing.

RAFTING AND CANOEING

The **Sjoa River,** close to Lillehammer, offers some of the most challenging rapids in the country. Contact **Heidal Rafting** (☎ 61/23–60–37).

SKIING

Lillehammer and the four other nearby skiing destinations are collectively called Lillehammer Ski Resorts (www.lillehammerskiresorts.com). Together, they have 35 lifts, 78 pistes, and more than 1,500 km (930 mi) of cross-country trails. Each destination has its own particular charm. A Lillehammer Ski Resorts Pass admits you to all five.

With both high mountain and forest terrain **Hafjell** (⊠ 10 km (6 mi) north of Lillehammer, ☎ 61/27–47–00) is the largest Alpine facility. Snow conditions are generally stable here. The Trollclub snowboard park is popular. There's also a childcare center, a ski school, and several après-ski spots.

Although it has the very challenging downhill course used in the 1994 Olympic Games, **Kvitfjell** (⊠ 50 km north of Lillehammer, ☎ 61/28–36–00) also has easier courses, including a family-friendly 2-km (1 mi) slope with a drop of 350 m (1150 ft). There's also a snowboard park and more than 200 km (124 mi) of prepared cross-country trails. **Gålå** (⊠ 70 km from Lillehammer, ☎ 61/29–85–28) is an all-around ski facility, with spectacular high mountain terrain and views of Jotunheimen and Rondane national parks. It has cross-country trails and organized activities that include ice fishing, snow rafting, sledding, winter riding, and sleigh riding.

Shopping

Most of Lillehammer's 250-odd shops are on or near Storgata street or nearby. From Lilletorget, you can walk to the old industrial area of Mesna Brug, where there's the Mesnasenter (Mesna Center) group of clothing and craft shops. **Husfliden** (⊠ Sigrid Undset pl., ☎ 61/26–70–70), one of the biggest and oldest home crafts stores in Europe, specializes in handknitted sweaters and traditional and handmade goods from the Gudbrandsdalen area. Glassblowing is demonstrated at **Lillehammer Kunst Glass** (⊠ Elvegt. 17, ☎ 61/25–79–80) where special souvenirs are also sold.

Gausdal

⓭ *18 km (11 mi) northwest of Lillehammer.*

The composer of Norway's national anthem and the 1903 Nobel Prize winner in literature, Bjørnstjerne Bjørnson, lived at **Aulestad,** in Gausdal, from 1875 until he died in 1910. After his wife, Karoline, died in 1934, their house was opened as a museum. ⊠ *2656 Follebu,* ☎ *61/22–41–10.* ▣ *NKr 50.* ☺ *Late May and Sept., daily 11–2:30; June and Aug., daily 10–3:30; July daily 10–5:30.*

The scenic, well-marked **Peer Gynt Vegen** (Peer Gynt Road) begins in Gausdal. It's named for the real-life man behind Ibsen's character. As you travel along the rolling hills sprinkled with old farmhouses and rich with views of the mountains of Rondane, Dovrefjell, and Jotunheimen, the road is only slightly narrower and just 3 km (2 mi) longer than the main route. It passes two major resorts, **Skeikampen/Gausdal** and **Golå/Wadahl,** before rejoining E6 at Vinstra.

En Route The E6 highway passes through **Vinstra,** the village of Peer Gynt, where, around mid-August every year, the Peer Gynt Festival celebrates the character and his lore.

Dining and Lodging

$$ ✕⊞ **Golå Høyfjellshotell og Hytter.** Tucked away in Peer Gynt terri-
★ tory north of Vinstra, this peaceful hotel is furnished in typical Norwegian country style. The restaurant's simple menu of fresh local fish and game is elegantly prepared. The trout is highly recommended. ✉ *2646 Golå,* ☎ *61/29–81–09,* FAX *61/29–85–40,* WEB *www.golaresort.com. 42 rooms. Restaurant, pool, cross-country skiing, downhill skiing, children's programs, meeting room. AE, DC, MC, V.*

Outdoor Activities and Sports

HIKING

You can pick up maps and the information-packed **"Peer Gynt"** pamphlet at the tourism office in Vinstra; then hike anywhere along the 50-km (31-mi) circular route, passing Peer's farm, cottages, and monument. **Norske Bygdeopplevelser** (☎ 61/28–99–70) organizes special mountain walking and cycling trips in Peer Gynt country.

SKIING

Skei (☎ 61/22–85–55), near Gausdal, has 125 years' experience as a ski resort. It has trails for downhill, telemark, snowboard, and cross-country. **Peer Gynt** (☎ 61/29–85–28) has respectable downhill slopes but is stronger as a cross-country venue. The one-day **Troll Pass** (NKr 195) ticket is good for admission to lifts at five sites in the area.

Lom

⓮ *At Otta, Route 15 turns off for the 62-km (38-mi) drive to Lom.*

Lom, in the middle of Jotunheimen national park, is a rustic town, with log-cabin architecture, a stave church from 1170, and plenty of decorative rosemaling.

Lom Stavkirke (Lom Stave Church), a mixture of old and new construction, is on the main road. The interior, including the pulpit, pews, windows, the gallery, and a large collection of paintings, is Baroque. ☎ *61/21–10–00.* ✉ *NKr 20.* ☉ *Mid-May–mid-June and mid-Aug.–mid-Sept., daily 10–4; mid-June–mid-Aug., daily 9–9.*

The information center for the Jotunheimen national park, **Norsk Fjellmuseum,** also has fascinating mountain-related exhibits. A permanent display profiles the Norwegian high mountains and the people who live there. ✉ *Town Center,* ☎ *61/21–16–00,* WEB *www.fjell.museum.no.* ☉ *Mid-June–mid-Aug., daily 9–9; mid-Aug.–mid-June, daily 9–4.*

Dining and Lodging

$$ ✕⊞ **Fossheim Turisthotell.** Kristofer Hoyland's cooking has made this
★ traditional hotel famous. Hoyland's a self-taught champion of the local cuisine and now a household name in Norway; his dishes are based on nature's kitchen, with liberal use of game, wild mushrooms, and berries. Try the hotel's famous fillet of reindeer or its breast of ptarmigan, a relative of the grouse. Built as a staging inn in 1897, the hotel has been updated several times. However, it retains its traditional character, with solid-timber walls and antique furnishings that make this an intimate and memorable place. ✉ *2686 Lom,* ☎ *61/21–95–00,* FAX *61/21–95–01,* WEB *www.infor.no/dhh. 54 rooms. Restaurant, bar. AE, DC, MC, V.*

$$ ⊞ **Vågå Hotel.** About halfway between Otta and Lom, this homey, no-frills hotel lies in the lovely mountain village of Vågå. The village has become known for mountain activities like summer hang-gliding competitions. ✉ *Rte. 15, Vågåmo,* ☎ *61/23–95–50,* FAX *61/23–95–51,*

WEB *www.vagahotel.no. 57 rooms. Restaurant, bar, indoor pool, meeting room. AE, D, MC, V.*

$ ⌂ **Elveseter Hotell.** There are many reasons to stay overnight at this unusual hotel, including a swimming pool in a barn dating from 1579. About 24 km (15 mi) from Lom in Bøverdalen, the family-owned Elveseter feels like a museum. ✉ *2687 Bøverdalen,* ☎ *61/21–20–00,* FAX *61/21–21–01,* WEB *www.elveseter-hotell.no. 100 rooms. Restaurant, bar, indoor pool, meeting room. AE, MC, V. Closed mid-Sept.–May. BP.*

Outdoor Activities and Sports

DOGSLEDDING
In Jotunheimen, **Magnar Aasheim and Kari Steinaug** (Sjoa Rafting, ☎ 88/00–63–90) have one of the biggest kennels in Norway, with more than 30 dogs. You can travel as a sled-bound observer or control your own team of four to six dogs, most of which are ridiculously friendly Siberian and Alaskan huskies.

FISHING
Lom Fiskeguiding DA (☎ 61/21–10–24) rents fishing boats and organizes fishing trips.

HIKING
In summer you can hike single-file (for safety purposes, in case of cracks and other dangers) on the ice and explore ice caves on the **Galdhøpiggen** glacier. Call Lom Fjellføring (☎ 61/21–21–42) or the tourist board. You can also rent mountaineering equipment and arrange for lessons through **Natur Opplevingar** (☎ 61/21–11–15).

HORSEBACK RIDING
Saddle up and take to the mountain trails with trips arranged by **Jotunheimen Hestesenter** (☎ 61/21–18–00).

NATIONAL PARKS
In this region are **Ormtjernkampen,** a virgin spruce forest, and **Jotunheimen,** a rougher area spiked with glaciers, as well as Norway's highest peak, the **Galdhøpiggen.**

RAFTING
Several local outfits cater to rafting needs, including **Lom Rafting** (☎ 61/21–29–29), and **Sjoa-Norwegian Wildlife and Rafting** (☎ 61/23–87–27). The companies will organize overnight trips and supply guides.

SKIING
To the east of the Gudbrandsdalen is the **Troll-løype** (Troll Trail), 250 km (155 mi) of country trails that vein across a vast plateau studded with mountains, including the Dovrefjells to the north. For information, contact the Otta Tourist Office. **Beitostølen** (9 km of downhill slopes, 150 km of cross-country trails; seven ski lifts), on the southern slopes of the Jotunheim range, has everything from torchlit night skiing to hang gliding. **Galdhøpiggen Sommerskisenter** (✉ 2686 Lom, ☎ 61/21–21–42 or 61/21–17–50) sits on a glacier, which makes it great for summer skiing.

Lesja

⑮ *159 km (99 mi) from Lom.*

As you follow Route E6 toward Lesja, the broad, fertile valleys and snow-capped mountains of the Upper Gudbrandsdal provide staggering scenery for the drive. The area around Lesja is trout-fishing country; Lesjaskogvatnet, the lake, has a mouth at either end, so the current changes in the middle.

JØRUNDGARD MIDDELALDER SENTER – Anyone who read Sigrid Undset's 1928 Nobel prize–winning trilogy, *Kristin Lavransdatter,* will remember that the tale's heroine grew up on a farm of the same name. The medieval farm, built for the 1995 Liv Ullmann movie, now serves as Jorundgård Medieval Center, a historical and cultural museum. ✉ *Sel,* ☎ *61/23–37–00,* WEB *www.jorundgard.no.* 🖼 *NKr 55, guided tours every ½ hr.* ☉ *June–mid-Sept., daily 10–6.*

Outdoor Activities and Sports

HIKING IN NATIONAL PARKS

The scrubby, flat, and wide **Rondane,** to the southeast of Lesja, is easily accessible for backpacking trips. As Norway's first national park, it was established in 1962 and contains 10 peaks that are more than 2 km (1-¼ mi) high. Wild reindeer still roam here, although road and railway construction has constricted their habitat.

At **Dovrefjell,** peaked to the north, is one of the last virtually intact high-mountain ecosystems in Europe. Wild reindeer, wolverines, wild musk ox, arctic fox, and rare plant species all make their home here. Snøhetta, the highest peak in the park at 2,286 m (7,500 ft), is a popular hiking destination. There are many restrictions regarding hiking in the area, so contact the tourist office before setting out.

TOURS

From 1932 to 1953, musk ox were transported from Greenland to the Dovrefjell, where about 60 still roam—bring binoculars to see them. For information on tours, call the Dombås Tourist Office. **Dovrefjell Aktivitetsenter** (☎ 61/24–15–55) organizes family rafting, moose safaris, mountain trips, and climbing and overnight wilderness camps. **Dovre Eventyr** (☎ 61/24–01–59) has local guides that lead tours of the local flora and fauna. They also offer musk-oxen safaris and mountain climbing courses.

Røros

16 *317 km (197 mi) from Lesja, 157 km (97 mi) from Trondheim.*

At the northern end of the Østerdal, the long valley to the east of Gudbrandsdalen, lies Røros, one of Norway's great mining towns. For more than 300 years practically everyone who lived in this one-company town was connected with the copper mines. Notice there are two main axes: one leads to the church, the other to the company.

Røros's main attraction is the **Old Town,** with its 250-year-old workers' cottages, slag dumps, and managers' houses, one of which is now City Hall. Descendants of the man who discovered the first copper ore in Røros still live in the oldest of the nearly 100 protected buildings. A 75-minute tour organized by the tourist office starts at the information office and ends at the church. ✉ *Peder Hiorts gt. 2,* ☎ *72/41–11–65.* 🖼 *NKr 45.* ☉ *Tours early June and late Aug.–mid-Sept., Mon.–Sat. at 11; late June–mid-Aug., Mon.–Sat. at 10, noon, 1, 2, and 3, Sun. at 1; mid-Sept.–May, Sat. at 11.*

The **Røroskirke** (Røros Church), which rises above all the other buildings in the town, is an eight-side stone structure from 1784 (the mines' symbol is on the tower). It can seat 1,600, quite surprising in a town with a population of only 3,500 today. The pulpit looms above the center of the altar, and seats encircle the top perimeter. ☎ *72/41–00–50.* 🖼 *NKr 25.* ☉ *Mid–late June, weekends 11–1; late June–mid-Aug., Mon.–Sat. 10–5, Sun. 2–4; mid-Aug.–mid-Sept., Mon.–Sat. 11–1; mid-Sept.–May, Sat. 11–1.*

The **Rørosmuseet** (Røros Museum), in an old smelting plant, documents the history of the mines, with working models in one-tenth scale demonstrating the methods used in mining. ⊠ *Near Rte. 30,* ☎ *72/41–05–00.* ⊡ *NKr 45.* ⊙ *Late July–mid-Aug., weekdays 10:30–6, weekends 10:30–4; mid-Aug.–late July, weekdays 11–3, weekends 11–2.*

OFF THE
BEATEN PATH

OLAVSGRUVA – The guided tour of Olaf's Mine, a former copper mine outside town and now a museum, takes visitors into the depths of the Earth, complete with sound-and-light effects. Bring warm clothing and good shoes, as the temperature belowground is about 5°C (41°F) year-round. ⊠ *Near Rte. 31,* ☎ *72/40–61–70.* ⊡ *NKr 50.* ⊙ *Guided tours early June and late Aug.–early Sept., Mon.–Sat. at 1 and 3, Sun. at noon; late June–mid-Aug., daily at 10:30, noon, 1:30, 3, 4:30, and 6; early Sept.–May, Sat. at 3.*

Dining and Lodging

If you want to explore the green, pastured mountains just south of Røros, more than a dozen farmhouses take overnight visitors. Some are hytter, but others, such as the **Vingelsgaard Gjestgiveri** (☎ 62/49–45–43), have entire wings devoted to guest rooms. Rates at Vingelsgaard are around 460 NKr per person. Contact **Vingelen Turistinformasjon** (☎ 62/49–46–65 or 62/49–46–83) for more information.

$$$ ✕⊡ **Bergstadens Hotel.** The lobby here can be very inviting, with many tables and chairs make the area seem intimate. The main draw is the restaurant , which serves traditional Norwegian fare ⊠ *Oslovn. 2, 7460,* ☎ *72/40–60–80,* ⅻ *72/41–60–81. 88 rooms, 4 suites. 2 restaurants, 2 bars, pub, pool, sauna, nightclub, meeting room. AE, DC, MC, V.*

Outdoor Activities and Sports

SKIING

At the northern end of the Gudbrandsdalen region, west of Røros, is **Oppdal** (45 km of alpine pistes, 186 km of cross-country trails; 10 ski lifts), a World Cup venue. Like most other areas, it has lighted trails and snow-making equipment.

Shopping

There are so many craftspeople in downtown Røros that the tourist office arranges tours of their workshops.

Interior Norway A to Z

To research prices, get advice from other travelers, and book travel arrangements, visit www.fodors.com.

LODGING

There are many farms available for a stay in the vicinity of Lillehammer, with a good number on the other side of Lake Mjøsa. For more information contact **Country Holidays in Troll Park** (⊠ Olympia Utvikling, ☎ 61/28–99–70). Rentals are available for stays of a week or longer.

CAR TRAVEL

The wide, two-lane Route E6 north from Oslo passes through Hamar and Lillehammer. Route 3 follows Østerdalen (the eastern valley) from Oslo. Route 30 at Tynset leads to Røros and E6 on to Trondheim, 156 km (97 mi) farther north.

Roads in the north become increasingly hilly and twisty as the terrain roughens into the central mountains. The northern end of the region is threaded by E16, E6, and Routes 51 and 3. Don't speed: high-tech markers at the roadside, particularly prevalent in the area of Vinstra and Otta, are actually cameras. Exceed the speed limit, and you may receive a ticket in the mail.

TRAIN TRAVEL
There are good train connections between Oslo and the major interior towns to the north. The region is served by the Oslo–Trondheim line and two other lines.

VISITOR INFORMATION
➤ TOURIST INFORMATION: **Dombås Tourist Office** (☎ 61/24–14–44). **Gjøvik** (✉ Jernbanegt. 2, ☎ 61/14–67–10). **Hamar** (✉ Vikingskipet, Olympia Hall, ☎ 62/52–12–17). **Lillehammer** (✉ Lilletorget, ☎ 61/25–02–99). **Lom** (☎ 61/21–29–90). **Otta** (✉ Otta, ☎ 61/23–66–50). **Øyer** (☎ 61/27–70–00). **Røros** (✉ Peder Hiorts gt. 2, ☎ 72/41–11–65). **Vågå** (✉ Vågå 37, ☎ 61/23–78–80). **Vinstra** (☎ 61/29–47–70).

9 THE WEST COAST: FJORD COUNTRY

The Norwegian fjords snake inland from the Russian border in the far north all the way to Norway's southern tip. In spectacular inlets like Sognefjord and Geirangerfjord, vertical walls shoot up out of the water, jagged snowcapped peaks blot out the sky, and water tumbles down off mountains in an endless variety of colors, from thundering turquoise to wispy white.

T HE INTRICATE OUTLINE OF THE FJORDS makes Norway's coastline of 21,347 km (13,264 mi) longer than the distance between the North and South Poles. Majestic and magical, the fjords can take any traveler's breath away in a moment. Lush green farmlands edge up the rounded mountain sides. Chiseled, cragged-edged, steep peaks seem to touch the blue skies.

The farther north you travel, the more rugged and wild the landscape. The motionless Sognefjord is the longest inlet, snaking 190 km (110 mi) inland. At the top of Sogn og Fjordane county is a group of fjords referred to as Nordfjord, with the massive Jostedalsbreen, mainland Europe's largest glacier, to the south. In the county of Møre og Romsdal, you'll see mountains that would seem more natural on the moon—all gray rock—as well as cliffs hanging over the water below. Geirangerfjord is the most spectacular fjord.

Boat cruises are the classic way of taking in this breathtaking landscape, but there's much to be gained by more up-close-and-personal experiences. You can walk or climb on one of Norway's 1,630 glaciers, remnants of the 30 ice ages that carved the fjords. Head to Eid and ride one of the ponylike Fjord horses, originally bred for farmwork. In Selje, visit the ruins of a 10th-century cloister. You can also fish for freshwater trout or river raft in the fjord waters.

The best way to see the fjord country is to make an almost circular tour—from Oslo to Åndalsnes, out to the coastal towns of Ålesund, Molde, and Kristiansund, then over Trollstigveien (the "Troll's Path" tourist road) to Geiranger. From there, take a ferry to Hellesylt, down to Stryn, around Loen and Olden and through the subglacial tunnel to Fjærland, and by ferry to Balestrand, connecting with another ferry down to Flåm. In Flåm the railroad connects with Myrdal on the Bergen line. Then the trip can either continue on to Bergen or back to Oslo.

Numbers in the margin correspond to points of interest on the West Coast map.

Åndalsnes

❶ *495 km (307 mi) from Bergen, 354 km (219 mi) from Trondheim.*

★ Åndalsnes is an industrial alpine village of 3,000 people. Walking and hiking are popular pastimes. The tourist office has special guides outlining trails and paths. Fishing trips on the fjord, taking four hours, leaving three times a day, cost NKr 250, and are arranged by the office. Six or seven different species of mostly white fish, such as cod, can be caught. The town is best known for three things: its position as the last stop on the railway, making it a gateway to fjord country; Trollstigveien (Trolls' Path); and Trollveggen (Trolls' Wall).

From **Horgheimseidet,** which used to have a hotel for elegant tourists—often European royalty—you can view **Trollveggen** (Troll Wall), Europe's highest vertical rock face at 3,300 ft. The birthplace of mountain-climbing sports in Scandinavia, this face attracts elite climbers from all over, drawn by its reputation for challenging climbs.

Trollstigveien, Norway's most popular tourist road, starts in Åndalsnes. The road took 100 men 20 summers (1916–1936) to build, in a constant struggle against the forces of rock and water. Often described as a masterpiece of road construction, the road snakes its way through 11 hairpin bends up the mountain to the peaks named **Bispen** (the Bishop), **Kongen** (the King), and **Dronningen** (the Queen), which are

The West Coast

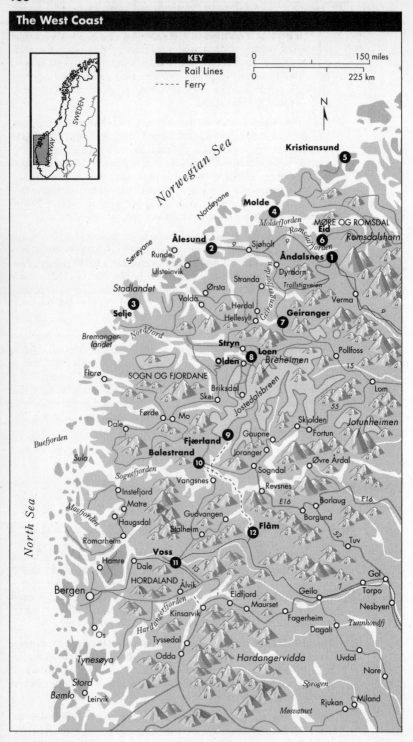

150 miles
0   225 km

N

NORWAY
SWEDEN

Norwegian Sea

Kristiansund ⑤

Nordøyane

Molde ④
Moldefjorden
Romsdalsfjorden

Ålesund ②
Sjøholt
Eid ⑥
MØRE OG ROMSDAL
Romsdalshorn

Runde
Åndalsnes ①

Ulsteinvik
Stranda
Dyrdorn
Trollstigveien

Stadlandet
Ørsta
Herdal
Verma

Volda
Hellesylt

Selje ③
Geiranger ⑦

Nordfjord
Stryn
Loen

Bremanger-
landet
Olden ⑧
Breheimen

Pollfoss

Florø
SOGN OG FJORDANE
Briksdal
Skei
Jostedalsbreen
15

Lom

Førde
Mo
Skjolden
55

Dale
Fjærland ⑨
Gaupne
Fortun
Jotunheimen

Buefjorden
Balestrand ⑩
Joranger

Sula
Sogndal
Øvre Ardal

Sognefjorden
Vangsnes
Revsnes

Instefjord
E16
Borlaug
E16

Matre
Gudvangen
Borgund

Masfjorden
Haugsdal
Stalheim
Flåm ⑫

Romarheim
52
Tuv

North Sea
Hamre
Voss ⑪
Gol

Dale
7
Torpo

HORDALAND
Ålvik
Geilo
Nesbyen

Bergen
Eidfjord
Maurset
Fagerheim
Tunnhovdfj

Kinsarvik
Dagali

Os
Tyssedal

Odda
Hardangervidda
Uvdal

Tynesøya
Nore

Stord
Sprogen

Bømlo
Leirvik
Rjukan
Miland

Møsvatnet

Hardangerfjorden

2,800 ft above sea level. The roads Trollstigveien and Ørneveien (at the Geiranger end) zigzag over the mountains separating two fjords. They're open only in summer. Halfway up, the road crosses a bridge over the waterfall **Stigfossen** (Path Falls), which has a vertical fall of nearly 600 ft. Walk to the lookout point, Stigrøra, by taking the 15-minute return path to the plateau. Signs show the way.

One of Norway's most famous mountaineers, Arne Randers Heen (1905–91), and his wife, Bodil Roland, founded the **Norsk Tindemuseum** (Norwegian Mountain Museum), which is dedicated to mountain climbing. Displays of Heen's equipment and photography follow the development of the sport and Heen's many feats. The mountain nearest to his heart was Romsdalshorn, 1,555-m (5,101-ft) high. He climbed that mountain 233 times, the last time when he was 85. He was the first to climb several mountains, especially those in northern Norway. ✉ *2 km (1 mi) south of* Andalsnes center, along E139, ☎ 71/22–12–74. ☉ Mid-June–mid-Aug., daily 1–5.

Lodging

$$ 🏨 **Grand Hotel Bellevue.** Travelers often begin their exploration of the region at this well-established hotel. All the rooms are done in bright yellow colors with old prints of the fjord on the walls. The hotel's restaurant, Trollstua, is known for its seafood dishes based on fresh catches by local fishermen. ✉ *Åndalsgt. 5, 6301,* ☎ *71/22–75–00,* 🖷 *71/22–60–38,* 🌐 *www.grandhotel.no. 86 rooms. Restaurant, bar, meeting room. AE, DC, MC, V.*

Ålesund

❷ *240 km (150 mi) west of Åndalsnes.*

★ On three islands and between two bright blue fjords is Ålesund, home to 38,000 inhabitants and one of Norway's largest harbors for exporting dried and fresh fish. About two thirds of its 1,040 wooden houses were destroyed by the fire of 1904. In the rush to shelter the 10,000 homeless victims, Kaiser Wilhelm II, who often vacationed here, led a swift rebuilding that married German art nouveau (*Jugend*) with Viking flourishes. Winding streets are crammed with buildings topped with turrets, spires, gables, dragonheads, and curlicues. Today, it's considered one of the few art nouveau cities in the world. Inquire at the tourism office for one of the insightful walking tours.

A little gem, the **Ålesunds Museum** highlights the city's past, including the escape route that the Norwegian Resistance established in World War II—its goal was the Shetland Islands. Handicrafts on display are done in the folk-art style of the area. You can also see the art nouveau room and learn more about the town's unique architecture. ✉ *R. Rønnebergsgt. 16,* ☎ *70/12–31–70.* 🖰 *NKr 30.* ☉ *Mid-June–Sept., Wed.–Sat. noon–5, Sun. noon–4.*

You can drive or take a bus (☎ 70/12–41–70) up nearby Aksla Mountain to a vantage point, **Kniven** (the knife), for a splendid view of the city—which absolutely glitters at night.

☾ **Atlanterhavsparken** Atlantic Sea-Park. Teeming with aquatic life, this is one of Scandinavia's largest aquariums. Right on the ocean 3 km (2 mi) west of town, the park emphasizes aquatic animals of the North Atlantic, including anglers, octopus, and lobster. Nemo, the park's adorable seal mascot, waddles freely throughout the complex. See the daily diving show at which the fish are fed. The divers actually enter a feeding frenzy of huge halibut and wolffish, which are sometimes aggressive. After your visit, have a picnic, hike, or take a refreshing swim at the adjoining Tueneset Park. Bus 18, which leaves from St. Olavs Plass, makes the 15-minute journey once every hour Monday through Saturday. ✉ *Tueneset,* ☎ *70/10–70–60,* 🕸 *www.atlanterhavsparken.no.* 💵 *NKr 85.* ⊘ *Mid-June–mid-Aug., weekdays 10–7, Sat. 10–5; mid-Aug.–mid-June, daily 11–4, Sun. noon–5.*

OFF THE BEATEN PATH **RUNDE –** Norway's southernmost major bird rock, Runde, is near Ålesund. It's one of the largest in Europe and a breeding ground for some 240 species, including puffins, gannets, and cormorants. The region's wildlife managers maintain many observation posts. During summertime, straying into the bird's nesting areas is strictly forbidden. A catamaran leaves from Skateflua quay in Ålesund for the 25-minute trip to Hareid, where it connects with a bus for the 50-km (31-mi) trip to Runde. A path leads from the bus stop to the nature reserve. Call the Runde tourist office for more information.

Dining and Lodging

$$$$ ✕ **Gullix.** The decor is over the top, but you can't fault the Spanish-inspired international menu of 52 dishes. Try the popular fish platter or sautéed monkfish garnished with shrimp, mussels, and crayfish; Norwegian bacalao; or grilled, marinated fillet of lamb. ✉ *Rådstugt. 5B,* ☎ *70/12–05–48. AE, DC, MC, V.*

$$ 🏨 **Comfort Home Hotel Bryggen.** A converted turn-of-the-20th-century fish warehouse, this hotel has warm stone walls and a glassed-in atrium. All rooms are doubles and have fantastic views. A light evening buffet is included in the rates. ✉ *Apotekergt. 1–3, 6004,* ☎ *70/12–64–00,* 🖷 *70/12–11–80. 85 rooms. Sauna, Turkish baths, fishing, meeting room. AE, DC, MC, V.*

$$ 🏨 **Quality Hotel Scandinavea Hotel.** Part of the Quality chain, this hotel ★ has impressive towers and arches and dates back to 1905. The modern rooms are beautifully decorated, especially those done in an art-nouveau style. ✉ *Løvenvoldgt. 8, 6002,* ☎ *70/15–78–00,* 🖷 *70/15–78–05,* 🕸 *www.choicehotels.no. 65 rooms. Restaurant, bar, pizzeria, meeting room. AE, DC, MC, V.*

$$ ✕ **Sjøbua.** Pick your own lobster from the large tank at this good restau-★ rant. The mixed fish and shellfish platter comes highly recommended. ✉ *Brunholmgt. 1,* ☎ *70/12–71–00. AE, DC, MC, V. Closed Sun.*

$–$$ ✕ **Fjellstua.** This mountaintop restaurant offers tremendous views over the surrounding peaks, islands, and fjords. Inside the old-fashioned brick building is a marine-blue interior accented by picture windows and natural stone. On the international menu, try the Norwegian bacalao, salmon, and lamb. ✉ *Top of Aksla mountain,* ☎ *70/10–74–00. AE, DC, MC, V. Closed Jan.*

$–$$ 🏨 **First Hotel Atlantica.** Reproduction van Gogh prints hang on the brightly colored walls of this hotel's cheery guest rooms. Most have views of mountains and the town harbor. ✉ *R. Rønnebergsgt. 4, 6004,* ☎ *70/12–91–00,* 🖷 *70/12–62–52,* 🕸 *www.firsthotels.com. 73 rooms. Restaurant, café. AE, DC, MC, V.*

Selje

③ *135 km (85 mi) southwest of Ålesund.*

From the town of the same name, the ruins of the **Selje Cloister,** on Selje Island, is a 15-minute boat ride away. The cloister's tower still stands. Dedicated to St. Sunniva, western Norway's patron saint, the cloister was built by the Benedictine order in the 10th century. It was on this island that St. Sunniva was martyred after fleeing her native Ireland when it was overrun by heathens. She died in St. Sunniva Cave, a large mountainside cavern. The island also has ruins of the first parish church, St. Sunniva Church; and St. Albanus Church, dedicated to the English saint. On the south side of the island, several Viking graves and remains of an Iron Age longhouse have been found. In summer, a boat departs several times daily from Selje harbor for two-hour guided tours of the island. ☎ *57/85–66–06.* ⊠ *NKr 110.* ⊙ *Late May–Sept., daily 10–5.*

Lodging

$$ 🏨 **Selje Hotel–Selje Spa Thalasso.** Set on a beautiful coastal beach, this spa is a popular choice for Norwegians. The health and well-being center has an outdoor Jacuzzi, spa treatments, massage, and skin and body care treatments. ⊠ *6740, Selje,* ☎ *57/85–88–80,* FAX *57/85–88–81,* WEB *www.seljehotel.no. 49 rooms. Restaurant, bar, lounge, indoor pool, hot tub, spa, dance club, meeting rooms. AE, DC, MC, V.*

Molde

❹ *69 km (43 mi) north of Ålesund on Route 668.*

Once known as the "City of Roses," Molde has kept its 19th-century nickname even though the only reminder today is the city hall rooftop rose garden that blooms in July and August. Now, Molde is best known for its annual jazz festival, which includes art exhibitions, street festivals, and jazz films as well as performances by international and national artists.

If you like to walk, take the footpath that leads uphill to the charming **Romsdalsmuseet** (Romsdal Open-Air Museum). On the way to the museum, stop at Reknes Park for a view of the 222 mountain peaks on the other side of the Romdalsfjord. Costumed tour guides lead you through the open-air museum's 40 sod farmhouses and churches dating back to the 14th century. See the collection of children's toys. During the jazz festival, the museum is a major venue for the larger concerts. Inquire about the museum's other attraction, Hjertøya, a fish museum 3 km (2 mi) from the city. ⊠ *Per Amdams veg 4,* ☎ *71/20–24–60.* ⊙ *Early June–mid-Aug., daily 11–6.*

Dining and Lodging

$$–$$$ ✕ **Lubbenes.** In a Swiss-style chalet, this is one of the best restaurants in the region. The grilled monkfish, steak, catfish, and bacalao come highly recommended—Lubbenes excels at serving updated versions of traditional Norwegian cuisine. ⊠ *Sanestrandsvn. 117,* ☎ *71/21–12–86. AE, DC, MC, V.*

$$–$$$ 🏨 **Rica Hotel Molde.** This hotel keeps up its chain's stylish business hotel image. Rooms are modern, light, airy, and comfortable. The hotel is a popular meeting place for locals as well as guests and has good harbor views. ⊠ *Storgt. 3, 6400,* ☎ *71/20–35–00,* FAX *71/20–35–01,* WEB *www.rica.no. 88 rooms, 3 suites. Restaurant, bar. AE, DC, MC, V.*

$$ 🏨 **Quality Hotel Alexandra Molde.** This premier hotel is named for
★ Britain's Princess Alexandra of Wales, who stayed here in the 1880s. Many of the elegant rich yellow and red rooms overlook the water. ⊠ *Storgt. 1–7, 6401,* ☎ *71/20–37–50,* FAX *71/20–37–87,* WEB *www.qualityhotels.no. 160 rooms, 11 suites. 2 restaurants, bar, indoor pool, sauna, gym, meeting room. AE, DC, MC, V.*

Kristiansund

❺ *68 km (42 mi) north of Molde on Route 64.*

By the 19th century, timber and klipfish had made Kristiansund one of Norway's biggest export ports. Today, Kristiansund is the offshore petroleum capital of central Norway: the Draugen and Åsgad oil fields are nearby. The city's lively harbor, Vågen, has the world's oldest collection of small boats. During World War II, almost everything in town was destroyed except for Vågen, where some well-preserved buildings remain.

A warehouse from the 18th century now houses the **Norwegian Coastal Cultural Center,** right on the harbor. Inside are a number of museums and shops, including **Woldbrygga,** a cooper's (barrel maker's) workshop in use from 1875 to 1965. The equipment is still operational. (🎫 NKr 20, ⊙ Sun. 1–4). **Milnbrygge,** the Norwegian Klippfisk Museum, pays tribute to the process and the history of the town's klippfisk industry—fishy smells and all. At the **Patrick Volkmar Roastery,** you can have a cup of coffee as well as browse through the wooden handicrafts, metal toys, and offbeat gifts available for sale. ✉ *Harbor,* 🕾 *71/67–15–78.* 🎫 *NKr 30.* ⊙ *Mid-June–mid-Aug., Mon.–Sat. noon–5, Sun. 1–4.*

OFF THE BEATEN PATH	**GRIP** – This group of 80 islands lies 15 km (9 mi) out in the open sea, a 2½-hour boat ride away. See the little stave church that was built around 1400 on the island's highest point, just 25 ft above sea level. Few people live year-round on the historic islands now, and most of those who come stay in summerhouses. 🕾 *71/58–54–54.* ⊙ *Mid-May–Aug., daily boats at 10:30 AM and 1:30 PM.*

Dining and Lodging

$$ ✕ **Smia Fiskerestaurant.** The antiques, exposed brick, and fireplace inside this 1787 house are in keeping with the food served. The dishes are based on *nordmørske mattradisjoner,* northern homemade food traditions that emphasize fish. Try the restaurant's famous fish soup; fish balls; or bacalao, the popular Mediterranean salt cod that's also a part of local culture. ✉ *Fosnagt. 30B,* 🕾 *71/67–11–70. AE, DC, MC, V.*

$$–$$$ 🏨 **Rica Hotel Kristiansund.** This popular business hotel opened a conference center in 2001. The art-filled rooms are calm and fairly standard. The Sky Bar, on the 10th floor, has a stunning view of the harbor. ✉ *Storgt. 41, 6508,* 🕾 *71/67–64–11,* 🖷 *71/67–79–12,* 🌐 *www.rica.no. 102 rooms. Restaurant, 2 bars, minibars, sauna, gym, nightclub, convention center, meeting rooms. AE, DC, MC, V.*

$$ 🏨 **Comfort Hotel Fosna.** Both the wooden furniture and black-and-white pictures of Norway make the rooms feel rustic and traditional in this waterfront hotel. Ask for a room with a view of the harbor: it's spectacular. An evening meal is included. ✉ *Hauggt. 16, 6501,* 🕾 *71/67–40–11,* 🖷 *71/67–76–59,* 🌐 *www.choicehotels.no. 50 rooms. Restaurant, outdoor café, pub, nightclub, meeting rooms. AE, DC, MC, V.*

Eid

❻   *In Nordfjordeid country, along E39, near Hornindals Vatnet Lake, Northern Europe's deepest lake.*

A small agricultural community of about 6,000, Eid offers such fjord-village attractions as mountain walks, dairy and farm visits, and skiing. The town is best known for the Fjord Horse, or Fjordhest—it even appears on its official shield. This Norwegian horse breed, one of the oldest, was bred for farmwork. It therefore played a big role in helping western Norway develop. Every May, the community hosts the State Stallion Show, which attracts horse enthusiasts from Norway and beyond.

The **Norsk Fjordhestsenter** is the official center for the breeding and use of the native Fjord horse. Open year-round, the center's summer tourist program features riding camps; riding and horsedrawn trips;

cabin rentals; mountain horseback riding; and day, two-day, and week-long trips. ✉ *Myroldhaug.* ☎ *57/86–02–33,* 𝔽𝔸𝕏 *57/86–02–67,* 𝕎𝔼𝔹 *www.norsk-fjordhestsenter.no.*

Outdoor Activities and Sports
FISHING

Trout, char, salmon, eel . . . whatever your favorite catch, an abundance can be caught in the Eidselv River. Fishing licenses range in price from NKr 25 to NKr 225 depending on the area and time allotted. Equipment and boat rentals, organized trips, and outfitter companies cater to sports fishing tourists. For information on equipment rental and organized trips, contact **Freshwater fishing** (☎ 57/86–27–23), **Eidselv River** (☎ 57/86–01–62), or **Fjord Fishing** (Tourist office, ☎ 57/86–13–75).

Geiranger

❼ *85 km (52½ mi) southwest of Åndalsnes, 413 km (256 mi) from Bergen.*

★ **Geiranger** is Norway's most spectacular and perhaps best known fjord. The 16-km-long (10-mi-long), 960-ft-deep Geirangerfjord's best-known attractions are its roaring waterfalls—the Seven Sisters, the Bridal Veil, and the Suitor. Perched on mountain ledges along the fjord, deserted farms at Skageflå and Knivsflå are now being restored and maintained by local enthusiasts.

The village of Geiranger, at the end of the fjord, is home to only 300 year-round residents, but in spring and summer its population swells to 5,000 due to tourists traveling from Hellesylt to the east. In winter, snow on the mountain roads means that the village is often isolated.

The most scenic route to Geiranger is the two-hour drive along Route 63 over Trollstigveien from Åndalsnes. Once you are here, the Ørneveien (Eagles' Road) down to Geiranger, completed in 1952 with 11 hairpin turns, leads directly to the fjord.

Outdoor Activities and Sports
HIKING

Trekking through this stunning fjord country can take a few hours or several days. Trails and paths are marked by signs or cairns with a red ᴛon them. Area tourist offices and bookshops have maps, and of course you can always ask local residents for directions or destinations.

Lodging
$$–$$$ 🏨 **Union Hotel.** One of the biggest hotels in the region, the Union is famous for its location near the fjords. Decked out in rosemaled wood furniture, the lobby has a country feel, although the rooms are modern. Ask for one of the rooms with good fjord views. ✉ 6216, ☎ 70/26–30–00, 𝔽𝔸𝕏 70/26–31–61, 𝕎𝔼𝔹 *www.union-hotel.no. 168 rooms, 13 suites. Restaurant, bar, 2 pools, sauna, Turkish bath, miniature golf, nightclub, solarium, playground. AE, DC, MC, V. Closed Jan.–Feb.*

Stryn, Loen, and Olden

❽ *If you continue on to Stryn from Geiranger, take the ferry across the Geiranger Fjord to Hellesylt, a 55-minute ride. It's about 50 km (30 mi) from Hellesylt to Stryn on Route 60.*

Stryn, Loen, and Olden, at the eastern end of Nordfjord, were among the first tourist destinations in the region. English salmon fishermen became the first tourists in the 1860s. By the end of the 19th century, more hotels had been built, and cruise ships added the area to their routes. Tourism grew into an important industry. Today, the most famous attraction in Stryn is the Briksdal Glacier, which lies between cascading waterfalls and high mountaintops. It's one arm of the Jostedal.

Covering the mountains between the Sognefjord and Nordfjord, **Jostedal Glacier** is the largest in Europe. Nearly ⅓ mi in parts, it has grown in recent years due to increased snowfall. There are 100 different known routes for crossing Jostedal Glacier: if you want to hike it, you must have a qualified guide. Contact the Jostedalsbreen National Park Center or another tourist office. Such hikes should only be attempted in summer; mountain boots and windproof clothing are both essential.

Many of Jostedal's arms are famous local tourist attractions in their own right. The best known arm, **Briksdal Glacier,** lies at the end of Oldedal Valley, about 20 km (12 mi) south from Olden. It can be visited by bicycle, car, or foot from April to October. The **Jostedalsbreen National Park Center** covers the glacier and the surrounding region in detail. Landscape models, mineral and photography collections, and animal dioramas all serve to get across the region's unique geography, flora, and fauna. An exhibit on local wildflowers showcases more than 300 species.

Outdoor Activities and Sports

HIKING

In addition to taking a guided walk on the glaciers, there are many other trails in this area. Ask at the Tourist Office for a walking map and hiking suggestions.

SKIING

The **Stryn Summer Ski Center** has earned a reputation as Northern Europe's best summer-skiing resort. The trails run over Tystig Glacier. The center has a ski school, a snowboard park, and a special children's June and July tow. ⊠ *Rte. 258, near Videseter.* ☎ *57/87–40–40,* ⅋ *57/87– 40–41,* WEB *www.stryn-sommerski.no.* ☉ *May–June and Aug.–Sept., daily 10–4.*

Dining and Lodging

$–$$$ ✕ **Kjenndalstova Kafé and Restaurant.** Sometimes called western Norway's best kept secret, this café–restaurant serves magnificent views as well as traditional dishes. Close to Kjendal's glacier, towering mountains, cascading waterfalls, and a pristine lake, the scenery alone is well worth a visit. The fried fresh trout or stew and dessert cakes come highly recommended. ⊠ *Prestestegen 15, Loen,* ☎ *945–38–385. AE, DC, MC, V. Closed Oct.–Apr.*

$–$$ ✕ **Briksdalsbre Fjellstove** (Briksdal Glacier Mountain Lodge). Right at Briksdal Glacier, this mountain lodge's cafeteria restaurant has a surprisingly well-regarded menu. The trout, the fillet of reindeer, and the deep-fried cod's jaws are all worth a try. Accommodation is also available, and as you'd expect from its location, a large gift shop is nearby. ⊠ *Briksdalbre,* ☎ *57/87–68–00. AE, DC, MC, V.*

$$–$$$ ✕▥ **Visnes Hotel.** Dating back to 1850, this nostalgic small hotel is done in a Swiss style. The hotel is located five minutes from Stryn's center. Specialities in the restaurant include smoked salmon and venison. The Norwegian dragon-style Villa Visnes, a restored 1898 conference center and apartment, is nearby and operated by the same owners. ⊠ *Prestestegen 1, 6781 Stryn,* ☎ *57/87–10–87,* ⅋ *57–87–20–75,* WEB *www.visnes.no. 15 rooms with bath. Restaurant, convention center. AE, DC, MC, V.*

$–$$ ✕▥ **Olden Fjordhotel.** Close to the fjord and cruise terminal, this hotel
★   is popular with travelers. Most of the simple, comfortable rooms have a balcony with fjord views. Special allergen-free and family rooms are

available. ✉ 6788, Olden, ☎ 57/87–34–00, FAX 57/87–33–81, WEB www.olden-hotel.no. 60 rooms. Restaurant, bar, nightclub, library. AE, DC, MC, V.

$$ ★ 🏨 Alexandra. This hotel was built in 1884 but has been entirely refurbished in a modern style. Through its use of stone and oak, the Alexandra is still the most luxurious hotel around. ✉ 6789 Loen, ☎ 57/87–50–00, FAX 57/87–50–51, WEB www.alexandra.no. 191 rooms, 9 suites. 2 restaurants, 3 bars, indoor pool, tennis court, gym, nightclub, convention center. AE, DC, MC, V.

Shopping

Kari Trestakk (✉ Olden, ☎ 57/87–33–27) sells pewter, rosemaling, trolls, dolls, Nordfjord's largest selection of Norwegian knitwear—including Dale of Norway—and other popular souvenirs. **Strynefjell Draktverkstad** (✉ Oppstryn, ☎ 57/87–72–20) specializes in stylish trousers, and skirts made of heavy wool. It's a 10-minute drive east of Stryn on Route 15.

Fjærland

❾ *From Olden it's 62 km (37 mi) of easy, though not particularly inspiring, terrain to Skei, at the base of Lake Jølster, where the road goes under the glacier for more than 6 km (4 mi) of the journey to Fjærland.*

Fjærland, until 1986, was without road connections altogether.

In 1991 the **Norsk Bremuseum** (Norwegian Glacier Museum) opened just north of Fjærland. It has a huge screen on which a film about glacier trekking plays and a fiberglass passage that shows what it's like beneath a glacier. ✉ *Fjærland.* ☎ *57/69–32–88,* WEB *www.bre. museum.no.* 🎫 *NKr 70.* ⏱ *June–Aug., daily 9–7; Apr.–May and Sept.–Oct., daily 10–4.*

OFF THE BEATEN PATH

ASTRUPTUNET – Halfway across the southern shore of Lake Jølster (about a 10-minute detour from the road to Fjærland) is Astruptunet, the farm of one of Norway's best-known artists, Nicolai Astrup (1880–1928). Astrup was especially known for his landscape paintings of western Norway. Set on a steep hill, this cluster of small sod houses was Astrup's home and studio until he died. His paintings and sketches are now available for viewing. The entertaining guides explain much about him and his family. The cozy café serves waffles and rømmegrøt (sour-cream porridge). ✉ *Sandal i Jølster.* ☎ *57/72–67–82 or 57/72–61–45,* WEB www.astruptunet.com. 🎫 NKr 50. ⏱ July, daily 10–6; late May–June and early–late Aug., daily 10–5; or by appointment.

Dining and Lodging

$$$ ✕🏨 Hotel Mundal. Artists, mountaineers, and tourists first began coming to the Mundal in the late 1800s via boat. The quiet, yellow-and-white gingerbread hotel, with Norwegian painted wood throughout, still retains its old-fashioned charm. Now descendants of the original owners run the hotel. The café serves wholesome, traditional Norwegian fare. ✉ *Town Center, 6848 Fjærland,* ☎ *57/69–31–01,* FAX *57/69–31–79,* WEB *www.fjordinfo.no/mundal. 35 rooms. Bar, café, lounge, billiards, library, meeting rooms. DC, MC, V. Closed mid-Sept.–mid-May.*

Shopping

You may not be able to read Norwegian, but you may still be fascinated by Mundal's **Den norske bokbyen** (☎ 57/69–31–01, WEB www.bokbyen.no). From June through August, the "Norwegian Book Town" has 150,000 used books, cartoons, magazines, and records for sale in various old buildings around town.

Audhild Vikens Vevstove (⊠ Skei, ☎ 57/72–81–25) specializes in handicrafts, particularly woven textiles.

Balestrand

🔟 *30 km (17 mi) up the fjord by ferry, 204 km (126 mi) by car to Fjærland.*

Balestrand is on the southern bank of **Sognefjord,** one of the longest and deepest fjords in the world. Along its wide banks are some of Norway's best fruit farms, with fertile soil and lush vegetation (the fruit blossoms in May are spectacular). Ferries are the lifeline of the region.

Lodging

$$–$$$$ 🏨 **Kvikne's Hotel.** Kings, presidents, movie stars, and famous artists
★ have stayed in this landmark hotel that dates back to 1913. While the inside of the Swiss-chalet-style hotel has been modernized, old-fashioned touches like a veranda and dragon-style furniture have been retained. The area is ideal if you're interested in swimming, hiking, rowing, and fishing. ⊠ *Balholm, 6898 Balestrand,* ☎ *57/69–42–00,* FAX *57/69–42–01,* WEB *www.kviknes.no. 210 rooms. 2 restaurants, gym, fishing. AE, DC, MC, V.*

Voss

🔟 *80 km (50 mi) south of Vangsnes, a one-hour train ride from Bergen.*

Set as it is between the Hardanger and Sogn fjords, Voss is in a handy place to begin an exploration of Fjord Norway. Once just considered a stopover, Voss now attracts visitors drawn by its concerts, festivals, farms, and other attractions. Norwegians know Voss best for its skiing and Vossajazz, its annual jazz festival. People come from all over Norway for the sheep's head's festival, a celebration of the culinary delicacy.

Dating back to 1277, the enchanting **Voss Kyrkje - Vangskyrkja** (Voss Church) still holds services every Sunday. Take a walk through to see the stained glass within. Special concerts are occasionally held here. ☎ *56/51–22–78.* ⊙ *Mid-June–mid-Sept., daily 10–4.* 🎫 *Free.*

Perched on the hillside overlooking Voss, **Mølstertunet** is an open-air museum. The 16 farm buildings here were built between 1600 and 1870. Along with handcrafted tools and other items, they reveal much about area farmers' lives and struggles. Along with Nesheimstunet Museum and the Old Vicarage at Oppheim, it makes up Voss Folkemuseum. ⊠ *Mølstervn. 143,* ☎ *56/51–15–11.* ⊙ *May–Sept., daily 10–5; Oct.–Apr., weekdays 10–3, Sun. noon–3.* 🎫 *NKr 35.*

The **Galleri Voss** shows the works of Norwegian and regional artists in an airy space. ⊠ *Stallgt. 6–8,* ☎ *56/51–90–18.* ⊙ *Wed.–Sat. 10–4, Sun. noon–3.*

Outdoor Activities and Sports

FISHING
The Tourist Information Office sells fishing licenses and has a "Voss Fishing Guide" to the nearly 500 lakes and rivers open for fishing in the area. Fishing licenses (one-day for NKr 50) are also sold at campsites and the post office.

HIKING
Walks and hikes are especially rewarding in this region, with spectacular mountain and water views everywhere. Be prepared for abrupt weather changes in spring and fall. Voss is a starting point for mountain hikes in Slølsheimen, Vikafjell, and the surrounding mountains. Contact the Voss Tourist Board for tips.

PARACHUTING

At **Bømoen Airstrip** (☎ 92/05–45–56), 5 km (3 mi) from downtown, there's an active parachuting club. Jumps can be booked daily from mid-June to late August.

PARAGLIDING

One of the best places to paraglide in Norway, Voss has easily accessed starting points and constant thermals. The tandem season runs roughly from June to August. To take a **tandem paraglider flight** (in which an instructor goes with you), you must weigh between 30–110 kg (70 to 240 pounds). The flight lasts an hour and costs NKr 650. Contact the **Voss Adventure Senter** (☎ 56/51–36–30).

RIVER SPORTS

Rivers around Voss are ideal for river paddling, kayaking, and other water sports. **Voss Ski & Surf** (☎ 56/51–30–43) offers one to three day courses in river kayaking for beginners and experienced kayakers alike. They also book tandem kayak trips with instructors, which start around NKr 750. The latest is their new two-person, apparently very stable, self-bailing, easy to maneuver mini-rafts that blend river kayaking and rafting. Rides cost NKr 590. The **Voss Rafting Senter** (☎ 56/51–05–25) offers rafting, river-boarding, and canyoning at prices beginning around NKr 500. **Nordic Ventures** (☎ 56/51–35–83) runs guided sea kayak tours through the waterfalls and mountains of Sognefjord from April to October starting at NKr 390.

SKIING

Voss and her varied mountain terrain are ideal for winter sports. An important alpine skiing center in Norway, it has 40 km of alpine slopes; one cable car; eight ski lifts; eight illuminated and two marked cross-country trails, a snowboard park, and the Voss School of Skiing. Call the Voss Tourist Board for details.

Lodging

$$$–$$$$ 🏨 **Fleischer's Hotel.** One of Norway's historic wooden and dragon-style hotels, Fleischer's makes guests feel as if they're living in the lap of luxury. The elegant decor and the first-class service makes stays memorable. Magdalene, the hotel's traditional restaurant, serves well-done renditions of sheep's head, grilled deer, fresh mountain trout, and salmon dishes. Steps away from the railway tracks that go to Bergen, the hotel has become closely linked with that of Voss itself. ✉ *Evangervegen 13, 5700,* ☎ *56/52–05–00,* FAX *56/52–05–01,* WEB *www.fleischers.no. 90 rooms. Restaurant, bar, pool, sauna, nightclub, solarium, children's programs, coin laundry, meeting rooms. AE, DC, MC, V.*

$$–$$$ 🏨 **Park Hotel Vossevangen.** Mountain and lakeside views make Voss's largest hotel a popular choice. The rooms are comfortable and of a generous size. They're decorated with burnished mahogany. Dining and entertainment options here include Café Stationen, an informal café; Stallen Pub, which has live entertainment; Pentagon, a disco; Pianissimo, a piano bar; and Elysée, a French restaurant. ✉ *5701,* ☎ *56/51–13–22,* FAX *56/51–00–39. 127 rooms. Restaurant, café, piano bar, pub, nightclub. AE, DC, MC, V.*

Flåm

⑫ *131 km (81 mi) east of Voss.*

One of the most scenic train routes in Europe zooms from Myrdal, high into the mountains and down to the town of Flåm. After the day-trippers have departed, it's a wonderful place to extend the tour and spend the night.

The **train ride to Myrdal** is only 20 km (12 mi) long, but it takes 40 minutes to travel the 2,850 ft up a steep mountain gorge and 53 minutes to go down. The line includes 20 tunnels. From Flåm it's also an easy drive back to Oslo on E16 along the Lærdal River, one of Norway's most famous salmon streams. It was King Harald's favorite.

Souvenirs

Saga Souvenirs (✉ Flåm train station, ☎ 57/63–22–44, WEB www. sagasouvenir.no) is one of the largest gift shops in Norway. The selection of traditional items includes knitwear, trolls, and jewelry.

Lodging

$$–$$$ 🏨 **Fretheim Hotell.** One of western Norway's most beautiful hotels, the Fretheim seems timeless. Staying true to the Fretheim's 1866 roots, the rooms are furnished simply. The bar has a spectacular view of the fjord. ✉ 5742 Flåm, ☎ 57/63–63–00, FAX 57/63–64–00, WEB www.fretheim-hotel.no. 121 rooms. 2 restaurants, bar, fishing. AE, MC, V.

The West Coast A to Z

To research prices, get advice from other travelers, and book travel arrangements, visit www.fodors.com.

AIR TRAVEL

CARRIERS
Braathens has nonstop flights to Ålesund from Oslo, Bergen, Trondheim, and Bodø. SAS flies between Ålesund and Oslo.

➤ AIRLINES AND CONTACTS: **Braathens** (☎ 81/52–00–00). **SAS** (☎ 70/10–49–00 in Ålesund).

AIRPORTS

Ålesund's Vigra Airport is 15 km (9 mi) from the center of town. It's a 25-minute ride from Vigra to town with Flybussen. Tickets cost NKr 50. Buses are scheduled according to flights—they leave the airport about 10 minutes after all arrivals and leave town about 60 or 70 minutes before each departure.

➤ AIRPORT INFORMATION: **Vigra** (☎ 70/11–48–00).

BOAT AND FERRY TRAVEL

Ferries are a way of life in western Norway, but they are seldom big enough or don't run often enough in summer, causing delays. Considerable hassle can be eliminated by reserving ahead, as cars with reservations board first. Call the tourist office of the area to which you're heading for ferry information (☞ Visitor Information).

The *Hurtigruten* (the coastal steamer) stops at Skansekaia in Ålesund, at noon. It then heads northward at 3. It returns at midnight and heads southward at 1 AM.

A catamaran runs between Ålesund and Molde at least twice daily. In addition to regular ferries to nearby islands, boats connect Ålesund with other points along the coast. Excursions by boat are available through the tourist office.

BUS TRAVEL

Bus routes are extensive. The tourist office has information about do-it-yourself tours by bus to the outlying districts. Three local bus companies serve Ålesund; all buses depart from the terminal on Kaiser Wilhelms Gate.

CAR TRAVEL

From Oslo, it's 450 km (295 mi) on Route E6 to Dombås and then Route 9 through Åndalsnes to Ålesund. The well-maintained two-lane road runs inland to Åndalsnes and then follows the coastline out to Ålesund.

EMERGENCY SERVICES
➤ CONTACTS: **Car Rescue** (☎ 70/14–18–33).

ROAD CONDITIONS
The 380-km (235-mi) drive from Bergen to Ålesund covers some of the most breathtaking scenery in the world. Roads are narrow two-lane ventures much of the time; passing is difficult, and in summer traffic can be heavy.

EMERGENCIES
Nordstjernen, a pharmacy in Ålesund, is open weekdays 9–5, Saturday 9–2, and Sunday 6 PM–8 PM.
➤ CONTACTS: **Emergency: Hospital** (☎ 70/10–50–00), **Doctor** (☎ 70/14–31–13). **Nordstjernen** (⊠ Korsegt. 8, Ålesund, ☎ 70/12–59–45).

TOURS
A 1½-hour guided stroll through Ålesund, concentrating mostly on the art nouveau buildings, departs from the tourist information center (Rådhuset) Saturday, Tuesday, and Thursday at 1 PM from mid-June to mid-August. Admission is NKr 45. Aak Fjellsportsenter in Åndalsnes specializes in walking tours of the area.

From Easter through September, **Jostedalen Breførlag** offers glacier tours, from an easy 1½-hour family trip on the Nigard branch (equipment is provided) to advanced glacier courses with rock and ice climbing.

Olden Aktiv Briksdalsbreen offer a Blue Ice Excursion of three to four hours, an easy glacier walk, and ice climbing, among others.

The **Stryn Fjell- og Breførarlag** organizes five- to six-hour walks on Bødalsbreen from May to September.

The **MS** *Geirangerfjord* offers 90-minute guided minicruises on the Geirangerfjord. Tickets are sold at the dock in Geiranger (NKr 70). The tours run June–August at 10, 11:45, 1:30, 3:30, and 5:30; in July, there's an additional tour at 8 PM.

Firdafly based in Sandane, offers plane tours over Jostedalsbreen.
➤ FEES AND SCHEDULES: **Aak Fjellsportsenter** (⊠ Øran Vest, 6300 Åndalsnes, ☎ 71/22–71–00, ▥ www.aak.no). **Olden Aktiv Briksdalsbreen** (⊠ 6792 Briksdalsbre, ☎ 57/87–38–88, ▥ www.briksdalsbreen.com). **Firdafly** (☎ 57/86–54–19). **Jostedalen Breførlag** (⊠ 5828 Gjerde, ☎ 57/68–31–11). **MS** *Geirangerfjord* (☎ 70/26–30–07). **Stryn Fjell- og Breførarlag** (Glacier Guiding Association; ⊠ 6792 Briksdalsbre, ☎ 57/87–68–00).

TRAIN TRAVEL
The *Dovrebanen* and *Raumabanen* between Oslo S Station and Åndalsnes via Dombås run three times daily in each direction for the 6½-hour ride. At Åndalsnes, buses wait outside the station to pick up passengers for points not served by the train. The 124-km (76-mi) trip to Ålesund takes close to two hours.

VISITOR INFORMATION
Fjord Norway in Bergen is a clearinghouse for information on all of western Norway. Its Web site is a good starting point for your fjord trip.
➤ TOURIST INFORMATION: **Ålesund** (⊠ Rådhuset, ☎ 70/12–58–04). **Åndalsnes** (⊠ Corner Nesgt. and Romsdalsvn., ☎ 71/22–16–22). **Balestrand** (⊠ Dockside, ☎ 57/69–12–55). **Bremanger** (⊠ Kalvåg,

☎ 57/79–69–00). **Eid** (✉ Eidsgt., ☎ 57/86–13–75). **Fjord Norway** ☎ 55/55–07–30, ⓦⓔⓑ www.fjordnorway.no). **Flåm** (✉ Railroad station, ☎ 57/63–21–06). **Geiranger** (✉ Dockside, ☎ 70/26–30–99). **Hellesylt** (✉ Dockside, ☎ 70/26–50–52). **Lærdal** (☎ 57/66–65–09). **Molde** (✉ Rådhuset, ☎ 71/25–71–33). **Nordfjord** (☎ 57/87–40–53). **Selje** (✉ Town Center, ☎ 57/85–66–06). **Runde** (☎ 70/01–37–90). **Sogndal** (☎ 57/67–30–83). **Stryn** (☎ 57/87–23–33). **Voss** (☎ 56/52–08–00).

10 TRONDHEIM TO THE NORTH CAPE

A narrow but immensely long strip of land stretches between Trondheim and Kirkenes in northern Norway. In this vast territory, you'll encounter dramatically different ways of life and a variety of geographical features, from the sawtooth, glacier-carved peaks of the Lofoten Islands to the world's strongest tidal current in Bodø.

T HOUSANDS OF ISLANDS AND SKERRIES hug the coast of northern Norway moving up from Trondheim to the northernmost point
of Europe. The coast continues even farther, straggling above Sweden and Finland to point a finger of land into Russia.

This area has many more small, quaint towns and fishing villages than
it has larger cities like bustling, high-tech Trondheim or Tromsø, sometimes called "Paris of the North." Views are often exquisite: glaciers,
fjords, rocky coasts, and celestial displays of the midnight sun in summer and northern lights (aurora borealis) in winter.

Basking in the midnight sun, one of Norway's most popular attractions, Nordkapp (North Cape) warmly welcomes thousands of summer visitors flocking there every year.

*Numbers in the margin correspond to points of interest on the Trond-
heim and the North map.*

Trondheim

❶ *494 km (307 mi) north of Oslo, 657 km (408 mi) northeast of Bergen.*

One of Scandinavia's oldest cities, Trondheim is Norway's third largest
with 150,000 inhabitants. Founded in 997 by Viking King Olav Tryggvasson, it was first named Nidaros (still the name of the cathedral),
a composite word referring to the city's location at the mouth of the
Nid River. Today, Trondheim is a university town as well as a center
for maritime and medical research, but the wide streets of the city center are still lined with brightly painted wooden houses and striking ware-
houses.Saint Olav formulated a Christian religious code for Norway
in 1024 while he was king. It was on his grave that **Nidaros Domkirke**
(Nidaros Cathedral) was built. The town became a pilgrimage site for
the Christians of northern Europe, and Olav was canonized in 1164.

Although construction began in 1070, the oldest existing parts of the
cathedral date from around 1150. It has been ravaged on several occasions by fire and rebuilt each time, generally in a Gothic style. Since
the Middle Ages, all Norway's kings have been crowned and blessed
in the cathedral. The crown jewels are on display here. Guided tours
are offered in English late June to late August, weekdays at 11, 2, and
4. ✉ *Kongsgårdsgt. 2,* ☎ *73/53–91–60.* 🎟 *NKr 35. Ticket also permits entry to Erkebispegården.* ☉ *Mid-June–mid-Aug., weekdays 9–
6, Sat. 9–2, Sun. 1–4; May–mid-June and mid-Aug.–mid-Sept., weekdays 9–3, Sat. 9–2, Sun. 1–4; mid-Sept.–Apr., weekdays noon–2:30,
Sat. 11:30–2, Sun. 1–3.*

Scandinavia's oldest secular building is the **Erkebispegården** (The
Archbishop's Palace). Dating from around 1160, it was the residence
of the archbishop until the Reformation in 1537. After that it was a
Danish governor's palace and later a military headquarters. The oldest buildings, which face the cathedral, are now used for official func-
tions by the state, county, and municipal governments. The Archbishop's
Palace museum has original sculptures from Nidaros Cathedral and
archaeological pieces from throughout its history.

Within the Erkebispegården is the **Rustkammeret** (Army Museum; ☎
73/99–58–31; ☉ June–Aug., weekdays 9–3, weekends 11–4; Mar.–May
and Sept.–Nov., weekends 11–4), which traces the development of the
army from Viking times to the present through displays of uniforms,
swords, and daggers. The **Hjemmefrontmuseet** (Resistance Museum;
☎ 73/99–58–31; ☉ June–Aug., weekdays 9–3, weekends 11–4; Mar.–

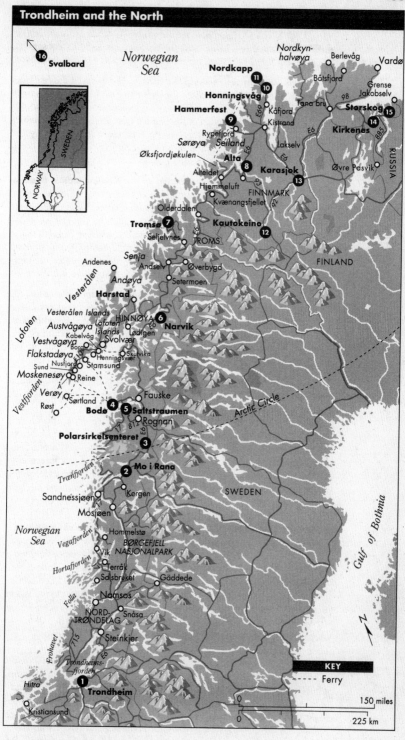

Norwegian
Sea

Nordkyn-
halvøya

16 **Svalbard**

Berlevåg Vardø

Nordkapp 11
10
Båtsfjord
Grense
Honningsvåg Tana bru Jakobselv
98
Kåfjord **Storskog**
Hammerfest 9 Kistrand 14 15
Rypefjord E6 **Kirkenes**
Sørøya Seiland Lakselv E6
Øksfjordjøkulen **Alta** 8
Alteidet **Karasjok** 13 RUSSIA
Hjemmeluft Øvre Pasvik
Kvænangsfjellet FINNMARK
Olderdalen **Kautokeino**
Tromsø 7
Seljelvnes TROMS
Andenes Senja
Andselv Øverbygd
Andøya Setermoen
Vesterålen FINLAND
Harstad
Vesterålen Islands Lofoten
Austvågøya Islands HINNØYA **Narvik** 6
Vestvågøya Kabelvåg Lødigen
Flakstadøya Borg Svolvær
Nusfjord Henningsvær Skutvika
Sund Stamsund
Moskenesøy Reine
Verøy Å Sørtland
Røst **Bodø** 4 5 **Saltstraumen**
Fauske Rognan
17 817 E6
Polarsirkelenteret 3
Arctic Circle
2 **Mo i Rana**
Trænfjorden
Sandnessjøen Korgen SWEDEN
Mosjøen
Norwegian
Sea Hommelstø
Vegafjorden **BØRGEFJELL
NASJONALPARK**
Vik
Hortafjorden Terråk
Salsbruket Gäddede
Folla Namsos
**NORD- Snåsa
TRØNDELAG**
715 Steinkjer
Gulf of Bothnia
Trondheims-
fjorden
Hitra 1 **Trondheim**
Kristiansund

N

KEY
- - - Ferry

0   150 miles
0   225 km

May and Sept.–Nov., weekends 11–4), also here, documents the oc-cupation of Norway during World War II. ⊠ *Trondheim,* ☎ *73/53–91–60.* ☒ *NKr 35. Ticket also permits entry to Nidaros Cathedral.* ☉ *Late June–late Aug., Mon.–Sat. 10–5, Sun. noon–5; late Aug.–late June, Mon.–Sat. 11–3, Sun. noon–4.*

In 1718 the **Kristiansten Festning** (Kristiansten Fort) saved the city from conquest by Sweden. Built after the great fire of 1681, it still stands watch over Trondheim. During Norway's occupation by Germany, 1940–45, members of the Norwegian Resistance were executed here; there's a plaque in their honor. The fort has a spectacular view of the city and its surroundings, the fjord, and mountains. ☎ *73/99–58–31.* ☉ *June–Aug., weekdays 10–3, weekends 11–4.*

The Tiffany windows are magnificent at the **Nordenfjeldske Kunstin-dustrimuseum** (National Museum of Decorative Arts), which houses an impressive collection of furniture, silver, and textiles. The Scandinavian Design section features a room interior designed by the Danish archi-tect Finn Juhl in 1952. The 1690 bridal crown by Adrian Bogarth is also memorable. ⊠ *Munkegt. 5,* ☎ *73/80–89–50,* WEB *www.nkim.museum.no.* ☒ *NKr 30.* ☉ *June–late Aug., weekdays 10–5, Sun. noon–5; late Aug.–May, Tues.–Wed. and Fri. 10–3, Thurs. 10–5, Sun. noon–4.*

Near Nidaros Cathedral, the **Trondheim Kunstmuseum** (Trondheim Art Gallery) houses more than 2,700 works of pictoral art that date from 1800 to the present. Regional artists represented include Håkon Bleken, Jakob Weidemann, Adolph Tidemand, Christian Krohg, and Harald Sol-berg. Many Danish artworks are also on view. ⊠ *Bispegt. 7B,* ☎ *73/53–81–80.* ☒ *NKr 30.* ☉ *June–Aug., daily 10–5.*

Near the ruins of King Sverre's medieval castle is the **Trøndelag Folke-museum,** which has open-air and outside sections. Re-creations of coastal, inland, and mountain village buildings depict life in Trønde-lag during the 18th and 19th centuries. Haltdalen stave church was built in 1170. "Old Town" includes a number of buildings moved from Trondheim's center, including a 1900 dentist's office and an old-fash-ioned grocery that still sells sweets. A public hall and exhibition cov-ers the ways that the stages of life have changed over the last 150 years. ⊠ *Sverresborg allé,* ☎ *73/89–01–00.* ☒ *NKr 70.* ☉ *June–Aug., daily 11–6; Sept.–May, 11–3, Sun. noon–4.*

OFF THE
BEATEN PATH

MUNKHOLMEN – Now a recreation area, the Monk's Island was where Trondheim held executions in ancient times. In the 11th century, Benedic-tine monks built a monastery on the island. In 1658, the monastery was converted into a prison and fort and, later, a customs house. Today, the island is a popular spot for swimming and recreation. Local handicrafts are on display in what was once a caretaker's house. Boats to the island depart from the fish market from late May to August. ☎ *73/80–63–00,* ☉ *Mid-May–early Sept. boats depart daily every hr on the hr 10–6; Aug. 20–24 and Aug. 27–31, departures start at noon.* ☒ *NKr 36.*

Norway's oldest institution of science, the **NTNU Vitenskapsmuseet** (NTNU Science Museum) covers flora and fauna, minerals and rocks, church history, southern Sámi (Lapp) culture, and archaeological finds. The eclectic exhibits have relics from the Bronze Age as well as eccle-siastical articles from the 13th to 18th centuries. ⊠ *Erling Skakkes gt. 47,* ☎ *73/59–21–45,* WEB *www.ntnu.no/vmuseet.* ☒ *NKr 25.* ☉ *May–mid-Sept., weekdays 9–4, weekends 11–4; mid-Sept.–Dec., Tues.–Fri. 9–2, weekends noon–4.*

Scandinavia's largest wooden palace, **Stiftsgården,** was built in 1774–78 as the private home of a prominent widow. Sold to the State in 1800, it's now the official royal residence in Trondheim. The architecture and interior is late baroque and highly representative of 18th-century high society's taste. Go on one of the guided tours taking place every hour on the hour, the last tour an hour before closing. The tours offer insight into the festivities centered around the coronations of the kings in Nidaros Domkirke. ✉ *Munkegt. 23,* ☎ *73/84–28–80.* 🔁 *NKr 40.* 🕙 *June–mid-June, Mon.-Sat. 10–3, Sun. noon–5; mid-June–mid-Aug., Mon.-Sat. 10–5, Sun. noon–5.*

Off Munkegate near the water, you can see an immense variety of seafood at **Ravnkloa Fiskehall** (Fish Market). A former 1725 prison now houses the little **Trondhjems Sjøfartsmuseum** (Maritime Museum). Models of sailing ships, figureheads, marine instruments, and photographs of local ships make up the exhibits. Standouts include a harpoon gun from a whaler and recovered cargo from the frigate *The Pearl,* which was wrecked in 1781. ✉ *Fjordgt. 6A,* ☎ *73/89–01–00.* 🔁 *NKr 25.* 🕙 *June–Aug., daily 10–4.*

OFF THE BEATEN PATH | **RINGVE MUSEUM –** If you have a taste for musical history and unusual museums you may want to spend some time at this museum, which is housed in an estate from the 1740s. The first part of the museum displays the main 1860 building of the estate. The second section looks at the development of instruments and styles of music throughout the ages, from "the invention of the piano" through jazz and pop. A hands-on exhibit lets you play Norwegian folk instruments. To get here, take a half-hour ride on Bus 3 or 4 from Munkegaten to Ringve Museum. ✉ *Lade Allé 60,* ☎ *73/92–24–11,* 🌐 *www.ringve.com.* 🔁 *NKr 70.* 🕙 *Jan.-mid-May and mid-Sept.–mid-Dec., Sun. 11–4; mid-May–June and Aug.-mid-Sept., daily 11–3; July, daily 11–5.*

Dining and Lodging

Trondheim is known for several local and regional dishes, including *surlaks* (marinated salmon served with sour cream). A sweet specialty is *tekake* (tea cake), which looks like a thick-crust pizza topped with a lattice pattern of cinnamon and sugar. The city's restaurant scene is spicing up, with Mexican, Asian, and other types of cuisine getting more common.

$$$ ✕ **Bryggen Restaurant.** In an elegant country style of blonde woods and rich greens and reds, this 240-year-old refurbished warehouse is one of the city's most popular restaurants. The international menu uses Norwegian ingredients such as fish and reindeer. The wine list is extensive, with many French and Italian choices. Most guests select one of the prix-fixe menus, which are constantly changing. ✉ *Øvre Bakklandet 66,* ☎ *73/87–42–42. Reservations essential. AE, DC, MC, V. Closed Sun. No lunch.*

$$$ ✕ **Havfruen Fiskerestaurant.** "The Mermaid" is Trondheim's foremost fish restaurant. Taking its cues from France as well as more locally, the restaurant excels at bouillabaisse as well as many other fish dishes, which change seasonally. The warm decor uses orange, greens, and reds accented by wood. ✉ *Kjøpmannsgt. 7,* ☎ *73/87–40–70. AE, DC, MC, V. Closed Sun. No lunch.*

$$ ✕ **East Sushi & Noodles.** Trondheim's only sushi bar also serves other Japanese dishes in a bright and elegant room. Besides an excellent wine list, Japanese beer and sake is also in stock. Come between 4 and 7 for less expensive "Happy Hour" sushi prices. ✉ *Munkegt. 39,* ☎ *73/52–10–20. AE, DC, MC, V.*

$$ ✕ **Grønn Pepper.** Tex-Mex is extremely popular throughout Norway, and this Trondheim restaurant serves a good rendition. Striped, vibrant Mexican blankets cover chairs on hardwood floors and dark wood furniture complements the fiery food on offer, which also includes some Cajun and Creole dishes. Mexican beer and tequila is also served. ✉ *Søndregt. 17 and Fjordgt. 7,* ☎ *73/51–66–44. AE, DC, MC, V.*

$$ ✕ **Vertshuset Tavern.** Housed in what was once a 1739 tavern in downtown Trondheim, this restaurant is now part of the Trøndelag Folk Museum. The Vertshuset serves traditional Norwegian food at reasonable prices. Popular local favorites include homemade fish cakes; rømmegrøt (sour-cream porridge); spekemat (cured meat); and Trøndelag klubb, the local kind of potato dumplings. ✉ *Sverresborg Allé 7,* ☎ *73/52–09–32. AE, DC, MC, V.*

$$–$$$$ ▦ **Britannia Hotel.** First opened in 1897, this classic Rica hotel has luxurious rooms with gold accents and dark wood furniture. The elegant Palmehaven Restaurant is often used for special occasions. ✉ *Dronningensgt. 5, 7401,* ☎ *73/800–800,* 𝐅𝐀𝐗 *73/800–801,* 𝐖𝐄𝐁 *www.britannia.no. 210 rooms. 2 restaurants, cocktail bar, piano bar, pub, meeting room. AE, DC, MC, V.*

$$–$$$$ ▦ **Radisson SAS Royal Garden Hotel.** Right on the river, this extrava-
★ ganza of glass is one of the reasons Radisson SAS is seen as Norway's best hotel chains. Superb service and beautiful decor makes stays here memorable. The atrium is filled with vivid plants and marble touches. Rooms are elegantly done in light blues and reds. In the middle of the hotel, Bakkus Mat & Vin is the perfect casual place for breakfast or dinner. ✉ *Kjøpmannsgt. 73, 7410,* ☎ *73/80–30–00,* 𝐅𝐀𝐗 *73/80–30–50,* 𝐖𝐄𝐁 *www.radissonsas.com. 298 rooms, 9 suites. Restaurant, bar, café, grill, indoor pool, sauna, gym. AE, DC, MC, V.*

$$–$$$ ▦ **Clarion Hotel Grand Olav.** In the same building as Trondheim's large concert hall, this reasonably priced hotel is centrally located. The vivid decor varies throughout but makes use of vibrant paintings and rich shades of reds, blues, and greens. Every Friday and Saturday night, the lobby turns into a popular piano bar. ✉ *Kjøpmannsgt. 48, 7010,* ☎ *73/80–80–80,* 𝐅𝐀𝐗 *73/80–80–81,* 𝐖𝐄𝐁 *www.choice.no. 112 rooms. Restaurant, bar, pub, gym. AE, DC, MC, V.*

$$ ▦ **Ambassadeur.** From the roof terrace of this first-rate modern hotel, you can see the deep-blue waters of the Trondheimsfjord reflect the dramatic and irregular coastline. The Ambassadeur is about 300 ft from the market square. Most rooms have fireplaces, and some have balconies. ✉ *Elvegt. 18, 7013,* ☎ *73/52–70–50,* 𝐅𝐀𝐗 *73/52–70–52. 34 rooms. Bar. AE, DC, MC, V.*

$$ ▦ **Comfort Home Hotel Bakeriet.** Inside a building used as a bakery
★ when it was built in 1863, this hotel has large, stylish rooms. Many business travelers stay here. There's no restaurant, but breakfast, afternoon waffles, and a hot evening meal are included in the room rate. ✉ *Brattørgt. 2, 7010,* ☎ *73/52–52–00,* 𝐅𝐀𝐗 *73/50–23–30. 109 rooms. In-room VCRs, sauna, Turkish baths. AE, DC, MC, V. MAP.*

Nightlife

Olavskvartalet is the neighborhood at the center of much of the city's nightlife, with dance clubs, live music, bars, and cafés. **Monte Cristo** (✉ Prinsensgt. 38–40, ☎ 73/52–18–80) has a restaurant, bar, and disco and is popular with people in their mid-20s and up. Students and younger people in search of cheap drinks, music, and dancing gravitate toward **Strossa** (✉ Elgesetergt. 1, ☎ 73/89–95–10). **Cafe Remis** (✉ Kjøpmannsgt. 12, ☎ 73/52–05–52) is the center for gay nightlife in Trondheim.

The bustling **Kontoret Bar & Spiseri** (✉ Nordregt. 24, ☎ 73/53–40-4–0) has 40 varieties of malt whiskey and excellent cognacs in all price ranges. Downtown, several fantastic places in the Elvehavna area include **Blæst** (☎ 73/60–01–00), a nightclub that includes a bar that's perfect for just chilling out; **Choco Boco** (☎ 73/600–300), a chocolate-obsessed café; **ESC. mediabar** (☎ 73/600–606), a news bar with a great selection of newspapers and magazines; and **Horgan's** (☎ 73/600–090), an American sports bar and eatery.

The Arts

Trondheim Symphony Orchestra (⊠ Olavskvartalet, Kjøpmannsgt. 46, ☎ 73/99–40–50) performs weekly concerts with internationally acclaimed soloists and conductors. In late July, the annual **St. Olav Festival in Trondheim** (⊠ Dronningensgt. 1B, ☎ 73/92–94–70, WEB www.olavsfestdagene.no) features a lively program of indoor and outdoor concerts, opera, and organ concerts at Nidaros Cathedral. Exhibits and children's activities are also staged. The **Modern Art Gallery** (⊠ Olav Tryggvasonsgt. 33, ☎ 73/87–36–80) shows contemporary art, watercolors, lithographs, and art posters from Norway and abroad.

Outdoor Activities and Sports

CYCLING

Some 300 **Trondheim Bysykkel City Bikes** can be borrowed in the city center. Parked in easy-to-see stands at central locations, the distinctive green bikes have shopping baskets. You'll need a 20-kroner piece to release the bike (you'll get it back upon its return).

Trondheim has an elevator called Trampe, that is a lift specifically designed for cyclists. The lift ascends the steep hill Brubakken near Gamle Bybro and takes cyclists nearly to Kristiansten festning. Contact the Tourist Office to get the card you need in order to use the Trampe.

FISHING

The **Nidelven** (Nid River) in Trondheim is one of Norway's best salmon and trout rivers, famous for its large salmon (the record is 70 lbs). You can fish right in the city, but you need a license. For further information and fishing licenses, contact **TOFA (Trondheim og Omland Jakt-og Fiskeadministrasjon)** (⊠ Leirfossvn. 76, ☎ 73/52–78–23, WEB www. tofa.org), the governing body that controls fishing and hunting in Trondheim and the surrounding area.

HIKING/WALKING

Take a walk or hike in and around Trondheim on one of many trails. **Bymarka,** a wooded area on Trondheim's outskirts, has a varied and well-developed network of trails. The **Ladestien** (Lade Trail) is a 14-km (9-mi) trail that goes along the Lade peninsula and offers great views of Trondheimsfjord. **The Nidelvstien Trail** runs along the river from Tempe to the Leirfossene waterfalls. Much of this trail is accessible to people with disabilities.

SKIING

Bymarka and **Estenstadmarka,** wooded areas on the periphery of Trondheim, are popular among cross-country skiers. Bymarka's Skistua (ski lodge) also has downhill runs.

Vassfjellet Skisenter (☎ 72/83–02–00), 8 km (5 mi) south of Trondheim city limits, has five tow lifts and 10 runs in all. There are facilities for downhill and Telemark skiing as well as snowboarding and tobogganing. In season (roughly mid-October through Easter), the center is open every day and ski buses run every evening and weekend.

SWIMMING

The Trondheimsfjord and lakes a little inland are both options for outdoor swimming. **Trondheim Pirbadet** (⊠ Havnegt. 12, ☎ 73/83–18–

00) is Norway's largest indoor swimming center. There's a wave pool, a sauna, and a Jacuzzi as well as a gym here.

Shopping

Trondheim's **Mercur Centre** (✉ Nordregt.) and **Trondheim Torg** shopping centers both have friendly staff and an interesting mix of shops.

For knitted sweaters by such makers as Oleana and Oda, try **Jens Hoff Garn & Ide** (✉ Olav Tryggvasongt. 20, ☎ 73/53–15-37). **Arne Ronning** (✉ Nordregt. 10, ☎ 73/53–13–30) carries fine sweaters by Dale of Norway. Founded in 1770 and Norway's oldest extant goldsmith, **Møllers Gullsmedforretning** (✉ Munkegt. 3) sells versions of the Trondheim Rose, the city symbol since the 1700s. Trondheim has its own branch of the handicraft store **Husfliden** (✉ Olav Tryggvasongt. 18, ☎ 73/83–32–30).

Mo i Rana

❷ *450 km (280 mi) north of Trondheim.*

Mo i Rana, meaning "Mo on the Ranafjord," is known as "the Arctic Circle city" because the Arctic Circle crosses the larger municipal area from east to west. The municipality has long been a center for iron and steel smelted from the ore supplied by nearby mines.

The **Grønligrotta** (Grønli Cave) is one of almost 200 caves 26 km (16 mi) northwest of Mo i Rana. With 7,920 ft of charted underground paths, many narrow passages, natural chimneys, and an underground river, it's one of Scandinavia's best-known show caves. For almost 100 years, tourists have been visiting the "grotta," and it's the only cave complex in Norway with built-in lighting. A 20-minute tour takes you several hundred feet inside. There's an underground waterfall, naturally formed potholes, and a formation carved by glacial flow over thousands of years. ✉ *Grønli* ☎ *75/13–25–86.* 🎫 *NKr 50.* ☉ *Mid-June–mid-Aug. Tours daily on the hr 10–7.*

OFF THE
BEATEN PATH

THE SVARTISEN GLACIER – Glacier fans can hike on the Svartisen, which literally means "black ice." The second-largest glacier in Norway covers 375 square km (144 square mi); the Arctic Circle crosses the glacier inside the Saltfjellet-Svartisen Nasjonale Park. Several main entrances to the park are accessible from Mo i Rana.

The easiest way to get to the glacier itself from Mo i Rana is to head north 32 km (20 mi) by car to Svartisvannet Lake. The Svartisbåten (Svartis Boat; ☎ 75/16–23–79) crosses the lake to within 2½ km (1½ mi) of the Østerdal arm of the glacier. From there it's a 3 km (2 mi) hike up to Austerdalsvatnet Lake and the glacier. Glacier walking is extremely hazardous and should never be attempted without a professional guide. Contact the Svartisen Tourist Center (☎ 75/75–00–11) for referrals. Four-hour guided tours of the Engenbreen glacial arm are offered by Svartisen bre-og turlag (☎ 75/75–00–11). No previous experience is necessary.

Polarsirkelsenteret

❸ *80 km (50 mi) north of Mo i Rana.*

A bleak stretch of treeless countryside marks the beginning of the Arctic Circle. The **Polarsirkelsenteret** (The Arctic Circle Center) is right on the line. Here you can build a small cairn as evidence you passed the circle. You can also take home an Arctic Circle certificate to show the folks back home. ✉ *Rte. E6, Rognan,* ☎ *75/16–60–66.* 🎫 *NKr 50.* ☉ *May–Sept.*

Bodø

4 *174 km (108 mi) north of the Polarsirkelsenteret.*

Bodø, a modern city of about 42,000 just above the Arctic Circle, is best known as the terminus of the Nordlandsbanen railroad and the *Hurtigruten* (a coastal boat), as well as the gateway to the Lofoten Islands and the North. The midnight sun is visible from June 2 to July 10 and the polar night descends December 15–29. Like many other coastal towns, it began as a small fishing community, but today it is a commercial and administrative center.

Bodø is the best base for boat excursions to the coastal bird colonies on the Væren Islands. The town is also known for the many sea eagles that soar high through town and perch on the rocks on nearby islands.

The **Nordland County Museum,** in one of the city's oldest buildings (1903), covers regional history, including both the fishing industry and the changes that the 20th century brought about. An exhibit on Sámi culture features a 350-year-old wooden box with inscribed runes. There's also silver treasure on display that dates back 1,000 years, to the Iron Age: these English and Arabic coins and jewelry were discovered in 1919. ⊠ *Prinsengt. 116,* ☎ *75/52–16–40,* WEB *www.museumsnett. no/nordlandsmuseet.* 🎫 *NKr 30.* ☉ *Late May–mid-Aug., weekdays 9–3, Sat. 10–3, Sun. noon–3; mid-Aug.–late May, weekdays 9–3, weekends noon–3.*

☾ Down the road from Bodø's airport and 15 minutes from the town's center, the 10,000 square meter (12,000 square yard) jumbo **Norsk Luftfartsmuseum** (Norwegian Aviation Museum) covers aviation in a building shaped like a propeller. The collection includes 34 airplanes, from an AVRO 504 built in 1913 to a Thunderwing Spitfire from 1993. Flight simulators let you see what an F-16 or a Harrier would be like. ⊠ *Olav V gt.,* ☎ *75/50–85–50,* WEB *www.luftfart.museum.no.* 🎫 *NKr 70.* ☉ *Mid June–mid-Aug., weekdays and Sun. 10–7, Sat. 10–5; Late-Aug.– early June, weekdays 10–4, weekends 11–5.*

Lodging

$–$$$ 🏨 **Radisson SAS Hotel Bodø.** In classic Radisson SAS style, this grandiose hotel pulses with life. The rooms make use of marble and brass and dark furniture; they're elegant and calm. Sjøsiden Restaurant is well regarded for its classy maritime feel and menu while Pizzakjeller'n has a more casual style and pizza, Tex-Mex, Norwegian, and international dishes. Moloen Bar is the perfect place for a nightcap or to dance the night away. ⊠ *Storgt. 2,* ☎ *75/52–41–00,* FAX *75/52–74–93,* WEB *www. radissonsas.com/bodono. 190 rooms. 2 restaurants, bar, nightclub. AE, DC, MC, V.*

$–$$ 🏨 **Golden Tulip Rainbow Nordlys Hotel.** Facing the harbor, this hotel is decorated in marine blues, with artsy fish-theme decor throughout. The rooms are cheerful and simply furnished. The Windjammer Café and Wine bar is a popular meeting place. ⊠ *Molovn. 14, 8003 Bodø,* ☎ *75/53–19–00,* WEB *www.rainbow-hotels.no. 153 rooms. Restaurant, café, bar, meeting rooms. AE, DC, MC, V.*

$ 🏨 **Norrøna Hotell.** If you're just passing through Bodø on the way to the Lofoten Islands, then consider this budget hotel. A no-frills establishment, it's plain and comfortable with a prime downtown location. Relax with friends and share a pint or two at the lively Picadilly pub. ⊠ *Storgt. 4B,* ☎ *75/52–55–50,* FAX *75/52–33–88,* WEB *www. norronahotell.bedre.no. 88 rooms. Restaurant, pub, sauna. AE, DC, MC, V.*

Outdoor Activities and Sports

BOATING

Boating is a popular pastime at Bodø. Boats for fishing and other activities can be rented at several places in town. Elvegård Camping (☎ 75/56–33–22) has boats equipped with outboard motors, fishing tackle, and quay facilities. Saltstraumen Fishing Camp (☎ 75/58–71–38) and Kjerringgøy Rorbu Camp (☎ 75/58–50–07) rent out smaller-size boats.

CYCLING

Heading out on bicycle is a great way to explore Bodø and the surrounding countryside. Destinasjon Bodø has bicycles for rent. They cost NKr 60 for 24 hours, NKr 110 for 48 hours, and NKr 160 for 72 hours.

HIKING/WALKING

The tourist office has a map outlining nearby trails. **Bodømarka** (Bodø Forest) has 35 km (22 mi) of flood-lit trails. **Bodø og Omegn Turistforening- BOT** (Bodø Mountain Touring Association; ☎ 75/52–48–90), the local chapter of the Norwegian Mountain Touring Association, owns and operates 12 cabins along trails in the area. The association has a youth group, and groups devoted to glacier walking, cave exploring, and rock climbing.

FISHING

Serious or amateur anglers can fish in local rivers and lakes for trout, char, and salmon. Destinasjon Bodø (☞ Visitor Information) has contacts for fishing licenses and for recommendations.

SKIING

Destinasjon Bodø (☞ Visitor Information) has advice on local skiing. They rent out skis, poles, boots, and clothing for NKr 100 a day.

Saltstraumen

⑤ *33 km (20 mi) southeast of Bodø on Route 80–17.*

Saltstraumen is a 3-km-long (2-mi-long) and 500-ft-wide section of water between the outer fjord, which joins with the sea, and the inner fjord basin. During high tide, the volume of water rushing through the strait and into the basin is so great that whirlpools form. In fact, every six hours, 400 million cubic meters (500 million cubic yards) of water rushes through the narrow sound. This is the legendary maelstrom (*malstrøm* in Norwegian)—and the strongest one in the world. That rush of water brings enormous quantities of fish, making the maelstrom a popular fishing spot.

On the shores of the world's strongest tidal current, visit **Saltstraumen Opplevelsesenter** (Saltstraumen Adventure Center). The center looks at 10,000 years of regional history, from the Ice Age, when humans first emerged here, through the Iron and Viking Ages on through the present. The maelstrom itself is covered. There's also an aquarium of local fish and a seal pond outdoors. ✉ *Saltstraumen, highway RV 17.* ☎ *75/56–06–55.* 🎫 *NKr 60.* ☉ *May–mid-June, daily 11–6; mid-June–late June and mid-Aug.–late Aug., daily 10–7; July–mid-Aug., daily 9–8; Sept., weekends 11–6.*

Every summer, the **World Saithe Fishing Championships** (☎ 75/54–8000) attract anglers from near and far to compete in catching saithe, also known as pollack. There are categories in fishing from either land or from a boat, as well as overall awards for the largest saithe caught.

Lodging

$$–$$$ 🏨 **Saltstraumen Hotel.** Although it's rather plain, the Saltstraumen's position practically on top of the maelstrom makes it a memorable place to stay. The restaurant serves delicious steamed halibut in butter sauce. The Saltstraumen Gallery has regional paintings and other graphic art on display. ⊠ *8056,* ☎ *75/58–76–85,* WEB *www.saltstraumen-hotel.no. 28 rooms, 7 bungalows. Restaurant, meeting room. AE, DC, MC, V.*

OFF THE BEATEN PATH **BLODVEIMUSEET –** Ninety minutes southeast of Bodø in Rognan, the Blood Road Museum re-creates the sinister atmosphere of an icy North Norway Nazi prison camp where Russian, Serb, and Polish prisoners of war were incarcerated by the Germans, 1942–45. **Saltdal Bygdetun,** a collection of historic houses, is a few yards away. ⊠ *Bygetunet, Saltnes, Rognan,* ☎ *75/68–22–90.* 🖭 *NKr 30.* ⊗ *Mid-June–mid-Aug., week-days 9–4, Sat. 1–4, Sun. 1–6.*

Narvik

❻ *336 km (210 mi) north of Saltstraumen.*

Narvik was originally established as an ice-free port for exporting Swedish iron ore mined around Kiruna. From mid-June to August you can take the seven-minute **Narvik Mountain Lift,** a cable car that of-fers a view of the Ofotenfjord, the mountains, and the city below. ☎ *76/96–04–94.* ⊗ *Mid-June–early Aug., noon–1 AM; early Aug.–late Aug., daily 1–9; spring and winter, same opening hrs as Narvik Ski Center.*

Narvik was rebuilt after being flattened during World War II. **Nord-land Røde Kors Krigsminnemuseum Museum** (Nordland Red Cross War Memorial) documents the German occupation with photos, models, and equipment. ⊠ *Torget–Narvik City Square,* ☎ *76/94–44–26.* 🖭 *NKr 35.* ⊗ *Mar.–early June and late Aug.–late Sept., daily 10–4; late-June–early Aug., daily 10–10.*

Lodging

$$–$$$ 🏨 **Grand Royal Hotel.** Considered Narvik's best, this elegant hotel is very popular. The fairly large rooms are light and airy. ⊠ *Kongensgt. 64, 8501,* ☎ *76/97–70–00,* FAX *76/97–70–07. 107 rooms. 2 restaurants, 2 bars, sauna, nightclub, convention center. AE, DC, MC, V.*

Outdoor Sports and Activities

Narvik Tourist Information is a great resource for finding out the many outdoor tours and activities available in this area.

DIVING

During World War II, more than 50 planes and 46 ships were shot down or sank in the Narvik area. Three of the 11 German battleships that were shot down are still under water. Ever since a ban on going near the wrecks has been lifted, Narvik has become a fascinating place for dives. There are several licensed, experienced guides who specialize in such dives. Contact Narvik Tourist Information.

FISHING

Fjord and sea fishing trips are organized year-round on the *Delphin,* a 14-meter (46-ft) fishing boat, and *Gåsten,* a former Swedish minesweeper, as well as other boats. Contact Narvik Tourist Information.

MOUNTAINEERING

Narvik's landscape makes it ideal for the botany, mountain, and glacier walks and tours led by **North Norwegian School of Mountaineering** (☎ 76/95–13–53). Climbing equipment is available for rent.

SKIING

Set amid fjord and mountains, the **Narvik Ski Center** (☎ 76/96–04–94) is known for its stunning natural setting.

October and November means that schools of killer whales are in the fjord around Narvik hunting Atlantic herring. Whale-spotting expeditions are organized by the tourist office around that time.

Lofoten and the Islands of the North

Extending out into the ocean north of Bodø are the Lofoten Islands, a 190-km (118-mi) chain of jagged peaks. In summer the idyll of farms, fjords, and fishing villages draws caravans of tourists, whereas in winter the coast facing the Arctic Ocean is one of Europe's stormiest. The midnight sun is visible here from May 25 to July 17. If you are lucky enough to be visiting on a clear midnight, drive over to the western side, where the spear-shape mountains give way to flat, sandy beaches that look oddly fluorescent in the hush of night. The sight is spectacular.

Until about 50 years ago fishing was the only source of income for the area (today tourism helps bolster the still thriving fisheries). As many as 6,000 boats with 30,000 anglers would mobilize between January and March for the Lofotfisket, the world's largest cod-fishing event. During the season they fished in open boats and took shelter during stormy nights in rorbuer, simple cabins built right on the water. Today many rorbuer have been converted into tourist lodgings, but Lofotfisket is still an annual tradition.

The best way to visit Lofoten is by car. **Svolvær,** the main town and administrative center for the villages on the islands, is connected with the other islands by express boat and ferry, and by coastal steamer and air to Bodø. It has a thriving summer art colony.

A drive on E10, from Svolvær to the outer tip of Lofoten (130 km [80 mi])—the town with the enigmatic name of **Å**—presents an opportunity to see how the islanders really live.

The Norwegian Fishing Village Museum is a spread-out fishing village with houses, a 19th-century cod-liver-oil factory, and a bread bakery. You can take home a souvenir bottle of cod-liver oil or a cod-liver oil lamp. ⊠ *Å, Highway E10, 10 km (6 mi) from Reine,* ☎ *76/09–14–88.* 🖾 *NKr 40.* ⊙ *Mid-June–mid-Aug., daily 11–6; mid-Aug.–Dec. and Jan.–mid-June, weekdays 11–3:30.*

At the **Lofoten Stockfish Museum,** a conventional fish processing plant concentrates on stockfish (fish dried in the open air without salt). Exhibits and videos explain how it's all done. ⊠ *Å,* ☎ *76/09–12–11.* 🖾 *NKr 35.* ⊙ *Early June–mid-June, weekdays 11–5; mid-June–Aug., daily 11–5.*

Just south of Svolvær, the hamlet of **Kabelvåg** provides the perfect introduction to the string of islands, their history, and their inhabitants. A cluster of **museums** less than a mile from the quiet village center sits on the site of an old fishing settlement. Restored fishing cabins displayed at the **Lofotmuseet** (The Lofoten Museum; ☎ 76/07–82–23) depict the rigorous life of a fishing community on the grassy edge of a fjord inlet. Next door, the **Galleri Espolin** (☎ 76/07–84–05) exhibits dark, haunting paintings and lithographs of fishermen in stormy weather. Kaare Espolin Johnsen, who died in 1994, was a nationally renowned artist. The **Lofot-Akvariet** (Lofoten Aquarium; ☎ 76/07–86–65) includes a salmon farm exhibit, an aquarium, and seal and otter ponds. ⊠ *Storvågan,* ☎ *76/07–86–65.* 🕸 *www.lofotakvariet.no.* 🖾 *NKr 70.* ⊙ *Mid-June–mid-Aug., daily 10–9; mid–late Aug. and early–mid-June, daily 10–6; Sept. and May, daily 11–3; Oct.–Nov. and Feb.–Apr., Sun.–Fri. 11–3.*

Southwest of Kabelvåg is Henningsvær. This village is home to **Lofoten House Gallery (Gallery Harr)** (☎ 76/07–15–73), which exhibits Lofoten-inspired paintings by acclaimed Norwegian artists, including Karl Erik Harr.

Viking enthusiasts might want to veer northwest to Borg, where archaeologists unearthed a long, low chieftain's house—the largest Viking building ever discovered. For the Vikings, the banqueting hall was a sacred place where religious and political rituals were carried out. Now rebuilt exactly as it was, the **Lofotr-The Viking Museum of Borg** houses the 1,000-year-old artifacts that were discovered here. They reveal contact with Germany, France, and England. ⊠ *Prestergårdsvn. 59,* ☎ *76/08–49–00,* 🌐 *www.lofotr.no.* 🖃 *NKr 80.* ☼ *Late May–early-Sept., daily 10–7.*

Other scenic stops include tucked-away **Nusfjord,** a 19th-century fishing village on an official European Conservation list; **Sund,** with its smithy and small fisheries museum; and festive **Reine.**

<table>
<tr><td>NEED A
BREAK?</td><td>The rustic **Gammelbua** (⊠ Reine, ☎ 76/09–22–22) serves excellent salmon mousse and chilled Norwegian beer. Locals and tourists flock here to eat, drink, and gossip.</td></tr>
</table>

Off the tip of Moskenesøy, the last island with a bridge, is **Moskenesstraumen,** another maelstrom that's not quite as dramatic as Saltstraumen.

North of the Lofotens are the **Vesterålen Islands,** with more fishing villages and rorbuer, and diverse vegetation. There are fewer tourists in Vesterålen, but more whale sightings. Puffins populate area cliffs, as in the Lofotens. The Coastal Steamer slithers in and around fjords of these more low-key islands.

East of Vesterålen on Hinnøya, Norway's largest island, is **Harstad,** where the year-round population of 23,000 swells to 42,000 during the annual June cultural festival (the line-up includes concerts, theater, and dance) and its July deep-sea fishing festival.

Dining and Lodging

Although hotels have popped up in some of the bigger fishing villages, staying in a rorbu (fisherman's cabin) is essential to the Lofoten experience. Rorbuer vary in size and comfort, some date back to the last century and others are new. If you do stay in a rorbu, it is worth your while to bring a few days' worth of food to stick in the refrigerator. Some villages have few cafés, and you may find that the closest thing to a grocery store is a gas station. Unless you have your own linens, you'll have to pay extra—usually about NKr 100.

$$–$$$ ✕ **Røkenes Gård.** Originally a 16th-century commercial trading house and inn, this has become a well-regarded restaurant. Dishes are based on fresh catches of the day and therefore vary, but try the fried saithe (pollack) or roasted lamb chops if they're available. ⊠ *Harstad,* ☎ *77/05–84–44. Reservations essential. AE, DC, MC, V.*

$$ ✕ **Fiskekrogen.** At this quayside restaurant in a fishing village, chef and owner Otto Asheim's specialties come highly recommended. They include fried catfish; bacalao; "homemade" caviar directly from the sea; and the Krogen seafood plate, a selection of fresh seasonal fare. ⊠ *Henningsvær,* ☎ *76/07–46–52. AE, DC, MC, V.*

$–$$ 🏠 **Henningsvær Rorbuer.** This small group of turn-of-the-20th-century rorbuer is just outside the center of Lofoten's most important fishing village. Breakfasts can be ordered from the cafeteria. Summer is extremely busy so reservations are essential for July. ✉ *8312 Henningsvær,* ☎ *76/07–46–00,* FAX *76/07–49–10. 19 1- or 2-bedroom rorbuer. Cafeteria, grill, sauna, laundry service.* V.

$–$$ ⊡ **Nusfjord Rorbuanlegg.** These secluded cabins are extremely attractive to families: many choose to stay weeks at a time. There's plenty to do—hiking, fishing, boating—in the surrounding area. For a glimpse at the midnight sun, drive to the other side of the island at Flakstad. Rowboats are included in the price of a rorbu, and you can rent fishing gear and motorboats. ✉ *8380 Ramberg,* ☎ *76/09–30–20,* FAX *76/09–33–78. 34 1- or 2-bedroom rorbuer. Restaurant, pub, coin laundry. AE, DC, MC,* V.

$–$$ ⊡ **Nyvågar Rorbuhotell.** This lodging and recreation complex is a 20-minute drive from the Svolvær airport and a two-minute walk from the group of museums near Kabelvåg. Activities are well organized, with fishing-boat tours, eagle safaris, and deep-sea rafting, as well as evening entertainment. The cabins are spotless. ✉ *8310 Kabelvåg, Storvågan,* ☎ *76/07–89–00,* FAX *76/06–97–01,* WEB *www.top.no. 60 rooms. Restaurant, meeting room. AE, DC, MC,* V.

$–$$ ⊡ **Rainbow Vestfjord Hotel.** This simple hotel has spacious rooms and a lovely view of the harbor beyond. It used to be a cod-liver-oil factory. ✉ *8301 Svolvær,* ☎ *76/07–08–70,* FAX *76/07–08–54. 63 rooms, 3 suites. Restaurant, bar, meeting room. AE, DC, MC,* V.

$–$$ ⊡ **Rica Hotel Svolvær.** While the exterior says rustic rorbu, this Rica hotel's interior says comfortable luxury. Accommodations are in separate all-wood rorbu cabins, which are comfortably appointed, each with its own waterfront veranda from which you can fish. The main lobby and restaurant are inside an unusual boat-shape building that has panoramic harbor views. ✉ *Lamholmen, 8301 Svolvær,* ☎ *76/07–22–22,* FAX *76/07–20–01,* WEB *www.rica.no. 147 rooms. Restaurant, bar, convention center. AE, DC, MC,* V.

Outdoor Activities and Sports

BIRD-WATCHING

A constant shrieking hum emanates from some of North Norway's arctic island cliffs, which pulsate with thousands of birds. From Moskenes, just north of Å, or from Bodø, you can take a ferry to the bird sanctuaries of **Værøy** and **Røst.** Many different types of seabirds inhabit the cliffs, particularly eider (sea ducks).

GOLF

The beautiful, 9-hole **Lofoten Golf Course** (☎ 76/07–20–02) has become famous for 24-hour-a-day summer golfing.

MOUNTAINEERING

The North Norwegian School of Mountaineering (☎ 76/07–49–11) calls the Lofoten Islands home. They have one-week or day mountaineering courses at different levels, guided mountain tours, and an equipment shop.

WHALE-WATCHING

The stretch of sea that lies north of Lofoten and Vesterålen is perhaps the best place to sight whales, porpoises, and white-beaked dolphins. Whale safari boat tours leave from the tip of Andøy, an island northwest of Hinnøya. Contact **Whale Safari** (☎ 76/11–56–00) for more information. Brush up on your knowledge of the sea-faring mammal at the island's **Whale Center** (Destination Lofoten, ☎ 76/07–30–00) before the trip. **Whale Tours A/S** (☎ 76/13–44–99) scours the sea for minke, sperm, and killer whales. Reservations are necessary for both excursions.

Shopping

Lofoten is a mecca for artists and craftspeople, who come for the spectacular scenery and the ever-changing light.

Probably the best-known craftsperson in the region is Tor Vegard Mørkved, better known as **Smeden i Sund** (the blacksmith at Sund; ☎ 76/09–36–29). Watch him make wrought-iron gift items. Åse and Åsvar Tangrand's **Glasshytta and Ceramics Workshop** (☎ 76/09–44–42), near Nusfjord, is a fun place to stop.

Tromsø

❼ *318 km (197 mi) northeast of Harstad.*

Tromsø surprised travelers visiting in the 1800s: they thought it very sophisticated and cultured for being so close to the North Pole. It looks the way a polar town should—with ice-capped mountain ridges and jagged architecture that is an echo of the peaks. The midnight sun shines from May 21 to July 21, and the city's total area—2,558 square km (987 square mi)—is the most expansive in Norway. Tromsø is just about the same size as the country of Luxembourg, but home to only 58,000 people. The city's center sits on a small, hilly island connected to the mainland by a slender bridge. The 13,000 students at the world's northernmost university are one reason the nightlife here is more lively than in many other northern cities.

The **Ishavskatedralen** (Arctic Cathedral) is the city's signature structure. Representing North Norwegian nature, culture, and faith, it's meant to evoke the shape of a Sámi tent as well as the iciness of a glacier. Inside, an immense stained-glass window, one of the largest in Europe, depicts the Second Coming. ✉ *Tromsdalen,* ☎ *77/63–76–11.* ☜ *NKr 20.* ☉ *May, daily 3–4:30; June–Aug., Mon.–Sat. 10–8, Sun. 1–8. Times may vary according to church services.*

The **Tromsø Museum, Universitetsmuseet** (Tromsø University Museum) is dedicated to the nature and culture of the region. Learn about the Sámi, and see a reconstructed Viking longhouse. Many of the exhibitions are great for children, including the lifesize dinosaur. ✉ *Universitetet, Lars Thørings v. 10,* ☎ *77/64–50–00,* [WEB] *www.imv.uit.no.* ☜ *NKr 30.* ☉ *June–Aug., daily 9–8; Sept.–May, weekdays 8:30–3:30, Sat. noon–3, Sun. 11–4.*

The **Polarmuseet i Tromsø** (Polar Museum), in an 1830s former customs warehouse, documents the history of the polar region, including a great deal on Norway's polar explorers and hunters. ✉ *Søndre Tollbugt. 11B,* ☎ *77/68–43–73,* [WEB] *troms.kulturnett.no/pol/.* ☜ *NKr 40.* ☉ *Mid-May–mid-June, daily 11–5; mid-June–Aug., daily 10–7; Sept.–mid-May, daily 11–3.*

Macks Ølbryggeri (Mack's Brewery). Established in Tromsø in 1877, the Mack's Brewery produces 21 types of beer. You can tour the brewery, take home a beer stein, and sample the product in the Ølhallen pub. ✉ *Storgt. 5–13,* ☎ *77/62–45–00,* [WEB] *www.mack.no.* ☜ *NKr 70.* ☉ *Guided tours Mon.–Thurs. Call ahead for hours.*

The science center **Polaria** examines life in and around the Norwegian and Arctic seas. Changing exhibits look at developments in Arctic research, and there's an aquarium with sea mammals, including seals. The cafeteria serves special Arctic dishes. ✉ *Hjarmar Johansens gt. 12,* ☎ *77/75–01–00,* [WEB] *www.polaria.no.* ☜ *NKr 70.* ☉ *Mid-May–mid-Aug., daily 10–7; mid-Aug.–mid-May, daily noon–5.*

Tromsø Botaniske Hage (Tromsø Botanic Garden). The world's northernmost botanical gardens has plants from the Antarctic and Arctic as well as mountain plants from all over the world. The garden has been designed as a natural landscape with terraces, slopes, a stream, and a pond. Guides are available by special arrangement. ⊠ *Tromsø University, Breivika,* WEB *www.imv.uit.no/homepage.htm.* ⌷ *Free.* ⊙ *Daily 24 hours.*

To get a sense of Tromsø's immensity and solitude, take the **Fjellheisen** (cable car) from behind the cathedral up to the mountains, just a few minutes out of the city center. **Storsteinen** (Big Rock), 1,386 ft above sea level, has a great city view. ☎ 77/63–87–37. ⌷ *NKr 60.* ⊙ *Mar., weekends 10–5; Apr.–mid-May, daily 10–5; mid-May–mid-Aug., daily 10–1; mid-Aug.–Sept., daily 10–5; Oct.–Feb. by appointment.*

OFF THE
BEATEN PATH

NORDLYSPLANETARIET – At the Northern Lights Planetarium, 112 projectors guarantee a 360° view of programs, which include a tour through the universe. It's just outside town. ⊠ *Hansine Hansensv. 17, Breivika,* ☎ *77/67–60–00.* ⌷ *NKr 50.* ⊙ *Shows in English: June–late Aug., weekdays 1:30 and 4:30; weekends 4:30; late Aug.–May, call for show times.*

Dining and Lodging

$$ ✕ **Vertshuset Skarven.** With a whitewashed and blue color scheme that recalls Greece, this is a landmark indoor and outdoor restaurant known for its fish dishes. Sample the fish soup, beef stew, or seal lasagna. The Skarvens Biffhus and Sjømatrestauranten Arctandria restaurants are also in the same building. ⊠ *Strandtorget 1,* ☎ 77/60–07–20. *Reservations essential. AE, DC, MC, V.*

$$$–$$$$ ☆ **Rica Ishavshotel.** Shaped like a ship, Tromsø's snazziest hotel is right at the harbor and stretches over the sound toward Ishavskatedralen. Inside, shiny wood furnishings with brass trimmings evoke the life of the sea. The hotel breakfast buffet is one of the best in Norway, even including vitamins. Guests represent a mixture of business executives, tourists, and those attending scientific conferences. ⊠ *Fr. Langes gt. 2, Box 196, 9252,* ☎ 77/66–64–00, FAX 77/66–64–44, WEB *www.rica.no. 180 rooms. 2 restaurants, 2 bars, convention center, meeting rooms. AE, DC, MC, V.*

$$–$$$$ ☷ **Radisson SAS Hotel Tromsø.** You can see splendid views over the Tromsø shoreline at this modern hotel. The standard rooms are tiny but still provide the signature classy Radisson SAS style and service. ⊠ *Sjøgt. 7, 9008,* ☎ 77/60–00–00, FAX 77/68–54–74, WEB *www.radissonsas.com. 195 rooms with bath, 2 suites. Restaurant, 2 bars, pizzeria, sauna, nightclub. AE, DC, MC, V.*

$$–$$$ ☷ **Comfort Home Hotel With.** This comfortable hotel on the waterfront has a great location with views to match. Breakfast and evening supper is included in the room price. The ever-popular top floor "relaxation room" has skylights. ⊠ *Sjøgt. 35–37, 9257,* ☎ 77/68–70–00, FAX 77/68–96–16, WEB *www.with.no. 76 rooms. Sauna, Turkish baths, meeting room. AE, DC, MC, V. MAP.*

$–$$ ☷ **Comfort Hotel Saga.** Centrally located on a pretty town square, this hotel has somewhat basic rooms that are loaded with blonde wood and warm colors. Its restaurant has affordable, hearty meals. ⊠ *Richard Withs pl. 2,* ☎ 77/68–11–80, FAX 77/68–23–80, WEB *www.sagahotel.com. 67 rooms. Restaurant, cafeteria. AE, DC, MC, V.*

Nightlife

Tromsø has vibrant nightlife for all tastes, whether you're seeking a quiet café, a lively pub, or a dance club. The best city view is likely at **Skibsbroen Bar,** the fifth floor of the Rica Ishavshotel or harborside at its more subdued **Galleriet Bar** (both ⊠ Fr. Langesgt. 2, ☎ 77/66–64–00), which has piano music almost every evening. Since 1928, polar explorers, Arctic skippers, hunters, whalers, and sealers have been meeting at Mack Brewery's **Ølhallen** (⊠ Storgt. 5, ☎ 77/62–45–80). **Meieriet Café & Storpub** (⊠ Grønnegt. 37–39, ☎ 77/61–36–39) is one of the city's largest, most popular, and yet still cozy cafés. Rock music and the city's largest selection of beer are at the **Blå Rock Café** (⊠ Strandgt. 14–16, ☎ 77/61–00–20), which has live concerts and DJs on weekends.

Victoria Fun Pub/Sub Circus/Amtmandens Dattar (⊠ Amtmanngt., ☎ 77/68–49–06), a lively evening entertainment complex, has something for everyone. Sub Circus has live bands and attracts a younger crowd while a broader range of ages head to the English-style Victoria. The smoky Amtmandens Dattar is an old, mellow café. The University's café and cultural center **DRIV** (⊠ Søndre Tollbod gt. 3, ☎ 77/60–07–76) is in a 1902 quayside building. Live concerts, theater, and other cultural events are all staged here.

Outdoor Activities and Sports

TROMSO Troms Turlag (☎ 77/68–51–75) organizes tours and courses and has overnight cabins.

DIVING

Atlanter'n Dykk (☎ 77/63–63–50) can help you get certified in scuba diving and then take you on a guided dive. They offer dives near wrecks, and even dives at night.

DOGSLEDDING

Some 20 km (12 mi) outside the city, **Tromsø Villmarkssenter** (☎ 77/69–60–02) organizes winter husky dogsledding trips and Sámi-style dinners, which take place around a campfire inside a *lavvu* (a Sámi tent).

HIKING AND WALKING

Tromsø has more than 100 km (62 mi) of walking and hiking trails in the mountains above the city. They're reachable by funicular. For guided mountain and glacier walking, contact **Bo-med-oss** (☎ 77/71–06-92) or **Svensby Tursenter** (☎ 77/71–22–25).

SAFARIS

Lofoten Opplevelser (☎ 76/07–50–01) organizes sea eagle expeditions on giant rubber dinghies.

SKIING

Since the mountains are eight minutes away by funicular, **Tromsø Alpine Ski Center** (☎ 77/60–66–80) is a convenient place to downhill ski. There are also 70 km of cross-country trails, 33 of which are floodlit around the clock in order to combat the long, dark days of winter.

En Route   The drive from Tromsø to Alta is mostly right along the coast. At one point you'll drive along the **Kvænangsfjellet ridge,** where Kautokeino Sámi spend the summer in turf huts—you might see a few of their reindeer along the way. Thirteen kilometers (eight miles) west of Alteidet you'll pass by **Øksfjordjøkelen,** the only glacier in Norway that calves (separates or breaks) into the sea.

Alta

❽ *409 km (253 mi) north of Tromsø, 217 km (134 mi) from the North Cape.*

At the turn of the millennium, Alta was officially renamed Nordlysbyen Alta (Northern Lights City Alta). This town of 13,500 is a major transportation center for the regions of West Finnmark and North Troms.

Most people spend the night here before making the final ascent to the North Cape.

Northern Europe's biggest canyon is nearby **Sautso, Alta Canyon,** the site of hiking, riverboat trips, and bus tours. At the **Alta Hydro-electric Power Station,** you can view the reservoir and concrete dam through a panoramic window. Contact the Destination Alta tourist office for more information.

OFF THE BEATEN PATH
ALTA MUSEUM – It's worth a trek to Hjemmeluft, southwest of the city, to see four groupings of 2,500- to 6,200-year-old prehistoric rock carvings, the largest in northern Europe. The pictographs were discovered in 1973 and form part of the museum. Changing exhibitions deal with prehistoric Finnmark and local history. ☎ 78/45–63–30. ☑ NKr 70. ◷ May and Sept., daily 9–6; early-June–mid-June and mid-Aug.–late Aug., daily 9–8; mid-June–mid-Aug., daily 8 AM–11 PM; Oct.–Apr., weekdays 9–3, weekends 11–4.

Lodging

$$–$$$ ⊡ **Rica Hotel Alta.** Everything is light and bright in this hotel, from the reflectors on the ceiling of public rooms to the white furniture in the bedrooms. It's a functional place to stay in the area. ⊠ Lokkevn. 1, 9501, ☎ 78/48–27–77, FAX 78/43–58–25, WEB www.rica.no. 154 rooms. 2 restaurants, 2 bars, lobby lounge, sauna, nightclub, meeting room. AE, DC, MC, V.

DOGSLEDDING
Roger Dahl's **Canyon Huskies** (⊠ Alta, ☎ 78/43–33–06) arranges all kinds of custom sled-dog tours along Finnmark's ancient travel routes. They can last a half-day, a full day, or longer.

Shopping
Manndalen Husflidslag (☎ 77/71–62–73) at Løkvoll in Manndalen, on E6 about 15 km (9 mi) west of Alta, is a center for Coastal Sámi weaving on vertical looms. Local weavers sell their rugs and wall hangings along with other regional crafts.

Hammerfest

❾ *145 km (90 mi) north of Alta.*

The world's northernmost town is one of the most widely visited and oldest places in North Norway. "Hammerfest" means "mooring place" and refers to the natural harbor formed by the crags in the mountain. In 1891, Hammerfest was tired of the months-long night that winter always brought. They decided to brighten the situation and purchased a generator from Thomas Edison. It was the first city in Europe to have electric street lamps.

Hammerfest is home to the **Isbjørn Klubben** (Royal and Ancient Polar Bear Society). Founded by two businessmen, their goal was to share the town's history as a center for hunting and business. All the exhibits depict some aspect of Arctic hunts. ⊠ Town Hall Basement, ☎ 78/41–31–10. ☑ Free. ◷ Sept.–mid-May, daily 11:30–1:30; mid-May–mid-June, daily 10–3, weekends 11–2; mid-June–mid-Aug., daily 7–6; mid–late Aug. daily 10–3, weekends 10–2.

Although it covers Finnmark's history from the Stone Age until today, the **Museum of Post-War Reconstruction** mainly focuses on World War II. At that time, Finnmark's population was forced to evacuate and the county was burnt to the ground. Through videos and sound reenactments, the museum recounts the residents' struggle to rebuild their lives.

✉ *Kirkegt. 21, Hammerfest,* ☎ *78/42–26–30.* ☉ *Early June–late Aug.,*
daily 10–6; late Aug.–early June, daily 11–2.

Mikkelgammen is a traditional Sámi turf hut in Hammerfest at which
you can learn something about Sámi culture and traditions. You can
gather around a campfire for a meal of *bidos,* a Sámi reindeer dish.
Joik, a kind of singing–chanting, is performed, and stories are told. You
can also participate in reindeer herding in winter. Contact the tourist
office for information on both programs.

Dining and Lodging

$$–$$$ ⛫ **Rica Hotel Hammerfest.** The rooms here are functional and small,
but comfortable enough. ✉ *Sørøygt. 15,* ☎ *78/41–13–33,* 𝔽𝔸𝕏 *78/41–*
13–11, 🖳 *www.rica.no. 48 rooms. Restaurant, bar, pizzeria, sauna,*
convention center. AE, DC, MC, V.

$$ ⛫ **Quality Hammerfest Hotel.** Right on the pleasant Rådhusplassen,
this guest house has handsome, harborview rooms for decent prices.
✉ *Strandgt. 2–4,* ☎ *78/42–96–00,* 𝔽𝔸𝕏 *78/42–96–60,* 🖳 *www.*
hammerfesthotel.no. 53 rooms. Restaurant, 2 pubs, bar, sauna. AE,
DC, MC, V.

Honningsvåg

🔟 *130 km (80 mi) from Hammerfest.*

Known as "the Town by the North Cape," Honningsvåg was completely
destroyed at the end of World War II, when the Germans burned every-
thing in their retreat. The town's central location and infrastructure have
made it one of the most important harbors in North Norway.

The **Nordkappmuseet** (North Cape Museum), on the third floor of Nord-
kapphuset (North Cape House), documents the history of the fishing
industry in the region as well as the history of tourism at the North
Cape. You can learn about how people have survived here for 10,000
years. ✉ *Fiskerivn. 4,* ☎ *78/47–28–33.* 🕮 *NKr 20.*

The destination of many travelers, **Knivskjelodden** (Crooked Knife) is
Europe's northernmost point. There's a spectacular view toward the
North Cape Plateau. Walk the world's northernmost hiking trail (18
km round-trip) to Knivskjelodden. Here you can write your name in
the hiking association's minute book and buy a diploma attesting to
your visit.

Lodging

$$ ⛫ **Rica Hotel Honningsvå.** Right on the harbor, the town's best hotel
has reasonably priced rooms. They're bright and cheerful, decorated
in yellow and light woods. Bryggen Restaurant is a favorite dining choice
for traditional fare. ✉ *Vågen 1, 9750,* ☎ *78/47–28–88,* 𝔽𝔸𝕏 *78/47–27–*
24, 🖳 *www.rica.no. 42 rooms, 4 mini-suites. Restaurant, bar. AE, DC,*
MC, V.

Nordkapp

⑪ *34 km (21 mi) from Honningsvåg.*

On your journey to the Nordkapp (North Cape), you'll see an incredible
treeless tundra, with crumbling mountains and sparse dwarf plants.
The sub-Arctic environment is very vulnerable, so take special care not
to disturb the plants. Walk only on marked trails and don't remove
stones, leave car marks or campfires, or remove stones. Because the
roads are closed in winter, the only access is from the tiny fishing village of Skarsvåg via Sno-Cat, a thump-and-bump ride that's as un-
forgettable as the beautifully bleak view.

The contrast between this near-barren territory and **The North Cape Hall,** the tourist center, is striking. Blasted into the interior of the plateau, the building is housed in a cave and includes an ecumenical chapel, souvenir shop, and post office. Exhibits trace the history of the Cape, from Richard Chancellor, an Englishman who drifted around it and named it in 1533, to Oscar II, king of Norway and Sweden, who climbed to the top of the plateau in 1873. Celebrate your pilgrimage to the Nordkapp at Café Kompasset, Restaurant Kompasset, or at the Grotten Bar coffee shop. ☎ 78/47–68–60, ꟿ *www.norway.com/north_cape.* ⬚ *Entrance to the hall NKr 175.* ☉ *Early Apr.–early Oct., 9–2.*

Outdoor Activities and Sports

BIRD SAFARI

Gjesvær Turistsenter (☎ 78/47–57–73) organizes bird safaris and deep-sea fishing. **Nordkapp Reiseliv** (☎ 78/47–25–99) books adventures and activities including bird safaris, deep-sea fishing, boat excursions, and various winter expeditions.

DIVING

Take a scuba dive at the top of Europe with **Nordkapp Dykkesenter** (☎ 78/47–22–22), which also provides deep-sea rafting, kayaking, ski and guided tours, and bike rentals.

RAFTING

Deep-sea rafting is as exhilarating as it is beautiful. Among the several tours offered is a three-hour trip to the North Cape. Call **Nordkapp Safari** (☎ 78/47–27–94).

Trondheim and the North Cape A to Z

To research prices, get advice from other travelers, and book travel arrangements, visit www.fodors.com.

AIR TRAVEL

CARRIERS

SAS, Braathens, and Widerøe are the main domestic carriers, and offer excellent connections throughout northern Norway. SAS flies to eight destinations, including Bodø, Tromsø, Alta, and Kirkenes. Braathens flies to five destinations, including Bodø and Tromsø. Widerøe specializes in northern Norway and flies to 19 destinations in the region, including Honningsvåg, the airport closest to the North Cape.

➤ AIRLINES AND CONTACTS: **Braathens** (☎ 815–20–000). **SAS** (☎ 810/03–300). **Widerøe** (☎ 810/01–200).

AIRPORTS

Trondheim's Værnes Airport is 32 km (21 mi) northeast of the city. With the exception of Harstad, all cities in northern Norway are served by airports less than 5 km (3 mi) from the center of town. Tromsø is a crossroads for air traffic between northern and southern Norway and is served by Braathens, SAS, and Widerøe. Honningsvåg is served by Widerøe.

➤ AIRPORT INFORMATION: **Honningsvåg** (☎ 78/47–29–92) **Tromsø Airport** (☎ 77/64–84–00). **Trondheim Værnes Airport** (☎ 74/84–30–00).

BOAT AND FERRY TRAVEL

Boat travel is ideal for Nordland. *Hurtigruten* (the coastal express boat, which goes to 35 ports from Bergen to Kirkenes) stops at Trondheim, southbound at St. Olav's Pier, Quay 16, northbound at Pier 1, Quay 7. Other stops between Trondheim and the North Cape include Bodø, Stamsund and Svolvær (Lofotens), Sortland (Vesterålen), Harstad,

Tromsø, Hammerfest, and Honningsvåg. Call the number below for information on *Hurtigruten* and local ferries.

It is possible to buy tickets for the *Hurtigruten* between any harbors right on the boats. OVDS, Ofotens og Vesterlens Dampskibsselskap, in partnership with TFDS (Troms Fylkes Dampskibsselskap), operates the Coastal Express ferries and express boats that serve many towns in the region.

Getting to the Lofoten Islands is easiest and most enjoyable by taking the *Hurtigruten* from Bodø or another of its ports of call along the coast. ➤ BOAT AND FERRY INFORMATION: **Hurtigruten–local ferry information** (☎ 77/64–82–00). **OVDS** (✉ Narvik, ☎ 76/96–76–96). **TFDS** (✉ Tromsø, ☎ 77/64–81–00; ✉ Trondheim, ☎ 73/51–51–20).

BUS TRAVEL

Bus 135 (*Østerdalsekspress*) runs overnight from Oslo to Trondheim via Røros. Buses also connect Bergen, Molde, and Ålesund with Trondheim.

Nor-Way Bussekspress can help you to put together a bus journey to destinations in the North. The Ekspress 2000 travels regularly among Oslo, Kautokeino, Alta, Nordkapp, and Hammerfest.

All local Trondheim buses stop at the Munkegata–Dronningens Gate intersection. Some routes end at the bus terminal at Trondheim Sentralstasjon. Tickets cost NKr 12 and allow free transfer between buses and streetcars (Gråkallbanen).

North of Bodø and Narvik (a five-hour bus ride from Bodø), beyond the reach of the railroad, buses go virtually everywhere, but they don't go often. Get a comprehensive bus schedule from a tourist office or travel agent before making plans. Local bus companies include Saltens Bilruter, Ofotens Bilruter, Tromsbuss, Midttuns Busser, Finnmark Fylkesrederi og Ruteselskap, and Ekspress 2000. ➤ BUS INFORMATION: **Ekspress 2000** (✉ Alta, ☎ 78/44–40–90). **Finnmark Fylkesrederi og Ruteselskap** (☎ 78/40–70–00). **Gråkallbanen** (Trondheim streetcars; ☎ 72/55–23–55). **Midttuns Busser** (✉ Tromsø, ☎ 77/67–27–87). **Nor-Way Bussekspress** (☎ 815/44–444). **Ofotens Bilruter** (✉ Narvik, ☎ 76/92–35–00). **Tromsbuss** (✉ Tromsø, ☎ 77/67–75–00). **Trondheim Sentralstasjon** (☎ 72/57–20–20) **Saltens Bilruter** (✉ Bodø, ☎ 75/50–90–00).

CAR RENTALS

Book a rental car as far in advance as possible. There's no better way to see the Lofoten and Vesterålen islands than by car. Nordkapp (take the plane to Honningsvåg) is another excursion best made by car. ➤ LOCAL AGENCIES: **Avis Bilutleie** (☎ 77/61–58–50). **Budget Bilutleie** (☎ 73/94–10–25). **Budget, Tromsø Airport** (☎ 77/66–19–00).

CAR TRAVEL

Trondheim is about 500 km (310 mi) from Oslo: seven to eight hours of driving. Speed limits are 80 kph (50 mph) much of the way. There are two alternatives, E6 through Gudbrandsdalen or Route 3 through Østerdalen. It's 727 km (450 mi) from Trondheim to Bodø on Route E6, which goes all the way to Kirkenes. There's an NKr 30 toll on E6 just east of Trondheim. The motorway toll also covers the NKr 11 toll (6 AM–10 PM) for cars entering the downtown area. Anyone who makes it to the North Cape *sans* tour bus will be congratulated with a NKr 150 toll.

The best way to see the Lofoten Islands is by car since bus service is often limited and there is much to see. The main tourist office in Svolvær can point you to local rental agencies, whose rates tend to be quite high. Short distances between neighboring villages are doable by bicycle if you plan to stay in one village for several days.

ROAD CONDITIONS

The roads aren't a problem in northern Norway—most are quite good, although there are always narrow and winding stretches, especially along fjords. Distances are formidable. Route 17—the *Kystriksvegen* (Coastal Highway) from Namsos to Bodø—is an excellent alternative to E6. Getting to Tromsø and the North Cape involves additional driving on narrower roads off E6. In the northern winter, near-blizzard conditions and icy roads sometimes make it necessary to drive in a convoy.

EMERGENCIES

The following pharmacies serve the Trondheim area: in Tromsø, Svaneapoteket is open daily 8:30–4:30 and 6–9. In Trondheim, Svaneapoteket is open weekdays 8:30–3 and Saturday 9–3.

➤ CONTACTS: **Svaneapoteket** (✉ Kongensgt. 14b, ☎ 73/52–23–01). **Svaneapoteket** (✉ Fr. Langesgt. 9, ☎ 77–60–14–80).

TAXIS

Taxi stands are in logical locations in downtown Trondheim. All taxis are connected to the central dispatching office. Numbers for taxis in Harstad, Narvik, and Tromsø are listed below by town.

➤ TAXI INFORMATION: **Harstad Taxi** (☎ 77/04–10–00). **Nordland Taxi, Narvik** (☎ 76/94–65–00). **Tromsø** (☎ 77/60–30–00). **Trøndertaxi** (✉ Trondheim; ☎ 73/90–90–73).

TOURS

In Tromsø, the tourist information office sells tickets for City Sightseeing (Dampskipskaia) and the MF *Polstjerna,* an Arctic vessel that runs a fishing tour in the waters around Tromsø Island. The Trondheim Tourist Association offers a number of tours. Tickets are sold at the tourist information office or at the start of the tour.

➤ CONTACTS: **Tromsø Tourist Information Office** (✉ Storgt. 61–63, 9253, ☎ 77/61–00–00).

TRAIN TRAVEL

The *Dovrebanen* has frequent departures daily and nightly on the Oslo–Trondheim route. Trains leave from Oslo S Station for the seven-to eight-hour journey. Trondheim is the gateway to the North, and two trains run daily in both directions on the 11-hour Trondheim–Bodø route. The *Nordlandsbanen* has three departures daily in each direction on the Bodø–Trondheim route, an 11-hour journey. The *Ofotbanen* has two departures daily in each direction on the Stockholm–Narvik route, a 21-hour journey. Call ahead for local information for summer trains from Narvik to the Swedish border.

➤ TRAIN INFORMATION: **Summer Train Information** (☎ 76/92–31–21). **Trondheim Train Information** (☎ 72/57–20–20).

VISITOR INFORMATION

➤ TOURIST INFORMATION: **Alta (Destinasjon Alta)** (✉ Top Of Norway, 9500 Løkkeveien, ☎ 78/45–50–00). **Bodø (Destinasjon Bodø)** (✉ Sjøgt. 21, 8001, ☎ 75/54–80–00). **Fauske** (✉ Salten Tourist Board, ☎ 75/64–32–38). **Hammerfest** (✉ 9600, ☎ 78/42–25–22). **Harstad** (✉ Torvet 8, 9400, ☎ 77/06–32–35). **Lofoten** (✉ 8301 Svolvær, ☎ 76/07–30–00). **Mo i Rana** (✉ , 8601 Mo, ☎ 75/13–92–00). **Narvik** (✉ Kongensgt. 66, 8505, ☎ 76/94–33–09). **Nordkapp** (✉ Fiskerivn. 4D Honningsvåg, ☎ 78/47–25–99). **Tromsø** (✉ Storgt. 61–63, 9253, ☎ 77/61–00–00). **Trondheim** (✉ Munkegt. 19, Torget 7001, ☎ 73/80–76–60).

11 SÁMILAND TO SVALBARD AND THE FINNISH-RUSSIAN CONNECTION

On the roof of Europe, atop the vast, windswept Finnmarksvidda, the Continent's only nomadic indigenous people, the reindeer-herding Sámi, roam. Most still live in traditional tents and dress in colorful costumes, although the most visible evidence of their lifestyle is roadside souvenir stands and tourist exhibits. The desolate expanses and treeless tundra makes an inspiring trekking destination—you're almost guaranteed an encounter with reindeer.

UROPE'S ONLY ANCIENT INDIGENOUS PEOPLE, the Sámi, recognize no national boundaries. Sámiland, formerly called Lapland, stretches from the Kola Peninsula in Russia through Finland, Sweden, and Norway. The majority of Sámi, some 35,000, live in Norway. Norwegian Sámiland is centered around the communities of Karasjok and Kautokeino, in the Finnmark region.

The traditional symbol of the Sámi is the reindeer herder, and about a third still live this way. The rest pursue other traditional professions such as fishing or newer occupations in their communities and cities. As you'd expect, the Sámi have their own language, music, art, and handicrafts. Take time to experience this traditional culture, whether it's expressed through the lavvus (their tents made of reindeer skin), their distinctive songs, or their cuisine, rich in reindeer and wild salmon dishes.

Numbers in the margin correspond to points of interest on the Trondheim and the North map in chapter 10.

Kautokeino

⑫ *129 km (80 mi) southeast of Alta.*

Kautokeino, with 3,000 inhabitants, is in the heart of Finnmarksvidda (the Finnmark mountain plateau). Because of such institutions as the Nordic Sámi Institute, Sámi Theater, and Sámi College, it has become center for the Sámi culture, research, and education.

OFF THE BEATEN PATH

MÁZE ZION – A mountain church stood from 1721 to 1768, but only ruins are here now. The headstones in the cemetery have names written in an old form of Sámi, in which special characters are used for each name. ⊠ *Highway 93, en route to Alta from Kautokeino.*

The beautiful **Pikefossen Falls,** on the Alta River between Kautokeino and Máze, were named after a girl ("pike" means girl) who mysteriously drowned here. If you stay in the area overnight in a Sámi tent (a lavvu), legend has it that you may hear the girl's screams in the falls.

Outdoor Activities and Sports

FISHING

Kautokeino has an abundance of lakes available for year-round fishing. Contact the **Kautokeino Environmental Office** (☎ 78/48–71–00).

HIKES AND OUTINGS

The plains and forests around Kautokeino make it excellent terrain for hiking year-round. In fact, it has one of the largest areas of untouched nature in northern Europe. Kautokeino intersects with the **Nordkalott Route,** an 800-km (500-mi) trail with ends in Kvikkjokk, Sweden, and Sulitjelma, Norway.

DNT, the Norwegian Mountain Touring Association, organizes special activities in the region. Contact the **Kautokeino Environmental Office** (☎ 78/48–71–00). The **Suohpatjávri Nature and Cultural Trail,** 7 km (4½ mi) south of Kautokeino, is popular. Along the 4½-km (2¾-mi) marked trail, there's a picnic area, a *jordgamme* (earth and turf hut), and a *siedi,* a sacrificial stone, which is a protected cultural monument.

Nightlife and the Arts

Traditional Sámi culture is celebrated at Kautokeino's longstanding annual **Easter Festival** (☎ 78/48–71–00, WEB www.saami-easterfestival.org), which features traditional craft exhibits as well as joik, a haunting kind of song that's sung as a solo with no accompaniment. Joik are usually songs of praise for nature. The festival also includes more recent cultural developments, including large Sámi weddings, reindeer races, concerts, theatrical performances, skiing, fishing competitions, and snowmobile rallies.

Shopping

Inside what was once a secret military facility, **Juhls' Silver Gallery** (☎ 78/48–61–89), home of Finnmark's first silversmith, carries the best selection of contemporary Sámi art— everything from paintings and posters to sculpture. Part Frank Lloyd Wright and part Buddhist temple, the interiors have been designed and decorated over 50 years by the Danish-German Frank and Regine Juhls. Don't miss the ornamental ceiling in the Afghan room. It was made to honor the Sámis.

Lodging

$ ☷ **Norlandia Kautokeino Hotel.** This standard hotel has comfortable rooms. The hotel restaurant serves Sámi dishes, Norwegian home fare, and international dishes. ✉ 9520, ☎ 78/48–62–05, FAX 78/48–67–01, WEB www.norlandia.no. 50 rooms. Restaurant, bar, sauna. AE, DC, MC, V. Closed mid-Dec.–Mar.

Karasjok

🚯 178 km (110 mi) northeast of Kautokeino.

A Sámiland crossroads as well as the Sámi capital, Karasjok has 2,900 residents and is 18 km (11 mi) from the Finnish border. Many of the most significant Sámi institutions are here, including Sámetinget, the Sámi Parliament; De Sámiske Samlinger, the Sámi Collections; and the Sámi Kunstnersenter, Sámi Artists' Center. If you're on the way to the North Cape, then Karasjok is a natural place to stop and take in the stunning scenery.

The **Sámiid Vuorká Dávvirat - De sámiske sáminger** (Sámi Collections) is an indoor as well as open-air museum dedicated to Sámi culture and history. It emphasizes the arts, reindeer herding, and the status of women in the Sámi community. There are also some of the real hunting pits used to catch wild reindeer. ✉ Museumsgt. 17, ☎ 78/46–99–50. ☷ NKr 25. ☉ Early June–mid-Aug., Mon.–Sat. 9–6, Sun. 10–6; mid-Aug.–Oct. and Apr.–early June, weekdays 9–3, weekends 10–3; Nov.–Mar., weekdays 9–3, weekends noon–3.

Karasjok Opplevelser A/S (☎ 78/46–88–10) organizes exciting authentic Sámiland adventures. These may include dining in a lavvu, visiting a Sámi camp, listening to Sámi songs, and heading to Basevuovdi (Helligskogen, or the Sacred Forest) for gold panning. From late fall to early spring you can go **reindeer sledding.** A Sámi guide takes you out on a wooden sled tied to a couple of unwieldy reindeer, and you'll clop through the barren, snow-covered scenery of Finnmark.

The **Sámi Artists' Center** holds 10 temporary art exhibitions of contemporary and traditional Sámi visual art. Guided tours must be arranged in advance. ✉ Jeagilvármádii 54, ☎ 78/46–90–02. ☷ Free. ☉ Mid-June–mid-Aug., daily 10–5; mid-Aug.–mid-June, weekdays 10–3, Sun. noon–5.

The **Sápmi** theme park showcases the everyday life, mythology, food traditions, and art and crafts of the Sámi. Experience first-hand the Siida, which are the Sámi settlements. You can also enjoy a Sámi meal and take home a handmade silver Sámi souvenir. ✉ Porsangervn. 1, ☎ 78/46–88–10, WEB www.sapmi.no. ☉ Mon.–Wed., Fri. 10–6, Thurs. 10–8, Sat. noon–9, Sun. noon–5.

Opened in late 2000, the stunning **Sametinget** (Sámi Parliament; ☎ 78/74–00–00) is well worth admiring. The building's form blends ancient Sámi forms with Scandinavian modernism. Inside, the walls are covered with Sámi art.

Dining and Lodging

$$–$$$ ✕▣ **Rica Hotel Karasjok.** Looking like a cozy ski chalet, this hotel has
★   bright, warm rooms accented with blonde woods, and blues and reds. The highly regarded Sámi restaurant, Storgammen, is in a gamme (turf hut). It serves centuries-old Sámi dishes, including reindeer in lingonberry sauce, cooked over an open fire. ✉ *Porsangervn. 1, 9730 Karasjok,* ☎ *78/46–74–00,* FAX *78/46–68–02,* WEB *www.rica.no. 56 rooms. 2 restaurants, bar, sauna, gym, nightclub, meeting rooms. AE, DC, MC, V.*

Outdoor Activities and Sports

DOGSLEDDING

Sven Engholm leads dogsledding tours in winter. You can lead your own dog sled, accompany one on skis, or just go along for the ride. Engholm also organizes gold panning, fishing trips, and wilderness tours. Dine in Barhta, a special gamme (turf hut), or rent a cabin. In summer, you can hike with the huskies. Contact **Engholms Husky** (☎ 78/46–71–66, WEB www.engholm.no) for information.

HIKING AND FISHING

Finnmarksvidda, the plateau between Alta and Karasjok, has marked trails with places to stay overnight in lodges, cabins, lavvu, and tents. Fishing and canoe trips can be organized with a guide during July and August. Rather than hike to the fishing lakes, you can take an airplane or a helicopter instead: contact **Nils Rolf Johnsen** (✉ Svenskebakken 35, 9730 Karasjok, ☎ 78/46–63–02), who handles fishing trips and wilderness adventures on the Finnmarksvidda Plains, or Karasjok Opplevelser A/S (☎ 78/46–88–10).

Shopping

Sámi crafts, particularly handmade knives, are a specialty in this area. **Samelandssenteret** (☎ 78/46–71–55), a shopping center, has a large collection of shops featuring northern crafts. See how an authentic Sámi knife is made at **Knivsmed Strømeng A/S** (☎ 78/46–71–05).

Kirkenes

⑭   *320 km (200 mi) northeast of Karasjok.*

At its very top, Norway hooks over Finland and touches Russia for 122 km (75 mi). The towns in east Finnmark have a more heterogeneous population than those in the rest of the country. A century ago, during hard times in Finland, many industrious Finns settled in this region, and their descendants keep the language alive there.

A good way to visit this part of Norway is to fly to Kirkenes and then explore the region by car. Kirkenes itself has 7,000 residents. The town was built up around Sydvaranger, an iron ore mining company that operated until 1996. Today, the town's industries include tourism and ship repair.

During the World War II, Kirkenes was bombed more than 300 times— only Malta was bombed more—and virtually all buildings had to be rebuilt. Many residents sought cover in subterranean tunnels dug for use as bomb shelters. One of them, **Andersgrotta,** is open to the public every summer for tours (special arrangements can be made the rest of the year). The tour includes a film covering its use during the war. *Tellef Dahls gt.,* ☎ *78/99–25–44.* ▣ *NKr 60.* ☉ *Opening hrs vary.*

Dedicated to the works of the Sámi artist John Andras Savio (1902–1938), the **Savio Museum** showcases his woodcutting, watercolors, and oils. Savio is best known for depicting Sámi life in the North. The museum also has changing temporary exhibits of contemporary Sámi art. ✉ *Kongensgt. 10B,* ☎ *78/99–92–12.*

Wedged between Russia and Finland, **Pasvikdalen** is a valley known for its flora and fauna: Norway's largest bear population shares the valley with species of plants and birds that can't be found anywhere else in the country.

OFF THE BEATEN PATH	**ST. GEORGS KAPELL** (St. Georg's Chapel) – Forty-five kilometers (28 miles) west of Kirkenes is the only Russian Orthodox chapel in Norway. This tiny building is where the Orthodox Skolt-sámi had their summer encampment. An annual outdoor mass is held the last Sunday in August, weather permitting.

Lodging

$$–$$$ 🏨 **Rica Arctic Hotel.** Centrally located, this hotel is the perfect choice for outdoor sports enthusiasts. It's the beginning of the world's largest forest, stretching all the way from Pasvikdalen to the Bering Strait. The spacious rooms are pleasant, with white-painted furniture and floral and light-color fabrics. ✉ *Kongensgt. 1–3, 9900,* ☎ *78/99–29–29,* ℻ *78/99–11–59,* 🌐 *www.rica.no. 80 rooms. Restaurant, bar, pool, sauna, gym, convention center. AE, DC, MC, V.*

Storskog

⑮ *About 15 km (9 mi) east of Kirkenes.*

Just east of Kirkenes is Storskog, for many years the only official land crossing between Norway and Russia. The tiny village of **Grense Jakobselv,** 50 km (30 mi) east of Kirkenes along the Russian border, is where King Oscar II built a chapel in 1869 as a protest against constant Russian encroachment in the area. Salmon river fishing is good and several beaches are popular.

OFF THE BEATEN PATH	**ØVRE PASVIK NATIONAL PARK –** The southernmost part of Finnmark, about 118 km (73 mi) south of Kirkenes, is Øvre Pasvik national park, a narrow tongue of land tucked between Finland and Russia. This subarctic evergreen forest is the western end of Siberia's taiga and supports many unique varieties of flora.

Svalbard

⑯ *640 km (400 mi) north of the North Cape.*

The islands of the Svalbard archipelago, the largest of which is Spitsbergen, have only officially been part of Norway since 1920. This wild, fragile area lies halfway between the North Pole and the mainland. Icelandic texts from 1194 contain the first known mention of Svalbard. After the Dutch navigator Willem Barents visited Svalbard in 1596, whaling and winter-long hunting and trapping were virtually all that happened here for the next 300 years.

In 1906, John M. Longyear established the first coal mine and named the area Longyear City. Now called Longyearbyen, Svalbard's capital has a population of 1,200. Quite surprisingly, it's a diverse community with excellent accommodations and restaurants. There's an abundance of organized exotic wilderness activities and tours such as dogsledding, snowmobiling, skiing, ice caving, igloo camping, and fossil hunting.

Svalbard has its share of sports and cultural events, too. Famous musicians and artists visit Svalbard during the year for special exhibitions and concerts. The Polar Jazz festival takes place at the end of January followed by the lively Sunfestival in early March. The Svalbard Ski Marathon is held late April–early May and the Spitsbergen Marathon runs the beginning of June.

Sixty percent of Svalbard is covered by glaciers; plants and other vegetation cover only 6%; the rest of the surface is just rocks. Remote and isolated, the only way to fly in is from Tromsø. Only a few cruise ships and other boats land here, and no roads connect the communities on Svalbard itself—people travel between them with snowmobiles.

The archipelago's climate is surprisingly mild, with periods of summer fog. The small amount of precipitation makes Svalbard a sort of Arctic desert. Permafrost covers all of Svalbard, which means only the top meter of earth thaws in summer. Because it's so far north, it has four months of the midnight sun (as well as four months of polar night).

Although they spend most of their time on ice floes, polar bears can be encountered anywhere on Svalbard because they give birth to their cubs on land. They are a genuine threat, so be sure to only travel outside the settlements with an experienced guide.

Once a pig farm, the **Svalbard Museum** profiles the early trapper period, various Svalbard expeditions, the war years, and the biology of the islands. Learn about the history of mining on the first floor: you can change into a miner's outfit and crawl into a copy of a mine tunnel. ⊠ *Longyearbyen,* ☎ *79/02–13–84,* ◔ *Call for hrs.*

Mine No. 3, the last mine in which coal was extracted using traditional methods, ended production in 1996. Special guided visits can be arranged throughout the year. The mine is just outside of Longyearbyen. Contact **Svalbard Wildlife Service** (☎ 79/02–10–35).

Dining and Lodging

$$$ ✕ **Huset.** Considered one of Longyearbyen's best restaurants, Huset serves fine Norwegian food in a relaxed, classy setting. A wintery, signature Kåre Tveter painting of Svalbard graces one wall. Dramatically covering another wall is the snowy skin of a polar bear who wandered into Longyearbyen and was shot in 1983. Try tartare of arctic char, the grouse, or reindeer dishes. Popular with locals as well as visitors, the restaurant is often fully booked. ⊠ *Longyearbyen,* ☎ *79/02–25–00. Reservations essential. AE, DC, MC, V.*

$$$–$$$$ 🏨 **Radisson SAS Polar Hotel, Spitsbergen.** The world's northernmost Radisson SAS hotel excels in warm service and style. Every room is understated and elegant with light walls, warm colors, and blonde and dark woods. An enormous window in the dining and bar area provides a view of Mount Hjorthavnfjellet across the waters of the Icefjord. In summer, you can watch the sun cross from one side of the mountain at dusk to the other at dawn. The Restaurant Nansen's exotic menu features seal and white grouse. Barents Pub is a popular meeting place for the town. Svalbard Polar Travel specially arranges tours and activities for hotel guests. ⊠ *Box 544, 9171 Longyearbyen,* ☎ *79/02–34–50,* 📠 *79/02–34–51,* 🌐 *www.radissonsas.com. 99 rooms, 5 suites. Restaurant, bar, sauna, meeting rooms. AE, DC, MC, V.*

$$–$$$$ ✕🏨 **Spitsbergen Funken Hotell.** This distinguished hotel is known for the relics that fill it as well as for the luxury and high level of service its staff provides. Each room is tastefully and elegantly decorated in dark woods and richly colored textiles. You can relax in a red burnished-leather couch by the library's roaring fireplace. At the Funktionærmessen

Restaurant, dine on interpretations of local cuisine that include reindeer spring rolls. In cooperation with Spitsbergen Travel, the hotel offers such activities as snowmobiling, dog sledding, glacier walking, hiking, and boat trips. ⊠ *9171, Longyearbyen,* ☎ *79/02–62–00,* FAX *79/02–62–01,* WEB *www.spitra.no. 88 rooms. Restaurant, bar, sauna, meeting rooms. AE, DC, MC, V.*

The Arts

To get a sense of frosty Svalbard during other times of the year, head to **Gallery Svalbard.** One of Norway's most admired artists, Kåe Tveter donated 40 illustrations of Svalbard to Gallery Svalbard. The "Arctic Light Over Svalbard" slide show is an eye-opening presentation of what makes this area special. Centuries-old Arctic region maps and old books fill an adjacent exhibition room. ☎ *79/02–23–40.*

Shopping

For such a remote and small town, Longyearbyen has a surprising number of spots for souvenir shopping, including the **Lompensenteret** (79/02–36–53) shopping center. **Svalbardbutikken** (79/02–25–20) is a group of stores selling groceries, wine and liquor, cameras, clothes, souvenirs, and other things you may need. Head to **Svalbard Arctic Sport** (☎ 79/02–32–90) for sportswear and clothes for the outdoors.

Sámiland to Svalbard A to Z

To research prices, get advice from other travelers, and book travel arrangements, visit www.fodors.com.

AIR TRAVEL

Braathens and SAS service the Longyearbyen Airport.
➤ CONTACTS: **Braathens** (79/02–45–00). **Longyearbyen Airport** (☎ 79/02–38–00). **SAS** (79/02–16–50).

CRUISE TRAVEL

Hurtigruten, the coastal express boat, now cruises from Tromsø to Svalbard, dipping down to the North Cape afterward. Contact Bergen Line for information.
➤ CONTACTS: **Bergen Line Travel Agents** (⊠ 405 Park Ave., New York, NY 10022, ☎ 212/319–1300). Tours

BOAT TOURS

Cavzo Safari is a riverboat excursion from Máze to Alta Dam that includes guided tours, listening to joik in a lavvu, and traditional dishes such as *bidos,* a reindeer dish.
➤ FEES AND SCHEDULES: **Cavzo Safari** (☎ 78/48–75–88).

TOURS IN AND AROUND KIRKENES

Several regional companies offer specialized tours in and around Kirkenes. Grensland–Sovjetreiser focuses on the Barents Region with nature, cultural, and adventure tours in northwest Russia. Kirkenes Opplevelser's salmon and crab fishing boat expeditions span the region from the Kirkenes fjord to the Arctic Ocean. Bugøynes Opplevelser A/S visits a fishing community on the Arctic Ocean, where Kamchatka crab is served. Their tours include trying out an Arctic sauna and swimming. Neiden Fjellstue plans deep-sea, ice fishing, and snowmobile trips; staying in mountain cabins; and dining and entertainment in a lavvu.
➤ FEES AND SCHEDULES: **Bugøynes Opplevelser A/S** (☎ 78/99–03–75). **Destination Kirkenes** (☎ 78/99–80–69). **Grensland–Sovjetreiser** (☎ 78/99–25–01). **Kirkenes Opplevelser** (☎ 91/53–62–31). **Neiden Fjellstue** (☎ 78/99–61–41).

Svalbard's environment is fragile, and polar bears are dangerous as well as numerous (there are around 2,000 to 3,000 in and around Svalbard). For these reasons, heading into the wilderness should only be done on an organized tour with an experienced guide.

Spitsbergen Travel (SPITRA) organizes a wide and exciting range of activities and tours including glacier walks, horseback riding, dogsledding, and arctic barbecues. Svalbard Polar Travel (SPOT) handles skiing, dogsledding, and snowmobile tours in winter and spring cruises around Spitsbergen and the northwest coast in spring and summer.

For winter camping trips, Basecamp Spitsbergen sets you up with your very own Alaskan husky dogsledding team—or a snowmobile. In summer, the company operates hikes, trips with packdogs or packhorses, charter boat tours, and camping excursions. Svalbard Wildlife Service organizes tours into the Arctic wilderness and day trips in the Longyearbyen area. The day trips may include mine visits, glacier walks, and boating.

➤ FEES AND SCHEDULES: **Basecamp Spitsbergen** (☎ 79/02–35–80). **Spitsbergen Travel (SPITRA)** (☎ 79/02–61–00). **Svalbard Polar Travel (SPOT)** (☎ 79/02–34–00). **Svalbard Wildlife Service** (☎ 79/02–10–35).

TRANSPORTATION AROUND SÁMILAND AND SVALBARD
(☞ Trondheim to the North Cape A to Z.)

VISITOR INFORMATION
➤ TOURIST INFORMATION: **Karasjok** (✉ 9730 Karasjok, ☎ 78/46–88–10). **Kautokeino** (✉ 9520 Kautokeino, ☎ 78/48–65–00). **Kirkenes** (✉ 9915 Kirkenes, ☎ 78/97–74–00). **Info-Svalbard** (✉ 9171 Longyearbyen, ☎ 79/02–55–50).

12 PORTRAITS OF NORWAY

In Norway at Christmas

Books and Videos

Norway at a Glance: A Chronology

IN NORWAY AT CHRISTMAS

Every culture reinvents the wheel. But every culture reinvents it slightly differently. In Norway, a traditional dining table may rest not on four legs, as tables usually do elsewhere, but on a cubic frame, like an imaginary cage that imprisons your feet while you eat.

I am a Chinese who has fallen in love with Norway. I was invited by my good friends Ole and Else to spend Christmas and New Year's with them in Oslo. It turned out to be the most marvelous Christmas of my fifty-two years.

It was one long feast, moving from household to household. On Christmas Eve we held hands and sang carols and danced ring-around-the-Christmas-tree. We skied at night on an illuminated track, whose lights switched off at ten, plunging us into obscurity on the downward slope. We played squash on the Norsk Hydro court and afterward relaxed in the sauna. We ushered in the New Year with fireworks on Oslo's frozen streets.

I am probably one of the few Chinese in two thousand years to have had such an intimate glimpse of Norwegian life. Of course, it is presumptuous of me to write about a people after an eight-day visit. Yet I have the feeling that Norwegians don't very much mind presumption (as long as it is straightforward and honest). Indeed, this exceptional tolerance of friendly rudeness bespeaks their generosity and is, to me, one of their most endearing qualities.

To begin with, to a Chinese who has seen something of the world, Norway is a most exotic country. Even ordinary, everyday things are done exotically here. For example, I saw my Norwegian friends: drink aquavit at breakfast; eat breakfast in the afternoon; turn on an electric switch to heat the sidewalk in front of their house; get a thrill out of driving their car like a bobsled; leave the house lights on day and night, when they went out and when they slept; wash their dishes with soap without rinsing them.

Norwegians also love to give gifts and make philosophical speeches at festive dinners. They decorate their Christmas trees not with angels but with strings of Norwegian flags. They don't find it necessary to have curtains around their showers, because it's simpler to build a drain on the bathroom floor. Cold dishes are de rigueur in the winter. There is a national horror of hot, spicy foods, and a national pact to ignore vegetables.

The Norwegians and the Chinese share certain cultural traits. The most striking is their common fondness for rituals. Confucius insisted on the importance of rituals as a collective code of behavior that gives order to life. The Master said, "To suppress the self and submit to ritual is to engage in Humanity." This precept might just as well apply to the Norwegians as to the Chinese.

At Christmas, all the traditional rituals are performed, some older than Christianity in Norway. A great deal of effort goes into making sure that they are done right. After each one—the baking of the gingerbread houses, the decorating of the tree—the excitement palpably mounts.

Christmas begins on the eve, with the hostess welcoming the guests to the dinner table. She assigns to each a specific seat according to a careful arrangement. The seating plan is the one touch of originality that marks the occasion. It is, in some ways, the hostess's signature for the evening. (You find seating charts of past banquets faithfully recorded in a family book.) It's quite touching to see a young hostess assign a seat to her own mother, who has undoubtedly done the same many times herself. It signals the passing of the torch from one generation of women to another.

Once the guests are seated and the candles lit, the feast begins. It begins with the dessert: rice pudding (reminiscent of the rice gruel that Chinese eat for breakfast and when ill, albeit without milk and butter). Toasts are offered, followed by a chorus of *skaals*.

Then comes raw fish of every kind—salmon, eel, herring, enough to send a sashimi-loving Japanese into ecstasy. From the sea, the food parade marches onto land. A whole side of roast pork, skin done to a golden crisp, is served with meatballs and sausage, and buried under potatoes. Throughout there is much toasting with aquavit.

Finally, after two hours the meal is done. You get up from the table and stagger into the living room. There, in a role reminiscent of her mother's, the little daughter of the house hands out the gifts—to each recipient with charming solemnity.

Great care is taken by each household to do everything the same way, so that, as with the retelling of a familiar tale, all expectations are happily satisfied. Once in a while, one may introduce an oddity, such as a Chinese guest from afar, to liven up the routine. But in general, surprises tend to raise eyebrows.

If, for the Chinese, rituals recall the teachings of Confucius, for the Norwegians they go back to the pagans. In spite of the electric sidewalks, the past is very much alive in the modern Norwegian psyche. The feasting, the speech-making, the gift-giving, and especially the generous hospitality and the importance of friendship are all part of the Viking tradition. Yuletide was a pagan celebration of the winter solstice. The birth of Christ was a later liturgical imposition. In some families these days, it is celebrated almost as an afterthought.

The other thing that the Norwegians share with the Chinese is their strong attachment to the family. Like the Chinese, the Norwegians belong to extended families, practically clans. But what defines a family in Norway is not at all clear. The relations are so complex and intertwined that, rather than family trees, the Norwegians seem to have family bushes. To begin with, there is one's spouse and one's brothers and sisters and their spouses. And then there is one's former spouse and his or her present spouse. The children of the former spouse of one's spouse are somewhat like nephew and nieces. Beyond that, there are the living-together arrangements and the progeny thereof, which take on quasi-family status.

It's not unusual for people who are divorced to remain good friends. Their old pictures sometimes hang in each other's bedrooms, Christmastime finds them reunited with their old partners and all of their children, old and new. At first, this kind of marital pluralism is slightly unsettling. What, no bad blood? No bitterness or jealousy?

I asked a young Norwegian if it upset him to be shuttling between his father's and mother's separate households. He looked at me with astonishment. "But that's normal," he said. "Every kid in my class is in the same situation."

His guileless reaction gave me food for thought. "And indeed what's wrong with that?" I asked myself. Why try to stay with an unhappy relationship when one feels the need to change? And once changed, why not try to reconcile the past with the present?

The Chinese family is a vertical structure. Like the society itself, it is hierarchical, ruled from the top down. Confucius said, "Let the prince be prince, the minister be minister be minister, the father be father, the son be son." Patriarchy and gerontocracy are the order of things: old men will rule, and the young will obey. Repression is inevitable under such a hierarchy. The collective always takes precedence over the individual; order always takes precedence over freedom. This denial of the self is responsible for much of the envy, backbiting, and hypocrisy common in Chinese communities.

The Norwegian family, on the other hand— or perhaps I should say the *new* Norwegian family—is horizontal. Like a strawberry plant, it spreads in all directions. Wherever it touches soil, it sprouts a new shoot. An obvious sign of this strawberry-patch kinship in the diminished importance of the family name. These days people are known mostly by first names. Children, too, often address their parents by their first names. As more and more households are headed by women, the old nuclear family is giving way to a fluid tribalism.

One way to understand the difference between the vertical and the horizontal cultures is to compare their concepts of space. To the Chinese, any space must have a center. The Chinese name for China, Zhongguo, means precisely Center Country. Every Chinese knows that the center of China is Beijing. Why? Because the vast expanse of China is not divided into time zones, and from the Pacific to Tibet every watch is set to Beijing time. Every Chinese also knows that the center of Beijing is the Forbidden City, the symbol of governmental power, and that inside the Forbidden City sits an old man whose word is law.

No one would dream of ordering Norway's space this way. Unlike elsewhere in Europe, you seldom see a square in a Norwegian town. People don't seem to feel the need to meet and sit in the sun and feed the pigeons. In some rural communities, the church stands not in the center of town but on a hill somewhere on the outskirts. The houses, in all forms and dispositions, are widely dispersed, disdaining to line up along a straight road. One gets the impression that zoning laws are not very strict in Norway.

The big question is, if the Norwegians are such confirmed individualists, how come they are so conformist? It's voluntary, true, they choose it, but it's conformity all the same. This is the question posed—but never answered—by Ibsen's plays.

For me, the key to understanding the Norwegians is to recognize that they are a nation of irreconciled opposites. They have taken on the contradictions of their seasons: the long happy summer days alternating with the gloomy nights of winter. They have inherited two pasts with totally different characters. For more than two hundred years, from the ninth to the eleventh centuries, they were the scourge of Europe. They raided Britain and discovered America; they ruled Kiev and besieged Paris; they served at the court of Byzantium, and—who knows?—maybe some of them even made it to China. Lusty, adventurous, destructive, and curious about the world, they were sea nomads, the maritime counterpart of the horsemen of Genghis Khan, who conquered Russia and China. Then, as suddenly as they burst upon the world in their splendid ships, the retreated, went back to their home in the north. They were converted to Christianity and not heard from again.

Why the seafaring Vikings turned into God-fearing Christians is one of those mysteries that history doesn't explain very well. What made them turn their gaze inward? Why did they change from thinking big to thinking small? What, finally made them give up violence for peaceful ways? There is no satisfactory answer.

In any case, as the final image of Ingmar Bergman's *Fanny and Alexander* so powerfully shows, there are two ghosts walking beside the Scandinavian soul: the ghost of the hard-drinking father and the ghost of the psalm-singing stepfather. They walk beside the boy, each with a hand on his shoulder, never exchanging a word.

So the Norwegian labors under a double identity. In one ear, the Viking ghost tells him to leave Norway, this cold, homogeneous, incurious community, and discover the world. Go! The center is elsewhere! There are wonderful places to see and fabulous riches to be had!

In his other ear, the Christian ghost tells him Stay! Go back to your roots! Embrace the tradition and preserve the social order.

This ambivalence is at the heart of Norway itself. You see it reflected on canvas in the National Gallery in Oslo. Among the painters of the late nineteenth century, one finds two divergent sensibilities: the naturalists, who took as their subject the Norwegian folk, and the cosmopolitans, who, having spent time in Paris or Rome, insisted that art was not sociology or geography but, simply and purely, a composition of color and light.

For eight centuries, Christian ethics held sway in Norway as in the rest of Europe. But since 1945 something important has changed. There is a gap between the values of the prewar and the postwar generations. Between the threat of nuclear destruction and the temptation of America, the influence of the church waned. More and more, people have stopped practicing their faith. As they do so, they are reverting to their ancestral Viking instincts.

One clue to this reemergence of pagan consciousness is the marital pluralism that I observed. Another clue, probably closely related, is women's push for equality, a push that has been more forceful and more widely accepted in Scandinavia than anywhere else. A third indication of this new pagan way, I believe—and here I'm sticking my neck out—is the nation's collective decision, in the seventies, to turn Norway overnight into an oil economy.

There have been a lot of arguments about the reasoning behind this decision, but none of them address the Viking-versus-Christian dilemma. If Norway had listened to its Christian voice, it would have been content to remain a frugal, hard-working nation, tending the farm or the machine. Instead, after the oil crisis of 1973, Norway chose the Viking solution and went for broke. It decided to plunder the sea.

Agrarian people, like the Chinese, are naturally patient: it takes time to make things grow. The Vikings, on the other hand never had patience. If they could survive by fishing and gathering berries, they would not care to cultivate. Whatever they could get by raiding, they would not care to make. It is still so today. Norwegians are willing to put all their ingenuity and technical skill into building gigantic derricks and drilling kilometers beneath the sea. They will do so in order to avoid making clothes and toys to compete with Hong Kong. This is the message I got from that magnificent Christmas feast: If it tastes good raw, *don't bother to cook it*. Take it raw. Don't transform. And nothing is rawer than oil.

In 1066, King Harald Hardraade left the shores of Norway to grab the big prize: the throne of England. At Stamford Bridge he was offered by his enemy seven feet of English ground, "and more—if you are taller." Harald fought and lost. By nightfall, mortally wounded, he said, "I will accept that piece of kingdom that was offered me this morning."

I said to my friend Ole—who, as an oil engineer at Norsk Hydro, has staked his whole future on a challenge against the North Sea—"One day your oil will be depleted, and then where will you be?" He grinned and said, echoing King Harald's insouciance, "And then I will have nothing."

— by Chunglu Tsen

Born in Shanghai, Chunglu Tsen grew up in Paris and received his education in England and the United States. Since 1974 he has worked as a translator for the United Nations in Geneva. This article appeared originally in the December 1990 issue of *Wigwag*.

WHAT TO READ AND WATCH BEFORE YOU GO

Books

A History of the Vikings (1984, 2001) recounts the story of the aggressive warriors and explorers who during the Middle Ages influenced a large portion of the world, extending from Constantinople to America. Gwyn Jones's lively account makes learning the history enjoyable.

One of the greatest influences on 20th-century drama and literature, Norwegian poet and dramatist Henrik Ibsen is best known for *Peer Gynt* (1867), *A Doll's House* (1879), and *Hedda Gabler* (1890). His classic plays are still being performed in theaters from Berlin to Beijing.

Three Norwegian novelists were awarded the Nobel Prize for Literature in the 20th century: Bjørnstjerne Bjørnson, Knut Hamsun, and Sigrid Undset. Bjørnson was renowned for his lyric poetry and authored the Norwegian national anthem, *Ja, vi elsker.* Hamsun won for *Growth of the Soil* in 1920. Undset was honored for her masterpiece *Kristin Lavransdatter* (1928). More recently, Jostein Gaarder achieved international literary acclaim for his bestseller *Sophie's World* (1997).

For Norway's past, turn to *Norway: A History from the Vikings to Our Own Times* (1998); Karsten Alnaæs's *A History of Norway in Words and Pictures* (2001); and T. K. Derry's *A History of Scandinavia* (1996). Stunning images of the Norwegian landscape have been captured in the coffee-table books *The Magic of Fjord Norway* (2000), by Per Eide and Olav Grinde; *Panorama Norway* (1996), by Pål Hermansen; and Trym Ivar Bergsmo's *Lofoten* (2001).

Films of Interest

A History of the Vikings (Oxford University Press, 1984) recounts the story of the aggressive warriors and explorers who during the Middle Ages influenced a large portion of the world, extending from Constantinople to America. Gwyn Jones's lively account makes learning the history enjoyable.

Living in Norway (Abbeville Press, 1993) is a glossy depiction of Norwegian interior design. In 1995, Liv Ullmann directed the epic film *Kristin Lavransdatter,* an adaptation of Sigrid Undset's trilogy set in 14th-century Norway.

NORWAY AT A GLANCE:
A CHRONOLOGY

2,000 BC Tribes from Southern Europe migrate toward Denmark. The majority of early settlers in Scandinavia were of Germanic origin.

ca. 770 AD The Viking Age begins. For the next 250 years, Scandinavians set sail on frequent expeditions stretching from the Baltic to the Irish seas and even to the Mediterranean as far as Sicily, employing superior ships and weapons and efficient military organization.

ca. 870 The first permanent settlers arrive in Iceland from western Norway.

ca. 900 Norwegians unite under Harald I Haarfager.

995 King Olaf I Tryggvasson introduces Christianity into Norway.

1000 Leif Eriksson visits America. Olaf I sends a mission to Christianize Iceland.

1016–1028 King Olaf II Haraldsson (St. Olaf) tries to complete conversion of Norway to Christianity. Killed at Stiklestad in battle with Danish king, he becomes patron saint of Norway.

1028–1035 Canute (Knud) the Great is king of England, Denmark (1018), and Norway (1028).

1045–1066 King Harald III (Hardraade) fights long war with Danes, then participates in and is killed during Norman invasion of England.

1217 Haakon IV becomes king of Norway, beginning its "Golden Age." His many reforms modernize the Norwegian administration; under Greenland and Iceland form unions with Norway in 1261. The Sagas are written during this time.

1319 Sweden and Norway form a union that lasts until 1335.

1349 The Black Death strikes Norway and kills two-thirds of the population.

1370 The Treaty of Stralsund gives the north German trading centers of the Hanseatic League free passage through Danish waters.

1397 The Kalmar Union is formed as a result of the dynastic ties between Sweden, Denmark, and Norway, the geographical position of the Scandinavian states, and the growing influence of Germans in the Baltic. Erik of Pomerania is crowned king of the Kalmar Union.

1520 Christian II, ruler of the Kalmar Union, executes 82 people who oppose the Scandinavian union, an event known as the "Stockholm blood bath." Sweden secedes from the Union three years later. Norway remains tied to Denmark and becomes a Danish province in 1536.

1536 The Reformation enters Scandinavia in the form of Lutheranism through the Hanseatic port of Bergen.

1559–1648 Norwegian trade flourishes.

1660 Peace of Copenhagen establishes modern boundaries of Denmark, Sweden, and Norway.

1811 University of Oslo is established.

1814 Sweden, after Napoleon's defeat at the Battle of Leipzig, attacks Denmark and forces the Danish surrender of Norway. On 17 May,

Norwegians adopt constitution at Eidsvoll. On 4 November, Norway is forced to accept Act of Union with Sweden.

1884   A parliamentary system is established in Norway.

1903   Bjørnstjerne Bjørnson awarded Nobel prize for literature.

1905   Norway's union with Sweden is dissolved.

1914   At the outbreak of World War I, Norway declares neutrality but is effectively blockaded.

1918   Norwegian women gain the right to vote.

1920   Norway joins the League of Nations. Novelist Knut Hansun receives Nobel Prize.

1928   Sigrid Undset receives Nobel Prize for literature.

1929–1937   Norway is ruled by a labor government.

1939   Norway declares neutrality in World War II.

1940   Germany occupies Norway.

1945   Norway joins the United Nations.

1946–1954   Norwegian statesman Trygve Lie presides as first Secretary-General of UN.

1949   Norway becomes a member of NATO.

1952   The Nordic Council, which promotes cooperation among the Nordic parliaments, is founded.

1968   Norway discovers oil in the North Sea.

1971   North Sea oil extraction begins, transforming the Norwegian economy.

1972   Norway declines membership in the EC.

1981   Gro Harlem Brundtland, a member of the Labor party, becomes Norway's first female prime minister.

1991   King Olav dies. King Harald V ascends the throne. His wife, Queen Sonja, becomes first queen since the death of Maud in 1938.

1993   Norway's Minister of Foreign Affairs Thorvald Stoltenberg is appointed peace negotiator to Bosnia and Herzegovina.

1994   Norway hosts the XVII Olympic Winter Games a Lillehammer.

1995   In a national referendum, Norwegians again decline membership in the EC.

NORWEGIAN VOCABULARY

	English	Norwegian	Pronunciation
Basics			
	Yes/no	Ja/nei	yah/nay
	Please	Vær så snill	**vehr** soh snihl
	Thank you much.	Tusen takk	**tews**-sehn tahkvery
	You're welcome.	Vær så god	**vehr** soh goo
	Excuse me.	Unnskyld	**ewn**-shewl
	Hello	God dag	goo **dahg**
	Goodbye	Ha det	**ha** day
	Today	i dag	ee **dahg**
	Tomorrow	i morgen	ee **moh**-ern
	Yesterday	i går	ee **gohr**
	Morning	morgen	**moh**-ern
	Afternoon	ettermiddag	**eh-terr**-mid-dahg
	Night	natt	naht
Numbers			
	1	en	ehn
	2	to	too
	3	tre	treh
	4	fire	**feer**-eh
	5	fem	fehm
	6	seks	sehks
	7	syv, sju	shew
	8	åtte	**oh**-teh
	9	ni	nee
	10	ti	tee
Days of the Week			
	Monday	mandag	mahn-dahg
	Tuesday	tirsdag	**teesh**-dahg
	Wednesday	onsdag	**oonss**-dahg
	Thursday	torsdag	**tohsh**-dahg
	Friday	fredag	**fray**-dahg
	Saturday	lørdag	**loor**-dahg
	Sunday	søndag	**suhn**-dahg
Useful Phrases			
	Do you speak English?	Snakker De engelsk?	snahk-kerr dee ehng-ehlsk
	I don't speak Norwegian.	Jeg snakker ikke norsk.	yay **snahk**-kerr **ik**-keh nohrshk
	I don't understand.	Jeg forstår ikke.	yay fosh-**tawr** **ik**-keh
	I don't know.	Jeg vet ikke.	yay veht **ik**-keh
	I am American/ British.	Jeg er amerikansk/ engelsk.	yay ehr ah-mehr-ee-kahnsk/ehng-ehlsk
	I am sick.	Jeg er dårlig.	yay ehr **dohr**-lee

Please call a doctor.	Vær så snill og ring etter en lege.	vehr soh snihl oh ring **eht**-ehr ehn **lay**-geh
Do you have vacant room?	Har du et rom som er ledig?	yay vil **yehr**-neh hah eht room
How much does it cost?	Hva koster det?	vah **koss**-terr deh
It's too expensive.	Det er for dyrt.	deh ehr for **deert**
Beautiful	vakker	**vah**-kehr
Help!	Hjelp!	yehlp
Stop!	Stopp!	stop
How do I get to . . .	Hvor er	voor ehr
the train station?	jernbanestasjonen	yehrn-bahn-eh sta-**shoon**-ern
the post office?	posthuset	**pohsst**-hewss
the tourist office?	turistkontoret	tew-**reest**-koon-toor-er
the hospital?	sykehuset	**see**-keh-hoo-seh
Does this bus go to . . . ?	Går denne bussen til . . . ?	gohr **den**-nah boos teel
Where is the W.C.?	Hvor er toalettene?	voor ehr too-ah-**leht**-te-ne
On the left	Til venstre	teel **vehn**-streh
On the right	Til høyre	teel **hooy**-reh
Straight ahead	Rett fram	reht **frahm**

Dining Out

menu	meny	meh-new
fork	gaffel	gahff-erl
knife	kniv	kneev
spoon	skje	shay
napkin	serviett	ssehr-vyeht
bread	brød	brur
butter	smør	smurr
milk	melk	mehlk
pepper	pepper	pehp-per
salt	salt	sahlt
sugar	sukker	sook-kerr
water/bottled water	vann	vahn
The check, please.	Jeg vil gjerne betale.	yay vil **yehr**-neh beh-**tah**-leh

INDEX

Icons and Symbols

★ Our special recommendations
✕ Restaurant
🏠 Lodging establishment
✕🏠 Lodging establishment whose lodging establishment warrants a special trip
👆 Good for kids (rubber duck)
☞ Sends you to another section of the guide for more information
✉ Address
☎ Telephone number
🕐 Opening and closing times
🎫 Admission prices

Numbers in white and black circles ③ ❸ that appear on the maps, in the margins, and within the tours correspond to one another.

NOTES

NOTES

NOTES

NOTES

NOTES

NOTES